W9-DJJ-314

In Other Words

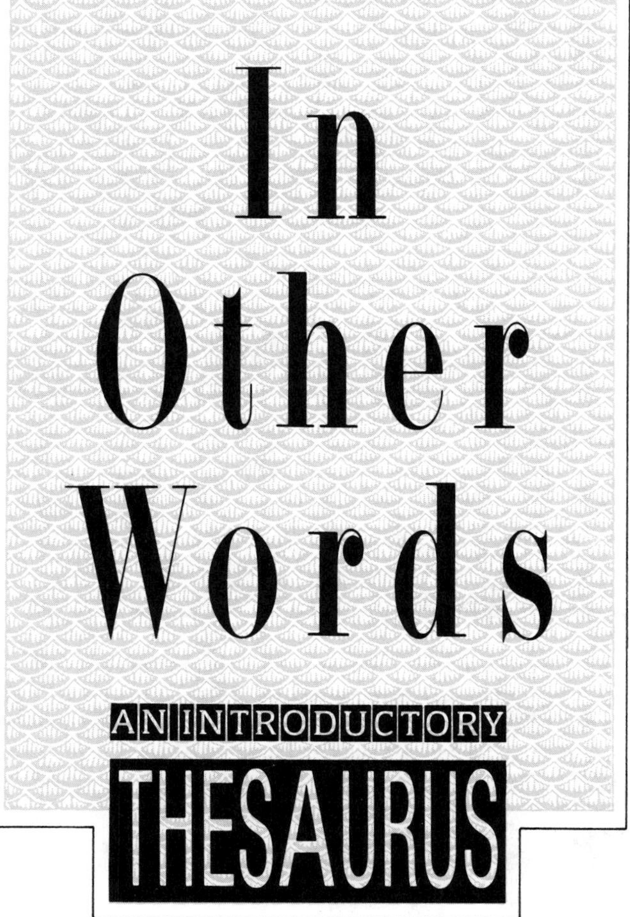

VERA DOBSON GOULD

PATRICIA J. HUGHES

The Publishers gratefully acknowledge the contribution of the many teachers who responded to our survey on the appropriateness of our word list and offered many helpful suggestions for the revision of this thesaurus.

We are especially grateful to the following for their insightful reviews:

David Boyd, Appleby College, Oakville, Ontario, Canada
Catherine Eddy, Vancouver Board of Education, B.C., Canada

ISBN 0-921156-11-1

Design: Wycliffe Smith
Editors: Maggie Goh, Elizabeth Siegel
Editorial Assistants: Amy Black, Jane Leonard, Sharon Rodriguez, Steffanie Schirop

Canadian Cataloguing in Publication Data

Gould, Vera Dobson
In other words

Rev. ed.
ISBN 0-921156-11-1

1. English language – Synonyms and antonyms – Dictionaries. I. Hughes, Patricia J. (Patricia Joyce), 1934- . II. Title.

PE1591.G68 1991 423'.1 C91-093345-6

1 2 3 4 5 95 94 93 92 91

Printed and bound in Canada by John Deyell Company

This revised edition of *In Other Words* is dedicated to the memory of the late Murray J. Dobson, whose creative ability and skilful planning resulted in the production of this book.

INTRODUCTION

This completely revised and updated edition of *In Other Words* is designed to continue the aims and purposes of the highly successful first edition, which sold over 100 000 copies. To reflect the changes in the language, some of the original entry words have been deleted because they are no longer in common use, while more than 1 000 new entries have been added. Altogether, the thesaurus contains more than 6 000 vocabulary entries. The new entries include the many words that have become part of the common vocabulary in the twenty years since the first edition was published, as well as words whose meanings have been modified through the years.

The book is designed for easy use. The source words are listed alphabetically in the colour bar on the left of each page. This eye-catching bar and the guide words at the top of each page make it easy to locate the source word.

Source words with more than one meaning are shown with separate entries according to usage: the first relating to use as a noun, the second to use as a verb, and the remaining to use as an adjective, adverb, and preposition. The part of speech of each form of the source word is indicated in italics as follows: *n.* for noun, *v.* for verb, *adj.* for adjective, *adv.* for adverb, and *prep.* for preposition. Where applicable, an alternate accepted spelling for the source word is indicated in brackets.

The list of synonyms or alternatives to the source words are listed in bold in the centre column. Following that is a sentence in which the source word is used, often in one of its extended forms. The sentence is a vital feature of this thesaurus in that, in most instances, it not only helps the user to understand the meaning of the source word, but it also shows a context in which the word is commonly used. The contrasting words cannot be substituted into the sentence in the way that the alternative words can, but the sentences do provide a basis for an explanation of the contrasting words.

Contrasting words are listed in the colour bar on the right-hand side of each page. Although most of these are antonyms, the editors have also included words which are near opposites in the belief that a broad definition of the opposite category is a helpful method of concept formation.

The editors intend that *In Other Words* will be used as a supplement to the dictionary. The book can be used initially to develop dictionary skills free of the confusion of the dictionary's diacritical marks, syllabication marks, multiple meanings, and often, small print.

Constant use of the book will extend the user's vocabulary. Research projects, student writing, independent study assignments, and private studies will all be helped by use of this book. Through such activities, independence and sound study habits will be developed.

It is the editors' hope that *In Other Words* will develop in users a deeper appreciation of the English language and greater skill in its use.

VERA DOBSON GOULD
PATRICIA J. HUGHES

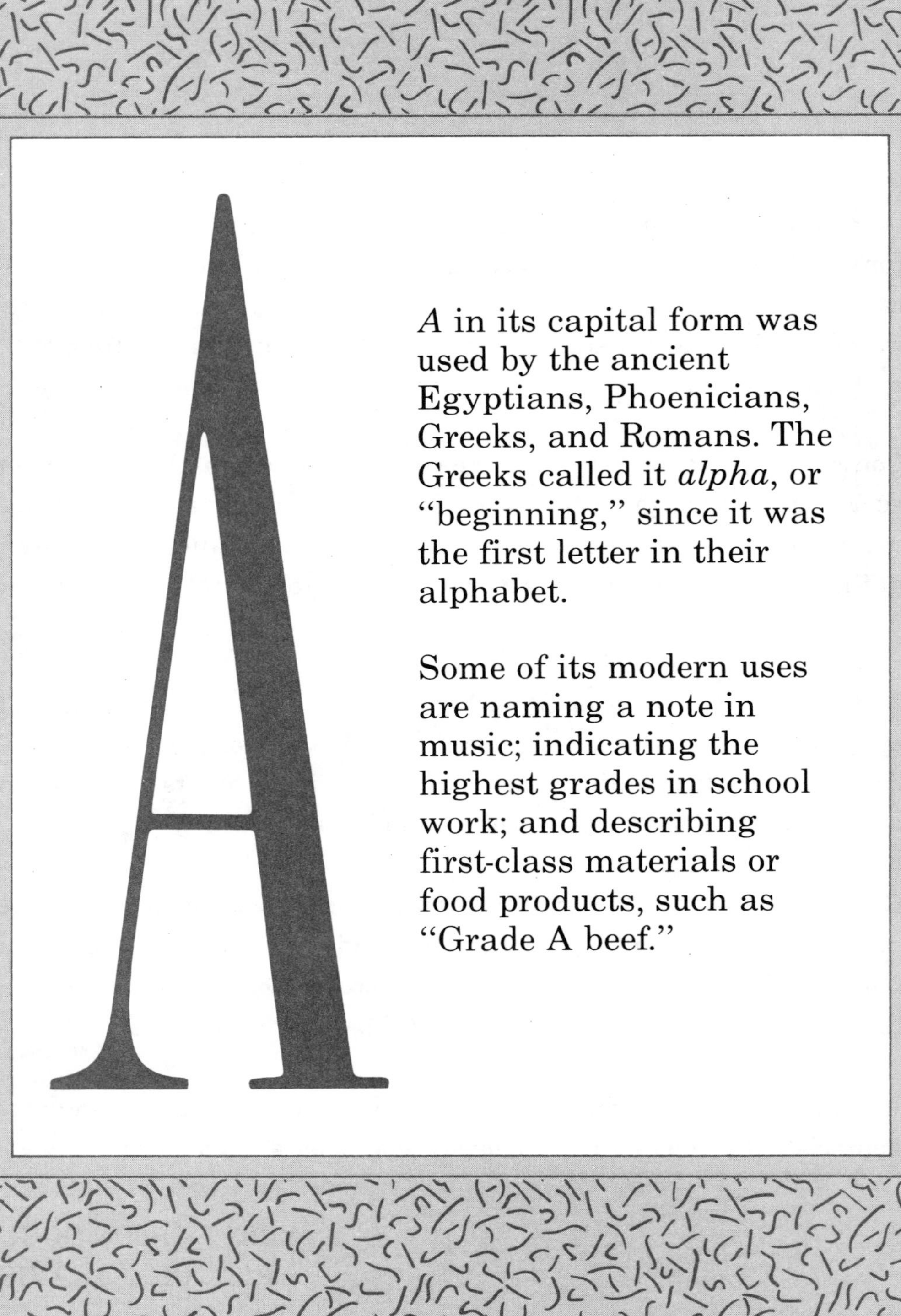

A in its capital form was used by the ancient Egyptians, Phoenicians, Greeks, and Romans. The Greeks called it *alpha*, or "beginning," since it was the first letter in their alphabet.

Some of its modern uses are naming a note in music; indicating the highest grades in school work; and describing first-class materials or food products, such as "Grade A beef."

abandon	**1.**	*v.*	**give up, surrender** In the last inning, the team abandoned all hope of winning.	**1.** *keep, maintain, retain*
	2.	*v.*	**desert, leave** The crew abandoned the ship when it hit an iceberg.	**2.** *retain, hold, keep, adopt*
abandoned	**1.**	*adj.*	**forsaken, deserted, left** The abandoned puppies were taken to the Humane Society.	**1.** *kept, retained, adopted*
	2.	*adj.*	**vacated, deserted** Signs warned us not to go near the abandoned mine.	**2.** *occupied, maintained*
abbreviate		*v.*	**shorten, lessen, reduce, condense, abridge** The word "August" can be abbreviated to "Aug." *n.* "Aug." is the abbreviation for August.	*lengthen, enlarge, expand, extend, increase*
abduct		*v.*	**kidnap, carry off, take away** The Prime Minister was abducted by terrorists. *n.* The abductors demanded a ransom for the release of the victim. *n.* The news of the abduction shocked everyone.	*free, restore, surrender, return*
ability		*n.*	**skill, capacity, capability, talent** Mozart showed his musical ability at an early age.	*incompetence, inability*
ablaze	**1.**	*adj.*	**aglow, blazing, brightly lit** The Christmas tree was ablaze with lights.	**1.** *dark, dim*
	2.	*adv.*	**on fire** The dead tree was set ablaze by lightning.	
able	**1.**	*adj.*	**capable of** Matt is able to speak three languages.	**1.** *unable to*
	2.	*adj.*	**clever, talented, qualified, skilful** Shen is an able student.	**2.** *stupid, dull, incompetent*
	3.	*adj.*	**powerful, vigorous, strong** Mina is an able athlete.	**3.** *weak, feeble, ineffective*
abnormal		*adj.*	**odd, unusual, peculiar, strange, queer, irregular, exceptional** Very cold weather is abnormal in the tropics.	*usual, common, normal, regular*

Word	No.	Part of speech	Synonyms / Example	Antonyms
aboard		*prep.*	**on** There were three people aboard the yacht.	*ashore, off*
abolish		*v.*	**eliminate, put an end to, annul, destroy, terminate** Environmental pollution must be abolished.	*retain, keep, hold, maintain*
about	1.	*prep.*	**concerning, regarding** He spoke about his plans for the future.	
	2.	*prep.*	**around, in** The tourists wandered about the ruins of the historical site.	
	3.	*adv.*	**around, nearly, approximately, almost** We are about the same size.	
above	1.	*adj.*	**preceding, previous** How are you? The above statement is a question.	**1.** *following, next*
	2.	*prep.*	**higher than** Her apartment is two floors above mine.	**2.** *below, beneath*
	3.	*adv.*	**overhead** Planes flew above.	**3.** *underneath*
aboveboard		*adj.*	**fair, open, honest, straightforward** This company is aboveboard in all its dealings.	*deceitful, dishonest, crooked*
abroad	1.	*adv.*	**at large, in circulation** Strange rumours are abroad.	**1.** *contained*
	2.	*adv.*	**out of one's country, overseas** Our family went abroad last summer.	**2.** *at home*
abrupt	1.	*adj.*	**sudden, hasty, unexpected** The car screeched to an abrupt stop at the lights. *adv.* He left abruptly without saying good-bye.	**1.** *gradual, expected, slow*
	2.	*adj.*	**very steep** My old car couldn't make the abrupt climb to the top of the hill.	**2.** *gradual*
	3.	*adj.*	**curt, sharp, blunt, to the point** His abrupt manner offended us.	**3.** *diplomatic, gentle, polite*
absent	1.	*adj.*	**away, not present** Sue is absent from school today because she is ill.	**1.** *present, on the spot*
	2.	*adj.*	**lacking** Trees are absent in the tundra region.	**2.** *existing, present*

absent-minded *adj.* **inattentive, forgetful, preoccupied, unaware**
The absent-minded boy forgot his books again.
attentive, interested, alert

absolute *adj.* **perfect, entire, complete, positive**
At the trial, the witness swore to tell the absolute truth.
adv. The evidence proved that she was absolutely right.
limited, incomplete, imperfect

absorb *v.* **soak up, suck in**
A sponge absorbs water.
exude

absorbed *adj.* **preoccupied, engrossed**
She was so absorbed in her book that she forgot the time.
distracted

abstain *v.* **refrain from, hold back**
Everyone should abstain from using drugs.
indulge, yield

absurd *adj.* **silly, foolish, ridiculous, crazy, preposterous, stupid, senseless, nonsensical**
Cows fly? What an absurd idea!
n. Do not bother me with such an absurdity.
wise, sound, logical, sensible, reasonable

abundance *n.* **plenty, full supply**
There is an abundance of fruits in the summer.
scarcity, shortage

abundant *adj.* **plentiful, rich, luxuriant**
Abundant vegetation grows in the tropical rain forests.
adv. Tropical foliage grows abundantly.
sparse, lean, meagre

abuse
1. *v.* **injure, mistreat, damage, harm**
He was fined for abusing his dog.
n. There are laws against child abuse.
1. *care for, protect, treat kindly*

2. *v.* **misuse, exploit**
The dictator abused her power by arresting those who opposed her.
2. *enhance*

accelerate *v.* **speed up, hurry, hasten**
The plane accelerated after takeoff.
retard, hinder, impede, slow down

accent
1. *n.* **manner of speech**
The visitor spoke English with a Spanish accent.

2. *n.* **emphasis**
The room was decorated with an Oriental accent.

Word	#	Part	Synonyms / Example	Antonyms
	3.	*v.*	**emphasize, heighten, intensify** The sound was accented by the microphone.	3. *detract from, lower, diminish*
accentuate		*v.*	**emphasize, stress** Her big smile accentuated how glad she was to see us.	*de-emphasize, minimize*
accept		*v.*	**agree to, consent to, receive** Gino accepted the invitation to the party. *n.* He sent the host a letter of acceptance.	*refuse, reject, decline*
acceptable		*adj.*	**agreeable, satisfactory, appropriate, fitting, suitable** The terms of the contract were mutually acceptable to us.	*unacceptable, inappropriate, unsatisfactory*
access		*n.*	**approach, entry** There is a hidden access to the cave.	*exit*
accessory	1.	*n.*	**assistant, partner, helper, accomplice** Two people were convicted as accessories to the crime.	1. *opponent, adversary*
	2.	*n.*	**extra, addition** A car telephone is a useful accessory.	
accident	1.	*n.*	**misfortune, mishap** He was injured in a skiing accident.	1. *good fortune*
	2.	*n.*	**chance, coincidence** We met by accident in the mall.	2. *design, plan, certainty*
accidental		*adj.*	**unexpected, unintentional** Our meeting was an accidental one. *adv.* The vase broke when I accidentally dropped it.	*deliberate, on purpose, intentional*
acclaim	1.	*n.*	**approval, praise** The anti-drug campaign was greeted with great acclaim.	1. *blame, criticism*
	2.	*v.*	**hail, call out, applaud** The firefighter was acclaimed a hero after she saved the child.	2. *condemn, blame, criticize*
accommodate	1.	*v.*	**serve, suit, house, hold** This room accommodates forty people comfortably.	1. *be inappropriate*
	2.	*v.*	**oblige, help, serve** Hotel staff try to accommodate their guests as far as possible.	2. *hinder, displease*

accommodation *n.* **lodging**
We had excellent accommodation on our trip.

accompany *v.* **escort, attend, go with**
I accompanied my mother to the store.

accomplish *v.* **achieve, complete**
She accomplished her goals through hard work.
adj. She is an accomplished pianist.
fail

accomplishment *n.* **performance, deed, attainment, achievement, feat**
Her parents are proud of her athletic accomplishments.
defeat, failure

accord
1. *n.* **agreement, harmony**
The argument was settled in complete accord.
2. *v.* **grant, concede, allow**
Tzen was accorded extra time to complete his homework.
1. *disagreement, discord*
2. *withhold, refuse*

account
1. *n.* **narrative, report, explanation, story**
Cartier wrote interesting accounts of his voyages.
2. *n.* **reason**
Do not go near the dumpsite on any account.

accumulate *v.* **collect, gather, save, assemble, hoard, gain**
If you do not clean the house regularly, the dust will accumulate.
scatter, disperse, spend, lose, distribute

accumulation *n.* **collection, store, mass, heap, stock**
An accumulation of books filled the shelves.
dispersion, scattering

accurate *adj.* **careful, precise, exact, truthful, sure, reliable, dependable, just, certain**
The eyewitness gave police an accurate description of the suspect.
adv. The witness reported accurately what he saw.
doubtful, uncertain, questionable, inaccurate, misleading, unjust, unreliable, vague

accusation *n.* **charge**
The accusation that she was lying proved to be false.

Word		Synonyms	Antonyms
accuse	*v.*	**charge, blame** The man was accused of robbery.	*clear, acquit*
accustom	*v.*	**become used to, familiarize** We soon accustomed ourselves to the new school.	
accustomed	*adj.*	**usual, regular, ordinary, familiar** The jogger followed his accustomed route in the park.	*uncommon, unusual, strange, unaccustomed*
ace	*n.*	**expert** As a golfer, Vic is an ace. *adj.* His excellent score indicates that he is an ace golfer.	*beginner, learner, novice*
achieve	*v.*	**accomplish, fulfil, perform, get, win, gain, capture** Kai achieved his goal after many years of hard work.	*fail, forsake, give up*
achievement	*n.*	**accomplishment, deed, feat, performance, act** It was a great achievement when human beings landed on the moon.	*failure, blunder*
acid	*adj.*	**sour, sharp, biting, pungent, tart** Too much vinegar in salad dressing gives it an acid taste.	*sweet, smooth*
acknowledge	*v.*	**admit, grant, confess, concede, say, accept, declare** The candidate acknowledged his defeat in the election.	*deny, refuse, decline*
acquainted	*adj.*	**known to, familiar** They were acquainted with each other from dance class. *n.* Jose is an old acquaintance of mine.	*unknown, strange*
acquire	*v.*	**get, gain, win, receive** David acquired fame after his book was published.	*lose, give*
acquit	*v.*	**pardon, forgive, clear, free, release** The accused was acquitted at the trial.	*convict, condemn*
acquittal	*n.*	**discharge, deliverance** Her name was cleared when she received an acquittal in court.	*conviction, condemnation*

Word	No.	Part of speech	Synonyms and example	Antonyms
acrid		*adj.*	**bitter, pungent, sour, acid** The burning material produced an acrid smell.	*sweet, pleasant, fragrant*
act	1.	*n.*	**deed, feat, accomplishment** Mother Teresa is admired for her acts of kindness.	
	2.	*v.*	**do, execute, operate, respond** The lifeguard acted quickly to save the swimmer who was in trouble.	**2.** *halt, cease, refrain, ignore, rest*
	3.	*v.*	**perform, impersonate, pretend, portray** She acted the role of Lady MacBeth superbly.	
action	1.	*n.*	**deed, feat, accomplishment, activity, movement, response** Quick action stopped the fire from spreading.	**1.** *inactivity, idleness, rest*
	2.	*n.*	**battle** My uncle died in action during World War II.	**2.** *peace*
active		*adj.*	**alert, quick, sharp, lively, spry, busy, energetic, vigorous** Grandma is an active eighty-year-old.	*idle, slow, inactive, dormant*
actual		*adj.*	**genuine, authentic, real** The diamond is an actual gem. *adv.* Are you actually leaving before the party is over?	*counterfeit, false, unreal, bogus, fictitious*
acute	1.	*adj.*	**sharp, severe, intense** The jogger felt an acute pain when she sprained her ankle.	**1.** *dull, mild*
	2.	*adj.*	**penetrating, piercing, shrill, high** An acute blast from the factory whistle halted all work.	**2.** *low, soft*
	3.	*adj.*	**keen, sensitive** Dogs have acute hearing.	**3.** *dull*
adamant		*adj.*	**stubborn, determined, firm, immovable** My parents are adamant about my curfew being nine o'clock. *adv.* They adamantly refuse to extend my curfew.	*yielding, pliable, submissive*
adapt	1.	*v.*	**adjust, suit, fit** We have adapted to the customs of our new country.	
	2.	*v.*	**alter, change, modify, remodel** Jo adapted the box to make a wagon.	

Word			Synonyms	Antonyms
add		*v.*	**increase, enlarge, extend, attach** We added another room to our house. *n.* The addition of another room made the house more comfortable.	*subtract, reduce, decrease, remove*
additional		*adj.*	**added, supplementary, more, extra** When I heard you were coming too, I ordered an additional ticket.	*less, fewer*
address	1.	*n.*	**location** Write your address on the envelope.	
	2.	*n.*	**speech, talk, oration** The graduation address was inspiring.	
	3.	*v.*	**greet, speak to, make a speech, deliver a speech** The Prime Minister addressed the country on national television	**3.** *ignore, overlook*
adept		*adj.*	**skilful, proficient, expert, able** Glenn is an adept carpenter.	*clumsy, unskilled, awkward*
adequate		*adj.*	**enough, suitable, sufficient, ample** Was there adequate time to complete your homework? *adv.* She is paid adequately for the job.	*insufficient, inadequate, lacking, deficient*
adhere		*v.*	**stick, cling, fasten, attach** Paste is used to adhere wallpaper to a wall.	*loosen, unfasten, separate, detach*
adhesive		*adj.*	**sticky, gummy** Adhesive tape has many uses.	*loose, free*
adjacent		*adj.*	**adjoining, neighbouring, bordering, next** I can hear music playing in the adjacent room.	*distant, far, detached*
adjust	1.	*v.*	**regulate, alter, change** Dad adjusted the television to make it clearer. *n.* The adjustment improved the picture.	**1.** *disarrange, jumble*
	2.	*v.*	**adapt, accustom, condition, get used to** Our friends from Singapore finally adjusted to the Canadian winter.	

Word			Synonyms	Antonyms
admirable		*adj.*	**worthy, excellent** The audience applauded the actress for her admirable performance. *adv.* She acted admirably despite the fact that she was not feeling well.	*unworthy, disgusting*
admiration		*n.*	**praise, appreciation, respect, approval, esteem** We were filled with admiration for the firefighters' courage.	*disapproval, contempt, disregard*
admire		*v.*	**appreciate, approve, applaud, respect, praise** We stopped to admire the scenery. *n.* Did an admirer send you the flowers?	*condemn, despise, dislike*
admit	1.	*v.*	**confess, acknowledge, grant, disclose** Be honest and admit your mistakes.	1. *deny, reject*
	2.	*v.*	**allow, permit, receive** This ticket admits one to the show.	
adolescent	1.	*n.*	**youth, teenager, teen, minor** An adolescent is a person who is between 13 and 18 years of age.	1. *grown-up, adult*
	2.	*adj.*	**juvenile, childish, immature** Throwing spitballs in class is adolescent behaviour.	2. *mature*
adopt		*v.*	**choose, take, assume, accept** The Shihs adopted a baby. *n.* The adoption of the baby pleased everyone.	*reject, repudiate*
adore		*v.*	**worship, cherish, love** The whole family adored the baby. *n.* The teenagers gazed in adoration at the rock star. *adj.* The baby was adorable.	*hate, detest, abhor, dislike*
adrift		*adv.*	**unfastened, untied, loose** The boat is adrift in the lake.	*moored, tied, fastened*
adult	1.	*n.*	**grown-up** The adults gave their consent to the children to go swimming.	1. *child, baby*
	2.	*adj.*	**mature, full-grown, developed** The school offers adult education classes for mature students.	2. *childish, immature, young*
advance	1.	*v.*	**go ahead, proceed, continue** The troops advanced toward the border.	1. *withdraw, recede*

Word	No.	Part of speech	Synonyms and example	Antonyms
	2.	*v.*	**improve, progress** The students passed their exams and advanced to the next level.	**2.** *decline, get worse*
advantage		*n.*	**benefit, gain, help, assistance** Height is an advantage for basketball players.	*hindrance, drawback, disadvantage*
adventure		*n.*	**daring enterprise, exciting incident, happening, experience** Skydiving was quite an adventure for us. *adj.* The adventurous woman sailed around the world alone.	
adversary		*n.*	**opponent, foe, enemy, rival, competitor** I beat my adversary in the election by just three votes!	*ally, friend, aid, associate*
adverse		*adj.*	**contrary, unfortunate, unfavourable, opposing** The adverse weather conditions made driving dangerous. *adv.* The umpire's decision affected the team adversely.	*favourable, desirable, agreeable*
adversity		*n.*	**bad luck, misfortune, distress, trouble** During their flight to safety, the refugees faced adversity with courage.	*good fortune, prosperity, good luck*
advertise		*v.*	**announce, publish, notify, proclaim, promote** The store advertised a special sale. *n.* The advertisement appeared in several newspapers. *n.* The advertiser was pleased with the response to it.	*conceal, suppress, hide*
advice		*n.*	**counsel, suggestion, guidance, direction** If you have a problem, go to your teacher for advice.	
advise		*v.*	**counsel, recommend, instruct, direct** Father advised me not to quit school.	*misdirect, lead astray*
affair	1.	*n.*	**happening, occasion, incident, event** The graduation dance will be a splendid affair.	

Entry	No.	Part	Synonyms / Example	Antonyms
	2.	*n.*	**concern, responsibility, duty, matter** Don't meddle with my personal affairs.	
affect	1.	*v.*	**influence, have an effect on** The cold weather has affected my health.	
	2.	*v.*	**move, touch, stir** The audience was greatly affected by the emotional performance.	**2.** *leave unmoved*
	3.	*v.*	**pretend** Min affected an air of innocence after spilling the milk.	
affected		*adj.*	**pretentious** Affected manners irritate people. *n.* Drop your affectations and be yourself.	*regular, ordinary, down-to-earth, normal*
affection		*n.*	**attachment, fondness, tenderness, goodwill, love** Biz has a deep affection for her sister. *adj.* She is an affectionate sister.	*dislike, hatred, aversion*
affirm		*v.*	**assert, declare, claim, maintain, ratify** The rebels affirmed their commitment to their cause. *n.* Their affirmation of commitment was inspiring.	*deny, disclaim, reject, veto*
afflict		*v.*	**distress, trouble, torment** Al was afflicted with measles. *n.* The affliction kept him in bed.	*relieve, comfort*
affluent		*adj.*	**rich, wealthy, prosperous** Every home in this affluent neighbourhood has a pool.	*poor, needy, destitute*
afraid		*adj.*	**timid, scared, frightened, fearful, alarmed, terrified** Are you afraid of snakes?	*brave, gallant, courageous, bold*
again		*adv.*	**over, another time, anew** I dare you to do that again.	*once*
age	1.	*n.*	**time, era, span, period** This is the age of space exploration.	
	2.	*n.*	**years of life, span of life** What is your age?	
	3.	*v.*	**grow feeble, decline** After his wife died, he seemed to age overnight.	

Word			Synonyms / Example	Antonyms
aged		*adj.*	**old, elderly** This community takes good care of the aged citizens.	*young, youthful*
aggravate		*v.*	**irritate, bother, annoy, irk, pester** Noise aggravates most people.	*calm, soothe, relieve, relax*
agile		*adj.*	**nimble, spry, dexterous** Gymnasts have to be agile to perform their routines. *n.* A gymnast's agility comes with years of training.	*awkward, clumsy*
agitate		*v.*	**excite, rouse, stir, disturb, annoy, bother, fluster** We were agitated by the bad news.	*calm, soothe, relieve, relax*
agony		*n.*	**torment, anguish, torture** Rani was in agony with a toothache. *adj.* She suffered with the agonizing pain until the tooth was pulled.	*joy, delight, pleasure*
agree	1.	*v.*	**consent, approve, accept** My friend agreed to help me with my project.	1. *refuse, oppose*
	2.	*v.*	**concur, coincide, match** I'm glad your ideas agree with mine.	2. *disagree, differ, contradict*
agreeable	1.	*adj.*	**pleasing, pleasant, inviting** Ali is well-liked because of his agreeable disposition.	1. *unpleasant, disagreeable*
	2.	*adj.*	**willing, approving** She nodded to show she was agreeable to the suggestion.	2. *against, unwilling*
	3.	*adj.*	**suitable** NASA waited for agreeable weather before launching the space shuttle.	3. *inappropriate, unsuitable*
agreement	1.	*n.*	**contract, treaty, promise, bargain** The two nations signed a trade agreement.	
	2.	*n.*	**accordance, harmony, conformity, correspondence** We are both in agreement about these proposals.	2. *disagreement*
ahead		*adv.*	**in advance, before, forward, onward** The first group of scouts walked far ahead of us.	*behind, backward*
aid	1.	*n.*	**help, assistance, support** We sent food and clothes as aid for the famine victims.	1. *hindrance, opposition*

Word	No.	Part	Synonyms / Example	Antonyms
	2.	*v.*	**help, assist, support** He aided the new student in English.	2. *hinder, block, injure, impede*
ailment		*n.*	**sickness, illness, disorder** Kirk suffers from a heart ailment.	
aim	1.	*n.*	**goal, mark, objective, purpose** His aim is to be a professional hockey player.	
	2.	*v.*	**point at, try for** The player aimed carefully before shooting the ball into the basket.	
aimless		*adj.*	**pointless, purposeless** Bob was told to take charge of his aimless life and act responsibly.	*planned, purposeful*
air	1.	*n.*	**atmosphere, sky** The plane climbed high into the air.	
	2.	*n.*	**appearance, manner, style, look, behaviour** Her easy manner gave her an air of confidence.	
	3.	*n.*	**breeze, draft, wind** Cold air came in when the door was opened.	
	4.	*v.*	**ventilate** We aired the cabin as soon as we arrived.	
airy	1.	*adj.*	**light, fluffy, delicate** The sponge cake was so airy it melted in your mouth.	1. *heavy, dull*
	2.	*adj.*	**gay, lively, joyous** The airy laughter of the young children filled the room.	2. *dull, dreary*
	3.	*adj.*	**breezy, ventilated, open** The high ceiling made the room airy.	3. *stuffy, confined*
alarm	1.	*n.*	**warning, alert** There's a fire in the building: Sound the alarm!	
	2.	*n.*	**excitement, fear, fright, terror, dread, panic** The cry caused much alarm.	2. *quietness, calm, peace*
	3.	*v.*	**frighten, agitate, disturb, excite** The children were alarmed when they heard gunshots. *adj.* There has been an alarming number of burglaries lately.	3. *calm, soothe, quiet*
alert	1.	*n.*	**warning, alarm** The boaters hurried to shore when the storm alert was announced over the radio.	

	2.	*adj.*	**watchful, wide-awake, attentive, vigilant** The alert ranger noticed the smoke and gave the alarm.	**2.** *drowsy, inattentive*
	3.	*adj.*	**active, nimble, lively, spry, agile** It is a challenge to keep up with his alert mind.	**3.** *sluggish, slow, inactive*
alibi		*n.*	**excuse, defence, case** The defendant claimed to have a foolproof alibi.	
alien	1.	*n.*	**foreigner, newcomer, stranger** Many people claim to have seen aliens from other planets.	**1.** *native, citizen*
	2.	*adj.*	**foreign, different, strange** Boris soon adapted to the alien customs of his new country.	**2.** *familiar, native, known*
allegiance		*n.*	**devotion, faithfulness, loyalty** Pledge allegiance to your country.	*disloyalty, treason*
alliance		*n.*	**connection, pact, union, league, federation** The three neighbouring countries formed a close alliance.	*separation, opposition*
allocate		*v.*	**apportion, assign, earmark** The funds were allocated to the various clubs. *n.* Since it considered everyone's needs, it was a fair allocation.	*deny, refuse, withhold*
allot	1.	*v.*	**assign, give** The teacher allotted the students a week to write the essay.	**1.** *keep, retain, withhold, withdraw*
	2.	*v.*	**divide, distribute, award** Will the prizes be allotted fairly? *n.* We received our allotment of books.	
allow		*v.*	**permit, let, grant, consent** The teacher allowed us to leave early.	*deny, refuse, forbid restrain, disallow*
allowance		*n.*	**pocket money, wage, salary** May gets a big allowance from her parents.	
alone	1.	*adv.*	**by oneself, solo, singly** All his friends were busy, so he went alone.	**1.** *accompanied, escorted*
	2.	*adj.*	**solely, only** He alone was left.	**2.** *numerous, many, several*

Word			Synonyms / Example	Antonyms
aloof	**1.**	*adj.*	**unsympathetic, cool, distant** His aloof manner made me wonder if he was upset with me.	**1.** *sympathetic, warm, sociable*
	2.	*adv.*	**apart, at a distance** The stranger stood aloof at the gathering.	**2.** *nearby, close*
also		*adv.*	**besides, too, in addition, likewise** My friends were going, so I also went.	*only, alone*
alter		*v.*	**change, modify, vary, adjust** The tailor altered the coat to fit me. *n.* The alterations made the coat fit much better.	*preserve, keep*
alternative		*n.*	**option, choice** What are my alternatives in this matter?	*obligation*
always		*adv.*	**forever, for all time, perpetually** They promised to love each other always.	*never, not at all*
amateur	**1.**	*n.*	**nonprofessional** Amateurs compete in sports for the love of it, not for fees.	**1.** *professional*
	2.	*n.*	**novice, beginner, trainee** For an amateur, she knows a lot about painting.	**2.** *expert*
amaze		*v.*	**overwhelm, surprise, astonish, astound** The magician amazed me with her tricks. *adj.* Making her assistant disappear into thin air was an amazing trick.	
amazement		*n.*	**surprise, astonishment, wonder, bewilderment** They stared in amazement at the athlete's great feats of strength.	*boredom*
ambition		*n.*	**desire, aspiration, enterprise** Her ambition was to lead the nation. *adj.* She works hard because she is ambitious.	*laziness, indifference*
amend		*v.*	**improve, better, correct, reform** The government amended the law to make it fairer. *n.* The amendments were well-received by the people.	*harm, impair, spoil, injure*

Word		Part of speech	Synonyms / Example	Antonyms
amiable		*adj.*	**good-natured, agreeable, pleasant, kindly, pleasing** Everyone likes her because she is such an amiable person.	*grouchy, irritable, ill-tempered, troublesome*
amount		*n.*	**total, full value, number** What is the amount of the bill?	
ample		*adj.*	**enough, abundant, copious** No one went hungry as there was ample food. *adv.* The hero was amply rewarded.	*insufficient, inadequate*
amplify		*v.*	**enlarge, increase, make louder** A microphone amplifies a speaker's voice. *n.* An amplifier increases the sound.	*reduce, shorten, lessen*
amuse		*v.*	**entertain, interest** The circus clowns amused the crowd. *adj.* The clown's big red nose was an amusing sight.	*bore, tire, annoy*
amusement		*n.*	**fun, diversion, entertainment** We watch movies for amusement. *adj.* Children love the rides in amusement parks.	*boredom, monotony*
ancient		*adj.*	**very old, aged** The ruins of the ancient pyramid were fascinating.	*modern, up-to-date, current, recent, young*
anger		*n.*	**rage, fury, ire, wrath** The beast's anger was frightening. *adj.* The angry animal lunged at the hunter. *adv.* The lion growled angrily at the hunter.	*mildness, patience, peace, calm*
angle		*n.*	**viewpoint, approach, position, slant, perspective** Let's discuss the problem from a different angle.	
anguish		*n.*	**agony, misery, torture, extreme pain, suffering, woe** The fire victim suffered great anguish from his burns.	*ease, comfort, relief*
animal	1.	*n.*	**beast, creature** We went to the zoo to see the animals.	

Word			Synonyms	Antonyms
	2.	*adj.*	**bestial, brutish, untamed, wild** In a fit of animal anger, he smashed the vase.	**2.** *tamed, cultivated*
animate	1.	*adj.*	**living, live** Plants and animals are animate.	**1.** *inanimate, lifeless*
	2.	*v.*	**activate, move to action** The walking doll was animated by batteries.	**2.** *neutralize, deactivate*
animated		*adj.*	**lively, vivacious, vibrant** The students were engaged in an animated debate.	*quiet, sober, dull, listless, inanimate*
annihilate		*v.*	**destroy, ruin, exterminate, eradicate** The town was annihilated by the tornado. *n.* The annihilation of the town by the tornado was complete.	*spare, preserve, save*
announce		*v.*	**proclaim, make known, tell, speak publicly, advertise, reveal, report, declare, notify** May and Ed announced their engagement. *n.* The engagement announcement was printed in the newspaper. *n.* Radio announcers must speak clearly.	*keep silent, conceal, hide, withhold*
annoy		*v.*	**aggravate, irritate, bother, pester, irk, badger, trouble** He annoys everyone with his bad behaviour. *n.* The dog's persistent barking was an annoyance. *adj.* Pushy salespeople are very annoying.	*soothe, calm, help*
annual		*adj.*	**yearly** Valentine's Day is an annual event. *adv.* Summer holidays occur annually.	
another		*adj.*	**additional, one more, different** Let's run another race after this one.	*same*
answer	1.	*n.*	**solution** I know the answer to the riddle.	**1.** *problem, question*
	2.	*n.*	**reply, retort, comeback, response** What was your answer when he asked you for a favour? *v.* We answered the letter right away.	**2.** *request, question, inquiry*

Word			Synonyms / Example	Antonyms
antagonize		*v.*	**repel, offend** Her selfish behaviour antagonized everyone in the class. *n.* She showed her antagonism by glaring at us.	*pacify, ingratiate*
anticipate		*v.*	**expect, predict, foresee** The enemy anticipated our attack and was prepared for it.	*be surprised, doubt*
anticipation		*n.*	**expectation** In anticipation of a big turnout, we rented a large hall.	
antique		*adj.*	**ancient, quaint, old-fashioned, timeworn, antiquated, very old** The antique jewellery was donated to the museum. *n.* Antiques are priceless because they represent a piece of the past.	*new, modern, recent, up-to-date, stylish, fashionable, current*
anxiety		*n.*	**concern, uneasiness, worry, anguish** Kit's illness caused us much anxiety.	*ease, contentment, peace*
anxious	1.	*adj.*	**troubled, worried, uneasy** Your parents are anxious when you are late.	1. *calm, relieved, unconcerned*
	2.	*adj.*	**desirous, fervent, eager** He was anxious to get a new car. *adv.* She anxiously awaits your return.	
apart		*adv.*	**aside, separately** Place those cups apart from the rest.	*together, side by side*
apathy		*n.*	**indifference, unconcern, insensitivity** Because of public apathy our environment has been drastically damaged. *adj.* We must change our apathetic attitudes before it is too late.	*concern, interest*
apex	1.	*n.*	**pinnacle, summit, peak** The mountaineers reached the apex of Mount Everest.	1. *base, foot, bottom*
	2.	*n.*	**climax** Winning the trophy was the apex of the team's career.	2. *depth, low point*

Word			Synonyms / Example	Antonyms
apparent		*adj.*	**obvious, probable, likely** The apparent cause of the fire was carelessness. *adv.* The accident was apparently the driver's fault.	*unlikely, doubtful*
appeal	1.	*n.*	**request, entreaty, petition** The prisoner's appeal for a new trial was granted.	1. *denial, refusal*
	2.	*v.*	**beg, plead, ask, pray, entreat** The police appealed to eyewitnesses for help.	2. *deny, refuse*
	3.	*v.*	**interest, engage, charm** Travelling appeals to many people. *n.* Travelling has great appeal for many people.	3. *disgust*
appealing		*adj.*	**enticing, attractive, charming** Her appealing personality won her many votes.	*unattractive, unpleasant, repulsive*
appear	1.	*v.*	**come into view, emerge** The sun appeared from behind the clouds.	1. *disappear, vanish*
	2.	*v.*	**seem, look** Judging from his appetite, the patient appears to be recovering. *n.* His healthy appearance cheered everyone.	
appetite		*n.*	**hunger, craving, longing** The aroma of freshly baked cookies whetted my appetite.	*aversion, dislike, distaste*
appetizing		*adj.*	**appealing, enticing** An appetizing aroma came from the kitchen.	*unattractive, repulsive, distasteful*
applaud	1.	*v.*	**clap, cheer** The audience applauded wildly after the performance. *n.* The applause was deafening.	1. *boo, deride, jeer*
	2.	*v.*	**approve, praise, acclaim** The government was applauded for its plans to clean the environment.	2. *disapprove, criticize*
apply	1.	*v.*	**use, practise, employ** Paul applied his new knowledge to the project.	
	2.	*v.*	**dedicate, direct** She applied herself to the job and finished it quickly.	
	3.	*v.*	**refer, fit, pertain** Safety rules apply everywhere.	
	4.	*v.*	**spread on, put on** We applied wax to the floor.	4. *remove, take off*

Word	#	Part	Synonyms / Example	Antonyms
	5.	*v.*	**make an application, request** Will you apply for a job this summer? *n.* I sent off my university application yesterday.	
appoint	1.	*v.*	**name, select, nominate** The committee appointed its new president. *n.* The appointment for the position was put to a vote.	1. *dismiss*
	2.	*v.*	**arrange, set, decide on** We appointed the date for the next meeting. *n.* I have an appointment tomorrow to see my dentist.	2. *cancel, change*
appreciate	1.	*v.*	**be thankful for, welcome, enjoy** Jan appreciated her friend's kindness. *n.* She sent flowers to express her appreciation.	1. *object to*
	2.	*v.*	**understand, realize, comprehend** It is difficult to appreciate the cost of education today.	
	3.	*v.*	**improve, inflate, rise in value** Property values have appreciated greatly in the last few years.	3. *depreciate, devalue*
apprehend		*v.*	**arrest, capture, seize, catch** The police apprehended the robbers at the scene of the crime.	*free, release, let go*
apprehension	1.	*n.*	**capture, seizure, arrest** After the criminals' apprehension, they were sent to jail.	1. *release*
	2.	*n.*	**trepidation, foreboding, dread** I was filled with apprehension about driving in the storm. *adj.* I am apprehensive about driving in a storm.	2. *calm, peace*
approach	1.	*n.*	**access, entrance, path** The approach to the cabin is hidden by trees.	1. *exit, departure*
	2.	*v.*	**move toward, come near** We approached the growling dog cautiously.	2. *leave, recede, depart, retreat*
appropriate		*adj.*	**suitable, fitting, proper, apt** Amy gave an appropriate answer to the question. *adv.* Dress appropriately for the party.	*inappropriate, improper, unsuitable*

Word			Synonyms and examples	Antonyms
approval		*n.*	**sanction, permission, assent** They asked for the committee's approval to proceed with the project. *v.* The committee approved of the project.	*disapproval*
approximate		*adj.*	**estimated, near** The approximate time of arrival is two o'clock. *adv.* The tree was approximately twice my height.	*correct, exact*
arduous		*adj.*	**trying, heavy, tiring, exhausting** Pushing the stalled car up the hill was arduous work.	*easy, effortless*
argue		*v.*	**dispute, debate, plead** The workers argued against Sunday shopping. *n.* The discussion turned into a heated argument.	*agree*
arid		*adj.*	**parched, dry, barren** It is difficult to grow crops in arid areas.	*well-watered, lush, fertile*
arms		*n.*	**weapons, munitions** Soldiers use arms in battle. *v.* The soldiers armed themselves for battle. *adj.* Armed robbers held up the bank.	
aroma		*n.*	**smell, fragrance, odour, scent** The aroma of freshly baked bread came from the bakery. *adj.* Roses are known for being aromatic.	
arouse		*v.*	**awaken, stir up, excite** The man was aroused from his sleep by a loud noise.	*calm, soothe*
arrange	1.	*v.*	**adjust, group, sort** Arrange these words in alphabetical order.	**1.** *scatter, jumble, disarrange*
	2.	*v.*	**plan, determine, prepare for** The students will arrange everything for the dance. *n.* The arrangements for the dance are going smoothly.	

Word		Part	Synonyms / Example	Antonyms
array	**1.**	*n.*	**display, arrangement** There was a splendid array of jewellery in the museum. *v.* The soldiers were arrayed for the battle.	
	2.	*v.*	**dress, outfit, clothe** The queen was magnificently arrayed for the ceremony.	
arrest	**1.**	*v.*	**catch, detain, capture, hold** The police arrested the suspects. *n.* Excellent police work led to the arrest.	**1.** *release, set free*
	2.	*v.*	**stop, check** Preventive medicine can help arrest the spread of disease.	**2.** *promote, foster*
arrive	**1.**	*v.*	**come** They will arrive on the next flight. *n.* We will meet them on their arrival at the airport.	**1.** *go, leave, depart*
	2.	*v.*	**reach, attain** After much deliberation, the students arrived at a decision.	
arrogance		*n.*	**vanity, contempt, conceit** His arrogance made him unpopular. *adj.* The arrogant boy refused to admit he had made a mistake.	*simplicity, humility*
art		*n.*	**skill, craft** She has spent years developing the art of quilt-making.	
artificial	**1.**	*adj.*	**imitation, synthetic, fake** An artificial lake was created in the new park.	**1.** *real, natural, genuine*
	2.	*adj.*	**pretended, phony, affected** Her artificial smile showed she was insincere.	**2.** *honest, sincere*
artist		*n.*	**expert, creator, author, musician, dancer, composer, painter, sculptor** A painter is one type of artist.	
ascend		*v.*	**rise, climb, scale, mount** The plane ascended suddenly to avoid the mountain top. *n.* Our ascent of the mountain tired us out.	*descend, go down*
ashen		*adj.*	**pale, wan, pallid** The boy turned ashen when he heard the bad news.	*flushed, rosy*

Word			Synonyms and examples	Antonyms
ask	**1.**	*v.*	**inquire, question** She always asks about you.	**1.** *tell, answer, inform*
	2.	*v.*	**request** The hospital asks for your support in their charity drive.	
	3.	*v.*	**require, demand, charge** That store asks higher prices than others.	**3.** *give*
assemble	**1.**	*v.*	**fit together, put together, combine, construct** She assembled the model jet.	**1.** *take apart, detach, dismantle, break*
	2.	*v.*	**gather together, meet, convene** The group assembles weekly. *n.* The school has a weekly assembly of all the students.	**2.** *scatter, disperse*
assert		*v.*	**claim, declare, insist** He asserted that the accident wasn't his fault. *n.* He will have to prove his assertion of innocence.	*deny*
assessment	**1.**	*n.*	**rate, appraisal, evaluation** According to the jeweller's assessment, my ring is worth one thousand dollars.	
	2.	*n.*	**tax, charge, fee** Each property owner must pay a new assessment for sewers.	
assign		*v.*	**allot, appoint, give** The teacher assigns homework. *n.* Our homework assignment is to research a famous inventor.	
assist		*v.*	**help, aid** He assisted the accident victim by giving her first aid. *n.* She came to my assistance when I had a problem.	*hinder, delay, oppose, obstruct*
associate	**1.**	*n.*	**partner, colleague, ally** He is meeting with his associate to discuss a business deal.	**1.** *competitor, rival, opponent*
	2.	*v.*	**work with, join with** I prefer to associate with people who have a positive attitude.	**2.** *avoid, ignore*
	3.	*v.*	**link, connect, correlate** Cats learn to associate the sound of a can opener with mealtime.	

Word	Part of speech	Synonyms and examples	Antonyms
association	*n.*	**union, society, body, group, club, company, organization** An association is being formed to protest against higher rents.	
assorted	*adj.*	**mixed, various, different** Assorted toys were collected for the children. *n.* There was a wide assortment of food at the banquet.	*all the same, identical*
assume	*v.*	**suppose, think, believe, guess** He never called back so we assumed he wasn't interested. *n.* He told us later that our assumption had been correct.	*know*
assumed	*adj.*	**false, phony** The author wrote under an assumed name to protect his identity.	*actual, real, true*
assurance	*n.*	**confidence, self-reliance** The experienced pilot flew the plane with assurance.	*nervousness, shyness, doubt*
assure	*v.*	**promise, guarantee, pledge** The baby-sitter assured us that she would take good care of the baby. *n.* We were relieved to hear this assurance.	*deny*
astonish	*v.*	**surprise, amaze, shock, astound** The young violinist's performance astonished the audience. *adj.* It was an astonishing performance. *n.* Her musical talent caused much astonishment.	
astound	*v.*	**shock, amaze, astonish** We were astounded by the news of the tragedy. *adj.* The pilots did some astounding flying feats.	
atomic	*adj.*	**small, minute, infinitesimal, molecular** A powerful microscope is used to see atomic objects.	*enormous, gigantic, huge*
attach	*v.*	**fasten, connect, join, unite, combine** We attached the trailer to the bumper of the car.	*sever, detach, disconnect, cut, separate*

Word			Synonyms	Antonyms
attachment		*n.*	**friendship, love, affection, devotion** There was a strong attachment between the friends.	*animosity, dislike, indifference*
attack	1.	*n.*	**invasion, assault, charge** The army made an attack on the rebel camp. *v.* The army attacked the enemy at dawn.	**1.** *retreat, surrender, withdrawal*
	2.	*n.*	**sudden occurrence** He had an attack of the flu.	
attain		*v.*	**get, gain, obtain, arrive at, accomplish, earn, reach** After much hard work, she attained her goal. *adj.* She had set herself an attainable goal.	*lose, fail, give up, surrender*
attempt		*v.*	**try, endeavour, strive** She attempted to jump over the high bar. *n.* It took her three attempts before she succeeded.	*avoid, shirk*
attend	1.	*v.*	**be present at, go to** Students must attend school regularly. *n.* The teacher recorded the class attendance.	**1.** *miss, be absent*
	2.	*v.*	**care for, look after** The nurse attended to the injured student.	**2.** *neglect*
attention	1.	*n.*	**care, thought, consideration** The patient received the best medical attention.	**1.** *neglect*
	2.	*n.*	**heed, notice, observance** Pay attention to the teacher.	**2.** *disregard*
attentive	1.	*adj.*	**alert, intent** The attentive audience listened to everything the speaker had to say.	**1.** *inattentive, unconcerned*
	2.	*adj.*	**courteous, polite, thoughtful** The attentive waiter received a large tip.	**2.** *impolite, careless, rude*
attire	1.	*n.*	**dress, apparel, clothing, clothes** Shorts are comfortable attire for hot weather.	
	2.	*v.*	**dress, array** The clown was attired in funny clothing.	**2.** *undress, disrobe*

Word	No.	Part	Synonyms and example	Antonyms
attitude	1.	*n.*	**manner, outlook, disposition** He has a positive attitude toward work.	
	2.	*n.*	**position, pose** The crowd stood in a quiet attitude.	
attract		*v.*	**draw, interest, appeal to** The computer show attracted a large crowd. *n.* The robot was a great attraction.	*offend, disgust, repulse*
attractive		*adj.*	**charming, lovely, pleasant, likeable, pretty** These new fashions are quite attractive.	*ugly, unpleasant*
attribute		*v.*	**credit, blame, accredit** The damage was attributed to a bomb blast.	
audacious	1.	*adj.*	**brave, plucky, daring, bold, fearless** The audacious mountain climber made it to the summit.	**1.** *timid, cowardly, frightened*
	2.	*adj.*	**reckless, risky, daring** The acrobats performed audacious feats on the tightrope.	**2.** *careful, cautious*
audible		*adj.*	**clear, distinct** The loon's cry was audible in the still night.	*faint, muffled*
audio		*n.*	**broadcast sound** The audio of the television program was excellent.	
augment		*v.*	**expand, add to, increase** The baseball team augmented their funds by selling candy.	*reduce, shrink, decrease*
auspices		*n.*	**charge, support, care** The bus trips were under the auspices of the school.	
austere		*adj.*	**severe, strict, stern** His austere expression prevented students from approaching him.	*kindly, easy, gentle*
authentic		*adj.*	**true, real, genuine, legitimate** The signature was authentic and not a forgery.	*counterfeit, false, fictitious*
authority	1.	*n.*	**control, command, power** Does he have the authority to do this?	

Word	No.	Part	Synonyms and example	Antonyms
	2.	*n.*	**scholar, specialist, expert** Jacques Cousteau is an authority on underwater research.	
automatic	1.	*adj.*	**involuntary, reflex, spontaneous** Blinking your eyes is an automatic action.	**1.** *planned, intended*
	2.	*adj.*	**mechanical, self-operating** The automatic door opened as I walked toward it.	**2.** *manual*
auxiliary	1.	*n.*	**helper, aid, assistant, supporter** The parents' auxiliary helps at the school.	**1.** *adversary, hinderer, antagonist*
	2.	*adj.*	**helping, supporting** The auxiliary motor on the boat enables it to go faster.	**2.** *main, chief, primary*
available		*adj.*	**obtainable, handy, free** We had to stand as there were no available seats on the train.	*unavailable, taken, occupied*
average	1.	*n.*	**mean, standard, norm** Her grades are above the class average.	
	2.	*adj.*	**normal, ordinary, usual** The study showed that the average family has two children.	**2.** *unusual, exceptional, extraordinary*
aversion		*n.*	**dislike, hatred, disgust** Their peaceful leader has an aversion to violence.	*affection, fondness*
avert		*v.*	**prevent, avoid, turn aside** The driver's quick action averted a serious accident.	
aviation		*n.*	**flying, flight, aeronautics** The Wright brothers are very important in the history of aviation.	
avid		*adj.*	**keen, eager, devoted** Marilyn is an avid reader of mysteries.	*unwilling, reluctant*
avoid		*v.*	**shun, evade, escape, dodge** He avoided speaking to her by crossing the street. *n.* The avoidance of a problem doesn't solve it.	*confront, meet, face, invite*
award	1.	*v.*	**give, grant, accord** The judges awarded the gold medal for figure skating to Anu.	**1.** *deny, refuse*

	2.	*n.*	**prize, honour, trophy** Awards at the Olympic Games are given for excellence.	
aware		*adj.*	**informed, knowledgeable, conscious of** I became aware of the fire when I smelled smoke.	*uninformed, unaware*
away	1.	*adj.*	**absent, gone, not present** The boss is away until three o'clock.	**1.** *present, here*
	2.	*adv.*	**aside, at a distance** Please go away and don't bother me.	**2.** *near*
awe		*n.*	**fear, reverence, wonder** Our first sight of Niagara Falls filled us with awe. *adj.* The size of Niagara Falls is awesome.	
awful		*adj.*	**dreadful, horrible, terrible, shocking, frightful, alarming** The awful accident shocked everyone.	*wonderful, terrific*
awkward	1.	*adj.*	**ungainly, gawky, clumsy** The circus bear's awkward movements amused the children.	**1.** *graceful, artful, easy*
	2.	*adj.*	**uncomfortable, embarrassing** There was an awkward silence when the results were announced.	**2.** *comfortable*
	3.	*adj.*	**inconvenient, difficult, troublesome** It will be awkward to get an appointment before Thursday.	**3.** *convenient, easy, handy*

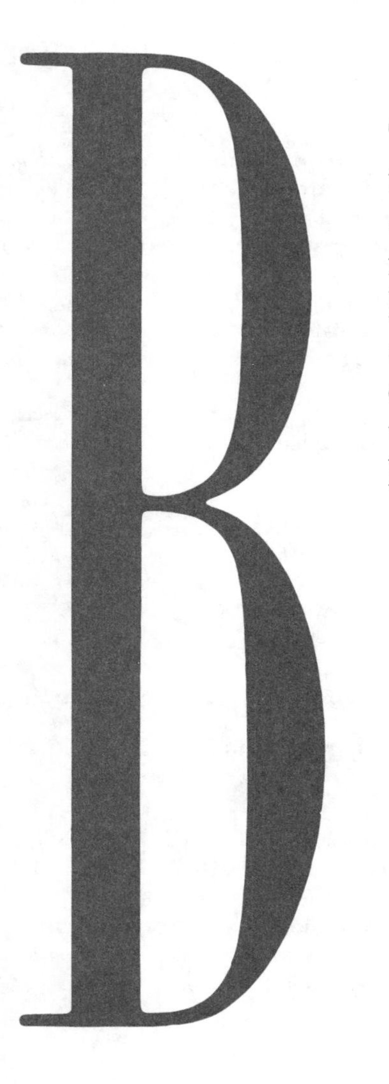

The Greeks made use of the Phoenician word *beth* and changed it to *beta*, from which comes the Roman letter *B*. Our alphabet gets its name by combining the Greek words for the first two letters, *alpha* and *beta*.

Word			Synonyms	Antonyms
babble		*n.*	**chatter, jabber, prattle, murmur** The excited babble of the crowd drowned out the music. *v.* A baby babbles before it learns how to talk.	
baby	**1.**	*n.*	**babe, infant, tot, toddler** Dad gently rocked the newborn baby to sleep.	**1.** *adult, grown-up*
	2.	*n.*	**young, offspring** Animals protect and feed their babies.	
bad	**1.**	*adj.*	**evil, wrong, vile, corrupt, wicked** In fairy tales, the bad characters are often punished in the end.	**1.** *honest, good, right*
	2.	*adj.*	**rotten, spoiled, foul, putrid, rancid, tainted** The smell of bad fish made me ill.	**2.** *pleasant, clean, pure, delicious, good, fresh*
	3.	*adj.*	**defective, deficient, inferior** Her handwriting is so bad that no one can read it.	**3.** *superior, excellent, correct*
	4.	*adj.*	**ill, diseased, ailing, sick** Ravi missed the trip because of bad health.	**4.** *well, healthy, hearty*
	5.	*adj.*	**harmful** Smoking is bad for one's health.	**5.** *good, helpful, beneficial*
	6.	*adj.*	**unfavourable, unfortunate, distressing** Did you hear the bad news about the car accident?	**6.** *good, favourable, fortunate*
baffle		*v.*	**puzzle, bewilder, confound, confuse, perplex** We were completely baffled by his strange behaviour.	*clarify*
balance	**1.**	*n.*	**scales, weighing machine** The butcher weighed the meat on the balance.	
	2.	*n.*	**equilibrium, equivalence, symmetry, steadiness, stability** Mary lost her balance and fell off the bike. *v.* She balanced herself carefully on the bike and rode off.	**2.** *imbalance, lopsidedness, instability*
	3.	*n.*	**cash on hand, credit surplus** She had a bank balance of five hundred dollars.	
	4.	*n.*	**remainder** I intend to take things easy for the balance of the year.	

Word	No.	Part of speech	Synonyms and example	Antonyms
balmy		*adj.*	**soft, soothing, gentle, mild, summerlike** The balmy spring weather melted the snow.	*harsh, unpleasant, strong, severe, wintery*
ban		*v.*	**forbid, prohibit, outlaw** Smoking is banned in many public buildings. *n.* There is also a ban on smoking in elevators.	*allow, permit, encourage*
band	1.	*n.*	**group, flock, herd, collection** The band of wild dogs roamed the plains searching for food.	1. *individual, one*
	2.	*n.*	**strip, stripe, ribbon, sash, belt** She wore a red band in her hair.	
	3.	*v.*	**unite, gather, join** The angry citizens banded together to protest the new taxes.	3. *disband, disperse, divide, separate*
bandit		*n.*	**thief, robber, outlaw** The bandits escaped in a van after they robbed the bank.	
banish		*v.*	**exile, dismiss, expel, evict** The spy was banished from the country after his arrest.	*welcome, accept*
bar		*v.*	**obstruct, forbid, block, restrain, keep out, prevent, exclude, ban** He was barred from the examination because he was caught cheating.	*permit, allow, admit, welcome*
bare	1.	*v.*	**disclose, divulge, reveal, uncover, make known** The actor bared the facts of the scandal in his memoirs.	1. *keep secret, hide, cover*
	2.	*adj.*	**uncovered, naked, unclothed, exposed, unprotected** At the campground, mosquitos attacked my bare arms and legs.	2. *clothed, covered, protected*
	3.	*adj.*	**simple, unadorned, modest, plain, unpretentious** Jin decorated the bare walls of her room with bright posters.	3. *ornamented, adorned, decorated, pretentious, fancy*
	4.	*adj.*	**empty, barren** The hungry kids were dismayed to find a bare refrigerator.	4. *full, well-stocked*
barely		*adv.*	**hardly, just, scarcely** We left late and barely caught our train.	*amply, sufficiently, adequately*

Word			Synonyms	Antonyms
bargain	1.	*n.*	**pact, agreement, deal, contract, promise** We made a bargain to help each other with our homework.	
	2.	*v.*	**haggle, negotiate** He bargained with the salesperson for a better deal.	
barren		*adj.*	**sterile, unproductive** Modern irrigation techniques have transformed barren deserts into farmland.	*fertile, fruitful, productive*
barrier		*n.*	**obstacle, hindrance, impediment, block, restriction** For many people, fear can be a mental barrier to adventure.	*entrance, opening, thoroughfare, way, path, trail*
base	1.	*n.*	**bottom, foot, foundation, support** The statue stood on a base of marble.	**1.** *summit, top, crest*
	2.	*v.*	**establish, found** Juri's opinions were based on thorough research.	
	3.	*adj.*	**low, mean, vile, unworthy, despicable, contemptible** The base acts of the secret police disgusted everyone.	**3.** *reputable, virtuous, noble, superior, esteemed, refined*
bashful		*adj.*	**shy, timid, retiring, reserved, modest** The bashful student would not speak in public.	*conceited, bold, forward*
basic		*adj.*	**essential, primary, central, principal, fundamental, necessary, required, indispensable** Food and shelter are a human's basic needs.	*dispensable, unnecessary*
bat	1.	*n.*	**stick, club** Try to hit the ball with a bat.	
	2.	*v.*	**hit, strike, sock, whack** Dan batted the ball across the field.	
battle	1.	*n.*	**fight, combat, conflict, clash, strife, contest, engagement** The battle between the two armies ended in a truce.	**1.** *peace, harmony, agreement, truce, armistice*
	2.	*v.*	**fight, struggle** The accident victim battled for her life.	**2.** *give in, quit, succumb, surrender, yield*
beam	1.	*n.*	**rafter, plank, girder** The construction worker riveted the steel beam into place.	

	2.	*n.*	**ray, gleam, glow** The laser beam is used in medical procedures and in warfare.	
	3.	*v.*	**transmit, give out, send, broadcast** Satellites beam television signals around the world.	**3.** *receive*
	4.	*v.*	**laugh, grin, smile brightly** Nida beamed when she saw her gift. *adj.* The beaming child opened the gift eagerly.	**4.** *frown, scowl, glower*
bear	1.	*v.*	**carry, transport, convey** Donkeys can bear heavy burdens.	**1.** *leave behind*
	2.	*v.*	**support, hold up** This small chair cannot bear the weight of an adult.	**2.** *drop, let go, collapse*
	3.	*v.*	**suffer, endure, tolerate, shoulder** The injured person bore the pain quietly. *adj.* The heat was more bearable after I changed into my shorts.	**3.** *succumb, give in*
	4.	*v.*	**yield, produce, generate** The apple tree bore delicious fruit.	**4.** *wither, be barren*
beast		*n.*	**brute, savage, creature** The wild beast lunged at the hunter.	
beat	1.	*v.*	**hit, strike, punch, whack, thump, pummel, thrash, pound, flog** Thugs brutally beat the old man. *n.* The police saved him from the beating.	
	2.	*v.*	**defeat, conquer, surpass, overcome** After a long struggle, Yun beat Nick in the chess game.	**2.** *surrender, give in*
beautiful		*adj.*	**handsome, pretty, good-looking, attractive, lovely, splendid, exquisite** Uri's beautiful photograph of a sunset won him a prize. *adv.* Some artists paint sunsets beautifully.	*unattractive, ugly*
beauty		*n.*	**loveliness, charm, splendour, handsomeness** The beauty of the tulip fields in Holland is world renowned.	*ugliness, unattractiveness*
becoming	1.	*adj.*	**fitting, proper, suitable** Shouting and pushing is not becoming behaviour.	**1.** *unsuitable, improper, unbecoming*

	2.	*adj.*	**pleasing, attractive, flattering** Chris complimented Ray on his becoming suit.	2. *unattractive*
before	1.	*adv.*	**previously, earlier, sooner, heretofore** I recognized the place because I had been there before.	1. *in the future, afterward*
	2.	*prep.*	**in front of, ahead of** There are many people before me in the line.	2. *behind, at the rear of, after*
	3.	*prep.*	**in advance of, previous to** I went to the dentist the day before yesterday.	3. *after, following*
befriend		*v.*	**help, favour, assist** The family befriended their new neighbours.	*hinder, impede*
beg	1.	*v.*	**beseech, implore, entreat, plead, ask** The prisoners begged for mercy at their trial.	1. *insist, require, demand*
	2.	*v.*	**ask for charity, ask for alms** The starving children begged for money on the streets. *n.* Tourists gave the beggars some money.	2. *give, endow, donate*
begin		*v.*	**commence, start, undertake, launch** We began our homework after dinner.	*finish, end, stop, complete, terminate*
beginner		*n.*	**novice, learner, amateur** A beginner in swimming should not go far from the shore.	*expert, ace, professional*
beginning		*n.*	**start, opening, origin, outset, source, commencement** I was late, so I missed the beginning of the movie.	*end, finish, close, completion, closing, conclusion, termination*
behaviour (also spelled behavior)		*n.*	**conduct, manners, actions, deportment, bearing** The children were on their best behaviour at the concert.	
behind	1.	*adv.*	**in the rear, aft, at the back** The animal's tail hung behind.	1. *in the front, fore, at the front*
	2.	*adv.*	**farther back** The slower walkers lagged behind.	2. *ahead*
	3.	*adv.*	**slow, late, not on time, tardy** The train should arrive soon, unless it's running behind.	3. *on time, on schedule, fast, ahead of schedule*

Word	No.	Part	Synonyms / Example	Antonyms
	4.	*prep.*	**at the back of, in the rear of** The child hid behind the door.	**4.** *in the front of*
	5.	*prep.*	**later than, after** The mail delivery is behind schedule today.	**5.** *earlier than, ahead*
	6.	*prep.*	**in support of, for** I know my friends will stand behind my actions.	**6.** *against*
believe		*v.*	**accept, think, have faith** I believe that you are telling the truth. *n.* It is my belief that you are telling the truth.	*doubt, deny, suspect*
bellow		*n.*	**howl, cry, roar, shout loudly** Lou let out a bellow of pain when he fell. *v.* The lumberjack bellowed a warning as the tree began to fall.	*whisper, whimper*
belongings		*n.*	**property, possessions** All their belongings were lost in the fire.	
below	1.	*adv.*	**beneath, underneath** I looked over the balcony and spotted my friend below.	**1.** *above*
	2.	*prep.*	**lower than, under** It gets cold when the temperature falls below zero degrees celsius.	**2.** *above, higher than*
	3.	*prep.*	**unworthy of, beneath** Bad language is below respect.	**3.** *worthy of, deserving of*
bend	1.	*n.*	**curve, turn** The car went out of control on the sharp bend in the road.	**1.** *straightaway*
	2.	*v.*	**curve, turn, twist** The electrician bent the wire around the base of the lamp.	**2.** *straighten, unwind, extend*
	3.	*v.*	**submit, yield** The people refused to bend to the dictator's demands.	**3.** *defy*
beneath	1.	*prep.*	**under, below, underneath, underfoot** We picnicked beneath a huge tree.	**1.** *above, on*
	2.	*prep.*	**unworthy of, undeserving of** Such a cruel dictator is beneath contempt.	**2.** *worthy of, deserving of*
benefit	1.	*n.*	**advantage, profit, favour, help** A good coach is a benefit for any team.	**1.** *disadvantage, loss, detriment*

	2.	*v.*	**help, aid, assist** Extra practice will benefit this team's game.	2. *hurt, harm, hinder, damage*
bent	1.	*adj.*	**determined, inclined** She is bent on winning a scholarship. *n.* With her bent for hard work she will most likely succeed.	1. *disinterested, indifferent*
	2.	*adj.*	**twisted, distorted, curved, crooked** The car had a bent fender from the accident.	2. *rigid, straight, erect*
bet		*n.*	**wager, gamble, stake** The gambler placed a bet at the casino. *v.* How much money did he bet?	
bewilder		*v.*	**puzzle, perplex, confuse, mystify, confound** His strange illness bewildered the doctors.	*inform, guide, instruct, enlighten*
bias		*n.*	**preference, leaning, partiality** The spectators had a bias for the home team.	*impartiality*
big		*adj.*	**huge, large, great, grand, vast, immense** The stadium was big enough to hold 60 000 people.	*small, little, petite, tiny*
bind		*v.*	**fasten, tie, secure, truss** We bound the package with a cord. *adj.* A contract is a binding document.	*loosen, unfasten, free, untie*
biting	1.	*adj.*	**bitter, piercing, penetrating, cutting, sharp, intense, harsh** The biting wind prevented us from skating outdoors.	
	2.	*adj.*	**pungent, stinging, sharp, tart** Pickles have a biting taste.	2. *bland*
	3.	*adj.*	**sarcastic** The debater resorted to biting remarks about the opposing team.	
bitter	1.	*adj.*	**biting, sour, sharp, pungent, tart, astringent** Spoiled nuts have a bitter taste.	1. *sweet, pleasing*
	2.	*adj.*	**harsh, cruel, unbearable** Many people died in the bitter winter.	2. *mild, gentle, kind*

blame

1. *n.* **fault, guilt, condemnation, depreciation**
Industries have to take the blame for environmental pollution.
1. credit, praise, commendation

2. *v.* **accuse, condemn, criticize, charge**
The driver was blamed for the accident because he had been speeding.
2. praise, commend, credit

bland

1. *adj.* **mild, soothing, gentle**
A warm spring breeze is bland.
1. severe, harsh, bitter

2. *adj.* **affable, polite, agreeable**
The police officer's bland manners helped us relax.
2. rude, abrasive, disagreeable, abrupt, harsh, severe

3. *adj.* **uninteresting, dull, flat**
Kit disliked the hospital's bland food.
3. exciting, interesting

blank

1. *n.* **void, empty space, hollow, opening**
Fill in the blanks on the form.

2. *adj.* **expressionless, vague, vacant, impassive**
The blank look on his face told us he was daydreaming.
2. excited, expressive

3. *adj.* **unused, empty, fresh**
Write your answers on a blank page.
3. used, inscribed

blaze

v. **flame, flare, burn**
The wood is blazing in the fireplace.
n. The firefighters had a difficult time extinguishing the blaze.

bleak

adj. **dismal, desolate, dreary, dull, bare, barren**
Bleak winter days can be very depressing.
balmy, pleasant, cheerful

blemish

1. *n.* **flaw, defect, imperfection**
A pimple is a blemish on the skin.
1. impeccability, perfection

2. *v.* **hurt, harm, injure, mar, spoil**
Tim's perfect attendance record was blemished when he fell ill.
2. enhance, help

blend

1. *n.* **mixture, combination**
The sauce was made from a blend of ten different spices.

2. *v.* **mix, combine, mingle, unite, fuse, merge**
Blend these ingredients together to make the pudding.
n. Use the electric blender.
2. separate, divide

Word	No.	Part	Synonyms / Example	Antonyms
bliss		*n.*	**joy, ecstasy, rapture** The bride and groom were in a state of bliss on their wedding day. *adj.* The ceremony was a blissful occasion.	*misery, woe, suffering, unhappiness*
block	1.	*n.*	**hindrance, obstruction, obstacle, barrier, restriction** The plumber cleared the block in our pipes.	1. *opening, aid*
	2.	*v.*	**close off, obstruct** Huge snow drifts blocked the mountain pass.	2. *clear, open up*
bloom		*v.*	**flower, blossom** Tulips bloom in the spring. *n.* Tulip blooms come in many colours.	*decay, wilt, shrivel*
blossom	1.	*v.*	**flower, bloom** Fruit trees blossom in the spring. *n.* Cherry blossoms are a sign of spring.	1. *wither, fade*
	2.	*v.*	**develop, grow** Over the years, José has blossomed into a very good writer.	2. *deteriorate, decline*
blot	1.	*n.*	**spot, stain, smudge, smear, blemish** The spilled coffee left an ugly blot on my shirt.	
	2.	*v.*	**dry, absorb, soak up** We blotted the spilled liquid with paper towels.	
blow	1.	*n.*	**hit, knock, rap, cuff, stroke, bang** A boxer has to suffer fierce blows to the body.	
	2.	*n.*	**misfortune, loss, disaster, calamity, catastrophe** The loss of her cat was a blow to Nan.	2. *blessing, comfort, relief*
	3.	*v.*	**fling, whirl, sweep, waft, flutter** The flags were blowing in the wind.	3. *remain still*
	4.	*v.*	**puff, exhale, pant** Take a deep breath and blow out the candles.	4. *inhale*
bluff		*v.*	**fool, mislead, trick, deceive** Hal tried to bluff his way into the show without a ticket. *n.* The usher saw through Hal's bluff and refused to let him in.	

Word			Synonyms	Antonyms
blunder	1.	*n.*	**error, mistake, oversight, slip** The careless cashier made costly blunders. *v.* The cashier blundered in her addition of my bill.	1. *correction, reparation*
	2.	*v.*	**stumble, trip, fall** The tired boy blundered down the stairs.	2. *glide*
blunt	1.	*adj.*	**dull, unsharpened** The scissors were too blunt to cut the fabric.	1. *sharp, keen*
	2.	*adj.*	**outspoken, curt, abrupt** Blunt remarks can hurt people's feelings.	2. *diplomatic, gentle, polite, tactful, subtle*
blur		*v.*	**obscure, dim, shadow, cloud, screen** The driver slowed down when the fog blurred her view. *n.* Everything was a blur in the fog.	*clear, focus*
boast		*v.*	**brag, show off** Richard boasted about his new convertible. *adj.* He was a boastful person.	*be humble*
body	1.	*n.*	**frame, physique, form, figure, build** Exercise builds strong bodies.	
	2.	*n.*	**corpse, remains, cadaver** Police found the victim's body in the bush.	
	3.	*n.*	**expanse, mass, area** An ocean is a large body of water.	
	4.	*n.*	**organization, corporation, association, group** The student body met with the principal about the new rules.	
bogus		*adj.*	**phony, fictitious, counterfeit, sham, false, fake, artificial** The bogus five dollar bill was difficult to detect.	*real, legitimate, genuine*
boisterous		*adj.*	**noisy, loud, rowdy, uproarious, unrestrained** The boisterous crowd at the soccer match was told to calm down.	*quiet, reserved, restrained, calm*
bold	1.	*adj.*	**daring, brave, fearless, intrepid, courageous, valiant, adventurous** Bold adventurers scaled the world's highest peak.	1. *timid, shy, cowardly*

Word	No.	Part	Synonyms / Example	Antonyms
	2.	*adj.*	**brazen, saucy, impudent, rude, impertinent** The bold child made faces at us.	**2.** *polite, courteous, well-behaved, mannerly*
boon		*n.*	**blessing, help, benefit, advantage** Thermal underwear is a boon in Arctic winters.	*hindrance, handicap, disadvantage*
boost	1.	*n.*	**shove, push** "Give me a boost over the wall," shouted Sheila.	**1.** *pull, haul, tow*
	2.	*v.*	**raise, improve, increase** The good news boosted morale.	**2.** *decrease, lower, decline*
border	1.	*n.*	**fringe, trim, edge, margin** Put a border along the hem of the dress.	**1.** *centre, inside, interior*
	2.	*n.*	**boundary, frontier** Canada and the United States share an undefended border.	**2.** *interior*
bother	1.	*n.*	**nuisance, irritation, annoyance** It's such a bother to work in this heat.	**1.** *assistance, aid, help*
	2.	*n.*	**worry, fuss, trouble** He makes a bother out of everything.	**2.** *joy, delight, pleasure*
	3.	*v.*	**pester, worry, badger, fuss, irritate, trouble** Don't bother me while I'm busy.	**3.** *help, aid, assist*
bound	1.	*v.*	**leap, jump, spring, vault** Deer bound through the forests.	
	2.	*adj.*	**obliged, obligated, compelled** We are legally bound to pay taxes.	**2.** *free*
	3.	*adj.*	**certain, sure** You're bound to catch a cold if you go out without your coat.	**3.** *uncertain*
boundless		*adj.*	**endless, unlimited, limitless, infinite** Outer space is boundless.	*limited, finite, restricted, confined*
brave	1.	*v.*	**face, defy, oppose** Columbus braved the mutiny among his crew.	**1.** *hide, run from*
	2.	*adj.*	**fearless, bold, valiant, heroic, courageous, adventurous, dauntless, daring, gallant** It takes a brave person to overcome a handicap.	**2.** *cowardly, frightened, timid, cringing, fearful*
bravery		*n.*	**courage, valour, daring, gallantry, fearlessness** She was commended for her bravery in rescuing the drowning child.	*cowardice, fearfulness*

Word	No.	Part	Synonyms and example	Antonyms
brazen	1.	*adj.*	**impudent, rude, impertinent, forward, saucy** The child will be scolded for such brazen behaviour.	**1.** *polite, retiring, shy, reserved, modest, withdrawn*
	2.	*adj.*	**brass, brassy, bronze** There are many brazen vases in antique shops.	
break	1.	*n.*	**crack, gap, split, rupture, rift, fracture, schism** The seal emerged through the break in the ice.	
	2.	*n.*	**rest, interval, pause** The workers took a half-hour break for lunch.	
	3.	*v.*	**crack, smash, shatter, split** The plate broke when it fell on the floor.	**3.** *mend, join, attach, fasten, piece together, bind*
	4.	*v.*	**injure, damage, ruin, destroy** The baby broke his sister's toy.	**4.** *restore, repair, fix, enhance*
	5.	*v.*	**reveal, disclose, make known** Radio and television break the latest news to the public.	**5.** *conceal, hide, shield*
breakable		*adj.*	**fragile, delicate, frail, weak** China plates are breakable.	*durable, strong, tough*
breakdown		*n.*	**collapse, disruption, stoppage** A computer breakdown caused the bank to close for the day.	*recovery, renewal*
brief	1.	*n.*	**summary, outline** The lawyer compiled a brief on the case.	
	2.	*adj.*	**short, terse, concise** A brief announcement of the event was made on television.	**2.** *lengthy, wordy, detailed*
	3.	*adj.*	**skimpy, small, slight, insufficient** Such a brief costume will attract attention.	**3.** *large, ample, sufficient*
bright	1.	*adj.*	**brilliant, shining, gleaming, glowing, lustrous, scintillating, sparkling, twinkling** Stars seem bright on clear nights. *adv.* Jewels shine brightly.	**1.** *dark, dull, clouded, gloomy, opaque, dreary*
	2.	*adj.*	**clever, brilliant, intelligent, alert** She is full of bright ideas.	**2.** *stupid, dull, unintelligent*
	3.	*adj.*	**promising, favourable, auspicious, hopeful** The scientist has a bright career ahead of her.	**3.** *obscure, doubtful, dubious*
brim	1.	*n.*	**edge, rim, lip, border, top** Please don't fill my cup to the brim.	**1.** *centre, interior*

Word	No.	Part	Synonyms and example	Antonyms
	2.	*v.*	**overflow** Her eyes brimmed with tears when she heard the bad news.	
bring	1.	*v.*	**carry, convey, bear, transport** Bring your lunch with you.	**1.** *send, remove*
	2.	*v.*	**draw, sell for, command, fetch, produce, earn, yield** Fresh fruits bring high prices in the winter.	
brink		*n.*	**edge, verge, limit** The mountain climber clung precariously to the brink of the cliff.	
brisk	1.	*adj.*	**quick, lively, energetic, stimulating** Each day the athlete has a brisk workout. *adv.* The sailboat moved briskly.	**1.** *slow, sluggish, lethargic, listless*
	2.	*adj.*	**sharp, keen** The sails caught the brisk wind.	**2.** *gentle, soft*
brittle		*adj.*	**fragile, delicate, breakable, frail, weak, easily broken** Thin glass such as crystal is brittle.	*durable, strong, tough*
broad	1.	*adj.*	**wide, large, extensive, widespread** Television news has a broad range of viewers.	**1.** *narrow, limited, restricted*
	2.	*adj.*	**liberal, tolerant** The speaker expressed some broad ideas.	**2.** *intolerant*
broken	1.	*adj.*	**defective, damaged, faulty, inoperable** Syl took the broken clock in for repair.	**1.** *operable, usable, in working order*
	2.	*adj.*	**shattered, destroyed, split, collapsed, smashed** His broken leg is healing slowly.	**2.** *whole, intact, sound*
brutal		*adj.*	**cruel, savage, pitiless, harsh, merciless, ruthless** Many soldiers were killed in the brutal battle. *n.* Many acts of brutality occur in wars.	*kind, considerate, humane, gentle, civilized*
buddy		*n.*	**chum, friend, playmate, comrade, pal** Tzen and Roger are buddies.	*rival, enemy, adversary, foe, stranger, alien*

Word			Synonyms / Example	Antonyms
build		*v.*	**erect, construct, raise, make, assemble, manufacture, put up, create** The house was built years ago.	*destroy, demolish, wreck, pull down, ruin, dismantle*
bulk		*n.*	**majority, preponderance, biggest share** In the election, which candidate got the bulk of the votes?	*minority, bit, portion, fraction*
burden		*v.*	**weigh down, hinder, hamper, oppress** They were burdened with big loans. *n.* The financial burden was too much for them to bear.	*lighten, unload, relieve, lessen*
burly		*adj.*	**strong, sturdy, husky** The bullies took off when they saw the burly guard approaching.	*puny, feeble, weak*
burn		*v.*	**set on fire, ignite, incinerate, cremate** The garbage was burned in the incinerator.	*put out, stifle, extinguish, quench, cool, smother*
burst		*v.*	**explode, blow up, erupt, rupture** The tire burst as the car sped along the highway.	
business		*n.*	**affair, concern, interest** "Your private life is none of my business," said the employer.	
bustle	1.	*n.*	**hustle, hurry, fuss, flurry, activity** Before the party, there was a great bustle in the kitchen.	**1.** *inactivity, quiet*
	2.	*v.*	**hustle, hurry, scurry** The performers bustled about the dressing room before the play began.	**2.** *linger, dawdle*
busy		*adj.*	**occupied, active, working, engaged, employed** The busy doctor had no time for lunch. *v.* The students busied themselves at the computers. *adv.* The children were working busily to meet the deadline.	*resting, relaxed, unoccupied, unemployed, idle, inactive*
buy		*v.*	**purchase, get, acquire, obtain** Ann bought a bracelet at the jewellers. *n.* It proved to be a good buy.	*sell, market, dispose of, vend, auction*

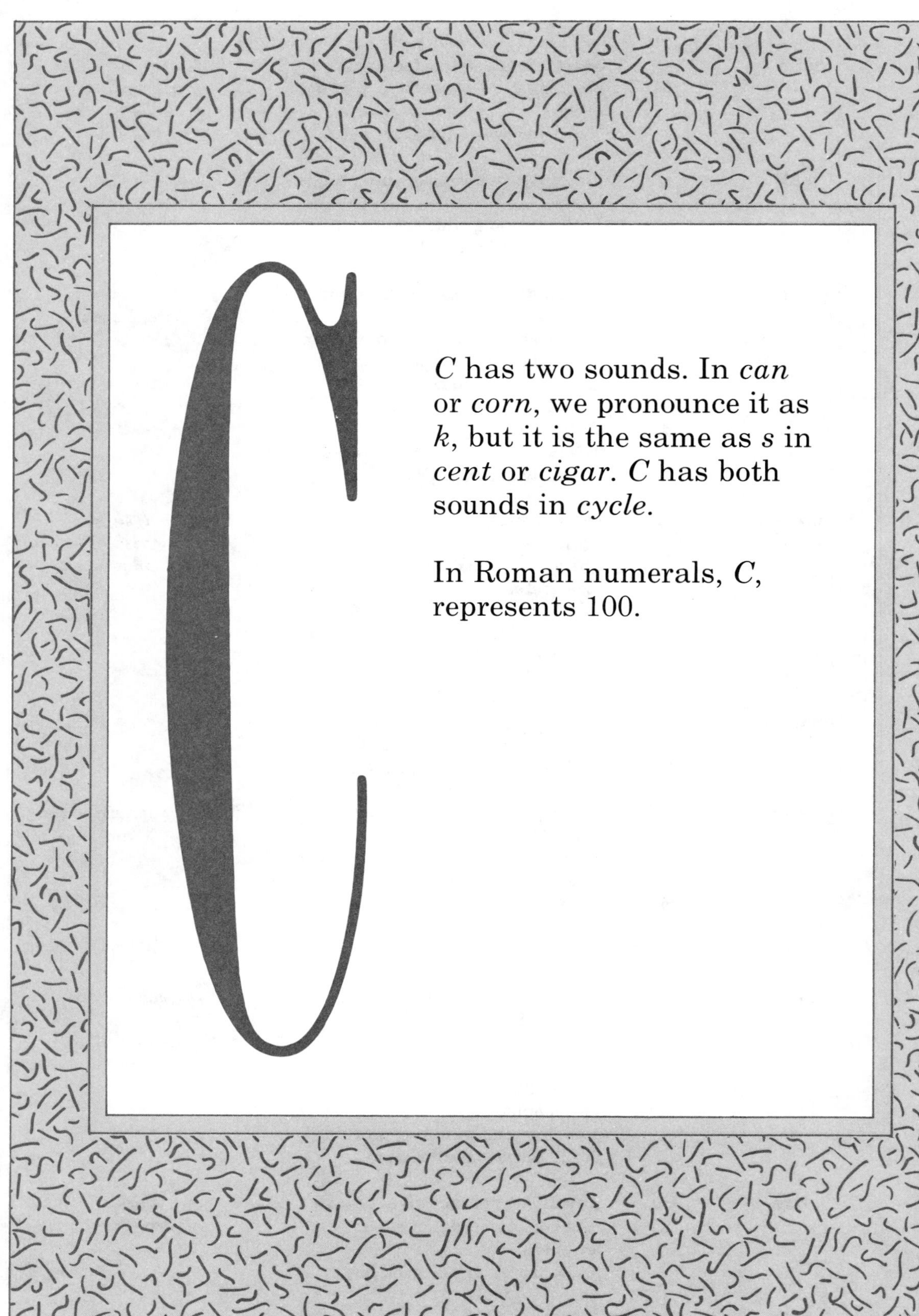

C has two sounds. In *can* or *corn*, we pronounce it as *k*, but it is the same as *s* in *cent* or *cigar*. *C* has both sounds in *cycle*.

In Roman numerals, *C*, represents 100.

Word			Synonyms and examples	Antonyms
cable	**1.**	*n.*	**cord, heavy chain, rope, wire** Underground cables carry electricity to homes across the city.	
	2.	*n.*	**cablegram, telegram, wire** The team sent a cable to inform us of their victory. *v.* We cabled the team our congratulations.	
cage	**1.**	*n.*	**coop, box, crate** Canaries are kept in cages in pet shops.	
	2.	*v.*	**enclose, confine, keep in** The zoo keeper caged the angry lion. *adj.* The caged lion roared ferociously.	**2.** *liberate, release, set free*
cake	**1.**	*n.*	**lump, mass, slab, loaf, bar, brick** Please put a cake of soap on the sink.	
	2.	*v.*	**harden, stiffen, set, congeal, thicken, solidify, pack** Mud cakes in the sun.	**2.** *soften, dissolve*
calamity		*n.*	**disaster, tragedy, catastrophe, misfortune** The destruction caused by the flood was a calamity for the town.	*blessing, benefit, good fortune, comfort, boon*
calculate		*v.*	**compute, count, appraise, figure** We calculated that we had just enough money for lunch. *n.* Fortunately, our calculation was accurate.	*guess, estimate*
call	**1.**	*n.*	**shout, cry, whoop, yell** The call for help awoke the family. *v.* He called for help at the top of his voice.	**1.** *whisper, murmur, silence*
	2.	*n.*	**visit, stop** Rani made a call at the hospital to see her friend. *v.* She called on her friend on her way home from school.	
	3.	*v.*	**telephone, phone** Yen called for an ambulance when she saw the accident.	
	4.	*v.*	**collect, convene, muster, assemble, summon** The organizers called the members to a meeting.	**4.** *scatter, send away, break up, dismiss*
callous	**1.**	*adj.*	**tough, hardened** Skin on the feet can become callous from ill-fitting shoes.	**1.** *soft, supple, tender, pliant, flexible*

	2.	*adj.*	**insensitive, unfeeling, indifferent, unconcerned** The callous person ignored the child's cries for help.	**2.** *sensitive, caring, compassionate, concerned*
calm	1.	*n.*	**tranquillity, peace, serenity, quiet** The calm of the night was shattered by the siren.	**1.** *disturbance, agitation, violence, turbulence*
	2.	*v.*	**ease, relax, soothe, pacify, tranquillize, quieten** Quiet music calms the nerves.	**2.** *agitate, excite, arouse, upset, disturb*
	3.	*adj.*	**quiet, peaceful, composed, placid, tranquil, serene** The boat glided languidly over the calm waters of the lake.	**3.** *violent, rough, turbulent, frantic, excited, agitated*
camouflage		*v.*	**disguise, mask, conceal, screen, cover** The hunters wore green to camouflage themselves in the woods. *n.* The polar bear's white coat acts as a camouflage in the snow.	*expose, reveal, display, uncover*
cancel	1.	*v.*	**cross out, delete, remove, eliminate** She cancelled Al's name from her guest list.	**1.** *maintain, keep*
	2.	*v.*	**eradicate, nullify, abandon, withdraw, void, rescind** I cancelled my subscription to the magazine. *n.* I sent a notice of cancellation.	**2.** *renew, restore, sustain, continue, keep*
candid	1.	*adj.*	**honest, open, straightforward** Ed's so honest you can always count on him for a candid opinion. *adv.* He candidly told Lin her essay was a disappointment.	**1.** *crafty, wily, deceitful, cunning, insincere*
	2.	*adj.*	**fair, impartial, just** The judge delivered a candid decision regarding the defendant.	**2.** *partial, unjust, biassed*
cantankerous		*adj.*	**grouchy, grumpy, cranky, ill-tempered, peevish, cross, irritable, disagreeable** The cantankerous child was sent to bed.	*pleasant, friendly, good-natured, calm, agreeable*
capable	1.	*adj.*	**competent, talented, proficient, able, skilful** The three most capable students received scholarships.	**1.** *incompetent, incapable*
	2.	*adj.*	**able to do, has potential for** Although she is young, she is capable of good work.	**2.** *incapable, unable to do*

capital

1. *n.* **cash, assets, money**
The owner invested $25 000 in capital in the business.

2. *adj.* **chief, main, principal, leading, primary, foremost, dominant**
A country's seat of government is found in its capital city.
2. subordinate, minor, lesser, least important

3. *adj.* **splendid, excellent, choice, delightful**
We had a capital time at the party.
3. unpleasant, poor, inferior

capsize

v. **upset, overturn, tip, invert**
The small boat capsized in the rough seas.
set upright

capsule

1. *n.* **spaceship, satellite, re-entry vehicle, spacecraft**
The space capsule separated from the rocket according to plan.

2. *n.* **container, can, receptacle**
Gelatin capsules are used to hold some medicines.

captain

n. **leader, chief, head, commander**
The captain explained the game plan to the team.
follower, subordinate

captivate

v. **charm, delight, enthral, fascinate, entrance, enrapture, dazzle**
The audience was completely captivated by her singing.
disgust, repel, horrify, disenchant

captive

1. *n.* **prisoner, convict, hostage**
The captives were taken to the jail.
1. free person

2. *adj.* **enslaved, imprisoned, restrained, jailed, incarcerated**
The guards treated the captive group roughly.
2. free, released, acquitted

captivity

n. **confinement, imprisonment, restraint, detention, incarceration**
Wild animals often die in captivity.
liberty, freedom, independence

capture

1. *v.* **catch, seize, trap, arrest, apprehend**
The police captured the robbers after a short chase.
n. The capture of the robbers was reported in the news.
adj. The captured robbers were taken to jail.
1. release, discharge, set free

2. *v.* **conquer, overwhelm, occupy**
The army captured the village after a short battle.
2. surrender

Word			Synonyms	Antonyms
	3.	*v.*	**attract, draw** The unusual painting captured a lot of attention from the press.	**3.** *repel*
car		*n.*	**automobile, auto, motor vehicle** Sal bought a car as soon as she got her driver's licence.	
care	1.	*n.*	**worry, anxiety, bother, concern** Few people are free from cares.	
	2.	*n.*	**heed, caution, precaution** "Take care when you drive home," urged Josef.	**2.** *neglect, carelessness, negligence*
	3.	*n.*	**attention, supervision** The twins were placed in the care of their aunt while their parents were away. *v.* They were well cared for by their aunt.	**3.** *disregard, neglect*
careful	1.	*adj.*	**thoughtful, considerate** The doctor's careful words calmed the patient's fears.	**1.** *inconsiderate, neglectful*
	2.	*adj.*	**exacting, precise, deliberate, accurate, thorough, meticulous** He took careful aim at the target before shooting.	**2.** *imprecise, inaccurate*
	3.	*adj.*	**cautious, vigilant, watchful, mindful, wary, alert** The students were told to be careful when experimenting in the laboratory.	**3.** *heedless, haphazard, careless*
careless		*adj.*	**thoughtless, rash** Hal failed the mathematics test because of careless mistakes. *n.* His teacher reprimanded him for his carelessness.	*cautious, careful*
cargo		*n.*	**load, freight, goods, shipment** The cargo was unloaded from the container ship.	
carry	1.	*v.*	**transport, bear, move, convey, transfer, haul, take** Rico carried the baby on his back.	**1.** *drop, let go, release, put down*
	2.	*v.*	**conduct, relay, transmit, transfer** Copper wiring carries electric current.	**2.** *repel, resist, repulse*
	3.	*v.*	**bear, sustain, support, shoulder, hold up, prop** In many buildings, pillars carry the weight of the roof.	**3.** *let fall, drop*

Word	No.	Part	Synonyms and example	Antonyms
case	1.	*n.*	**box, container, carton, crate, receptacle** The cases of fruit were shipped in refrigerated freight cars.	
	2.	*n.*	**example, instance, occurrence, circumstance, event, situation** In this particular case, the dentist decided to extract the tooth.	
cash		*n.*	**money, coins, bills, funds, legal tender, currency** Customers could only pay cash for the sale items.	
cast	1.	*n.*	**mould, form, shape** His broken leg was put in a plaster cast.	
	2.	*n.*	**performers, actors, actresses, players, troupe, company, dramatis personae** The play's cast included a famous actress.	**2.** *audience*
	3.	*n.*	**look, appearance, complexion** The man's face has a pallid cast.	
	4.	*v.*	**heave, fling, throw, hurl, pitch, project, propel** The children cast stones into the lake.	**4.** *catch, hold, seize, trap, grip*
casual	1.	*adj.*	**accidental, chance, unplanned, unintentional, inadvertent** The two friends had a casual meeting at the reception.	**1.** *planned, contrived, intentional*
	2.	*adj.*	**infrequent, random, erratic, irregular, occasional** The farmer hires casual workers in the summer.	**2.** *frequent, regular, constant, certain*
	3.	*adj.*	**indifferent, unconcerned, blasé, apathetic, nonchalant** He was warned about his casual attitude toward his work. *adv.* He casually told the boss he didn't care if he was fired.	**3.** *concerned, enthusiastic, ardent*
	4.	*adj.*	**informal, relaxed** The party will be a casual affair, so come in casual clothes.	**4.** *formal, rigid, stern*
catastrophe		*n.*	**calamity, disaster, misfortune, mishap, debacle** A huge earthquake or flood is a natural catastrophe.	*benefit, advantage, boon, good fortune, blessing, comfort, help*
catch	1.	*n.*	**buckle, clasp, hook, fastener, clamp, snap** I couldn't fasten the catch on my necklace.	

Word			Synonyms	Antonyms
	2.	*v.*	**snatch, grab, snare, seize, pluck, hold on to** The drowning child caught the rope.	**2.** *let go, free, release, miss*
	3.	*v.*	**apprehend, capture, arrest, trap, seize** The police officer caught the burglar.	**3.** *free*
	4.	*v.*	**overtake, overhaul, pass** The runner caught the leader in the race.	**4.** *lag behind, falter*
category		*n.*	**classification, section, level, division, class, rank, type, sort** The books were divided into two categories — fiction and nonfiction.	
cause	1.	*n.*	**reason, inducement, origin** A cigarette was the cause of the fire.	**1.** *effect, result, outcome*
	2.	*n.*	**reason, goal, purpose** They raised money for a good cause.	
	3.	*v.*	**make, compel, provoke** Her illness was caused by overwork.	**3.** *prevent, stop, prohibit*
caution	1.	*n.*	**care, heed, notice, discretion, attention** One should use caution when crossing the streets.	**1.** *rashness, recklessness, foolhardiness, indiscretion*
	2.	*v.*	**warn, advise** Our parents cautioned us to drive carefully.	
cautious		*adj.*	**careful, wary, watchful** The cautious cyclists avoided the busy street. *adv.* She rode cautiously along the side of the road.	*rash, careless, thoughtless, unthinking*
cavity	1.	*n.*	**hole, opening, gap** The dentist found two cavities in the patient's teeth.	**1.** *filling*
	2.	*n.*	**cavern, basin, excavation, depression, hole, hollow** The heavy rains caused a cavity to develop under the road.	**2.** *hill, elevation*
cease		*v.*	**stop, halt, terminate, end** The noise in the classroom ceased when the teacher walked in.	*begin, start, initiate*
cede		*v.*	**yield, grant, surrender, assign, turn over, relinquish** The farmlands were ceded to the government.	*hold, occupy, retain, keep, save, maintain*

Word	No.	Part	Synonyms and example	Antonyms
celebrate		*v.*	**commemorate, observe, keep** New Year's day is celebrated on January 1.	*disregard, forget, overlook*
celebration	1.	*n.*	**observance, party, fete, commemoration, jubilee** The Canada Day celebrations usually include a parade.	
	2.	*n.*	**gaiety, merrymaking** There will be a celebration if we win the game. *v.* The team celebrated its victory with a party.	**2.** *sadness, sorrow, grief, mourning, solemnity*
celebrity		*n.*	**well-known person, famous person, star, notable** Crowds waited at the airport for the celebrity's arrival.	*unknown*
celestial	1.	*adj.*	**heavenly, of the sky** The stars are celestial bodies.	**1.** *earthly, terrestrial*
	2.	*adj.*	**divine, ethereal, holy, angelic** The congregation was inspired by the celestial music from the organ.	
cell	1.	*n.*	**enclosure, cubicle** The prisoner was confined in a cell.	
	2.	*n.*	**small unit, division, portion** All living things are composed of cells.	
cement	1.	*n.*	**concrete** The workers paved the sidewalk with cement.	
	2.	*v.*	**join, bind, fasten, connect, unite** The bench was cemented to the ground to prevent it from being stolen.	**2.** *separate, undo, disconnect*
central		*adj.*	**main, chief, leading, principal** Who is the central character in the novel?	*subsidiary, auxiliary, secondary*
centre (also spelled center)	1.	*n.*	**midpoint, middle, heart, core, midst, nucleus** It is expensive to buy property in the centre of a city. *adj.* Central locations are most desired and therefore expensive.	**1.** *outside, exterior, rim, circumference, perimeter, edge*
	2.	*v.*	**concentrate, focus, converge on** The discussion centred on the coming elections. *n.* The film star was the centre of everyone's attention.	**2.** *decentralize, spread out, branch out*

Word			Synonyms and example	Antonyms
ceremony		*n.*	**ritual, rite, performance** The Wongs had a traditional wedding ceremony. *adj.* They wore ceremonial dress for the occasion.	
certain	1.	*adj.*	**confident, sure, assured, definite, positive** Liz was certain that she would win the first prize.	**1.** *doubtful, uncertain, indefinite, dubious*
	2.	*adj.*	**destined, sure, inevitable, predestined, unavoidable, unchangeable** That invention will have certain success!	**2.** *doubtful, avoidable, changeable*
	3.	*adj.*	**some, a few** Certain people enjoy window shopping.	**3.** *many, most, all*
chain	1.	*n.*	**series, succession, progression** The marriage was the first in a chain of happy events.	
	2.	*v.*	**tie, moor, hold, tether, attach, connect, fasten, secure** Ken chained his bicycle to the tree.	**2.** *untie, loosen, untether, release, set free*
challenge	1.	*n.*	**dare** Sven accepted Jim's challenge to a race. *v.* Ric challenged Jo to a match.	
	2.	*n.*	**effort** Learning to use the computer was a real challenge for me.	
	3.	*v.*	**defy, question, doubt, object to** Lee challenged the decision of the referee.	**3.** *grant, accept, agree with*
champion	1.	*n.*	**winner, victor, conqueror** It takes years of intense training to become an Olympic champion.	**1.** *loser*
	2.	*n.*	**protector, supporter, defender, ally, upholder, guardian** Mother Teresa is a champion of the sick and needy. *v.* She champions the cause of the needy.	**2.** *enemy, foe, rival, adversary*
	3.	*adj.*	**unbeaten, best, superior** Who is the champion speller?	**3.** *worst, poorest*
chance	1.	*n.*	**luck, fortune, accident** Lin and Tom met by chance at the rodeo.	**1.** *purpose, design, plan*
	2.	*n.*	**opportunity, opening, occasion, possibility** I have a chance to make more money on this new job.	

	3.	*v.*	**venture, gamble, risk, wager** They were warned not to chance their money on the project.	
change	1.	*n.*	**coins, coppers, silver** Sasha dumped the change out of his pockets.	
	2.	*n.*	**adjustment, variation, shift, alteration, substitution, deviation** A change of plans will be necessary if it rains.	**2.** *continuance, constancy*
	3.	*n.*	**switch, swap, replacement, exchange, substitute** The actors made a quick change of costumes between acts.	
	4.	*v.*	**adjust, shift, swerve** The wind changed direction.	**4.** *continue, keep, hold, remain, retain*
changeable		*adj.*	**variable, unsettled, unstable, doubtful, fluctuating** Spring weather is changeable.	*reliable, steady, dependable, constant*
chaos		*n.*	**confusion, disorder, turmoil, tumult, anarchy, discord, disarray, shambles** The tornado left the town in utter chaos. *adj.* It was a chaotic sight!	*order*
character	1.	*n.*	**personality, disposition, nature, temperament** The principal has a pleasant character and is well-liked.	
	2.	*n.*	**figure, symbol, letter, sign, mark** Chinese characters started off as pictures.	
characteristic	1.	*n.*	**quality, trait, peculiarity, attribute** A curly tail is a characteristic of pigs.	
	2.	*adj.*	**distinctive, typical, peculiar** Each fruit has its own characteristic taste.	
charade		*n.*	**deception, fake, trick, sham, pretence, forgery** The smile was a charade to conceal her disappointment.	*fact, reality*
charge	1.	*n.*	**cost, price, amount, expense** The show was poorly attended as the charge was too high.	
	2.	*v.*	**command, bid, instruct, tell, demand, order, direct** The judge charged the jury to state its verdict.	**2.** *request, ask, desire, invite*

	3.	*v.*	**attack, rush, stampede, assail** The bull charged at the matador.	**3.** *retreat, recoil, withdraw, fall back*
charm	1.	*n.*	**magic, spell, enchantment, sorcery** In the Irish legend, the leprechaun cast a charm on the village.	
	2.	*n.*	**good-luck piece, amulet, talisman** Many people believe charms can protect them or bring them luck.	**2.** *curse*
	3.	*n.*	**grace, enchanting personality, attractiveness** The actor turned on his charm for his fans.	**3.** *awkwardness, clumsiness*
	4.	*v.*	**enchant, delight, entice, please, captivate, enrapture, enthral, entrance, fascinate, beguile** Everyone was charmed by his warmth and sincerity. *adj.* Children enjoy listening to charming tales of long ago.	**4.** *tire, bore, weary, repel, disgust, displease, annoy, irritate, disturb, repulse, disenchant*
chart		*n.*	**map, graph, plan, draft, plot, diagram** The flow chart showed the steps we had to take to complete the assignment. *v.* We charted our course of action before beginning.	
chase		*v.*	**pursue, hunt, trail, track, follow** The hounds chased the foxes.	*avoid, flee, evade, shun, dodge*
chat		*v.*	**talk, converse, chatter** Yan and Jim chatted about their old school. *n.* The friends had an interesting chat.	*be quiet*
chatter		*v.*	**jabber, prattle, babble, gabble** The monkeys chattered endlessly. *n.* The chatter annoyed the zoo keeper.	
cheap		*adj.*	**low-priced, inexpensive, cut-rate, thrifty** They went to the market to look for cheap furniture.	*expensive, costly, dear, high-priced*
cheat		*v.*	**swindle, deceive, trick, defraud, mislead, dupe, hoodwink** Tina was cheated out of a fortune by a con person. *n.* Police are looking for the cheat.	*be trustworthy, be reliable*

Entry	No.	Part	Synonyms / Example	Antonyms
check	1.	*n.*	**examination, investigation, analysis, inquiry** The police ran a check on the fingerprints through the computer.	
	2.	*n.*	**rein, control, restraint, curb** A dog should be kept in check in a park.	2. *liberty*
	3.	*v.*	**examine, inspect, verify** Lu checked the dictionary for the meaning of the word.	3. *ignore*
	4.	*v.*	**retard, slow, reduce, lessen, decrease, lower, minimize** Yetta checked the car's speed on the wet pavement.	4. *hasten, increase, accelerate, speed up, advance, quicken*
	5.	*v.*	**control, moderate, curb** Dad told Kim to check his tongue. *n.* He was told to keep a check on his temper.	5. *loosen, free*
cheer	1.	*n.*	**yell, shout, cry, hurrah, applause, encouragement** Cheers from the crowd encouraged the team. *v.* The crowd cheered the home team to victory. *adj.* Who was that leading the cheering section?	1. *jeer, ridicule, boo*
	2.	*n.*	**happiness, joy, mirth, festivity, celebration, gladness** Christmas is a time of cheer.	2. *sorrow, grief, sadness, gloom, melancholy*
	3.	*v.*	**brighten, console, support, help, encourage, comfort** Visitors cheer patients in a hospital.	3. *depress, discourage, dishearten*
cheerful	1.	*adj.*	**bright, glad, happy, joyful, merry, sunny** She greeted everyone with a cheerful smile. *adv.* She cheerfully welcomed her guests.	1. *sad, unhappy, gloomy, glum, depressed*
	2.	*adj.*	**bright, sunny, sparkling, comfortable, pleasant, appealing** The children were delighted with their cheerful classroom.	2. *dull, drab, unappealing, unpleasant, gloomy, dreary*
cherish	1.	*v.*	**treasure, prize, value, love, idolize, protect** Animals cherish their young.	1. *abandon, give up, desert, forsake, reject, disown*
	2.	*v.*	**cling to, keep in mind** For many years, the patient cherished the hope of being cured.	2. *discard, reject, dispense with*
chest	1.	*n.*	**case, box, cabinet, bin, container** The medicine chest was kept out of the children's reach.	

Word			Synonyms	Antonyms
	2.	*n.*	**bosom, breast** The coach pounded his chest in frustration.	
chew		*v.*	**gnaw, crunch, grind, munch, masticate** Nan was told to chew her food carefully.	
chic		*adj.*	**stylish, smart, elegant, fashionable** Erin's chic hairdo drew admiring looks.	*dowdy, unstylish, unfashionable*
chief	1.	*n.*	**head, boss, leader, director, manager, administrator** Who is the chief of the local fire department?	**1.** *subordinate, attendant*
	2.	*adj.*	**main, foremost, leading, first, principal, greatest, prime** Oil is the chief export of Iran.	**2.** *last, least, slightest, minor*
child		*n.*	**infant, baby, tot, youngster, minor** Who's minding the children while their parents are away?	*adult, grown-up*
childish	1.	*adj.*	**childlike, infantile, juvenile, young, babyish, immature** They laughed at the baby's childish babble.	**1.** *adult, grown, mature, old*
	2.	*adj.*	**silly, stupid, foolish, absurd** Ian was annoyed by Lee's childish behaviour.	**2.** *wise, clever, sensible*
chill	1.	*n.*	**coolness, crispness, coldness, sharpness** Ed shivered in the chill of the night. *adj.* The chilly breeze made us shiver.	**1.** *warmth*
	2.	*v.*	**cool, refrigerate, frost, make cold** Mike chilled the pop before the party.	**2.** *heat, warm*
chip	1.	*n.*	**piece, part, small chunk, bit, fragment, slice, wedge, flake** The floor of the carpenter's workshop was covered with wood chips.	**1.** *whole, entirety*
	2.	*v.*	**break, crack, splinter, fragment, whittle, chisel** Borje chipped a hole in the ice to catch the fish.	**2.** *join, unite, blend, mend, repair*

chirp		*v.*	**sing, call, warble, trill** The birds chirped happily at daybreak.	
choice	1.	*n.*	**selection, option, preference, election, choosing** Simi is my choice for a writing partner.	
	2.	*n.*	**variety, quantity, diversity, assortment, mixture, medley** There is a wide choice of dishes on the menu.	***2.*** *limitation, restriction*
choke	1.	*v.*	**strangle, stifle, suffocate, asphyxiate, throttle, smother** The tight collar almost choked the pup.	
	2.	*v.*	**suppress, hold back, control** The angry customer choked back a rude reply.	***2.*** *release, let out, let go*
choose		*v.*	**pick, select, decide on, elect, prefer** The judges took a long time to choose a winner.	*discard, reject, refuse, dismiss, decline, leave*
chop		*v.*	**cut, cleave, lop, hew, fell, hack, slash, whack** Machetes were used to chop through the undergrowth of the jungle.	
chore		*n.*	**job, task, duty** Ali finished his chores before watching television.	
chronic		*adj.*	**persistent, continuing, constant, continual** Doctors couldn't do anything about his chronic cough.	*temporary*
chubby		*adj.*	**fat, plump, pudgy, hefty, chunky, stout, portly** No more candies for the chubby child.	*slim, slight, thin, skinny, lean, slender*
chuckle		*v.*	**giggle, laugh, snicker** The audience chuckled when Dad snored in the middle of the concert.	*cry, weep, sob*
chum		*n.*	**pal, friend, companion, buddy, comrade, mate, ally, playmate** They have been chums since they were in kindergarten.	*enemy, foe, opponent, rival, antagonist, stranger, adversary*

Word			Synonyms	Antonyms
civil		*adj.*	**polite, courteous, refined, cultured** The salesperson treated the angry customer in a civil manner.	*impolite, rude, discourteous*
claim	**1.**	*n.*	**title, right** State your claim to the property.	**1.** *disclaimer*
	2.	*v.*	**insist, assert** The suspect claimed he was innocent.	**2.** *disclaim, renounce, reject, disown*
	3.	*v.*	**take** The accident claimed many lives.	**3.** *give, restore, return*
clamour	**1.**	*n.*	**noise, commotion, protest, outcry, uproar** The no-smoking rule caused a clamour in the office.	**1.** *quiet, calm, peace*
	2.	*v.*	**shout, demand** The smokers clamoured for their right to smoke.	
clamp	**1.**	*n.*	**lock, fastener, catch, snap, clasp, brace, vise** The test tube was held in place by a clamp.	
	2.	*n.*	**restriction, control** The police have put a clamp on drinking and driving. *v.* The police are clamping down on drunk drivers.	**2.** *freedom*
clap	**1.**	*n.*	**crash, bang, burst** The clap of thunder frightened the baby.	
	2.	*v.*	**applaud, cheer, acclaim, praise, approve** The audience clapped thunderously as the actor took his bow.	**2.** *boo, jeer, disapprove*
clarify	**1.**	*v.*	**make clear, explain, elucidate, define** Josie asked the coach to clarify the rules of the game.	**1.** *confuse, tangle, muddle, befuddle, mislead, perplex*
	2.	*v.*	**purify, refine, filter, cleanse, clean** Filtration plants clarified the water so it would be safe to drink.	**2.** *pollute, dirty, soil, contaminate*
clash	**1.**	*n.*	**quarrel, disagreement, conflict, argument, dispute** They had a clash in opinion about politics, and argued all evening.	**1.** *agreement, accord, harmony, understanding*
	2.	*v.*	**disagree, differ, conflict** His views clashed with mine.	**2.** *agree, concur, coincide, harmonize*

Word			Synonyms	Antonyms
clasp	1.	*n.*	**hook, catch, buckle, clamp, fastener, pin** The gold clasp on the bracelet became loose.	
	2.	*v.*	**grip, grasp, clutch, hold, embrace** The mother clasped the baby to her breast.	**2.** *release, let go, drop, relinquish*
class	1.	*n.*	**grade, rank, quality, type, degree, order** The company president flies first class.	
	2.	*v.*	**rank, grade, identify, mark, classify** The laboratory classed the virus as a lethal one.	
classic		*adj.*	**excellent, first-class** Kit had a big collection of classic music tapes and compact discs.	*inferior, minor, second-class*
classify		*v.*	**sort, grade, select, arrange, categorize, systematize, organize** A government agency classifies meat according to its quality.	*disorganize, disarrange, disorder, muddle, confuse, scatter*
clatter		*n.*	**noise, racket, rattle, clash** Try not to make a clatter when stacking the dishes. *v.* The dishes clattered to the floor.	*silence, quiet*
claw		*v.*	**tear, scratch, rip open, rip apart** The hungry bears clawed at the sacks of food.	
clean	1.	*v.*	**scour, wash down, scrub, cleanse** The housekeeper cleaned the apartment weekly.	**1.** *dirty, soil*
	2.	*v.*	**cleanse, purify, disinfect, clarify, sterilize** The operating instruments were cleaned in a special disinfectant.	**2.** *pollute, infect, poison, contaminate*
	3.	*adj.*	**spotless, stainless, untarnished** The clean silverware sparkled.	**3.** *stained, soiled, tarnished, dirty*
	4.	*adj.*	**sanitary, pure, purified** Fish caught in clean waters are safe to eat.	**4.** *unsanitary, impure, polluted, contaminated*
	5.	*adj.*	**clear-cut, distinct, sharp, well-defined, precise** The skyscrapers cut a clean silhouette against the sky.	**5.** *indistinct, cluttered*
clear	1.	*v.*	**clean, cleanse, purify** She opened a window to clear the air in the smoky room.	**1.** *pollute, contaminate*

	2.	*v.*	**remove, rid, empty** Pesticides cleared the area of mosquitoes.	2. *fill, occupy*
	3.	*v.*	**clarify, explain** Farida's explanation cleared up the mystery.	3. *confuse, muddle, puzzle, confound*
	4.	*v.*	**acquit, release, excuse, absolve, exonerate** The jury believed the suspect was innocent, and cleared him of all charges.	4. *implicate, accuse, charge*
	5.	*v.*	**receive, get, make, realize, earn** We cleared a handsome profit on the sale of the house.	5. *lose, miss out on, suffer a loss*
	6.	*adj.*	**transparent** We could see the bottom of the sea through the crystal clear water.	6. *opaque*
	7.	*adj.*	**sunny, cloudless, bright, fair** It was a clear day, with not a cloud in the sky.	7. *dark, dismal, cloudy, dreary*
	8.	*adj.*	**distinct, audible** Announcers need to have clear voices.	8. *indistinct, inaudible*
	9.	*adj.*	**distinct, precise, sharp, definite, explicit** Li has a clear understanding of the problem.	9. *obstructed, blocked, indistinct, obscured*
	10.	*adv.*	**totally, fully, completely, entirely** The laser beam cut clear through the metal.	10. *somewhat, partially, partly*
clement	1.	*adj.*	**mild, fair, balmy, pleasant** Everyone was out enjoying the clement weather.	1. *severe, bitter, unpleasant*
	2.	*adj.*	**lenient, merciful, forgiving** The clement judge awarded a light sentence.	2. *ruthless, harsh*
clever	1.	*adj.*	**intelligent, bright, talented, skilful, expert, smart, adroit, accomplished, proficient, capable** The clever student won a scholarship for college.	1. *dull, unintelligent, inept, stupid, foolish*
	2.	*adj.*	**witty, keen** The play's success rested on its clever dialogue.	2. *dull, boring, silly*
client		*n.*	**customer, patron, buyer, purchaser, shopper** The new lawyer advertised for clients.	*seller, dealer, vendor*
cliff		*n.*	**bluff, precipice, steep hill** The house was perched on the edge of the cliff.	*plain, prairie, steppe, moor*

climax		*n.*	**peak, culmination, apex, highest point, turning point** The climax of the story was when the identity of the killer was revealed.	*anticlimax, lowest point*
climb		*v.*	**ascend, go up, scale, rise** The child climbed to the top of the ladder. *n.* Dave made a fast climb to the top of the company.	*go down, descend, come down, fall*
cling	**1.**	*v.*	**stick, adhere, attach** The plastic wrap clings to the sandwich.	**1.** *fall, slip, loosen*
	2.	*v.*	**grasp, hold tightly, clutch, grip, clench** The boy clung to the overturned canoe.	**2.** *let go, drop, release*
clip	**1.**	*n.*	**fastener, holder** She put a clip in her unruly hair.	
	2.	*v.*	**snip, crop, cut** Ari clipped the article from the newspaper.	
cloak	**1.**	*n.*	**cape, wrap, mantle** She wore a long cloak to protect herself from the rain.	
	2.	*v.*	**hide, disguise, cover, mask, camouflage, conceal, obscure** The spy's true identity is cloaked in secrecy.	**2.** *reveal, disclose, uncover, make known, exhibit*
close	**1.**	*n.*	**conclusion, end, finish, completion, termination** The audience stayed until the close of the show.	**1.** *beginning, start, commencement, opening*
	2.	*v.*	**conclude, finish, end, terminate** When did the exhibition close?	**2.** *begin, open, start, commence*
	3.	*v.*	**block, shut off, seal, bar** The police closed the highway because of the bad accident.	**3.** *open*
	4.	*v.*	**shut, fasten** He closed the door to keep out the flies.	**4.** *open*
	5.	*adj.*	**sticky, stuffy, unventilated, heavy, stale, oppressive** The air in the room became close after all the windows were shut.	**5.** *fresh, brisk, refreshing, exhilarating*
	6.	*adj.*	**intimate, dear, familiar** They have been close friends since childhood.	**6.** *estranged, unfamiliar, distant*
	7.	*adj.*	**stingy, cheap, miserly** Miserly people are close with their money.	**7.** *generous, liberal*

	8.	*adj.*	**confined, cramped, restricted, tight, narrow, compact** Close quarters can cause some people to feel claustrophobic.	**8.** *spacious, roomy, large*
	9.	*adv.*	**near, nearby, adjacent** The subdivision was built close to the shopping centre.	**9.** *at a distance, removed*
clothes		*n.*	**apparel, attire, clothing, garb, garments** The children packed their old clothes for camp.	
clothing		*n.*	**clothes, attire, apparel, garb, garments** She wore sturdy clothing for the hike through the woods.	
cloudy	1.	*adj.*	**overcast, misty, murky, hazy** Cloudy skies prevented the viewing of the eclipse.	**1.** *clear, fair*
	2.	*adj.*	**opaque, murky, thick, filmy** We couldn't see the bottom of the pool through the cloudy water.	**2.** *clear, transparent, translucent*
club	1.	*n.*	**organization, group, order, association** The tennis club was recruiting members.	
	2.	*n.*	**weapon, stick, bat, mallet** Some primitive hunters used clubs to kill their prey.	
	3.	*v.*	**hit, strike, whack, pound, beat, batter** The robber clubbed his victim on the head.	
clue		*n.*	**hint, sign, guide** The police searched for clues to help them identify the robber.	
clump	1.	*n.*	**cluster, group, batch, bundle** Jill hid behind the clump of bushes.	
	2.	*n.*	**thump, bump, thud** The clump of heavy footsteps woke her up. *v.* The men clumped up the stairs in their boots.	
clumsy		*adj.*	**awkward, ungainly, unskilful, bungling, cumbersome** The clumsy waiter bumped into the table and dropped the plates. *adv.* The skater fell clumsily on the ice.	*coordinated, dexterous, graceful, smooth*

Word	No.	Part of speech	Synonyms and example	Antonyms
clutch		*v.*	**grab, grasp, grip, seize, hold, clench, clasp, squeeze** Luke clutched the reeds as he fell into the river.	*relinquish, let go, release, drop*
coach	1.	*n.*	**trainer, instructor, tutor** The coach of the soccer team was well-known for discipline.	
	2.	*v.*	**train, drill, instruct** The quarterback of the football squad coached the junior team.	
coarse	1.	*adj.*	**rough, ragged, harsh** The coarse wool irritated my skin.	**1.** *smooth, fine, polished*
	2.	*adj.*	**crude, vulgar** We found his coarse jokes offensive.	**2.** *refined*
coast	1.	*n.*	**shore, seaboard** There are fine beaches on the coast of Jamaica.	
	2.	*v.*	**glide, float, drift** The toboggans coasted downhill.	**2.** *steer, direct*
coat	1.	*n.*	**topcoat, overcoat, jacket, cloak** The heavy winter coat kept her warm.	
	2.	*v.*	**cover, wrap, envelop** The beaches were coated in oil from the tanker's spill. *n.* A thick coat of oil covered the beach.	
coax		*v.*	**persuade, urge, cajole** She coaxed her shy friend into coming to the party.	*discourage, dissuade, coerce*
coerce		*v.*	**compel, force, make, oblige, drive** Was the suspect coerced into giving the confession?	*persuade, convince, coax*
coil		*v.*	**wind, wrap around, twine, twist, twirl, spiral, curl** The vine coiled around the tree. *n.* Electric coils heated the garage.	*uncoil, unwind, ravel, loosen, untangle, uncurl*
cold	1.	*adj.*	**cool, frosty, freezing, chilly** It was too cold to go outside.	**1.** *warm, hot, heated*
	2.	*adj.*	**reserved, indifferent, unfriendly** Pierre had difficulty making friends because of his cold personality.	**2.** *friendly, amiable, outgoing*

collapse *v.* **topple, cave in, fall down**
The houses collapsed in the hurricane.
n. Jin found it difficult to accept the collapse of her business.
rise, lift, build, erect, construct

collect
1. *v.* **assemble, amass, gather, congregate**
Fans collected outside the stage door after the show.
1. *disperse, scatter*
2. *v.* **raise, solicit, obtain, secure, glean**
The students collected money for the heart fund.
2. *dispense, dispose*
3. *v.* **accumulate, gather, compile, save**
Do you collect stamps?
n. Colin is an avid stamp collector.
n. He has a fine stamp collection.
3. *throw away, give away, get rid of*

collide
1. *v.* **hit, smash, strike, crash, bump**
The two oil tankers collided in the heavy fog.
n. The car collision was caused by slippery roads.
1. *avoid, evade, elude*
2. *v.* **clash, conflict, disagree, oppose, differ**
During the panel discussion, the two politicians collided in their views.
n. Such a heated collision was expected.
2. *agree, parallel, resemble*

colloquial *adj.* **informal, popular, everyday**
The English teacher didn't like his students to use colloquial expressions in their essays.
formal, conventional

colossal *adj.* **giant, mammoth, enormous, huge, vast, immense**
Dinosaurs were colossal creatures.
minute, tiny, miniature, small

colour (also spelled color)
1. *n.* **brilliance, brightness, vividness**
Costumes of the various ethnic groups added to the colour of the pageant.
adj. Her colourful clothes made her stand out in the crowd.
1. *drabness, dullness, plainness*
2. *n.* **tint, stain, tone, shade, dye**
The red colour of the dye came out in the wash.
v. Vic coloured his hair to hide the white in it.
3. *v.* **distort, warp, twist, bend, misrepresent, mislead**
The journalist coloured the report with her own prejudices.
3. *state verbatim*

Word	No.	Part	Synonyms and example	Antonyms
combat	1.	*n.*	**battle, conflict, struggle, fight, fray, contest** The troops were engaged in heavy combat.	1. *peace, concord, amity*
	2.	*v.*	**battle, fight, struggle, oppose, resist** Science combats disease.	2. *give up, give in, submit, surrender*
combination		*n.*	**mixture, mix, blend, union** Purple is a combination of red and blue.	*separation, division*
combine	1.	*v.*	**join, unite, link, couple, connect, attach** The two subway lines combine at this station.	1. *uncouple, unlink, detach, separate, divide, disengage*
	2.	*v.*	**consolidate, merge, unite, amalgamate** The scientists combined their efforts in researching a cure for cancer.	2. *separate, divide*
come	1.	*v.*	**arrive, reach, appear** Our neighbours came home from Italy yesterday.	1. *leave, go, depart*
	2.	*v.*	**approach, draw near, advance** "Come this way," ordered the usher.	2. *go, leave, depart, wait, stay*
	3.	*v.*	**reach, stretch, expand to, extend** Her hair comes to her waist.	3. *contract, shrink*
	4.	*v.*	**develop, mature, become, evolve, progress, turn into** We hope something will come out of the peace talks between the two warring countries.	4. *regress, remain, stay, continue*
comfort	1.	*v.*	**console, cheer, gladden, reassure** Friends comforted the grieving family. *n.* The friends were a great comfort in their time of sorrow.	1. *discourage, dishearten, depress*
	2.	*v.*	**ease, soothe, soften, calm, alleviate** The doctor prescribed drugs to comfort the patient's pain. *n.* The drugs helped him to sleep in comfort.	2. *worsen*
comfortable	1.	*adj.*	**contented, relaxed, satisfied** Ariel was comfortable sitting by the fire. *adv.* She snuggled comfortably into the big armchair.	1. *uneasy, disturbed, ill-at-ease*

	2.	*adj.*	**sufficient, ample, suitable, enough, adequate** The teacher gave the students a comfortable period of time to complete their project.	**2.** *insufficient, inadequate, meagre*
command	1.	*n.*	**demand, order, direction** Troops have to obey the captain's commands.	**1.** *request, invitation, offer*
	2.	*n.*	**power, control, authority** The general has command over the army.	
	3.	*v.*	**order, charge, direct, instruct, demand** The officer commanded the troops to fire on the enemy.	**3.** *request, ask, wish, desire*
commence		*v.*	**begin, start** Opening ceremonies will commence at two o'clock.	*end, finish, stop, conclude, complete*
comment		*n.*	**remark, opinion, statement** He was criticized for the mean comments he made about the singer. *v.* Everyone commented about his bad behaviour.	
commerce		*n.*	**business, trade, marketing, merchandising** Vancouver, Toronto, and Montreal are centres of commerce in Canada. *adj.* These cities are of commercial importance.	
commit	1.	*v.*	**perform, do, perpetrate** A teen gang committed the chain of robberies.	
	2.	*v.*	**entrust, assign, put in safekeeping** The patient was committed to the doctor's care.	**2.** *dismiss, discharge, relieve of*
commodity		*n.*	**merchandise, stocks, goods for sale** Commodities such as rubber and oil are traded on the market.	
common	1.	*adj.*	**ordinary, everyday, commonplace, customary, typical, usual** TV sets are common in homes today.	**1.** *unique, extraordinary, novel*
	2.	*adj.*	**frequent, usual, familiar, habitual, constant, regular** Tourists are a common sight in this historical town.	**2.** *irregular, infrequent, occasional*

	3.	*adj.*	**general, prevalent, well-known, widespread, public** It is common knowledge that Batman's sidekick is Robin.	**3.** *obscure, limited, restricted*
	4.	*adj.*	**communal, shared, mutual, joint** The estate is the common property of the family members.	**4.** *private, individual, personal*
commotion		*n.*	**uproar, disturbance, confusion, stir** When the bat flew into the tent it caused a commotion.	*order, quiet, calm*
communicate	1.	*v.*	**inform, advise, tell, reveal, divulge, disclose, notify, declare** News of the disaster was communicated to the people via TV and radio.	**1.** *keep secret, censor, conceal*
	2.	*v.*	**correspond with, confer, contact, share information** The branch offices communicate by fax daily. *n.* The branch offices keep in close communication.	**2.** *be out of reach, be removed from*
community	1.	*n.*	**likeness, unity, similarity, uniformity** Community of interest helps people to work together.	**1.** *diversity, difference*
	2.	*adj.*	**public, joint, cooperative, group** The arena was built to support community activities.	**2.** *private, individual*
compact	1.	*n.*	**case, container, box** Face powder is carried in a compact.	
	2.	*n.*	**agreement, contract, bargain, promise, pact** The two countries signed a defence compact.	
	3.	*adj.*	**close, thick, full, dense, compressed** Cabbage leaves form a compact head.	**3.** *wide-open, loose*
	4.	*adj.*	**small** Her compact car is easy to handle.	**4** *big, large, roomy*
companion		*n.*	**friend, chum, comrade, buddy, pal, mate** They have been constant companions for years.	*enemy, foe, stranger*
company	1.	*n.*	**business, firm, corporation** She is the president of the company.	

	2. *n.*	**visitors, guests, callers** We're having company for dinner this weekend.	
compare	*v.*	**contrast, test, analyse, examine** She compared the two brands to see which was the better buy. *n.* We did a comparison of prices before we made our choice.	
compartment	*n.*	**section, part, portion** The map is in the glove compartment of the car.	
compassion	*n.*	**pity, sympathy, consideration, tenderness, understanding, kindness** They felt compassion for the refugees and their terrible plight. *adj.* The refugees were grateful to their compassionate benefactors.	*severity, cruelty, hardheartedness, sharpness, unkindness*
compatible	*adj.*	**agreeable, harmonious, amicable, congruous** Jeff was glad to find a compatible roommate at college.	*incompatible, opposed*
compel	*v.*	**force, coerce, impel, make** Poor weather compelled the travellers to stay another night.	*help, assist*
compete	*v.*	**rival, contest, vie** The skiers competed for the Cup. *n.* It was a difficult competition. *n.* The competitors performed well. *adj.* Everyone was fiercely competitive.	*cooperate*
competent	*adj.*	**capable, able, efficient, skilled** Akiko is a competent skater.	*incompetent, unable, inefficient, unskilled*
compile	*v.*	**gather, collect, accumulate, assemble** Nan compiled a list of books to read during the holidays.	*scatter, disperse*
complacent	*adj.*	**smug, self-satisfied, unconcerned, contented** Pam was told to get rid of her complacent attitude toward her studies and to work hard. *n.* She failed the examination because of her complacency.	*discontented, dissatisfied, anxious*

Word		Synonyms	Antonyms
complain	*v.*	**grumble, object to, protest, disapprove, criticize** Customers complained of poor service in the restaurant. *n.* Their complaints resulted in some improvements.	*approve, praise, recommend*
complete	1. *v.*	**finish, conclude** Charles completed his homework before dinner.	1. *start, begin, commence*
	2. *adj.*	**entire, whole, total, full** The library has a complete set of the encyclopedia.	2. *partial, incomplete*
completely	*adv.*	**entirely, fully, totally, utterly, wholly, absolutely, perfectly** We were completely satisfied with the new television set.	*somewhat, partly, partially*
complex	1. *adj.*	**multiple, mixed, composite, compound** The human body needs complex vitamins to remain healthy.	1. *single, homogeneous*
	2. *adj.*	**complicated, intricate, involved, confusing** The case proved too complex for the local police.	2. *understandable, apparent, clear*
complicated	*adj.*	**intricate, complex, involved, difficult** We had trouble understanding her long, complicated story.	*simple, easy, uncomplicated, uninvolved*
compliment	1. *n.*	**praise, acclaim, approval, congratulations** The producer received many compliments on the excellent movie.	1. *abuse, reproof, disapproval, criticism*
	2. *v.*	**congratulate, praise, commend** We complimented Lim on her superb cooking.	2. *disapprove, criticize*
comply	*v.*	**meet, conform, submit, acquiesce** Students have to comply with the school's rules and regulations.	*differ, conflict, disagree*
component	1. *n.*	**part, piece, segment, ingredient, section** Television sets are made of many essential components.	1. *whole, total, aggregate*
	2. *adj.*	**basic, primary, fundamental, integral, central, main, necessary** The battery is a component part of a flashlight.	2. *incidental, superficial, insignificant, unessential*

Word			Synonyms and Example	Antonyms
compose	1.	*v.*	**create, originate, form, write, score, design** She composed a song for the school's centennial celebrations. *n.* The composer was congratulated for her fine musical composition.	
	2.	*v.*	**constitute, comprise, make up** Water is composed of hydrogen and oxygen.	2. *exclude*
comprehend		*v.*	**understand, grasp, perceive, discern, know** The audience couldn't comprehend the speaker's speech. *n.* The speech was beyond comprehension.	*misunderstand, misinterpret, misconstrue, mistake*
compute		*v.*	**calculate, measure, count, reckon, figure** He computed the cost of the supplies. *n.* Is your school equipped with computers?	*guess, speculate*
comrade		*n.*	**chum, friend, companion, associate, confidant** Jen and Yun remained comrades after graduation.	*enemy, foe, stranger*
conceal		*v.*	**hide, cover, screen, mask, disguise, camouflage** He concealed his disappointment behind a smile.	*reveal, expose, uncover*
concede		*v.*	**yield, grant, admit, allow** They conceded that the best team won the championship.	*deny, refuse*
conceit		*n.*	**vanity, self-admiration, egotism** Ann was full of conceit after winning first prize.	*modesty, humility*
concentrate	1.	*v.*	**pay attention, think** Sam was told to concentrate on his studies if he wished to graduate. *n.* He listened to the lecture with deep concentration.	1. *ignore, be inattentive*
	2.	*v.*	**gather, assemble, amass, congregate, combine, accumulate** The theatres are concentrated in the city.	2. *disperse, spread, scatter, separate, disband*
concept		*n.*	**idea, theory, notion** A democratic country believes in the concept of equality for its citizens.	

Word			Synonyms	Antonyms
concerned	1.	*adj.*	**interested, involved, affected** Concerned citizens protested against the proposed dumpsite.	1. *disinterested, unconcerned, indifferent*
	2.	*adj.*	**bothered, upset, distressed, disturbed, worried, anxious, troubled, agitated** We were concerned when the skiers did not return by nightfall.	2. *calm, at ease, unconcerned, undisturbed, placid, unperturbed*
concert	1.	*n.*	**recital, musical performance** Min performed at a charity concert.	
	2.	*n.*	**agreement, harmony, concord, accord, unity, union** The nations signed the treaty in concert.	2. *disagreement, disunity, discord, strife, dispute*
concise		*adj.*	**brief, short, condensed, succinct, terse** Daryl gave a concise report of the meeting.	*long, lengthy, extended, expanded*
conclude	1.	*v.*	**finish, stop, end, terminate, complete, cease** We were glad when the movie concluded happily.	1. *begin, start, commence*
	2.	*v.*	**arrange, settle** Canada and the United States concluded a trade agreement.	2. *discontinue, cease, end, break off*
	3.	*v.*	**reason, presume, deduce, infer, assume, judge** After studying the X-rays, the doctor concluded that Kit was suffering from lung cancer.	3. *doubt, question*
conclusion	1.	*n.*	**end, finish, completion, termination** At the conclusion of the play, the mystery was still unsolved.	1. *beginning, start, introduction, prelude*
	2.	*n.*	**result, decision, judgment, resolution, finding** After examining the patient, the surgeon reached the conclusion that an operation was not necessary.	
concrete	1.	*n.*	**cement** The streets were paved in concrete.	
	2.	*adj.*	**definite, particular, precise, exact, solid, real, detailed, specific** The lawyer needed concrete evidence to convince the jury that the accused was guilty.	2. *inaccurate, obscure, inexact, ambiguous, indecisive*

Word	#	Part	Synonyms / Example	Antonyms
concur		*v.*	**agree, approve, assent, consent** The judges concurred in their choice of a winner.	*disagree, dispute, disapprove, object*
condemn	1.	*v.*	**find guilty, convict** After studying the evidence, the jury condemned him as a spy.	**1.** *acquit, excuse, pardon, exonerate, forgive*
	2.	*v.*	**doom, sentence** The murderers were condemned to death.	
	3.	*v.*	**denounce, criticize** The chemical plant was condemned for polluting our water supply. *n.* A letter of condemnation was sent to the chemical plant.	**3.** *praise, hail*
condense		*v.*	**abridge, abbreviate, summarize** Phil condensed his novel for publication in a magazine.	*lengthen, extend, expand*
condition	1.	*n.*	**shape, state** The old car is in excellent condition.	
	2.	*n.*	**requirement, stipulation, contingency, specification** The main condition for the sale is that the buyer must pay cash.	
	3.	*v.*	**accustom, train** The astronauts were conditioned for weightlessness in space.	
conduct	1.	*n.*	**behaviour, actions, demeanour** He was thrown out of the concert for disorderly conduct.	
	2.	*v.*	**behave, act** She conducted herself with dignity throughout the ordeal.	
	3.	*v.*	**direct, guide, lead, manage** Syl conducted the visitors on a tour of the city. *n.* She works as a tour conductor.	
	4.	*v.*	**carry, send, transmit, convey, transfer** Those pipes conduct heat throughout the building.	
confess		*v.*	**admit, concede, acknowledge, own up, disclose, divulge** He confessed that he had cheated in the examination. *n.* He made his confession to the principal.	*withhold, hide, conceal*
confide	1.	*v.*	**reveal, tell, admit, disclose, divulge** Win confided her problems to her parents.	**1.** *conceal, keep secret*

Entry	No.	Part	Synonyms / Example	Antonyms
	2.	*v.*	**entrust, charge, delegate, assign** The student council funds are confided to the treasurer.	2. *maintain, keep, retain*
confidence	1.	*n.*	**trust** I have full confidence in my doctor.	1. *distrust*
	2.	*n.*	**assurance, security** Ron's air of confidence inspires his teammates.	2. *fear, nervousness, insecurity*
confident	1.	*adj.*	**positive, sure, certain, convinced** The coach is confident that the team will win.	1. *doubtful, uncertain*
	2.	*adj.*	**self-assured, sure of oneself** The two most confident students were selected for the debating team.	2. *insecure, timid, unsure*
confidential		*adj.*	**secret, private, classified, privy, personal** The teacher wrote a confidential report on the graduating students.	*public, open*
configuration		*n.*	**pattern, shape, outline, form, contour** Astronomers study the many configurations of stars in the universe.	
confine	1.	*v.*	**hold back, restrain, limit** Let's confine this meeting to urgent matters only.	1. *release, let out, let loose*
	2.	*v.*	**imprison, cage, shut up, incarcerate** The hostage was confined in a cell.	2. *release, set free, liberate*
confirm		*v.*	**approve, endorse, ratify, affirm, sanction, validate** The airline confirmed the reservation on the flight to Calgary. *n.* Ian phoned for a confirmation of his appointment.	*cancel, veto, refuse, revoke, rescind*
confiscate		*v.*	**impound, usurp, seize, appropriate, secure, take, commandeer** The customs officer confiscated the illegal merchandise.	*return, restore, compensate, atone, make good, make amends*
conflict	1.	*n.*	**fight, struggle, strife, battle, encounter, clash, contest** It was hoped that the conflict would not develop into a major war.	1. *peace, concord, collaboration*

	2.	*n.*	**hostility, dispute, disagreement, dissension, antagonism** Their differing ideas created conflict between the two friends. *v.* His ideas conflicted with Kay's.	**2.** *concurrence, agreement, cooperation*
conflicting		*adj.*	**contrary, opposing, contradictory, clashing** The leaders held conflicting views about trade regulations.	*like, compatible, similar, parallel*
conform		*v.*	**comply, adapt, follow, obey** Citizens must conform to the laws of the country. *n.* Conformity to the law is expected of citizens. *n.* A person who follows the rules is a conformist.	*conflict, disagree, differ*
confound		*v.*	**confuse, bewilder, perplex, dismay, puzzle** The maze confounded the children, and they couldn't find their way out.	
confront		*v.*	**face, resist, oppose** The neighbours confronted each other over the fence. *n.* It was a nasty confrontation.	*comply, agree*
confuse	1.	*v.*	**muddle, bewilder, puzzle, fluster, jumble, unsettle, rattle, agitate, mix up, confound, disturb** We were confused by the conflicting reports of the witnesses.	**1.** *assist, clarify, untangle*
	2.	*v.*	**mistake, mix up** People often confuse Pat with her sister Pam.	**2.** *distinguish*
confusion	1.	*n.*	**disorder, disarray** It took months to sort out the confusion at the new store.	**1.** *order*
	2.	*n.*	**bewilderment, commotion, agitation, fracas** The crowd was thrown into confusion when the fire alarm sounded.	**2.** *quiet, calm*
congenial		*adj.*	**agreeable, compatible, sympathetic, pleasant** Congenial classmates help make school enjoyable.	*disagreeable, incompatible, unsympathetic, unpleasant*

Word	Sense	Part of speech	Synonyms and examples	Antonyms
congratulate		*v.*	**rejoice with, wish well, compliment** The winner was congratulated by the mayor. *n.* Congratulations poured in from all over the world.	*rebuke, criticize*
congregate		*v.*	**convene, meet, converge, gather, collect, assemble** Fans congregated outside the hotel waiting for the star to appear. *n.* The congregation sang during the church service.	*disperse, disband, separate, scatter, break up*
connect	1.	*v.*	**unite, attach, join, combine, link, fasten** The electrician connected the wires. *n.* The telephone connection was so poor that I could hardly hear.	1. *disconnect, unfasten, untie*
	2.	*v.*	**associate, relate** The two families are connected by marriage. *n.* His connection with the Smith family helped him get the job.	2. *disassociate, shun*
conquer	1.	*v.*	**subdue, defeat, vanquish, crush, triumph, prevail, win** Alexander the Great conquered many parts of the world. *n.* He was a remarkable conqueror. *n.* His conquests are recorded in all the history books.	1. *lose, retreat, yield*
	2.	*v.*	**overcome** Andrew conquered his fear of water and learned to swim.	2. *yield, give in to*
conscious	1.	*adj.*	**awake, alert** Rea was conscious soon after the operation. *n.* She regained consciousness in the recovery room.	1. *unconscious, insensible*
	2.	*adj.*	**informed, aware, discerning, cognizant** Kelly made a conscious decision to return to school.	2. *uninformed, unaware*
consensus		*n.*	**agreement, accord, consent** The school's decision to become co-educational was arrived at by a concensus of the board of governors.	*disagreement, discord*
consent	1.	*n.*	**assent, approval, permission, agreement** We had to get our parents' consent to go on the school trip.	1. *refusal, disagreement, denial, dissent*

	2.	*v.*	**allow, approve, agree, concur, comply, accede, permit** The judge consented to the accused person's request for bail.	**2.** *reject, deny, decline, negate, refuse, disagree, disapprove*
consequence	1.	*n.*	**outcome, end, result, product, effect, outgrowth** People are responsible for the consequences of their actions.	**1.** *cause, origin, beginning, source*
	2.	*n.*	**importance, significance** Marie Curie's discoveries about radioactivity were of great consequence to humanity.	**2.** *unimportance, insignificance, inconsequence, triviality, paltriness*
conservation		*n.*	**protection, preservation, maintenance, keeping** The government is concerned with the conservation of the nation's natural resources.	*destruction, waste, misuse, consumption, dissolution*
conservative		*adj.*	**moderate, careful, cautious** She is a conservative investor who does not take risks.	*changing, risky*
conserve		*v.*	**store, save up, reserve, keep back, lay away, accumulate** During the heat wave the people were told to conserve water.	*waste, use, use up, empty, squander, spend, consume, go through*
consider		*v.*	**think about, ponder, contemplate, deliberate, reflect on, examine** Have you considered which university you're going to? *n.* Shen has given the question a lot of consideration.	*ignore, reject, disregard, deny, refuse*
considerable	1.	*adj.*	**important, noteworthy, significant** The mayor has considerable influence on the council's decision.	**1.** *insignificant, ordinary, immaterial, nonessential*
	2.	*adj.*	**ample, bountiful, much, abundant, plentiful, substantial** Canada is blessed with considerable natural resources.	**2.** *small, scant, insufficient, insubstantial, meagre*
considerate		*adj.*	**thoughtful, kind, humane, solicitous, caring** Carlo is always considerate of his parents.	*inconsiderate, neglectful, thoughtless, remiss, indifferent*
consist		*v.*	**comprise, include** The human body consists of about 65% water.	*exclude*

consistent

1. *adj.* **uniform, regular, constant**
Will has been a consistent part of her life for the last ten years.
adj. They have been seeing each other consistently for ten years.
— *1. inconsistent, divergent*

2. *adj.* **compatible, in agreement with, matching, conforming, congruous**
The weather is consistent with the season.
— *2. incongruous, discrepant, incompatible, disagreeing*

console

v. **comfort, solace, encourage**
Claude consoled his sister after her cat disappeared.
n. She was so stricken with grief that she was beyond consolation.
— *annoy, trouble, hurt, distress*

consolidate

1. *v.* **combine, unite, condense, compress, put together**
The two small publishing houses consolidated into one.
n. The consolidation resulted in a large, profitable organization.
— *1. scatter, cut, sever, separate, divide*

2. *v.* **fortify, strengthen, build up, add to, increase**
The merger of the companies consolidated their financial position.
— *2. weaken, tear down, cripple*

conspicuous

1. *adj.* **notable, prominent, eminent, outstanding, celebrated, illustrious, well-known, renowned**
She played a conspicuous role in the country's fight for independence.
— *1. unimportant, unknown*

2. *adj.* **evident, obvious, prominent, noticeable, glaring, visible**
The solitary tree was conspicuous on the prairie.
— *2. hidden, screened, concealed, obscured, covered*

conspire

v. **plot, scheme, contrive**
The army conspired to overthrow the government.
n. It was a well-planned conspiracy.

constant

1. *adj.* **steady, uniform, continual, even, unchanging, incessant, lasting, nonstop, perpetual**
Planets move around the sun in a constant motion.
adv. Planets rotate constantly around the sun.
— *1. uneven, interrupted, intermittent, periodic, occasional, spasmodic, sporadic, now and then*

	2.	*adj.*	**faithful, devoted, loyal, steadfast, fast, firm, staunch, unwavering, unchanging, abiding, permanent, dependable** Gim and Fred have been constant companions for years.	**2.** *unreliable, inconsistent, uncertain*
constraint	1.	*n.*	**force, pressure, compulsion, coercion** The accused confessed under constraint.	**1.** *free will*
	2.	*n.*	**shyness, reserve, bashfulness, timidity, restraint** On being presented with the award, the winner showed constraint.	**2.** *bravado*
	3.	*n.*	**captivity, detention, confinement, arrest, restriction** The men held the thief in constraint till the police arrived.	**3.** *freedom, liberty*
construct		*v.*	**build, erect, make, compose** They constructed a bridge over the river. *n.* The construction of the bridge took a year.	*dismantle, tear down, take apart*
consume	1.	*v.*	**destroy, exhaust, waste, demolish** The building was totally consumed by fire.	**1.** *preserve, save, protect*
	2.	*v.*	**use, utilize, spend** Dad's old car consumes a lot of gas. *n.* The car's gas consumption is high.	**2.** *hoard, collect, gather, accumulate*
	3.	*v.*	**eat, drink, swallow, devour** At the party, the children consumed all the cake.	
	4.	*v.*	**take up, wrap up, engross** Golf consumes all her spare time. *adj.* She has a consuming interest in golf.	
consumer		*n.*	**user, buyer, shopper, customer, purchaser** North Americans are big consumers of processed foods.	
contact	1.	*n.*	**touch, connection, meeting, junction** Electric wires must be in contact to complete a circuit.	**1.** *distance, separation*
	2.	*v.*	**communicate, talk to, reach** Mission Control contacted the astronauts in the spacecraft. *n.* They have had no contact with their former neighbours for years.	

Word			Synonyms	Antonyms
contagious		*adj.*	**transferable, catching, communicable, infectious, transmissible** Measles is a contagious disease, hence patients are usually kept in isolation.	*non-communicable, non-contagious*
contain	**1.**	*v.*	**hold, include, comprise, be composed of, consist of** The parcel contained many gifts for the children. *n.* A vase is a container for flowers.	
	2.	*v.*	**restrain, restrict, hold, keep back, stop, check, impede** Don couldn't contain his excitement when he heard the news.	**2.** *release, let go, relinquish*
contaminate		*v.*	**pollute, infect, corrupt, dirty, soil, sully** Factory wastes can contaminate lakes and rivers. *n.* Bacteria can cause contamination of the water supply. *adj.* Contaminated water will make people ill.	*purify, cleanse, clean, clarify, refine, filter*
contemporary	**1.**	*n.*	**peer, counterpart** Winston Churchill and Franklin Roosevelt were political contemporaries.	
	2.	*adj.*	**current, present, modern** Sheila bought contemporary furniture for her apartment.	**2.** *old-fashioned, dated*
	3.	*adj.*	**simultaneous, coexistent** Pollution and nuclear warfare are contemporary social issues.	
contempt	**1.**	*n.*	**scorn, disdain, derision, malice** He was charged with contempt of the law.	**1.** *respect, esteem, honour, regard, admiration*
	2.	*n.*	**shame, dishonour, disgrace** The people showed their contempt for the traitor.	**2.** *praise, honour*
content		*adj.*	**satisfied, pleased, happy, gratified** Manny is content with his new home. *v.* He contented himself with a small house. *n.* He lived a life of contentment.	*discontented, unhappy, displeased, dissatisfied*

Word	#	Part of speech	Synonyms / Example	Antonyms
contents		*n.*	**ingredients, parts, substances, elements, components, constituents** Should the contents of all prepared foods be listed?	
contest	1.	*n.*	**competition, match, challenge** The students took part in a writing contest.	
	2.	*n.*	**battle, fight, feud, dispute, fray, conflict** There was a nasty legal contest for the custody of the children. *n.* They were both tough contestants.	
	3.	*v.*	**argue, debate, question, oppose** They contested their grandmother's will in court.	**3.** *defend, uphold, agree with, accept*
context		*n.*	**text, meaning, substance** There was a misunderstanding because he was quoted out of context.	
continual	1.	*adj.*	**constant, uninterrupted, unbroken, regular** Because of the infection, Jo heard a continual ringing in her ears.	**1.** *interrupted, broken, irregular, sporadic*
	2.	*adj.*	**ceaseless, lasting, unending, perpetual, endless, permanent** John F. Kennedy's grave is marked with a continual flame. *adj.* The flame burns continually.	**2.** *fleeting, brief, short, transitory, passing, momentary, temporary*
continue	1.	*v.*	**stay, linger, remain** The monsoon continued all week.	**1.** *leave, go, depart*
	2.	*v.*	**resume, begin again, take up again, recommence, renew** After lunch, the students continued their discussion.	**2.** *discontinue, postpone, stop, halt*
	3.	*v.*	**persist, persevere, keep on, progress, press onward** Terry Fox continued on his run despite the pain.	**3.** *end, give up, cease*
contract	1.	*n.*	**agreement, pact** The bride and groom signed the marriage contract.	
	2.	*v.*	**shrink, decrease, constrict, lessen, reduce** Metal contracts in the cold.	**2.** *stretch, expand, enlarge*
contradict	1.	*v.*	**refute, deny, disclaim** The defendant contradicted the charge made against him.	**1.** *admit, accept, affirm*

Word	No.	Part of speech	Synonyms and example	Antonyms
	2.	*v.*	**oppose, confront, defy** The two witnesses contradicted each other. *n.* One witness's story was a complete contradiction of the other's.	2. *back up, side with*
contribute		*v.*	**give, subscribe, donate** They contribute time and money to charity. *n.* They made a generous contribution to the hospital fund.	*receive, accept*
contrite		*adj.*	**repentant, regretful, sorry** The contrite boy promised never to steal again.	*unrepentant*
controversial		*adj.*	**debatable, contentious, disputable, questionable** Capital punishment is a controversial issue.	*incontestable, indisputable*
controversy		*n*	**dispute, debate, argument, altercation** The controversy over capital punishment is widely debated.	*agreement, accord*
convene		*v.*	**assemble, meet, gather, collect, congregate, convoke** The council convened at eight o'clock. *n.* Delegates voted at the annual convention.	*disperse, scatter, break up, dissolve*
convenient	1.	*adj.*	**advantageous, ready, useful, timesaving, labour-saving, available** Frozen dinners are convenient for those who work.	1. *unserviceable, disadvantageous*
	2.	*adj.*	**near, handy, easy to reach, accessible** Neighbourhood stores are convenient places to shop.	2. *far, distant, inaccessible*
conventional	1.	*adj.*	**customary, regular, standard, typical, commonplace, usual, prevailing, common** The bride wore a conventional white gown.	1. *unusual, unpopular, atypical*
	2.	*adj.*	**correct, right, established, sanctioned** The conventional curtsy was given to the Queen.	2. *unconventional, unorthodox*

converse *v.* **talk, chat, speak, discuss**
Emilie conversed in French with the storekeeper.
n. They had an interesting conversation.

convert *v.* **change, alter, transform, make over, revise**
They converted the old house into an office.
n. The conversion took two years to complete.

convey
1. *v.* **transport, send, carry, move, dispatch**
The new cars were conveyed by rail to the port.
Antonyms: 1. *keep, preserve, retain*
2. *v.* **transmit, conduct, pass on, communicate**
Please convey my regards to Yang.

convict
1. *n.* **prisoner, captive, criminal, felon**
The convict was captured in the swamp.
Antonyms: 1. *free person*
2. *v.* **find guilty, sentence**
The defendant was convicted of the charge.
n. The conviction will be appealed in a higher court.
Antonyms: 2. *acquit, find not guilty, liberate, clear*

conviction *n.* **belief, view, persuasion**
She had strong convictions on the issue.
Antonyms: *doubt, uncertainty, misgiving*

convince *v.* **persuade, assure, prove to**
The suspect convinced the police that she had been wrongfully arrested.
adj. She had convincing evidence of her innocence.
Antonyms: *be doubtful, be sceptical*

cool
1. *v.* **get cold, lose heat**
Sim let the soup cool before eating it.
Antonyms: 1. *heat, thaw, warm*
2. *adj.* **chilly, nippy**
Cool breezes caused the group to go indoors.
Antonyms: 2. *warm, hot, tepid, heated*
3. *adj.* **unruffled, calm, composed, deliberate**
Astronauts are trained to remain cool under stress.
Antonyms: 3. *ruffled, anxious, rash, excitable, wild*

cooperate		*v.*	**work together, collaborate, join forces, join in, work side by side** Schools cooperate with businesses to train students for the workplace. *n.* They work in cooperation. *adj.* This cooperative venture benefits everyone.	*act independently*
cope		*v.*	**endure, contend, tolerate, face, put up with, live through, suffer** He had to cope with a series of tragedies.	*avoid, resist, elude, evade*
copy	**1.**	*n.*	**facsimile, simulation, replica, duplicate, reproduction** Give Ali a copy of this letter.	**1.** *original*
	2.	*v.*	**duplicate, reproduce, reprint, transcribe** The designer copied someone's designs.	**2.** *originate, introduce*
	3.	*v.*	**imitate, match, mirror, repeat, follow, emulate, mimic** Children often copy the behaviour of their parents.	**3.** *avoid, shun, abandon*
cord		*n.*	**string, rope, twine** The package was tied with cord.	
cordial		*adj.*	**warm, friendly, genial, affable** The popular speaker received a cordial welcome.	*cold, distant, aloof, discourteous*
core		*n.*	**essence, heart, kernel, nucleus, hub** Acid rain is at the core of the pollution problem.	*edge, exterior*
correct	**1.**	*v.*	**repair, make right, improve, rectify, amend** Sheena had to correct the mistakes she had made in the test. *n.* She had to make many corrections.	**1.** *err, mistake*
	2.	*adj.*	**true, accurate, right, exact, precise, perfect** The first response given was correct.	**2.** *inaccurate, wrong, incorrect, imprecise, false*
	3.	*adj.*	**fitting, proper, appropriate, suitable** Is there a correct way to address the head of state?	**3.** *inappropriate, unsuitable, improper*
correspond	**1.**	*v.*	**match, harmonize, resemble** Actual sales corresponded with the forecast.	**1.** *vary, differ, clash*

Word	No.	Part	Synonyms / Example	Antonyms
	2.	*v.*	**write to, exchange letters** She corresponded with her former neighbour for years. *n.* Their correspondence lasted many years.	
corrode		*v.*	**destroy, erode, deteriorate, decay, degenerate, eat away** Acid corrodes metal. *n.* How can such corrosion be prevented?	*build, construct, establish*
corrupt	1.	*v.*	**taint, make immoral** Young people may be corrupted by bad company.	**1.** *improve, ennoble, purify*
	2.	*adj.*	**evil, wicked, immoral, dishonest** The corrupt dictator was finally overthrown. *n.* The overthrow of the dictator ended years of corruption in the country.	**2.** *good, moral, honest, upright*
cosmetic		*adj.*	**restorative, corrective, beautifying** He required cosmetic surgery to remove the scars caused by the fire.	
cost	1.	*n.*	**price, charge, worth, expense, value** The cost of houses is too high for the average person.	
	2.	*n.*	**damage, hurt, detriment** The nation won the battle at a great cost in lives.	
costly		*adj.*	**expensive, dear, high-priced, valuable, precious** Diamonds are costly gems.	*cheap, inexpensive, low-priced*
costume		*n.*	**suit, outfit, dress, apparel, clothes, garb** The guests wore national costumes for the event.	
council		*n.*	**assembly, gathering, bureau, cabinet, committee, board** Who will be the head of the students' council? *n.* Noni is one of the student councillors.	
counsel	1.	*n.*	**advice, suggestion, recommendation, guidance** Lawyers provide counsel.	

	2.	*v.*	**advise, guide, suggest** The guidance teacher counselled the students. *n.* Teachers often act as counsellors for the students.	
count	1.	*v.*	**figure, calculate, tally, score, compute, add up, total** The cashier counted out the change. *n.* What was the final count?	
	2.	*v.*	**depend, rely, trust** Aisha counted on her family for help.	
counterfeit		*adj.*	**artificial, false, forged, bogus, fraudulent, invalid, fictitious** They were arrested for trying to shop with counterfeit money.	*real, genuine, authentic, valid*
countless		*adj.*	**incalculable, innumerable, myriad, uncountable, limitless** We were attacked by countless mosquitoes.	*few*
couple	1.	*n.*	**pair, twosome, set** Lyn and Phil make a handsome couple.	**1.** *single, one, individual, separate*
	2.	*v.*	**tie, join, link, unite, pair, connect** The trailer was coupled to the van.	**2.** *separate, detach, untie, disconnect*
courage		*n.*	**bravery, spirit, boldness, nerve, fearlessness, valour, audacity, mettle, gallantry** She was awarded a medal for her courage in rescuing the child. *adj.* The courageous woman plunged into the river to save the child.	*fear, cowardice, timidity*
course		*n.*	**route, path, circuit, direction** They charted out a course of action.	
courtesy		*n.*	**politeness, respect, manners** Senior citizens should be accorded courtesy. *adj.* The courteous boy gave up his seat to the elderly man.	*rudeness, disrespect*
cover	1.	*n.*	**lid, top, covering, cap, seal** Put the cover on the paint pot to prevent the paint from hardening.	
	2.	*v.*	**conceal, hide, screen, mask, camouflage, disguise** The bird covered its nest with leaves.	**2.** *reveal, open, uncover, disclose*
	3.	*v.*	**wrap, enclose, encase, envelop** Cover the turkey with foil before roasting it.	**3.** *unwrap, uncover*

4. *v.* **cross, travel, journey, traverse**
The runner covered the distance in record time.

5. *v.* **report upon, recount, broadcast**
Megan was assigned by the newspaper to cover the Olympic Games.

cowardly *adj.* **fearful, timid, cowering**
The cowardly person ignored the victim's cries of help.
adv. He shut his ears and slunk away cowardly.
courageous, brave, bold, fearless

cozy *adj.* **snug, comfortable, warm**
Amy snuggled into her cozy bed.
uncomfortable

crack 1. *n.* **opening, slit, break, chink, cut**
The earthquake caused cracks to appear in many buildings.

2. *n.* **snap, crackle, stroke**
Circus lions respond to the crack of the trainer's whip.

3. *v.* **split, open, splinter, burst, break, snap, cleave**
The stone cracked the car's windshield.
adj. The cracked windshield had to be replaced.
3. *join, attach, connect, link, tie, bind, mend*

crafty *adj.* **wily, foxy, sly, cunning, tricky**
The crafty fox waited in the bushes for the lamb.
direct, honest, straightforward, sincere

cram 1. *v.* **stuff, jam, ram, pack**
The room was crammed with furniture.
1. *empty, remove*

2. *v.* **gorge, satiate**
The children crammed themselves with ice cream and cake at the party.
2. *disgorge*

3. *v.* **study hurriedly**
Shen is cramming for the test.

cramp 1. *n.* **spasm, kink, stitch, crick**
The swimmer got a cramp in his leg and had to get out of the pool.

2. *v.* **confine, restrict**
The prisoners were cramped together in a tiny cell.
adj. She got a sore back from sitting in a cramped position.

Word	Sense	Part of speech	Synonyms and examples	Antonyms
cranky		*adj.*	**cross, disagreeable, irritable, grouchy, cantankerous, grumpy, peevish, ill-tempered** Some people get cranky when they are tired.	*good-natured, pleasant, calm, agreeable*
crash	1.	*n.*	**clatter, clash, din, noise** The loud crash awoke the neighbourhood.	
	2.	*n.*	**collision, impact, smash** Plane crashes are more common in bad weather. *v.* The two cars crashed on the slippery road.	
crave		*v.*	**need, want, desire, covet, long for, yearn, hanker** The lonely child craved attention.	*loathe, be revolted by*
crawl	1.	*v.*	**creep, wriggle, worm** The spider crawled up the wall.	
	2.	*v.*	**plod, drag** The traffic crawled along the slippery road. *n.* Traffic was reduced to a crawl in rush hour.	**2.** *progress, advance*
crazy		*adj.*	**mad, insane, demented** You will lose money if you invest in that crazy scheme.	*sane, sensible*
create	1.	*v.*	**make, originate, invent, design, conceive, devise, formulate, compose, produce** Michelangelo created wonderful works of art. *n.* The Statue of Liberty is an inspiring creation. *adj.* Artists are creative individuals.	**1.** *end, destroy, finish, wipe out, exterminate, nullify, demolish, dismantle*
	2.	*v.*	**cause, produce** The scientists created a stir with the announcement of their discovery.	**2.** *prevent*
credit	1.	*n.*	**belief, faith, credence, confidence** The teacher gave little credit to his excuse for not completing his homework.	**1.** *disbelief, doubt, suspicion*
	2.	*n.*	**instalment buying** She couldn't afford the television, so she bought it on credit.	**2.** *cash*
	3.	*n.*	**recognition, honour, praise** The credit for the success of the team belongs to the coach. *v.* The coach should be credited for his training.	**3.** *blame, dishonour criticism*

	4.	*v.*	**believe in, rely on, trust, acknowledge** It was difficult to credit the journalist's story as there was no evidence to support it.	4. *doubt, deny, suspect*
credulous		*adj.*	**gullible, naive, trusting, unsophisticated, simple, innocent** The credulous man paid $500 for a stone with magic powers!	*experienced, sophisticated, suspicious*
crest	1.	*n.*	**top, crown, pinnacle, highest point, summit, peak, height** The view from the crest of the hill was spectacular.	1. *bottom, base, foot*
	2.	*n.*	**emblem, coat of arms** The school's crest is sewn on the blazer pocket.	
crevice		*n.*	**chasm, cleft, gap, fissure** The mountaineer slipped and plunged into the crevice.	
crew		*n.*	**team, squad, group, company** The crew of the space shuttle underwent rigorous training before the flight.	
crime		*n.*	**felony, offence, misdemeanour, wrongdoing, misdeed, illegality** The accused was found guilty of committing the crime of kidnapping. *adj.* The crime rate has risen alarmingly in the city.	*legality*
criminal	1.	*n.*	**lawbreaker, felon, culprit, offender** Criminals often serve time in prison.	
	2.	*adj.*	**unlawful, illegal, felonious** Robbery is a criminal offence.	2. *lawful, legal*
cripple		*v.*	**hurt, injure, disable, enfeeble, incapacitate** The town was crippled by the hurricane. *adj.* The Red Cross sent aid to the people in the crippled town.	*strengthen, invigorate, stimulate, energize*
crisp	1.	*adj.*	**firm, fresh, stiff** Crisp lettuce is needed in salads.	1. *limp, soft, pliant*
	2.	*adj.*	**brisk, bracing, invigorating, fresh, stimulating, refreshing, exhilarating** We were refreshed by the crisp morning air.	2. *dull, boring, tedious*

	3.	*adj.*	**terse, abrupt, short, brief** The government issued a crisp statement about the crisis.	3. *verbose, loquacious, lengthy*
critical	1.	*adj.*	**disapproving, faultfinding** Elle received a highly critical report of her work from her boss.	1. *endorsing, supportive, positive*
	2.	*adj.*	**crucial, life-threatening, dangerous** The patient was in a critical condition after the operation.	2. *stable*
	3.	*adj.*	**vital, crucial** Your support has been critical to the success of this project.	3. *unimportant, irrelevant*
criticize	1.	*v.*	**reprove, censure, reprimand, reproach, find fault with** The teenagers were criticized for their rowdy behaviour. *n.* Most people do not like criticism.	1. *praise, approve, endorse, support*
	2.	*v.*	**study, probe, scrutinize, examine, analyse, review, evaluate** The newspaper reviewer criticized the new ballet. *n.* The critics were full of praise for the new ballet.	
crooked	1.	*adj.*	**winding, curved, bent, askew, zigzag** Let's take the crooked path into the park.	1. *straight, direct*
	2.	*adj.*	**dishonest, criminal, corrupt, illegal, unlawful** The public must be protected from crooked dealers.	2. *honest, legal, straightforward, trustworthy*
crop	1.	*n.*	**harvest, yield, product** Excellent weather results in large farm crops.	
	2.	*v.*	**cut, trim, shorten** The photographer cropped the border of the photo.	2. *enlarge, extend, increase*
cross	1.	*n.*	**hybrid, mixture, crossbreed** The puppy is a cross between a spaniel and a terrier.	1. *purebred, thoroughbred, pedigree, full-blood*
	2.	*n.*	**affliction, obstacle, misfortune, trial, hardship** That disease is an awful cross to bear!	2. *blessing, benefit, advantage*
	3.	*v.*	**sail, navigate, travel, traverse** Vikings crossed the Atlantic Ocean.	
	4.	*v.*	**intersect** The town is situated where two major roads cross.	4. *parallel*

Word	No.	Part	Synonyms / Example	Antonyms
	5.	*adj.*	**annoyed, angry** Helen was cross with Vic for being late.	**5.** *even-tempered, pleasant, calm*
crouch	1.	*v.*	**squat, bend, stoop** The runners crouched at the starting line of the race.	**1.** *stretch, stand up*
	2.	*v.*	**cower, cringe, grovel** The prisoners crouched in terror.	**2.** *spurn, scorn, disdain*
crowd	1.	*n.*	**mob, throng, swarm, mass, multitude, horde** Police were called to control the crowd outside the stadium.	
	2.	*v.*	**shove, press, push, cram, squeeze, stuff, jam** During rush hour, people crowded into the subway car.	
crown	1.	*n.*	**coronet, tiara, diadem** The queen wore a magnificent crown during her coronation.	
	2.	*n.*	**top, crest, apex, pinnacle, summit, top** The hikers reached the crown of the hill.	**2.** *bottom, base, foot*
	3.	*v.*	**adorn, make complete, make perfect** The wedding cake will be crowned with roses.	
crowning		*adj.*	**supreme, highest, ultimate, chief, paramount, principal, main, best** Beautiful hair is her crowning glory.	*secondary, worst, poorest, lowest*
crucial	1.	*adj.*	**critical, significant, urgent, important** Choosing the right university is a crucial decision for most young people.	**1.** *insignificant, unimportant, inconsequential*
	2.	*adj.*	**trying, hard, difficult, taxing, disturbing** The family went through a crucial period when Kit fell ill.	**2.** *easy, satisfying, rewarding*
crude	1.	*adj.*	**homemade, rough, rudimentary** The campers built a crude shelter with twigs and blankets.	**1.** *sophisticated, refined*
	2.	*adj.*	**raw, natural, unprocessed** Crude oil is processed in refineries.	**2.** *refined, processed*
	3.	*adj.*	**uncouth, vulgar, coarse, rude** Most people avoid those with crude manners.	**3.** *couth, mannerly, polite, refined*

	4.	*adj.*	**clumsy, ungainly, awkward** The boxer's crude footwork cost him the match.	4. *smooth, graceful, dexterous*
cruel	1.	*adj.*	**brutal, painful, distressing** He lost his fortune by a cruel twist of fate.	1. *pleasing*
	2.	*adj.*	**pitiless, callous, merciless, unrelenting, ruthless** The solders attacked with cruel determination.	2. *merciful, compassionate*
cruise		*n.*	**voyage, sail, trip** A cruise is a relaxing way to spend a vacation. *v.* The family cruised in the Caribbean last winter.	
crumble		*v.*	**break up, disintegrate, decay** Buildings crumbled during the earthquake.	*build, put together, unite, combine*
crunch		*v.*	**bite, chew, munch, gnaw** The children crunched happily on the candy. *adj.* They enjoy crunchy peanuts.	
crush	1.	*v.*	**squash, smash, pulverize** The machine crushed the stones into gravel.	
	2.	*v.*	**defeat, beat, overwhelm, annihilate** The army crushed the rebellion.	2. *yield, give up, concede, relinquish*
crust		*n.*	**shell, casing, surface, coating** Everyone loves Ric's crisp pie crusts.	*interior, centre, inside*
cry	1.	*n.*	**shout, call, yell** We were alarmed when we heard a cry in the dark. *v.* The accident victim cried for help.	1. *whisper, murmur, silence*
	2.	*v.*	**mourn, weep, sob** The movie was so sad that everyone in the audience cried.	2. *laugh, rejoice, exult*
culprit		*n.*	**offender, felon, criminal, wrongdoer** After months of investigation, the police identified the culprit responsible for the thefts.	*innocent*
cultivate	1.	*v.*	**dig, plough, make grow, garden, till, farm, plant** Homesteaders cultivated the land.	1. *reap, destroy*

	2.	*v.*	**encourage, promote, help, advance, further, assist, bolster, foster, support, champion** Mom cultivated our interest in music by taking us to many concerts.	2. *discourage, impede, retard, weaken, hinder*
cunning		*adj.*	**clever, sly, crafty, wily, shrewd, smart, foxy** Todd was not taken in by the cunning ways of the salesperson.	*stupid, foolish, simple*
curb	1.	*n.*	**guard, protection, restraint, barrier, check** Leashes act as curbs on pets.	
	2.	*n.*	**edge, border, rim, ledge** People sat on the curbs of the sidewalks to watch the parade.	2. *interior, centre*
	3.	*v.*	**restrain, hold, check, restrict, retard, impede, subdue** She has learned to curb her hot temper.	3. *release, let go, free, liberate*
cure	1.	*n.*	**remedy, correction** Scientists are still trying to find a cure for cancer.	1. *cause, origin, reason, source*
	2.	*v.*	**restore, heal, make healthy** After months of treatment, the patient was cured of hepatitis.	2. *infect, contaminate*
	3.	*v.*	**preserve, salt, pickle** People cured meat and fish before the refrigerator was invented.	
curious	1.	*adj.*	**inquiring, eager, searching, inquisitive, interested** Curious children ask many questions. *n.* Children have a natural curiosity about everything.	1. *indifferent, uninterested, disinterested*
	2.	*adj.*	**strange, odd, queer, unique, unusual, rare, exceptional** It is curious that no one has heard from Ben in a year.	2. *normal, common, usual*
curl		*v.*	**twist, bend, coil, roll up, curve, crimp, wave** Tracie curled her hair into ringlets.	*straighten*
current		*adj.*	**contemporary, prevailing, up-to-date** Moshe writes a current affairs column for the newspaper.	*out-of-date, dated*
currently		*adv.*	**presently, now** This record is currently at the top of the list.	

Word			Synonyms	Antonyms
curt		*adj.*	**brief, short, concise, terse, abrupt** Paul returned her wave with a curt nod of the head.	*lengthy, wordy, verbose, detailed*
curtail		*v.*	**shorten, lessen, cramp, decrease, clip, abbreviate, reduce, abridge** Ho had to curtail his spending in order to save for college.	*lengthen, increase, extend, add, expand*
custom		*n.*	**fashion, practice, manner, habit, routine** In China, it is the custom for students to bow when the teacher enters the classroom.	*irregularity, oddity*
customary		*adj.*	**conventional, usual, routine, habitual, common, regular** It is customary in North America to shake hands when you meet.	*irregular, unusual, uncommon, rare, odd*
customer		*n.*	**purchaser, buyer, client, consumer** Many stores believe in the policy that the customer is always right.	*seller, dealer, retailer, vendor, merchant, marketer*
cut	1.	*n.*	**gash, groove, slit, slash, puncture, incision, gouge, opening, penetration** Jay got a nasty cut on his head when he fell. *v.* He cut himself badly in the fall.	**1.** *closure*
	2.	*n.*	**piece, slice, chunk** Sirloin steak is an expensive cut of beef.	
	3.	*n.*	**segment, slice, portion, part, section, piece** That cut from the movie is a classic.	**3.** *whole, entirety*
	4.	*n.*	**shape, form, construction** Designer gowns are known for their excellent cut.	
	5.	*n.*	**lessening, reduction, decrease** The government announced a cut in taxes just before the election. *v.* The company closed two branches to cut costs.	**5.** *increase, inflation, expansion*
	6.	*n.*	**insult, indignity, abuse, offence** Sue's thoughtless remark was a cut to me! *v.* I was cut to the quick by her remarks.	**6.** *tribute, praise, courtesy*
	7.	*v.*	**clip, snip, trim** Carm cuts my hair. *n.* She always gives me a good hair cut.	

8. *v.* **record, tape**
The singer recently cut a compact disc.

cynical *adj.* **unbelieving, sneering, sarcastic, scornful**
His cynical friends did not think he could win first prize.
n. It was discouraging to have such cynics for friends.
idealistic, believing, optimistic, genial

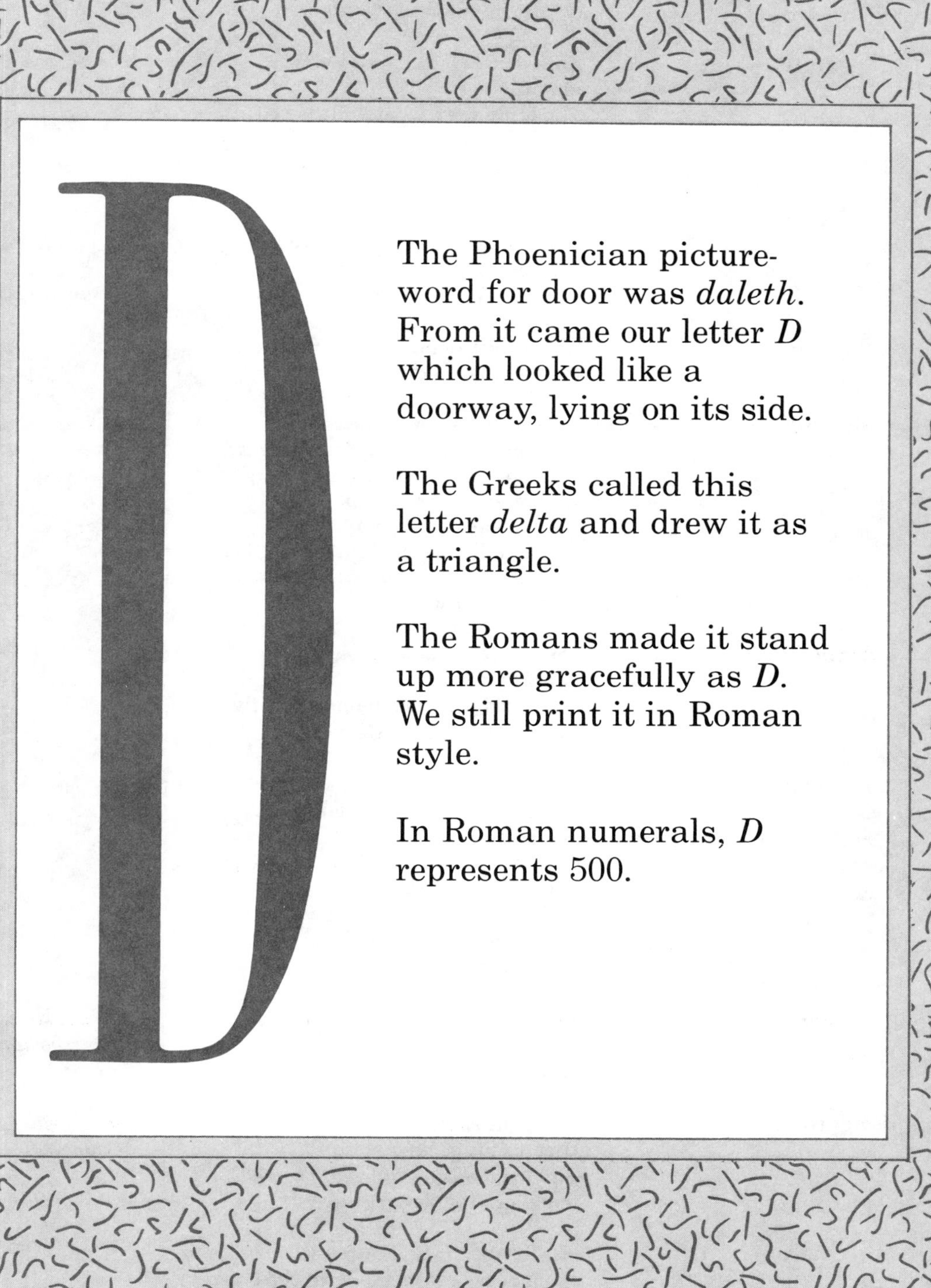

The Phoenician picture-word for door was *daleth.* From it came our letter *D* which looked like a doorway, lying on its side.

The Greeks called this letter *delta* and drew it as a triangle.

The Romans made it stand up more gracefully as *D.* We still print it in Roman style.

In Roman numerals, *D* represents 500.

Word		Part	Synonyms / Examples	Antonyms
daily		*adv.*	**every day, each day** We should exercise daily. *adj.* Mom's daily drive to work takes twenty minutes.	*rarely, irregularly*
dainty		*adj.*	**delicate, refined, exquisite, elegant** The bride wore a dainty lace veil. *adv.* The flower girl walked daintily down the aisle.	*coarse, inelegant, harsh*
dam	1.	*n.*	**barrier, wall** The engineer built a dam to control the flow of the river.	
	2.	*v.*	**clog, choke, hinder, obstruct, block** The beaver dammed the creek and flooded the roadway.	**2.** *clear, open*
damage	1.	*n.*	**injury, harm, hurt, loss** The earthquake caused widespread damage.	**1.** *improvement, benefit, advantage, reward*
	2.	*v.*	**injure, hurt, harm, spoil** He damaged the radio when he accidentally dropped it. *adj.* Damaged goods are often sold at reduced prices.	**2.** *repair, mend, fix, improve*
damages		*n.*	**reparations, compensation, reimbursement** The court awarded damages of five thousand dollars to the victims.	
damp		*adj.*	**soggy, moist, wet, clammy** The jogger's shirt was damp with perspiration. *v.* The clothes on the line were dampened by the rain. *n.* We shampooed the rugs yesterday and I can still feel the dampness.	*dry, parched, arid*
danger		*n.*	**peril, hazard, risk, menace** The children were warned of the danger of playing with fire.	*safety, security, preservation, protection*
dangerous		*adj.*	**risky, unsafe, perilous, threatening, hazardous** The icy roads and blowing snow made driving dangerous.	*safe, secure, sure, protected*
dare	1.	*v.*	**challenge, defy, confront** Doug dared me to ski down the steep slope. *n.* I accepted his dare.	

Word	Sense	Part	Synonyms / Example	Antonyms
	2.	*v.*	**venture, attempt, take a chance, endeavour, risk** I didn't dare skip class.	2. *fear, avoid*
daring		*adj.*	**bold, brave, adventurous, courageous, fearless** The daring firefighter dashed into the burning house to save the child.	*bashful, shy, timid, cowardly, afraid, frightened*
dark		*adj.*	**dim, gloomy, murky, shady** He groped his way through the dark room. *n.* Take a flashlight so you don't get lost in the dark. *n.* When the power went out we were left in complete darkness. *v.* Darken the room so we can show some movies.	*bright, clear, light, brilliant, vivid*
dart	1.	*n.*	**arrow, missile** Ian aimed carefully and threw the dart at the bull's-eye.	
	2.	*v.*	**rush, dash, run, race, hurry** She darted home for a quick meal before leaving again.	2. *dally, linger, loiter, dawdle*
dash	1.	*n.*	**small quantity, touch, sprinkling, pinch, trace** This soup needs just a dash of salt.	1. *large amount, a lot*
	2.	*n.*	**race, run, sprint** Which runner won the fifty-metre dash?	
	3.	*v.*	**race, rush, run, hurry, dart** Lim dashed into the classroom just before the bell rang.	3. *amble, loiter, dawdle*
	4.	*v.*	**disappoint, frustrate, spoil** The storm dashed our hopes for a picnic.	4. *encourage, increase, raise*
data		*n.*	**information, facts, evidence, results, statistics** The research data has been input into the computer.	
date	1.	*n.*	**time, day, span, period** We remember important dates in history.	
	2.	*n.*	**appointment, visit, rendezvous, engagement** Jo and I made a date to go to a movie.	
	3.	*v.*	**mark, register, record, assign a time to, chronicle** All important documents should be dated.	

Word			Synonyms	Antonyms
	4.	*v.*	**escort, go out with, associate with, take out** Naz has been dating Ray for some time now.	
dated		*adj.*	**old-fashioned, out-of-date** His dated views were rejected by the class.	*contemporary, fresh, modern*
dawdle		*v.*	**dally, linger, loiter, waste time, loaf, idle** Greg dawdled on his way home and was late for supper.	*hurry, speed, race, dart*
dawn	1.	*n.*	**origin, beginning, birth** The invention of the computer was the dawn of the "information age."	**1.** *end*
	2.	*n.*	**daybreak, sunrise** The canoes set out at dawn to get an early start.	**2.** *evening, sunset, dusk*
	3.	*v.*	**to understand, to realize** After failing her tests, it finally dawned on her that she should work harder.	
daydream		*n.*	**fancy, reverie, fantasy** In her daydream Shan imagined that she was rich and famous. *v.* Seeing the musical made Bill daydream about being a dancer.	
daze		*v.*	**stun, bewilder, mix up, shock** The boxer was dazed by the blow to his head. *n.* They found the accident victim walking around in a daze.	
dazzle		*v.*	**blind, confuse, daze, overpower, astonish, amaze** The sudden glare of the car's headlights dazzled the cyclist. *adj.* The dazzling lights blinded the driver.	
dead		*adj.*	**lifeless, deceased, extinct** The victim was dead when the ambulance arrived.	*alive, live, living, animated*
deaden		*v.*	**muffle, smother, cushion, blunt, dull, repress** The thick carpet deadened the sound of our footsteps.	*increase, amplify*

Word		Part	Synonyms / Example	Antonyms
deadly		*adj.*	**fatal, destructive, harmful, poisonous, lethal** The cobra produces a venom which makes its bite deadly.	*strengthening, health-giving, stimulating, vital*
deal	**1.**	*n.*	**arrangement, contract, agreement, compromise** Let's make a deal to study together.	
	2.	*v.*	**do business with, trade, bargain** I deal with Moe because she has the best prices.	
	3.	*v.*	**give out, hand out, distribute** Life has dealt him many hard knocks.	**3.** *collect, gather, assemble*
	4.	*v.*	**handle, treat, attend to** The guidance counsellor will deal with the student's problems.	**4.** *avoid, ignore, disregard*
dealer		*n.*	**trader, merchant, distributor** He is a used-car dealer.	*buyer, customer, purchaser*
dear	**1.**	*adj.*	**loved, cherished, close, favourite** I was upset when my dear friend moved away.	**1.** *disliked, despised, unimportant*
	2.	*adj.*	**expensive, costly** The price of that bike is too dear for my budget.	**2.** *low-priced, cheap, inexpensive, worthless*
debate	**1.**	*n.*	**discussion, contest, war of words** They held a heated debate on the pros and cons of the plan.	
	2.	*v.*	**argue, discuss, dispute, question, contend** The issue of child custody was hotly debated by the lawyers. *adj.* Who will win is debatable right now.	**2.** *agree, concede*
debris		*n.*	**remains, rubble, wreckage, ruins** The town was reduced to a pile of debris after the earthquake.	
debt		*n.*	**dues, money owing, obligation, bill, liability** I will settle my debts when I get my pay. *n.* A debtor is one who owes money.	*credit, asset*
decay		*v.*	**rot, decompose, spoil, waste away, decline** Meat decays rapidly in the heat. *n.* Tooth decay can be caused by eating too much sugar.	*bloom, grow, flourish*

Word			Synonyms	Antonyms
deceive		*v.*	**cheat, bluff, fool, trick, mislead, swindle** The salesperson deceived me into buying a faulty car. *n.* Consumers must be aware of deceit by disreputable businesses.	*be honest, advise, counsel, help*
decent	1.	*adj.*	**respectable, proper, appropriate, ethical, nice** It was very decent of you to help me. *n.* Please have the decency not to say anything rude to them.	1. *indecent, improper*
	2.	*adj.*	**fair, suitable, adequate** We were happy to pay a decent price for the car.	2. *unfair, inadequate*
decide		*v.*	**determine, rule, conclude, settle, judge** We decided on Hawaii for our holiday.	*put off, delay, postpone, hesitate*
decision		*n.*	**verdict, conclusion, ruling, decree, resolution** We made the right decision.	*procrastination, deferment*
decisive	1.	*adj.*	**determined, firm** A decisive person makes a good leader.	1. *indecisive, uncertain*
	2.	*adj.*	**convincing, crucial, definite, absolute** Lord Nelson won a decisive victory at the Battle of Waterloo.	2. *uncertain, unimportant*
deck	1.	*n.*	**floor, surface, platform** They sunbathed on the deck in the backyard.	
	2.	*v.*	**adorn, decorate, beautify** The room was decked with lovely flowers.	2. *deface, mar, spoil*
declare		*v.*	**proclaim, announce, reveal, assert** The government declared war on drug pushers. *n.* The declaration was applauded by the people.	*conceal, hide, withhold*
decline	1.	*v.*	**refuse, say no, reject** I declined her invitation because I had another engagement.	1. *accept, say yes, consent*

Word			Synonyms	Antonyms
	2.	*v.*	**lose value, cheapen, drop, fall, lower, decrease, weaken** Cigarette sales declined last year because fewer people are smoking. *n.* The decline in business meant the store had to close down.	2. *increase, improve, gain, rise*
decompose		*v.*	**decay, rot, spoil, disintegrate** The garbage decomposed in the hot weather and began to smell.	
decorate		*v.*	**beautify, adorn, array, trim** We decorated the gym with streamers for the dance. *n.* The decorations for the party are beautiful.	*deface, mar, spoil*
decrease		*v.*	**reduce, lessen, lower, deflate, shrink, weaken, diminish** The driver decreased his speed as he approached the sharp curve. *n.* In the winter there is a decrease in the demand for ice cream.	*increase, enlarge, swell, expand*
decrepit		*adj.*	**broken-down, worn-out** The decrepit car was towed to the junkyard.	*well-kept*
deed		*n.*	**act, feat, action, effort, accomplishment** Lou is remembered for his many charitable deeds.	
deep	1.	*adj.*	**far down** Brian fell into a deep pit in the ground. *adv.* The workers dug deep in the ground to make a well.	1. *shallow*
	2.	*adj.*	**intense, profound** Jay was in deep despair over the loss of his dog.	2. *light*
deface		*v.*	**injure, mar, disfigure, deform, scar, mark** Vandals defaced the wall by painting graffiti on it.	*beautify, adorn, decorate*
defeat	1.	*n.*	**failure, loss, setback** Our team suffered a crushing defeat in the tournament.	1. *success, victory, triumph, conquest*
	2.	*v.*	**beat, trounce, vanquish, subdue, conquer, overcome** Napoleon was defeated at the Battle of Waterloo.	2. *surrender, yield, submit*

Word			Synonyms	Antonyms
defect	1.	*n.*	**weak point, flaw, fault, imperfection** A defect in the brakes caused the accident. *adj.* Defective brakes can cause an accident.	1. *improvement, advantage*
	2.	*v.*	**run away, forsake, abandon, leave** He defected from his homeland because of the harsh government.	2. *stay*
defend		*v.*	**protect, guard, support, shield, secure** The bear defended her cub against the hunter. *n.* The activist spoke in defence of animal rights. *adj.* She is defensive of her right to take a stand.	*desert, abandon, leave, resign*
defer	1.	*v.*	**put off, delay, postpone, suspend** His examination was deferred because of his illness.	1. *expedite, hasten, quicken, advance*
	2.	*v.*	**yield, surrender, give in** He deferred to his parents' wishes in his choice of a school.	2. *defy*
defiance		*n.*	**opposition, disobedience, challenge, rebellion** Defiance of orders will bring punishment. *adj.* The defiant student was suspended for breaking school rules.	*support, obedience*
deficient		*adj.*	**short, inadequate, defective, insufficient** Water rationing was imposed because of deficient rainfall. *n.* A deficiency of vitamins in your diet can make you ill.	*excessive, sufficient, ample, satisfactory*
define		*v.*	**describe, state, explain** She defined her goals in a speech. *n.* He looked up the definition of the word in the dictionary.	*confuse*
definite		*adj.*	**sure, decided, distinct, clear** They set a definite date for the wedding.	*indefinite, indistinct, undecided, uncertain*
deflate		*v.*	**exhaust, reduce, flatten** Ian's confidence was deflated when he failed the test.	*inflate, expand*

Word			Synonyms	Antonyms
deform		*v.*	**twist, warp, injure, mutilate, distort, disfigure** His face was deformed with hatred at the sight of his enemy.	*enhance, make better*
deformed		*adj.*	**misshapen, disfigured** The puppy was born with a deformed leg. *n.* The deformity of his leg made it difficult for him to walk.	*perfect, whole*
defraud		*v.*	**cheat, swindle, deceive, rob** They were arrested for defrauding their employer.	*reward, assist, help*
defy		*v.*	**mock, oppose, resist, challenge** He was fined for defying the law.	*obey, conform to, agree*
degree		*n.*	**measure, amount, extent, rate, grade, mark** She has a large degree of support on this issue.	
dehydrate		*v.*	**dry up, remove water from, dry, parch** Raisins are made by dehydrating grapes.	*moisten, wet*
dejected		*adj.*	**unhappy, downcast, discouraged, low-spirited** She was dejected after being turned down for the job.	*happy, cheerful, merry*
delay	1.	*n.*	**setback, hesitation, reprieve, deferment** Rain caused a delay in the start of the ball game.	1. *progress, speed, advance*
	2.	*v.*	**hinder, retard, postpone, defer, detain** A traffic jam delayed the arrival of the bus.	2. *advance, hurry, hasten*
delegate	1.	*n.*	**ambassador, representative, envoy, commissioner** Every country sent a delegate to the conference.	
	2.	*v.*	**authorize, entrust, appoint, assign, nominate** The dance committee delegated Suli to decorate the gym. *n.* The committee agreed on the delegation of duties to all members.	

Word			Synonyms	Antonyms
delete		*v.*	**erase, remove, take out, cancel, omit** Two chapters were deleted to shorten the book. *n.* The author protested against the deletion of the two chapters.	*insert, add*
deliberate	1.	*v.*	**consider, examine, think over, ponder, contemplate** We deliberated on a new plan to raise funds. *n.* After much deliberation we decided to adopt the new policy.	1. *pass over, reject, discard*
	2.	*adj.*	**intentional, conscious, calculated, careful** The basketball player took deliberate aim at the basket and scored. *adv.* She deliberately said something that would hurt him.	2. *hasty, unintentional, careless*
delicate		*adj.*	**fragile, frail, fine, tender, dainty** Kim needs special care because of her delicate health.	*rough, coarse*
delicious		*adj.*	**enjoyable, sweet, tasteful, pleasing** Can I get the recipe for those delicious cookies?	*unpalatable, unsavoury, distasteful*
delight	1.	*n.*	**joy, pleasure, happiness** It was a delight to see all my old friends again.	1. *sorrow, pain, distress*
	2.	*v.*	**please, charm, make happy, enchant, entertain** She delighted us with her stories.	2. *disappoint, sadden, displease*
deliver	1.	*v.*	**hand over, transfer, bring, dispense, give out** The messenger delivered the parcel. *n.* She put the delivery in the mailbox.	1. *hold, keep, retain*
	2.	*v.*	**rescue, save, liberate, free, release** The police delivered the child from his kidnappers.	2. *hold, keep, retain*
delude		*v.*	**trick, deceive, fool, mislead, dupe** Do not be deluded by false advertising.	*counsel, aid, help*
deluxe		*adj.*	**grand, fine, elegant, choice, super** We stayed in a deluxe hotel on our holiday.	*ordinary, regular*

Word			Synonyms and example	Antonyms
demand	1.	*n.*	**need, requirement, want** There is a great demand for trained nurses.	
	2.	*v.*	**claim, ask, urge, require** The striking workers demanded better pay.	**2.** *give, offer, present*
demolish		*v.*	**wreck, destroy, ruin, level, smash, raze** The house was demolished as it was unsafe. *n.* The demolition of the building was done with explosives.	*construct, build, make, restore*
demonstrate		*v.*	**prove, show, illustrate, explain, exhibit, display** Pablo will demonstrate how his invention works. *n.* The gymnast gave a demonstration on the bar.	*hide, conceal, cover*
denote		*v.*	**mark, indicate, mean** That arrow sign denotes right turns only.	
dense		*adj.*	**compact, solid, close, thick** He cleared a path through the dense forest.	*thin, scanty, sparse*
dent		*n.*	**nick, indentation, hollow** She put a dent in the can when she dropped it. *v.* She dented the car fender in an accident.	
deny		*v.*	**contradict, dispute, reject** He denied that he had taken my book. *n.* The evidence made his denial of guilt hard to believe.	*reveal, admit, agree, concede*
depart		*v.*	**go away, leave, withdraw, start, quit, exit** The bus departs from the station at noon. *n.* The plane's departure was delayed by fog.	*remain, stay, wait, arrive*
depend		*v.*	**trust, rely on, count on** You can always depend on Sam to do a good job.	*distrust*
dependable		*adj.*	**reliable, trustworthy, steady, unfailing, loyal** Elle is a dependable babysitter.	*undependable, unreliable*

Word	Sense	Part of speech	Synonyms and example	Antonyms
depict		*v.*	**describe, portray, represent, draw** The author depicted the pioneers as strong people.	
deplete		*v.*	**use up, reduce, decrease, drain, lessen** The costly gift greatly depleted our funds.	*increase, strengthen, fill*
deplore		*v.*	**mourn, grieve, regret, lament** The activists deplored the use of animals for scientific experiments. *adj.* They denounced it as a deplorable act.	*rejoice, cheer, delight in, revel*
deport		*v.*	**banish, exile, cast out** He was deported from the country for his crimes.	*import, bring in*
deposit	1.	*n.*	**partial payment, instalment** In order to rent a movie you must leave a deposit.	**1.** *withdrawal*
	2.	*v.*	**place, put in, drop** Deposit waste paper in the basket.	**2.** *withdraw, take out, remove*
deprive		*v.*	**take from, strip, rob, divest** The fire deprived the family of all its possessions.	*give, add, assist*
depth	1.	*n.*	**deepness, measure, extent** The depth of the lake is ten metres.	
	2.	*n.*	**abyss, bottom, base** The diver explored the ocean depths for sunken treasure.	
derelict		*adj.*	**abandoned, broken, deserted, neglected** The roof of the derelict house sagged in the middle.	*cared for*
derive		*v.*	**obtain, gain, receive, acquire** The students derived much satisfaction from their success.	*forfeit, lose, divest*
descend		*v.*	**go down, drop, slip, slide, settle, sink** The elevator descended swiftly from the top to the first floor.	*ascend, go up, climb*
descent	1.	*n.*	**sinking, coming down, drop, decline** Our ears popped as the plane made its descent.	**1.** *rise, growth*

Word	No.	Part	Synonyms / Example	Antonyms
	2.	*n.*	**slope, fall, slant** The descent of the hill is quite steep here.	2. *ascent, climb, rise*
describe		*v.*	**talk about, explain, outline, express, illustrate** The actor was described as being tall, dark, and handsome. *n.* He did not fit the description.	
desert		*n.*	**wastelands, deserted area, barren plains** Few types of vegetation can grow in a desert.	
desert		*v.*	**abandon, forsake, leave, quit** He deserted his family and moved to the city.	*remain, stay, continue*
deserve		*v.*	**have the right to, be worthy of, merit, earn** Lee deserved the award for her brilliant work.	*be unworthy of*
design	1.	*n.*	**pattern, decoration** The wallpaper design is too busy for this small room.	
	2.	*n.*	**blueprint, outline, sketch, plan** Ann created a design for a new car.	
	3.	*v.*	**think up, create, plan** Alma designed a new computer program.	
desirable		*adj.*	**good, acceptable, advisable, valuable, worthy** We bought the house because it is in a desirable neighbourhood.	*undesirable, bad, harmful*
desire	1.	*n.*	**longing, wish, craving, yearning** Kit had a strong desire to succeed.	1. *hatred, dislike, disgust, aversion*
	2.	*v.*	**want, require, crave, long for** The weary traveller desired food and rest.	
desolate		*adj.*	**lonely, forlorn, miserable, bleak, wretched, barren, abandoned** Antarctica is a desolate continent.	*pleasant, lovely, enjoyable, inhabited*
despair	1.	*n.*	**hopelessness, gloom, discouragement, depression** The workers were in despair when the plant closed down.	1. *hope, courage*
	2.	*v.*	**lose hope, give up** After a long search, he despaired of ever finding his lost dog.	2. *hope, expect, anticipate*

Word		Part of speech	Synonyms and example	Antonyms
desperate	1.	*adj.*	**reckless, careless, wild, rash** The desperate man robbed the bank in broad daylight.	**1.** *calm, careful, collected*
	2.	*adj.*	**drastic, daring, bold** A desperate attempt was made to save the trapped miners.	**2.** *confident*
	3.	*adj.*	**despairing, hopeless, despondent, in great need of** I am desperate for a job because I need money. *n.* Out of desperation, the hungry children begged for food on the street corner.	**3.** *contented, satisfied*
despicable		*adj.*	**mean, base, disgraceful** Child abuse is a despicable act.	*kind, worthy*
despise		*v.*	**scorn, hate, abhor, detest, loathe** The athletes were despised for their use of illegal drugs.	*love, cherish, admire, exalt, respect, esteem*
destiny		*n.*	**fate, fortune, lot** The fortune teller said it was my destiny to be famous.	
destitute		*adj.*	**poor, needy, impoverished** They were left destitute after the business failed.	*rich, affluent, well-to-do, wealthy*
destroy		*v.*	**ruin, wreck, smash, demolish, do away with** The art collection was destroyed by fire.	*create, construct, build, add, renew, repair, save, preserve*
destruction		*n.*	**ruin, waste, devastation, demolition** The flood caused total destruction of the town.	*restoration, production, preservation*
detach		*v.*	**divide, separate, unfasten, disconnect, sever** At the campsite Dad detached the trailer from the car.	*unite, join, connect, attach, fasten*
detail		*n.*	**feature, item, fact, aspect, portion** She took care of every little detail of the party.	*whole, total, sum*
detain		*v.*	**delay, hold, retard, hinder, keep** The suspects were detained by the police for questioning.	*free, let go, deliver*

Word			Synonyms and examples	Antonyms
detect		*v.*	**notice, see, discover, observe, determine** I detected from his red eyes that he had been crying. *n.* Careful research led to the detection of the problem. *adj.* Although she tried to hide it, her fear was detectable.	*miss, omit, pass by*
detective		*n.*	**scout, investigator, sleuth, private eye** The detective studied the clues to solve the mystery.	
detention		*n.*	**restraint, confinement** John was given a detention for misbehaving in class.	*freedom, release*
deter		*v.*	**dissuade, caution, discourage, hinder** The unfavourable reviews of the movie deterred me from seeing it.	*encourage, persuade, urge, promote*
deteriorate		*v.*	**decay, become worse, decline, degenerate, decrease** His health deteriorated rapidly. *n.* Acid rain has led to the deterioration of our lakes.	*improve, get better*
determination		*n.*	**persistence, resolution, conviction, stubbornness, obstinacy** It takes a great deal of determination to overcome a failure. *adj.* The determined salesperson wouldn't take no for an answer.	*indecision, unsteadiness*
determine	1.	*v.*	**settle, decide, fix upon, resolve** The examination results will determine my future.	1. *confuse, muddle, unsettle*
	2.	*v.*	**find out, learn, discover** Have the police determined the cause of the accident?	2. *conceal, suppress, ignore*
detest		*v.*	**hate, loathe, despise, abhor** She detests him because he is a bully.	*like, prefer, love*
develop	1.	*v.*	**expand, enlarge, extend, refine, build up** Develop your outline into a story. *n.* Exercise is essential for the development of muscles.	1. *reduce, condense, shorten, abbreviate*
	2.	*v.*	**make visible, disclose, unfold** Images on film are developed into photographs by a chemical process.	2. *conceal, hide*

	3.	*v.*	**grow up, mature, evolve, advance** The tadpole developed into a frog.	3. *deteriorate*
device	1.	*n.*	**apparatus, invention, contraption, gadget, mechanism** The garlic press is a handy little device.	
	2.	*n.*	**scheme, trick, design, ruse, plan** What device did the swindler use to get you to give him the money?	
devise		*v.*	**invent, design, construct, plan, think up** The young inventors devised a new video game.	
devote		*v.*	**dedicate, apply, set apart, give** Yun devotes many hours to her violin.	*waste, squander, abuse*
devotion		*n.*	**attachment, commitment, dedication, loyalty** The teacher's devotion to duty earned her an award.	*indifference, neglect, carelessness*
devour		*v.*	**swallow, eat, gobble, consume, take in** He devoured the hamburger in two bites.	
dexterity		*n.*	**proficiency, skill, ability** Lin demonstrated her dexterity on the trampoline. *adj.* The dexterous typist could do 70 words a minute.	*awkwardness, inaptitude*
diagnose		*v.*	**identify, conclude, analyse** The doctor diagnosed June's symptoms as the mumps. *n.* Her diagnosis proved correct.	
diagram		*n.*	**plan, illustration, sketch, layout** The diagram showed how to set up the equipment.	
dialogue		*n.*	**talk, conference, exchange, conversation** The dialogue between the play's characters revealed their personalities.	
dictate	1.	*v.*	**order, command, direct, instruct** The organizer dictated where everything should be sent.	1. *beg, ask, plead*

	2.	*v.*	**tell, speak, deliver** The teacher dictated a paragraph in French for the students to record. *n.* The students wrote the teacher's dictation in their notebooks.	
dictator		*n.*	**tyrant, ruler, despot, oppressor, autocrat, leader** The ruthless dictator was overthrown in a coup.	
die	1.	*v.*	**expire, perish, pass away, succumb** Many people die from heart attacks.	**1.** *live, exist, survive*
	2.	*v.*	**decline, wither, fade, weaken** The applause died as the musician began the first piece.	**2.** *flourish, grow, increase, continue*
differ	1.	*v.*	**clash, disagree, object, dispute** They differed on the issue of capital punishment.	**1.** *agree, concede*
	2.	*v.*	**vary, contrast, diverge** The identical twins look alike, but differ in their personalities. *n.* There is not much difference between the copy and the original.	**2.** *resemble, match*
different		*adj.*	**unlike, unusual, distinct, diverse, separate** I changed into different clothes when I got home.	*similar, alike, same*
difficult		*adj.*	**hard, tough, complicated, bothersome, troublesome, awkward** It was difficult to trudge through the high snowdrifts.	*easy, simple, manageable*
difficulty	1.	*n.*	**hardship, burden, barrier, obstacle, hindrance, complication** Despite her illness and other difficulties, she finished the project.	**1.** *aid, assistance, help*
	2.	*n.*	**mess, muddle, trouble, crisis** The gambler had many losses and now is in financial difficulty.	**2.** *ease, comfort*
digest	1.	*v.*	**summarize, condense** Digest your project into a one-page explanation. *n.* The author made a digest of his story for a magazine.	**1.** *expand, enlarge*
	2.	*v.*	**dissolve, assimilate, convert, absorb, consume** Chewing your food makes it easier to digest.	

Word		Part of speech	Synonyms and example	Antonyms
dignity		*n.*	**grandeur, nobility, stateliness, self-respect, importance, honour** Everyone admires the Queen's dignity. *adj.* His dignified behaviour in the debate won him respect.	
dilapidated		*adj.*	**neglected, ruined, decrepit, broken-down** The dilapidated building was pulled down because it was an eyesore.	*in good repair, cared for, attended, preserved*
dilate		*v.*	**enlarge, swell, expand, widen** The pupil dilates in the dark to let more light into the eye.	*shrink, narrow, contract*
dilemma		*n.*	**predicament, scrape, fix, quandary** She was in a dilemma as to whom to take to the ball game.	*solution*
diligent		*adj.*	**hard-working, industrious, attentive, careful** The diligent student was at the top of her class. *adv.* She worked diligently on her project and won an award.	*lazy, careless, slow*
dilute		*v.*	**weaken, thin out, reduce** We diluted the soup by adding water.	*thicken, condense*
dim		*adj.*	**obscure, faint, indistinct, hazy, dull** We couldn't read in the dim light.	*bright, clear, distinct, brilliant*
diminish		*v.*	**decrease, lessen, reduce, shrink, dwindle** We waited until the snowfall diminished before setting off.	*increase, expand*
din		*n.*	**clamour, roar, noise, racket, pandemonium** Our neighbours complained about the din of our party.	*silence, quiet, calm, stillness*
dingy		*adj.*	**dirty, grimy, faded, shabby** We cleaned and painted the dingy apartment before moving in.	*clean, spotless, bright*
dip	1.	*v.*	**slope, decline, bend, tilt, plunge, drop** The plane dipped so suddenly that we were afraid something was wrong.	**1.** *ascend, increase, rise*

	2.	*v.*	**submerge, immerse, dunk, rinse** Tom dipped his donut in his coffee. *n.* She took a dip in the lake to cool off.	2. *lift, raise*
direct	1.	*v.*	**manage, control, conduct, lead, supervise** Hannah directed the class play. *n.* She did a good job as the director.	1. *serve, follow*
	2.	*v.*	**aim, conduct, lead, guide, indicate, point the way** The tour guide directed us to a good restaurant.	2. *follow*
	3.	*adj.*	**straight, even, true, shortest, uninterrupted** Take the direct route to school.	3. *indirect, crooked, roundabout, complicated*
	4.	*adj.*	**candid, frank, blunt, straightforward** She is a sincere person and always gives a direct answer.	4. *deceptive, misleading, indirect*
direction	1.	*n.*	**course, aim, route, path, way** If you go in that direction you will be heading north.	
	2.	*n.*	**recipe, instruction, order, plan** Follow the directions on the box to put the model together.	
directly		*adv.*	**immediately, at once, instantly** Come directly home after the movie.	*later*
dirt	1.	*n.*	**filth, grime** The floor was covered with dirt and needed a scrubbing.	
	2.	*n.*	**earth, loam, soil** The gardener spread a load of dirt over the flower beds.	
dirty		*adj.*	**soiled, filthy, polluted, grubby, unclean, messy** We loaded the dishwasher with the dirty dishes.	*clean, decent, unspoiled, neat, sanitary*
disability		*n.*	**weakness, inability, defect, infirmity, handicap** Her disability means she must walk with a cane.	*fitness, ability, power, strength*
disable		*v.*	**cripple, maim, impair** He was disabled in the war. *adj.* The disabled man travelled across the country in a wheelchair.	*heal, mend*

Word	No.	Part	Synonyms / Example	Antonyms
disagree		*v.*	**differ, argue, dispute, vary** I disagree with your opinion because it is based on incorrect information. *n.* They settled their disagreement after long negotiations.	*agree, concur, accept*
disagreeable		*adj.*	**nasty, unpleasant, bad-tempered, grouchy, bothersome** The disagreeable boy had no friends.	*pleasant, agreeable*
disappear		*v.*	**leave, depart, fade, pass out of sight, vanish** The moon disappeared behind dark clouds. *n.* We were puzzled by Sal's sudden disappearance.	*appear, arrive, come*
disapprove		*v.*	**condemn, object to, dislike** We disapprove of smoking in our house. *n.* He expressed his disapproval by frowning.	*like, approve*
disaster		*n.*	**calamity, misfortune, mishap, catastrophe, tragedy** The earthquake was a terrible disaster. *adj.* The school play was a disastrous failure.	*good fortune, blessing, benefit, advantage*
discard		*v.*	**throw away, dump, reject** The librarian has discarded all the torn books.	*keep, preserve, save*
discern		*v.*	**see, observe, notice, detect, perceive** I could discern from her frown that she was unhappy.	*disregard, overlook*
discharge	1.	*v.*	**release, unload, project, emit** The factory discharged its chemical waste into the lake. *n.* The discharge of the cannon made a loud boom.	1. *load*
	2.	*v.*	**release, set free, let go, dismiss** He was discharged from his job for tardiness. *n.* The discharge of the hostages was a welcome relief.	2. *keep, hold*
discipline	1.	*n.*	**self-control, order, restraint, regulation** Please show some discipline and settle down to work.	1. *chaos, disorder, confusion*

Word		Part	Synonyms / Example	Antonyms
	2.	*v.*	**chastise, punish, correct** The child was disciplined for being rude.	2. *reward*
disclose		*v.*	**tell, make known, reveal** He disclosed his secret to me, but didn't tell anyone else. *n.* His disclosure of the secret upset me.	*hide, conceal*
discount		*n.*	**reduction, saving, markdown, deduction** Will you give me a discount on this toy since it's damaged? *v.* The store discounted all clothing for the sale.	*increase, markup*
discover		*v.*	**find, locate, find out, detect, invent, uncover** In our explorations we discovered a wonderful picnic spot. *n.* We were given a reward for our discovery of the missing money.	*miss, overlook*
discreet		*adj.*	**careful, polite, cautious, reserved, sensible, guarded** The undercover detective was very discreet in his inquiries. *n.* She is easily offended so use discretion when you deal with her.	*foolish, reckless, indiscreet, rash, impetuous*
discrepancy		*n.*	**difference, disagreement, inconsistency** The discrepancies between his story and everyone else's indicated that he was lying.	*accord, agreement*
discriminate		*v.*	**judge, show prejudice, distinguish, separate** Employers should not discriminate between male and female employees. *n.* Discrimination between the sexes by employers is unlawful.	
discuss		*v.*	**talk over, debate, consider** She discussed her college plans with her parents. *n.* They had an in-depth discussion on her choice of college.	
disdain	1.	*n.*	**dislike, scorn, contempt** Our offer was rejected with disdain.	1. *regard, respect, admiration, esteem*
	2.	*v.*	**snub, spurn, despise, scorn** The salesperson disdained the price we offered for the car.	2. *like, admire*

Word			Synonyms and examples	Antonyms
disease		*n.*	**infection, illness, malady, ailment** Chicken pox is a common childhood disease.	*health, vigour*
disgrace	**1.**	*n.*	**shame, disfavour, reproach, dishonour** He was in disgrace after the scandal became public.	**1.** *favour, honour, respect*
	2.	*v.*	**degrade, defame, shame** They disgraced themselves with their terrible behaviour. *adj.* Their rude behaviour was disgraceful.	**2.** *glorify, honour*
disguise	**1.**	*n.*	**mask, veil, costume, camouflage** No one could guess the identity of the person behind the disguise.	
	2.	*v.*	**conceal, camouflage, hide, mask** The celebrity disguised herself with a wig and sunglasses.	**2.** *reveal, uncover*
disgust	**1.**	*n.*	**dislike, distaste, aversion, loathing** Their cruel actions filled me with disgust.	**1.** *approval, liking, admiration*
	2.	*v.*	**repel, sicken, offend, revolt** It disgusts me when people chew with their mouth open. *adj.* Cockroaches are disgusting insects to have in your home.	**2.** *attract, appeal*
dishonest		*adj.*	**crooked, deceitful, false, sneaky** The dishonest students cheated in the examinations. *n.* They were punished for their dishonesty.	*honest, true, lawful, honourable*
dismal		*adj.*	**dreary, dingy, gloomy, sombre** Everything seems dismal on a grey day.	*bright, gay, joyful, happy, cheerful*
dismay	**1.**	*n.*	**alarm, concern, anxiety, distress, fright, dread** The traveller showed dismay at the loss of his wallet.	**1.** *confidence, relief, joy, happiness*
	2.	*v.*	**frighten, scare, alarm, distress, dishearten** We were dismayed when we realized that we were lost.	**2.** *relieve, cheer, encourage*
dismiss	**1.**	*v.*	**let out, discharge, send off** The students were dismissed when the class was finished. *n.* They went home after their dismissal from class.	**1.** *retain, keep, hold*

	2.	*v.*	**reject, discard, spurn** She dismissed the idea because it was impractical.	2. *retain, consider*
disorder	1.	*n.*	**illness, sickness, malady, indisposition** Kevin missed school because of a stomach disorder.	1. *health*
	2.	*n.*	**disturbance, uprising, rumpus, commotion, riot** The country was plunged into disorder when the president died. *adj.* The police arrested the mob for disorderly conduct.	2. *order, peace*
	3.	*n.*	**clutter, muddle, mess, confusion** They left their room in a dreadful disorder.	3. *order, arrangement*
dispatch	1.	*n.*	**quickness, speed, efficiency, promptness, haste** Kay does all her work with great dispatch.	1. *slowness, inefficiency*
	2	*v.*	**send, transmit, forward** An ambulance was dispatched to the scene of the accident.	2. *receive, get, obtain*
dispel		*v.*	**remove, scatter, dismiss, drive away** The smooth flight dispelled our fear of flying.	
dispense		*v.*	**distribute, give out, assign** Drugs are dispensed by a pharmacist in a drugstore.	*keep, retain*
disperse		*v.*	**scatter, break up, disband** The police dispersed the rowdy crowd of spectators after the game.	*gather, collect, assemble*
displace		*v.*	**move, transfer, disarrange, shift, dislocate** Many people were displaced by the war and sent to refugee camps.	*arrange, place, put in order*
display	1.	*n.*	**exhibition, presentation, show, demonstration** The art display in the hall is from our class.	
	2.	*v.*	**exhibit, arrange, show, demonstrate, present** We displayed our arts and crafts at the fair.	2. *hide, conceal, cover*

Word			Synonyms and examples	Antonyms
dispose		*v.*	**throw away, get rid of, dump** The city disposes of our garbage at the dump. *n.* Our school has special bins for the disposal of recyclable materials. *adj.* Disposable diapers are a great convenience but they are bad for the environment.	*retain, keep*
dispute	1.	*n.*	**disagreement, argument, quarrel, debate** The children had a dispute over whose turn it was.	1. *agreement, harmony*
	2.	*v.*	**contradict, debate, argue, quarrel** She disputed his claim that the eldest child should go first.	2. *agree, harmonize, concur*
disrupt		*v.*	**interrupt, upset, disturb** The principal's speech was disrupted by a noisy student. *n.* The fire alarm caused a major disruption in the play.	
dissect		*v.*	**cut, slice, section, analyse** The biology students dissected a frog so that they could study it.	
dissolve		*v.*	**melt, thaw, disintegrate** The instructions said to dissolve the drink crystals in water.	*solidify, harden*
distance	1.	*n.*	**length, space, interval, span** What is the distance from Montreal to Vancouver?	
	2.	*n.*	**background, horizon** I could see them in the distance through my binoculars.	2. *nearness*
distant	1.	*adj.*	**faraway** Our new neighbours moved here from a distant country.	1. *neighbouring, close, nearby, near*
	2.	*adj.*	**remote, far-off** Sue likes to speculate on what life will be like in the distant future.	2. *near, immediate*
distinct		*adj.*	**clear, definite, plain, special** The distinct sound of crying was heard outside the window. *adv.* We distinctly heard his voice above the din.	*mixed, unclear, complicated*
distinguish	1.	*v.*	**differentiate, separate, specify, identify** I can't distinguish between the copy and the original.	

	2.	*v.*	**detect, discover, see** We could barely distinguish the cars through the thick fog.	
	3.	*v.*	**give honour, acknowledge, become famous** She has distinguished herself as the fastest runner in the school.	
distinguished		*adj.*	**famous, celebrated, notable, prominent** Everyone wanted the distinguished writer's autograph.	*unknown, obscure*
distort		*v.*	**twist, misrepresent, slant** The reporter distorted the news story to make it sensational. *n.* The distortion of news is unethical.	
distract		*v.*	**divert, confuse, draw away** The class was distracted by a loud noise. *n.* The phone call was a welcome distraction from my chores.	*focus, concentrate*
distress		*n.*	**discomfort, pain, concern, unhappiness, worry, trouble** Kit's illness caused us great distress. *v.* We were all distressed by the bad news.	*pleasure, joy, mirth, satisfaction, happiness*
distribute		*v.*	**give out, deal, hand out, share, dispense** The leader distributed the supplies to the team. *n.* We stood in line for the distribution of the books.	*hoard, keep, collect*
disturb		*v.*	**annoy, bother, irritate, unsettle, interrupt, upset** The noise of the sirens disturbed the peace of the night. *n.* They were thrown out of the theatre for causing a disturbance.	*soothe, pacify, calm, appease, compose*
dive		*v.*	**plunge, dart, rush into, leap into** The lifeguard dived into the pool to save the drowning child. *n.* The plane took a nose dive into the bushes.	
diverse		*adj.*	**different, unlike, varied** Our school has students from diverse cultural backgrounds.	*same, identical*

Word			Synonyms	Antonyms
diversion	**1.**	*n.*	**hobby, pastime, amusement, enjoyment** Dad's favourite diversion is golf.	
	2.	*n.*	**change, deflection, detour** The dam caused a diversion in the flow of the river.	
divert		*v.*	**sidetrack, turn aside, change** Traffic was diverted to avoid the flooded areas.	
divide		*v.*	**part, separate, share, distribute** The host divided the cake among all the guests. *n.* A fence marked the division of the two yards. *adj.* A number is even if it is divisible by two.	*join, unite, attach, connect*
divulge		*v.*	**tell, reveal, disclose** Don't divulge my secret to anyone.	*hide, keep secret, conceal*
dizzy		*adj.*	**giddy, silly, confused, shaky** Great heights often make people feel dizzy.	*clear-headed, steady, calm*
do		*v.*	**perform, act, accomplish, achieve, make, bring about** How will you do your project?	
docile		*adj.*	**orderly, quiet, meek, humble, obedient** The docile dog quietly trotted behind its owner.	*determined, stubborn, disobedient*
dock	**1.**	*n.*	**wharf, pier, landing, quay** Several boats were tied to the dock.	
	2.	*v.*	**join, hook up, link** The shuttle docked at the space station.	
dodge		*v.*	**lurch, duck, sidestep, avoid, evade** He dodged out of the bike's path just in time.	*meet, approach, face*
dole	**1.**	*n.*	**welfare, handout, charity** The jobless person lived on the dole.	
	2.	*v.*	**give, distribute, hand out, deal** The parents doled out the children's allowances.	**2.** *keep, hoard, collect*

Word		Part	Synonyms and example	Antonyms
doleful		*adj.*	**sad, unhappy, dismal, gloomy, dejected** The child looked doleful when she broke her toy.	*cheerful, joyous, merry, happy*
domain		*n.*	**territory, land, estate, kingdom, area** The ruler's domain stretched from sea to sea.	
domestic		*adj.*	**tame, settled** Most dogs are domestic animals, but there are still some wild ones.	*wild, untamed*
dominant		*adj.*	**chief, ruling, controlling** Peter's dominant characteristic is his good nature.	*obscure*
dominate		*v.*	**control, rule, direct, command** He dominated the meeting by not letting anyone else speak.	
dominion	1.	*n.*	**power, sway, rule, command, control** The new king took dominion over all the land.	
	2.	*n.*	**land, region, territory, realm, domain** The ruler issued new laws over all of her dominion.	
donate		*v.*	**give, contribute, grant** Mr. Shih donates blood regularly to the Red Cross. *n.* The charity was asking for donations of food and clothes.	*keep, retain*
dormant		*adj.*	**sleeping, hibernating, asleep, inactive** Many animals are dormant during the winter season.	*awake, moving, active*
dot		*n.*	**speck, spot, fleck, mark, point** Mark a dot to show where to put the nail. *v.* She was very careful to dot all of her i's.	
double	1.	*n.*	**twin, mate, duplicate** Make doubles of the photographs so that we'll have an extra set.	**1.** *opposite*
	2.	*v.*	**multiply, make twice as much** He doubled his sales and made twice as much money.	

Word	No.	Part	Synonyms / Example	Antonyms
	3.	*adj.*	**twofold, dual** She does the work of two people but she is not paid double wages. *adv.* Our employer pays us double to work on holidays.	3. *single*
doubt	1.	*n.*	**suspicion, disbelief, distrust** Her suspicious behaviour casts doubts on her intentions.	1. *belief, certainty, trust, faith*
	2.	*v.*	**suspect, be uncertain, distrust, question** His stories are so wild that I doubt if they are true.	2. *believe, trust, be convinced*
doubtful		*adj.*	**indefinite, uncertain, undecided, hesitant** We are doubtful about his chance for success.	*sure, certain, definite, positive*
dowdy		*adj.*	**shabby, sloppy, unattractive, frumpy** He finally threw his dowdy, old hat in the garbage.	*neat, chic, smart, tidy*
downcast		*adj.*	**sad, discouraged, depressed, unhappy** The players were downcast when they lost the game.	*happy, glad, encouraged*
downpour		*n.*	**rainstorm, shower, cloudburst, deluge** We were caught without umbrellas in a downpour.	
drab		*adj.*	**dull, monotonous, faded, unchanging, unattractive** The drab room was brightened with new wallpaper.	*exciting, bright, colourful*
draft	1.	*n.*	**sketch, outline, plan, blueprint** He is now revising the first draft of his essay. *v.* She drafted a design from which to make her model.	
	2.	*n.*	**recruitment, selection, conscription** The football coach is conducting a draft for new players. *v.* Many people were drafted into the army during the war.	
	3.	*n.*	**breeze, current of air, wind** There is a cool draft coming in that window. *adj.* A drafty room is uncomfortable.	

Word	No.	Part	Synonyms / Example	Antonyms
	4.	*n.*	**postal order, money order, cashier's cheque** Suli's grandmother sent her a draft for fifty dollars for her birthday.	
drag	1.	*v.*	**tug, tow, pull, draw, lug** Toni dragged her sled up the hill.	1. *push, shove*
	2.	*v.*	**dawdle, lag, go slowly** Time seemed to drag by while we waited for the bell to ring.	2. *progress, rush*
drain	1.	*n.*	**pipe, trench, outlet, duct** Pour the dirty water down the drain in the sink.	
	2.	*v.*	**filter, flow** Three rivers drain into this valley.	
	3.	*v.*	**empty, draw out, exhaust** All her energy was drained by her illness.	3. *fill*
drama	1.	*n.*	**the stage, acting, theatre** Craig studied drama for several years to become an actor.	
	2.	*n.*	**play, piece, work, show, production** My class is putting on a historical drama for the parents.	
dramatic		*adj.*	**exciting, striking** We watched the dramatic events of the riots on television.	*dull, ordinary, bland*
drastic		*adj.*	**extreme, dangerous, radical, desperate** Putting a lock on the refrigerator is a drastic way to diet.	*moderate, cautious*
draw	1.	*v.*	**pull, haul, drag, attract, bring** The tow truck drew the car to the garage.	1. *push, shove, repel*
	2.	*v.*	**sketch, design, depict** Tjin drew a picture of the scene to show to her friends. *n.* She framed her drawing and displayed it on the wall.	
drawn		*adj.*	**haggard, pinched, wrinkled, strained** The drawn look on her face told us something was wrong.	*smooth, unwrinkled, relaxed*
dread	1.	*n.*	**fear, anxiety, horror, terror, fright, alarm** The strange sounds in the night filled me with dread.	1. *hope, courage, calm, confidence*

	2.	*v.*	**be afraid of, fear** She dreaded writing the test because she hadn't studied for it.	**2.** *look forward to*
dreadful		*adj.*	**awful, serious, terrible** We heard the dreadful news about the accident.	*harmless, pleasing, lovely*
dream	1.	*n.*	**vision, nightmare, trance, fantasy** Last night I dreamt that I won the lottery.	**1.** *reality*
	2.	*v.*	**imagine, fancy, visualize, hallucinate, fantasize** I dream of being a famous writer someday.	
dreary		*adj.*	**dismal, dingy, gloomy, cheerless** It's dreary to work in an office without windows.	*bright, joyful, cheerful*
drench		*v.*	**douse, soak, saturate, wet** Without a raincoat, you'll be drenched in that downpour.	*dry, parch*
dress	1.	*n.*	**clothing, clothes, garments, attire, costume, covering** Casual dress will be fine for the barbecue.	
	2.	*v.*	**clothe, robe, attire, outfit** I have to shower and then dress for the party.	**2.** *strip, disrobe*
drift	1.	*n.*	**heap, mass, pile, bank** The children jumped into the huge drifts of snow.	
	2.	*n.*	**trend, flow, direction, course** I knew what he was leading up to from the drift of the conversation.	
	3.	*v.*	**sail, float, be carried along** The clouds drifted slowly across the blue sky.	**3.** *be motionless*
drill	1.	*v.*	**bore, punch, puncture, pierce** She drilled a hole in the wall to run a wire through. *n.* I used an electric drill to bore the holes.	
	2.	*v.*	**exercise, train, practise, rehearse** The teacher drilled the performers in their routine. *n.* A fire drill teaches you what to do in a real fire.	

Word			Synonyms	Antonyms
drip		*v.*	**trickle, dribble, drop** My wet clothes dripped water on the floor. *adj.* We were dripping wet after being caught in the rain.	
drive	1.	*n.*	**energy, impulse, force** Ali has the drive and ambition to be very successful.	
	2.	*v.*	**compel, make, prod, urge** His parents drive him to try harder.	**2.** *discourage, hinder, restrain*
	3.	*v.*	**steer, navigate, direct** I am taking lessons to learn how to drive a car. *n.* We went for a drive in the new car.	
droop		*v.*	**hang down, sag, sink, lower** The flowers drooped in the intense heat.	*rise, revive, perk up*
drop	1.	*n.*	**drip, globule, bead, trickle, speck, dab** Dew drops were shining on the roses.	
	2.	*v.*	**fall, slide, lower, topple** The temperature dropped from twenty to fifteen degrees. *n.* The lake froze when there was a drop in temperature.	**2.** *lift, raise, go up*
	3.	*v.*	**let go, release, omit, exclude** He was dropped from the team for missing practices.	**3.** *include, add to, pick up*
drown	1.	*v.*	**swamp, overwhelm, engulf, submerge** The audience drowned the speaker with loud boos.	
	2.	*v.*	**suffocate, extinguish** The mouse drowned in the large puddle.	**2.** *resuscitate, revive, revitalize, bring back to life*
drowsy		*adj.*	**sleepy, lazy, tired, slow** The drowsy child was put to bed.	*alert, lively*
dry	1.	*adj.*	**arid, parched, dehydrated** Few plants can survive in the dry desert.	**1.** *wet, soggy, damp, moist*
	2.	*adj.*	**dull, boring, tedious, uninteresting** I fell asleep while listening to a dry speech.	**2.** *interesting, witty, stimulating*

Word	No.	Part of speech	Meaning and example	Antonyms
dual		*adj.*	**twofold, double** Two can play this video game at once because it has dual controls.	*single*
dub		*v.*	**re-record, blend, add sounds** English dialogue was dubbed into the German film.	
dubious	1.	*adj.*	**uncertain, doubtful, hesitant, undecided** I am dubious about my chance for success in that difficult exam.	1. *certain, sure, positive, definite*
	2.	*adj.*	**questionable, suspicious** Ugly rumours are circulating about his dubious past.	
due	1.	*adj.*	**unpaid, owing, payable, outstanding** The customer paid the amount due on his account.	1. *settled, paid*
	2.	*adj.*	**scheduled, expected** The flight from London is due at four-thirty.	
	3.	*adj.*	**proper, suitable, deserved** We were taught to treat our elders with due respect.	3. *improper, unsuitable*
dull	1.	*adj.*	**boring, dry, uninteresting, tedious** He slept through the dull movie.	1. *interesting, stimulating, fascinating*
	2.	*adj.*	**gloomy, dismal, murky, dim** The grey clouds covering the sun made it a dull day.	2. *bright, cheerful, gay*
	3.	*adj.*	**stupid, slow** He does poorly in school not because he is dull, but because he is lazy.	3. *clever, intelligent, smart, witty, bright, keen*
	4.	*adj.*	**blunt, unsharpened** Please sharpen this dull knife.	4. *sharp*
	5.	*adj.*	**faint, soft, low** I just barely could hear a dull knocking on the door.	5. *distinct, loud*
dumb		*adj.*	**mute, silent, unable to speak** We were struck dumb with surprise when we heard the news.	*able to speak, vocal*
dump	1.	*n.*	**garbage disposal, rubbish heap, junk pile** The garbage trucks take the garbage to the dump.	
	2.	*v.*	**empty, unload** The trucks dumped the gravel at the construction site.	2. *fill, load*

Word			Synonyms	Antonyms
dupe		*v.*	**trick, fool, deceive** I was duped into buying a broken bike.	*guide, assist*
duplicate	**1.**	*n.*	**imitation, replica, copy, facsimile, double** I sent a duplicate of my certificate and kept the original.	**1.** *original*
	2.	*v.*	**copy, reproduce** She was punished for duplicating her mother's signature on a note.	**2.** *originate*
durable		*adj.*	**lasting, sound, strong, substantial, sturdy** We chose durable furniture for the children's room.	*weak, fragile, flimsy*
duration		*n.*	**period, term, extent, span** I was sick for the duration of the holiday.	
duty	**1.**	*n.*	**obligation, responsibility** We should place duty before pleasure.	
	2.	*n.*	**job, task, work** Your duties include market research.	**2.** *entertainment*
	3.	*n.*	**customs, tax, tariff** We had to pay duty to bring our purchases across the border.	
dwell	**1.**	*v.*	**inhabit, live, occupy, reside** The blue heron dwells in swampy regions. *n.* I visited the struggling actor in his humble dwelling.	**1.** *move, leave*
	2.	*v.*	**ponder, brood, think or speak about, harp on** Don't dwell on your past; look ahead to the future.	**2.** *forget, dismiss, overlook*
dwindle		*v.*	**shrink, decline, fade, lessen** Hopes of finding the lost children dwindled with each passing day.	*increase, grow, multiply, expand*
dye		*v.*	**stain, colour, tint** I dyed my white shirt a deep blue. *n.* We used yellow and blue dye to turn the fabric green.	*bleach*
dynamic		*adj.*	**active, powerful, vigorous, forceful, energetic** The business is thriving under the new owner's dynamic leadership.	*slow, dull*

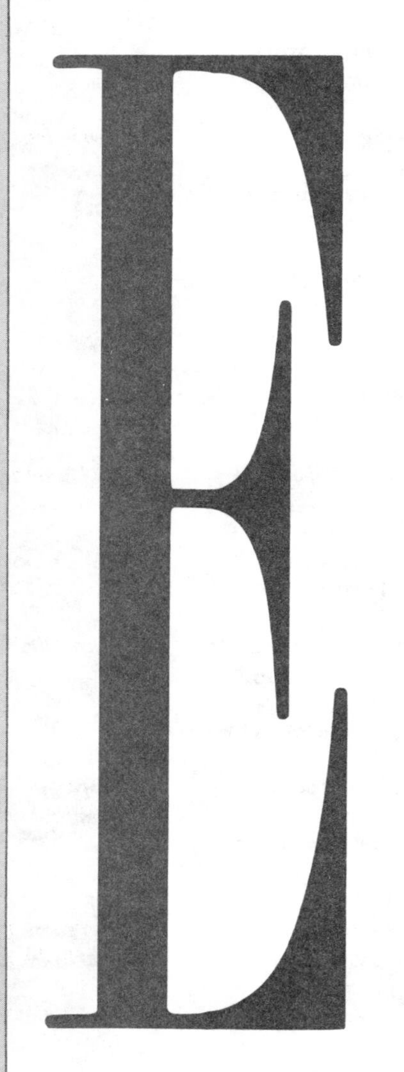

E is used more often than any other letter in our alphabet. Not only does it represent two vowel sounds by itself (*pen, seen*), but it may also change the sounds of other vowels when it ends a word (*hop, hope*).

The Romans used *E* to represent 250.

eager *adj.* **keen, enthusiastic, anxious, zealous, fervent, ardent**
The eager students completed their project in a day.
adv. Fans waited eagerly for the arrival of their favourite rock star.
indifferent, apathetic, unconcerned, uninterested

eagerness *n.* **zest, enthusiasm, anticipation, excitement, desire, readiness**
We were touched by their eagerness to help.
unwillingness, resentfulness, opposition, aversion

early
1. *adj.* **long ago, ancient**
Early peoples lived in caves.
1. contemporary, modern, recent
2. *adj.* **recent, new, fresh**
Tulips are early signs of spring.
2. old, late
3. *adv.* **in advance, ahead of time, beforehand, prematurely**
She arrived early for the party.
adj. We had an early dinner because we were so hungry.
3. late, slow, behind time, tardily

earn
1. *v.* **deserve, merit, rate, win**
They have earned the gold medals.
1. usurp, fail, forfeit
2. *v.* **get, obtain, acquire, profit, gain**
He earns his living as a cook.
n. Most people are wage earners.
2. spend, consume, exhaust

earnest *adj.* **zealous, eager, ardent, sincere, serious, fervent**
Earnest efforts are being made to reduce pollution.
adv. Activists are working earnestly to help save our environment.
indifferent, uninterested, insincere, flippant

earnings *n.* **pay, payment, income, salary, wages, receipts, returns**
People spend most of their earnings on housing and food.
expenses, outlay

ease
1. *n.* **rest, respite, repose, calmness, comfort**
The patient was put at ease after the treatment.
1. pain, unrest, discomfort, irritation
2. *n.* **facility, skill, dexterity, adroitness**
Ian jumped over the fence with ease.
2. difficulty, trouble, clumsiness, ineptitude
3. *n.* **leisure, pleasure, contentment, comfort, well-being**
Everyone envies Peter's life of ease.
3. adversity, hardship, discomfort
4. *v.* **relieve, reduce, soothe, lessen**
Take a pill to ease your headache.
4. increase, irritate, aggravate

Word		POS	Synonyms / Example	Antonyms
easy	1.	*adj.*	**simple, effortless, uninvolved, uncomplicated** We were relieved that it was an easy test.	1. *difficult, complex, involved, complicated*
	2.	*adj.*	**calm, peaceful, mild, serene, gentle, affable** The president's easy manners made everyone relax.	2. *raucous, irritating, strident, harsh*
eat	1.	*v.*	**devour, dine, digest, consume, sup** The hungry child ate all the food. *n.* Eating is a pleasure for some.	1. *fast, starve*
	2.	*v.*	**corrode, erode, wear away** Rust eats into the metal on cars.	2. *build, increase, improve*
ebb		*v.*	**recede, fall back, decline, decrease, subside, withdraw, wane, regress** The ocean tide ebbs daily. *n.* Beaches become wider with the ebb of the tide.	*rise, increase, advance, enlarge, grow, intensify*
eccentric		*adj.*	**unusual, odd, strange, bizarre, singular, unconventional, nonconformist** People avoid her because of her eccentric behaviour. *n.* She is known as an eccentric.	*usual, common, ordinary, conventional, conformist*
eclipse		*v.*	**darken, dim, conceal, cover, overshadow** Jay's career was eclipsed by his brother's. *n.* Will there be a total or partial eclipse of the moon?	*disclose, expose*
economize		*v.*	**be thrifty, conserve, scrimp, be frugal, save** Naomi economized on food when she was unemployed. *adj.* She looked for an economical way to survive. *n.* A sense of economy is necessary.	*waste, spend, splurge*
ecstasy		*n.*	**joy, delight, rapture, bliss, gladness, happiness, pleasure** They were in ecstasy over winning an Olympic gold medal. *adj.* They were ecstatic about their victory.	*sadness, discontent, dejection, depression*

edge	1.	*n.*	**brink, verge, brim, periphery, border, outside, rim** Zinnias were planted along the edge of the lawn. *v.* Flowers edged the lawn.	**1.** *centre, inside, interior*
	2.	*n.*	**blade** The razor's edge is sharp.	
educate		*v.*	**teach, instruct, tutor, train, enlighten, develop** Teachers educate their pupils. *n.* In many countries, education is compulsory until the age of sixteen.	*misinform*
eerie		*adj.*	**strange, peculiar, weird, ghostly, frightful, ominous, mysterious** The eerie scream made my hair stand on end.	*usual, ordinary, common*
effect	1.	*n.*	**result, consequence, conclusion, outcome, outgrowth, aftermath** The effect of hours of hard work was an impressive victory.	**1.** *cause, reason, rationale*
	2.	*n.*	**impression, influence** Her inspirational words had a lasting effect on us.	
	3.	*v.*	**accomplish, achieve, cause, bring about, realize** It is difficult to effect change.	**3.** *prevent*
effective		*adj.*	**productive, efficient, competent, capable** This new drug is effective in curing headaches. *adv.* It effectively gets rid of headaches.	*ineffective, unproductive*
efficient	1.	*adj.*	**capable, adept, effective, proficient, productive, competent, skilful** The efficient secretary will be promoted. *n.* His efficiency is much admired. *adv.* He worked efficiently on the project.	**1.** *inefficient, unskilled, incompetent, ineffective, incapable*
	2.	*adj.*	**economical, suitable, serviceable** Gas is an efficient way to heat the house.	**2.** *uneconomical, wasteful, unsuitable*
effort	1.	*n.*	**work, toil, labour, exertion** Their success was the result of years of effort.	**1.** *inactivity, rest, idleness*
	2.	*n.*	**attempt, undertaking, venture** Fund raising efforts are done by volunteers.	

Word		Part of speech	Synonyms and example	Antonyms
eject		*v.*	**oust, exclude, expel, dismiss, remove, evict** The conductor ejected the rowdy person from the bus.	*admit, let in, receive, allow, welcome, include*
elaborate	1.	*adj.*	**ornate, decorated, ornamented, adorned** Many cathedrals have elaborate interiors.	**1.** *plain, simple, unadorned, ordinary*
	2.	*adj.*	**gaudy, showy, ostentatious, pretentious** She wore an elaborate gown to the ball.	**2.** *plain, simple*
	3.	*adj.*	**detailed, complicated, complex, intricate, involved** They drew up elaborate plans for a plaza. *adv.* Some plazas are designed elaborately.	**3.** *simple, plain, uncomplicated*
	4.	*v.*	**expand, extend, embellish, enlarge** He elaborated on his ideas in his new book.	**4.** *condense, abridge, reduce, lessen*
elapse		*v.*	**slip away, pass, go by, transpire** How many hours elapsed before help came?	
elasticity		*n.*	**spring, resilience, flexibility** Human muscles have elasticity. *adj.* Rubber bands are elastic.	*hardness, brittleness, rigidity*
elated		*adj.*	**overjoyed, happy, delighted, ecstatic** The runner was elated with his victory.	*depressed, gloomy, disappointed, downhearted*
elder		*adj.*	**senior, older** She asked her elder sister for advice.	*younger, junior*
elect		*v.*	**choose, select, vote for** Jo was elected class president. *n.* The election was a close one.	*cast out, reject*
elegant	1.	*adj.*	**tasteful, classic, fancy** We dined in an elegant restaurant. *adv.* It was elegantly decorated.	**1.** *crude*
	2.	*adj.*	**cultured, dignified, refined, aristocratic** The elegant woman proved to be a princess. *n.* There was a distinct air of elegance about her.	**2.** *crude, unrefined, uncouth*

Word			Synonyms	Antonyms
elementary	1.	*adj.*	**rudimentary, introductory, simple** Kim learned elementary arithmetic in grade one.	1. *advanced, difficult, complicated*
	2.	*adj.*	**fundamental, basic, essential** An elementary education is required in North America.	
elevate	1.	*v.*	**raise, lift, heighten, hoist** Elevate the platform to allow the performers to be seen. *n.* A hill is an elevation. *n.* Elevators move people from one floor to another.	1. *lower, depress*
	2.	*v.*	**promote, advance, improve, upgrade** The officer was elevated to the rank of colonel.	2. *demote, downgrade*
elicit		*v.*	**extract, obtain, draw out** Excellent questions elicited thoughtful answers.	*instil, put in*
eligible		*adj.*	**qualified, suitable, fit** There are many eligible candidates for the job.	*ineligible, unfit, unauthorized, unqualified*
eliminate		*v.*	**remove, eject, discard, expel** Which teams will be eliminated from the playoffs? *n.* Six teams face elimination.	*include, accept*
elude		*v.*	**avoid, evade, dodge, avert, escape** The escaped convict eluded arrest for many years.	*face, meet, encounter, seek*
emancipate		*v.*	**liberate, free, release, deliver** President Lincoln emancipated the slaves in the Southern United States in 1863. *n.* The emancipation of slaves came after years of struggle.	*restrain, confine, imprison, enslave*
embark	1.	*v.*	**board, load** Many of the ship's passengers embarked at Halifax. *n.* Halifax was the port of embarkation.	1. *disembark*
	2.	*v.*	**set out, begin, start** He embarked on his new job with both fear and eagerness.	2. *conclude, end*

Word			Synonyms and examples	Antonyms
embarrass		*v.*	**disconcert, chagrin, distress, vex, bother, upset** The actor was embarrassed when he forgot his lines. *adj.* What an embarrassing moment! *n.* He blushed in embarrassment.	*encourage, help, assist, assure, reassure*
emerge	1.	*v.*	**appear, come out** A large crowd emerged from the stadium at the end of the game.	**1.** *disappear, hide, go in*
	2.	*v.*	**become known** The truth finally emerged after hours of questioning.	
emergency		*n.*	**crisis, dilemma, distress** Nurses are trained to stay calm during emergencies.	*routine, normalcy*
eminent	1.	*adj.*	**famous, noted, renowned, exalted, important, celebrated, prominent** The eminent scientists were applauded for their latest discovery.	**1.** *unknown, obscure, unheard of, unimportant*
	2.	*adj.*	**high, elevated, raised, lofty** The church on the hill is in an eminent position.	**2.** *low, depressed*
emit		*v.*	**give off, radiate, beam, discharge, send out** Cars emit carbon monoxide. *n.* Such emissions pollute the air.	*absorb, take in, consume, ingest, receive*
emotion		*n.*	**feeling, sentiment, passion** Humans experience many different emotions.	
emotional		*adj.*	**stirring, moving** Watching our team receive their gold medal was an emotional moment for us.	*unemotional, apathetic*
emphasize		*v.*	**stress, accent, accentuate, highlight** Commercials emphasize the qualities of the products which are for sale. *n.* The main emphasis of any commercial is the product.	*negate*
employ	1.	*v.*	**hire, engage, contract** The factory employs hundreds of workers. *n.* Many people are seeking employment here. *n.* The factory owner is the employer. *n.* The workers are the employees.	**1.** *dismiss, let go, fire*

	2.	*v.*	**use, apply, utilize** Nuclear weapons have been employed in war.	
empty	1.	*v.*	**flow out, drain, discharge** The St. Lawrence River empties into the Atlantic Ocean.	**1.** *flow in, absorb*
	2.	*v.*	**clear out, pour out, clean out** Please empty your desks before you leave.	**2.** *fill, pack*
	3.	*adj.*	**bare, vacant, unoccupied, hollow, blank, void** The empty lot will be turned into a park.	**3.** *full, filled, occupied*
	4.	*adj.*	**meaningless, senseless, vacuous, insincere** The speech contained empty promises.	**4.** *meaningful, purposeful*
enable		*v.*	**make possible, allow, let, permit, empower** Computers enable us to do many jobs much faster.	*prohibit, prevent, obstruct, impede*
enchant		*v.*	**delight, please, charm, thrill, bewitch, captivate, fascinate** The singer enchanted the audience. *adj.* It was an enchanting performance.	*disgust, repel, offend, displease*
enclose	1.	*v.*	**encompass, surround, encircle, circle, contain, ring** Hedges enclosed the gardens. *n.* Horses are kept in enclosures.	
	2.	*v.*	**insert, put in, include** Enclose the invoice with the cheque.	**2.** *exclude, take out, remove*
encompass	1.	*v.*	**enclose, circle, encircle, ring, surround** The army encompassed the town so that no one could escape.	
	2.	*v.*	**include, contain, consist of** The entire farm encompassed four hectares.	**2.** *exclude, lack*
encounter	1.	*n.*	**meeting, appointment, rendezvous** Brief encounters with friends are pleasant.	
	2.	*n.*	**conflict, fight, battle, confrontation, struggle, skirmish, engagement** Fierce border encounters between the nations led to war.	**2.** *withdrawal, retreat*

	3.	*v.*	**meet, come across, find, stumble across** Will scientists encounter life on other planets?	3. *leave, part*
encourage	1.	*v.*	**cheer, hearten, inspire, comfort, reassure** The doctor's news encouraged the patient to fight the disease. *adj.* The encouraging news cheered everyone. *n.* Patients need all the encouragement they can get.	1. *discourage, dishearten, depress*
	2.	*v.*	**stimulate, spur, bolster** The company offered free gifts to encourage sales.	2. *discourage, hinder, deter, obstruct*
encroach		*v.*	**trespass, infringe, invade, intrude, violate** His questions encroached upon our privacy.	
end	1.	*n.*	**tip, point, edge, tail, extremity** The emergency exit is at the end of the corridor.	1. *centre, middle*
	2.	*n.*	**conclusion, close, finish, finale, completion** Did you watch the end of the movie?	2. *beginning, start, opening, outset*
	3.	*n.*	**aim, purpose, intention, goal, object** There is no obvious end to the argument.	
	4.	*n.*	**demise, death** President Kennedy met his end in Dallas.	4. *origin, birth, beginning*
	5.	*v.*	**finish, stop, halt, cease, terminate, discontinue, conclude** Please end this meaningless argument.	5. *begin, start, commence, initiate*
endanger		*v.*	**imperil, jeopardize** Hunting has endangered many species of animals.	*save, preserve, protect*
endeavour (also spelled endeavor)		*v.*	**try, attempt, aim, struggle, strive** Captain Scott endeavoured to reach the South Pole. *n.* He made an honest endeavour to improve his grades.	*quit, give up*
endless	1.	*adj.*	**limitless, unbounded, measureless, uninterrupted, continuous** Outer space is endless.	1. *fixed, bounded*

	2.	*adj.*	**perpetual, eternal, everlasting, ceaseless** Without an education, many people live in an endless cycle of poverty.	**2.** *temporary, fleeting*
endorse		*v.*	**approve, sanction, support, stand up for** Famous people often endorse products in advertisements. *n.* They earn large sums of money from the endorsements.	*censure, condemn, denounce*
endow		*v.*	**bequeath, bestow, give** She endowed her paintings to the gallery. *n.* The art gallery appreciated the endowment.	*receive, acquire, obtain*
endure	1.	*v.*	**last, continue, remain, persist, stay, linger** Her contribution to society will endure forever. *adj.* She made an enduring contribution to society.	**1.** *cease, end, stop*
	2.	*v.*	**suffer, tolerate, bear, undergo** The arthritic patient endured great pain. *n.* Such pain is beyond endurance.	
enemy		*n.*	**foe, adversary, antagonist, opponent, attacker** The politician has made many enemies.	*friend, ally, helper, supporter*
energetic		*adj.*	**lively, active, vigorous, vital, industrious** The energetic child refused to go to bed.	*lazy, inactive, sluggish*
energy	1.	*n.*	**force, power, strength, vigour, vitality, drive** Proper diet and exercise is essential for physical energy.	
	2.	*n.*	**power, force** Home appliances use a lot of electrical energy.	
enforce		*v.*	**execute, compel, oblige, impose** The police enforce law and order. *n.* Law enforcement is necessary for stability in a country.	*abandon, evade, negate*
engage	1.	*v.*	**employ, hire, contract, retain** Who engaged that plumber for the job?	**1.** *dismiss, discharge, release*

	2.	*v.*	**involve, occupy, absorb** They are engaged in a discussion.	
	3.	*v.*	**commit, promise, pledge** We are engaged to be married. *n.* We announced our engagement last week.	
engulf		*v.*	**swallow up, inundate, submerge, immerse, flood, swamp** The tidal wave engulfed the coastal town.	*emerge, rise, come up*
enhance		*v.*	**magnify, intensify, heighten, increase, advance, augment** Winning the award will enhance the dancer's career.	*lessen, decrease, diminish, reduce, shorten*
enigma		*n.*	**puzzle, riddle, mystery, secret, bafflement, conundrum** The cause of the illness is an enigma.	
enjoy		*v.*	**delight in, like, be fond of** Misha enjoys singing. *adj.* Do you find singing enjoyable?	*dislike, hate, deplore*
enjoyment		*n.*	**pleasure, delight, happiness, joy, gladness** Television gives most people hours of enjoyment.	*unhappiness, sorrow, sadness, grief, misery*
enlarge		*v.*	**expand, increase, extend, augment** The family enlarged their house by adding two rooms. *n.* She made an enlargement of the picture to hang on the wall.	*decrease, reduce, make smaller*
enormous		*adj.*	**huge, immense, tremendous, vast, colossal, monstrous** Enormous amounts of money are spent on space research.	*tiny, minute, little, small, petite, diminutive*
enough		*adj.*	**ample, sufficient, adequate** We didn't have enough time to complete the test.	*insufficient, inadequate, deficient, scant*
enrich		*v.*	**improve, better** These cereals are enriched with vitamins. *n.* People seek enrichment in their lifestyles.	*destroy, deteriorate*
enter	1.	*v.*	**come into, go in, set foot in** Please knock before you enter.	**1.** *leave, exit, depart*

Word	No.	Part	Synonyms / Example	Antonyms
	2.	*v.*	**register, record, inscribe, list, file, post** Guests entered their names in the book.	**2.** *erase, remove*
	3.	*v.*	**join, enrol** Has Jon entered the race?	**3.** *quit, leave, withdraw*
	4.	*v.*	**begin, start, take up** At age fifty, Sam entered a new career as a writer.	**4.** *end, give up*
enterprise		*n.*	**project, task, adventure, venture, scheme, undertaking, attempt, endeavour, pursuit** Searching for the *Titanic* was a bold enterprise.	
enterprising		*adj.*	**bold, venturesome, adventurous, daring** Enterprising employees often reach the top.	*cautious, careful, hesitant, timid*
entertain	1.	*v.*	**amuse, delight, beguile, charm** Puppet shows entertain children. *n.* Rock stars are popular entertainers.	**1.** *bore, tire, weary*
	2.	*v.*	**host, welcome, receive** The Prime Minister entertained the royal visitors.	**2.** *neglect, exclude, ignore, shun*
enthusiasm		*n.*	**eagerness, zeal, fervour, zest, energy, ardour, zeal** The speaker aroused enthusiasm for his cause. *adj.* The enthusiastic listeners gave the speaker a standing ovation.	*indifference, ennui, apathy, boredom*
entice		*v.*	**lure, attract, draw, charm, tempt** They were enticed into a life of crime by the prospect of big money. *adj.* Money is often an enticement that is hard to resist.	*repel, repulse*
entire		*adj.*	**complete, whole, total** The entire room is painted yellow. *adv.* The room is entirely yellow.	*incomplete, partial*
entrance	1.	*n.*	**doorway, access, entry, approach** The host greeted the guests at the entrance.	**1.** *exit, outlet*
	2.	*n.*	**arrival, entry** The movie star made a dramatic entrance at the party.	**2.** *departure, exit*

Word			Synonyms / Example	Antonyms
entreat		*v.*	**beg, ask, urge, implore, plead with, beseech** The sick child entreated the nurse to stay.	*command, demand*
enumerate		*v.*	**list, count, compute, number, detail, calculate, reckon** Census takers enumerated the population of the country. *n.* How accurate is the enumeration?	*miscount*
environment		*n.*	**surroundings, habitat** Acid rain harms the natural environment.	
envy	1.	*n.*	**jealousy** The loser's envy was obvious. *adj.* Her colleagues were envious of her success.	1. *good will*
	2.	*v.*	**desire, covet** Many people envy her confidence.	
epidemic		*n.*	**pestilence, scourge, blight, plague** A flu epidemic caused illness across the country.	
episode	1.	*n.*	**instalment, part** One episode of the television series is shown nightly.	1. *whole, entirety*
	2.	*n.*	**occurrence, happening, occasion, incident** The Vietnam War will be remembered as a dreadful episode in history.	
epoch		*n.*	**era, age, period, time** Computers have led humans into an exciting epoch in history.	
equal	1.	*n.*	**match, counterpart, peer** The two tennis players are ranked as equals.	
	2.	*v.*	**correspond, be identical to, parallel, match** The students equalled each other in ability.	2. *differ, vary, deviate from*
	3.	*adj.*	**identical, like, matching, same, even, uniform** Equal amounts of water and sugar were added to the sauce.	3. *unequal, uneven, different, varying, disparate*
equip		*v.*	**furnish, supply, outfit, provide** The car was equipped with a phone and a stereo.	*strip, remove*

Word	No.	Part	Synonyms / Example	Antonyms
equitable		*adj.*	**fair, just, proper, impartial, proportionate** There should be equitable opportunities for all races. *adv.* The money will be shared equitably.	*unfair, unjust, disproportionate, partial*
equivalent		*adj.*	**equal, interchangeable, commensurate, correspondent, synonymous** The fractions 2/4 and 1/2 are equivalent.	*unequal, uneven*
era		*n.*	**period, epoch, generation, age, time** Dinosaurs lived in the prehistoric era.	
eradicate		*v.*	**exterminate, abolish, destroy, eliminate, erase** Drug dealers must be eradicated.	*save, protect, preserve, defend, guard, shelter*
erase	1.	*v.*	**blot out, remove, scratch out, rub out, cancel** Liquid whitener erases typing errors. *n.* Pencil erasers are made of rubber.	1. *retain, keep, enter*
	2.	*v.*	**obliterate, wipe out, remove all trace of, eliminate, eradicate** Nuclear war could erase all forms of life on earth.	2. *protect, preserve*
erect	1.	*v.*	**build, construct, raise** The council voted to erect a new city hall.	1. *demolish, remove, tear down*
	2.	*v.*	**assemble, put together, set up, fit together** Sonja erected a model spaceship from the parts in the kit.	2. *take apart, dismantle, disassemble, undo*
	3.	*v.*	**establish, found, form, institute, organize, create** The fund was erected to fight cancer.	3. *eradicate*
	4.	*adj.*	**upright, vertical, perpendicular** The soldier stood erect at his post.	4. *horizontal, flat, prone, level*
erode		*v.*	**disintegrate, break down, eat away, wear down** Wind erodes topsoil. *n.* Soil erosion is a serious problem for farmers.	*preserve, protect*
err		*v.*	**be mistaken, blunder, fail, misjudge** The player erred in his decision to steal a base.	*be correct, be right*

Word			Synonyms and example	Antonyms
errand		*n.*	**message, task, mission** We hired a student to run errands for the staff.	
erratic		*adj.*	**variable, unpredictable, inconsistent, irregular, changeable** His erratic behaviour caused us concern.	*consistent, reliable, steady, constant*
error		*n.*	**mistake, blunder, fault, faux pas** An error in addition was made by almost every student in the class. *adj.* Her smile gave us the erroneous impression that all was well.	
erupt		*v.*	**explode, emit, eject, discharge, burst forth** Molten lava erupted from the volcano. *n.* The volcanic eruption was a spectacular sight.	*lie dormant*
escape	1.	*n.*	**flight, retreat, withdrawal** The criminal's escape terrified the town.	**1.** *retention, imprisonment, capture*
	2.	*v.*	**flee, evade, avoid, elude** Did everyone in the building escape the fire?	**2.** *stay, remain, confront, incur*
escort		*v.*	**accompany, go with, attend** Bodyguards escorted the sports star through the crowd. *n.* Bodyguards are his constant escorts.	
espionage		*n.*	**spying, reconnaissance** Industrial espionage does occur in highly competitive industries.	
essential		*adj.*	**necessary, vital, important, indispensable, fundamental** The formula listed the essential ingredients.	*unnecessary, trivial, unimportant*
establish	1.	*v.*	**set up, build, install, found, erect** Explorers established settlements in North America.	**1.** *break up, dismantle*
	2.	*v.*	**prove, verify, confirm, authenticate, validate** The licence established the identity of the driver.	**2.** *disprove, refute, deny*

Word			Synonyms and examples	Antonyms
esteem		*n.*	**respect, honour, regard, admiration, favour** Our school principal is held in great esteem.	*disrespect, dishonour, disregard*
estimate		*n.*	**appraisal, evaluation, assessment, valuation** When is the real estate agent giving an estimate on the property? *v.* A realtor estimated the value of the house.	
eternal		*adj.*	**everlasting, unending, endless, perpetual, permanent, ceaseless** Earth is in an eternal orbit of the sun. *adv.* We will be eternally grateful for your help.	*temporary, brief, fleeting*
ethics		*n.*	**morality, conduct, code of right and wrong** Lawyers and medical doctors have a code of ethics to guide them. *adj.* He is an ethical man and can be trusted totally.	
evacuate	1.	*v.*	**empty, clear, quit, vacate, abandon, leave** Coastal towns were evacuated before the hurricane struck. *n.* The evacuation of the towns saved many lives.	**1.** *stay, remain*
	2.	*v.*	**void, empty, exhaust, remove** Air was evacuated from the beaker during the experiment.	**2.** *fill, retain, maintain*
evade		*v.*	**avoid, elude, get away from, escape** The witness evaded the lawyer's question.	*confront, meet, face*
evaluate		*v.*	**appraise, judge, assess, estimate** Insurance adjustors evaluated the cost of damages.	
evaporate	1.	*v.*	**dissolve, vanish, disappear, fade** Our hopes of victory evaporated in the final round.	**1.** *appear, emerge, materialize*
	2.	*v.*	**vaporize** Water evaporates when boiled.	**2.** *liquefy, solidify*
even	1.	*adj.*	**smooth, level, flat, regular** The floor has an even surface.	**1.** *uneven, rough, irregular*
	2.	*adj.*	**same, identical, equal, tied** The score at the end of the game was even.	**2.** *uneven, unequal*

Word			Synonyms	Antonyms
event	1.	*n.*	**happening, incident, occurrence, experience, occasion** Our holidays were full of exciting events.	
	2.	*n.*	**chance, case, possibility** The picnic will be cancelled in the event of rain.	2. *absence*
eventually		*adv.*	**ultimately, in the end, finally** Eventually there will be a cure for cancer.	
every		*adj.*	**each, all** Every citizen has a responsibility to vote.	
evict		*v.*	**oust, remove, put out, eject, dismiss** The tenants were evicted from their homes for not paying their rent. *n.* The tenants pleaded with the landlord to delay the eviction.	*receive, reinstate, restore*
evident		*adj.*	**apparent, clear, obvious, visible, unmistakable, plain** It was evident that the marathon runner was tiring. *adv.* The runner is evidently tired.	*concealed, hidden, obscure*
evil	1.	*n.*	**wrong, wickedness, corruption** No evil exists in Utopia.	1. *virtue, good, goodness*
	2.	*adj.*	**wicked, bad, corrupt, sinful** In the fairy tale, the evil creature was punished.	2. *kind, virtuous, good*
exact	1.	*adj.*	**precise, accurate, correct, perfect** The storekeeper had the exact change. *adv.* She made sure that she cut the cake exactly into eighths.	1. *incorrect, inaccurate*
	2.	*adj.*	**sharp, distinct, clear-cut, lucid, definite, obvious, clear** Exact silhouettes are easy to identify.	2. *blurred, unclear, indistinct, obscure, indiscernible*
	3.	*adj.*	**strict, demanding, rigorous, severe, stringent, rigid, exacting** Commanding officers issue exact orders.	3. *flexible, lax, undemanding*

Word			Synonyms	Antonyms
exaggerate		*v.*	**magnify, enlarge, expand, stretch, overstate** The reporters exaggerated the seriousness of the incident. *adj.* The exaggerated account of the incident alarmed many people. *n.* The reporters were reprimanded for their exaggeration of the truth.	*minimize, lessen, understate*
examine	**1.**	*v.*	**check, inspect, observe, investigate, survey, probe, search, scrutinize, check out** Scientists carefully examined the fossils. *n.* The prehistoric remains will undergo thorough examinations.	**1.** *neglect, ignore, disregard*
	2.	*v.*	**test, question** We were examined in mathematics. *n.* It was a tough examination.	
example		*n.*	**illustration, representation, model, pattern, sample, specimen, prototype** Lena was named as an example of a model student.	
exasperate		*v.*	**irritate, annoy, peeve, aggravate, upset, bother, anger** The teacher was exasperated with the students for their lack of attention. *n.* Ed quit his job in exasperation.	*please, soothe, satisfy, calm, comfort, console*
excavate		*v.*	**dig, shovel, empty, hollow out, open up, uncover** Archaeologists excavate historical sites.	*fill in, fill, bury, close, cover*
exceed		*v.*	**surpass, excel, outpace, outdo, outstrip, pass, go beyond** Her success exceeded all expectations.	*fall behind, lag, fall short of*
excel		*v.*	**beat others, surpass others, be superior, do better than** Kim excels in mathematics.	*be inferior to, fail*
excellent		*adj.*	**superior, superb, admirable, outstanding, wonderful, great** The prize-winning stories are excellent. *adv.* The prize winners write excellently.	*poor, inferior, imperfect*

Word	Part of speech	Synonyms and example	Antonyms
except	*prep.*	**excluding, omitting, saving, without, but, exempting, aside from, other than, barring** The whole family went except for Ian.	*including, inclusive, together with, as well as*
exceptional	*adj.*	**unusual, rare, special, unique, extraordinary, uncommon** Luciano Pavarotti is an exceptional opera singer. *adv.* He sings exceptionally well.	*usual, common, ordinary, regular, normal*
excess	*n.*	**abundance, surplus, oversupply** There is an excess of wheat this year. *adj.* The excess wheat will be exported.	*scarcity, lack, deficiency, dearth, shortage*
excessive	*adj.*	**superfluous, exorbitant, extravagant** Excessive rainfall can ruin crops.	*scant, lean, poor, insufficient, inadequate, meagre*
exchange	*n.*	**interchange, transaction, swap** There is an exchange of gifts at Christmas. *v.* We exchange gifts on Christmas Day.	
excite	*v.*	**arouse, stir, stimulate, agitate, provoke, animate, thrill** The roller coaster ride excited the children. *adj.* An excited group of spectators waited for the launch of the space shuttle. *n.* The space shuttle's flight caused great excitement.	*calm, soothe, quiet, pacify, relax, subdue*
exclaim	*v.*	**shout, call out, say loudly, cry out, yell** "Watch out!" exclaimed the waiter when I almost bumped into him. *n.* His exclamation startled me.	*murmur, mutter, whisper, mumble*
exclude	*v.*	**bar, ban, shut out, reject, prohibit, keep out** The feisty hockey player was excluded from the playoffs. *n.* The rival fans applauded the exclusion.	*allow, admit, welcome, include*
excrete	*v.*	**shed, emit, discharge, eliminate** The body excretes sweat through the pores in the skin.	*soak up, absorb, retain*

excursion		*n.*	**trip, jaunt, journey, outing, expedition** Bus excursions to New York City are popular.	
excuse	1.	*n.*	**reason, explanation, defence** Is there an excuse for your lateness?	
	2.	*v.*	**pardon, forgive, overlook** Please excuse me for not coming to your party.	**2.** *accuse, blame*
execute	1.	*v.*	**kill, put to death, slay** The rebels executed the dictator. *n.* Executions were frequent during the French Revolution.	**1.** *rescue, save, protect, preserve*
	2.	*v.*	**perform, do, complete, finish, achieve, accomplish** Which figure skater executed the best spin?	
exempt		*adj.*	**free, clear, excused, absolved** Antiques are exempt from customs duty.	*responsible, liable, subject to*
exertion		*n.*	**effort, struggle, work, action** Physical exertion can tire you if you are unfit.	*rest, repose, relaxation*
exhaust	1.	*v.*	**use up, consume, deplete** The stranded survivors exhausted their food supply.	**1.** *preserve, save, store, keep, restore, replenish*
	2.	*v.*	**tire, weary, fatigue, weaken, debilitate** The long climb up the mountain exhausted everyone. *n.* Marathon runners can collapse from exhaustion.	**2.** *refreshen, strengthen, invigorate*
exhibit	1.	*n.*	**show, display, presentation** Handicrafts were on exhibit at the fair.	
	2.	*v.*	**expose, reveal, display, show, present** The latest software will be exhibited at the computer fair.	**2.** *conceal, hide, cover*
exhilarate			**enliven, excite, stimulate, invigorate, gladden, refresh** The good news exhilarated all of us.	*depress*
exile	1.	*n.*	**banishment, expulsion, deportation, expatriation** Napoleon spent his exile on the island of Elba. *n.* Napoleon was an exile on Elba.	**1.** *repatriation*

Word			Synonyms / Example	Antonyms
	2.	*v.*	**cast out, banish, expel, deport** The government exiled the former leader.	2. *repatriate*
exist		*v.*	**live, survive, be, endure** Dinosaurs existed a long time ago. *n.* The refugees led a miserable existence in the camps.	*die, pass away*
exit	1.	*n.*	**way out, outlet** Fire exits in public buildings are mandatory by law.	1. *entrance, way in*
	2.	*n.*	**departure, withdrawal** The leading character made a dramatic exit from the stage.	2. *arrival, entrance*
	3.	*v.*	**leave, depart, go out** Exit by the main door.	3. *enter, go in, arrive*
exotic		*adj.*	**foreign, unusual, fascinating, different** Travel posters often show pictures of exotic places.	*local, common, ordinary*
expand		*v.*	**grow, extend, dilate, amplify, swell, stretch, inflate** Mercury expands and contracts with changes in temperature. *n.* The expansion of the company resulted in the hiring of more people.	*contract, shrink, reduce, decrease, deflate*
expanse		*n.*	**extent, area, space, stretch** We drove across the vast expanses of the prairies.	
expedition		*n.*	**excursion, voyage, journey, trip, quest** Cook's expedition circumnavigated the world.	
expel		*v.*	**eject, oust, dismiss, exclude, discharge, evict, suspend, remove** Our school expels students who drink or take drugs. *n.* Students face expulsion if they drink or take drugs.	*admit, include, welcome, let in, receive*
expense		*n.*	**cost, amount, charge, outlay, price** Enormous expenses were incurred in the search for the *Titanic.*	*profit, income, return, gain, saving*
expensive		*adj.*	**costly, high-priced, dear** Emeralds are expensive jewels.	*inexpensive, cheap, low-priced*

Word			Synonyms and examples	Antonyms
experience	1.	*n.*	**training, background, practice** The job applicant had no previous experience with computers. *adj.* The company hired an experienced computer programmer.	1. *inexperience*
	2.	*v.*	**encounter, undergo, live through, endure** The refugees experienced many hardships. *n.* They hope to forget their bad experiences.	2. *avoid, escape*
experiment		*n.*	**investigation, trial, test, examination, research** Scientists conduct experiments to prove their hypotheses. *v.* Scientists experimented with the new source of energy.	
expert	1.	*n.*	**authority, specialist, master** Art experts evaluated the painting.	1. *novice, beginner*
	2.	*adj.*	**accomplished, skilful, adept, proficient, practised, able** Expert divers are needed to retrieve the sunken treasure. *adv.* The divers expertly recovered the sunken treasure.	2. *inept, inexperienced*
explain		*v.*	**clarify, describe, make clear, clear up** Explain the meaning of the word. *n.* The explanation helped Ann understand the problem.	*puzzle, confuse, confound, perplex, mystify, baffle*
explicit		*adj.*	**detailed, clear, definite, precise** The witness gave an explicit description of the accident.	*confused, vague, sketchy*
explode		*v.*	**burst, blow up, detonate** Bombs exploded as the terrorists attacked. *n.* The loud explosions frightened us. *n.* Explosives must be handled with caution. *adj.* Explosive devices are dangerous.	
exploit	1.	*n.*	**deed, feat, achievement, venture, escapade** Flying the first space shuttle was a daring exploit.	
	2.	*v.*	**use, take advantage of** The gambler exploited the other players' weaknesses.	2. *help, aid, assist*

Word	No.	Part of speech	Synonyms / Example	Antonyms
explore		*v.*	**search, examine, investigate, inquire into** Astronauts are exploring space. *n.* Henry Hudson was an explorer.	
export		*v.*	**ship, send out** Canada exports wheat. *n.* Japan's exports include cars.	*import, bring in*
expose	1.	*v.*	**uncover, bare, reveal, show** She exposed her wound to help it dry.	**1.** *cover, conceal, hide*
	2.	*v.*	**disclose, bring to light, show up, uncover, make known** The truth was exposed after months of investigation.	**2.** *conceal, hide*
express	1.	*v.*	**tell, voice, state, utter, speak, declare, reveal, communicate** Everyone must learn to express their ideas clearly.	**1.** *keep silent, remain silent, withhold*
	2.	*v.*	**ship, dispatch, forward, send, deliver rapidly** Export companies express goods around the world. *n.* Certain items are sent by express.	
expressive		*adj.*	**eloquent, dramatic, stirring, emphatic, strong, spirited, meaningful, stimulating** Expressive speakers capture the audience's attention. *adv.* Do you speak expressively?	*indifferent, boring, dull, uninspiring, inarticulate*
exquisite		*adj.*	**delicate, choice, fine, precise, exact, dainty** Everyone admired the exquisite details on the cameo ring. *adv.* The ring was designed exquisitely.	*ordinary, common, coarse, mediocre, average*
extend	1.	*v.*	**offer, give, impart** We extend our best wishes to you.	**1.** *get, receive*
	2.	*v.*	**expand, enlarge, increase, lengthen, stretch** We extended our holiday by a week. *n.* The extension to our house will be completed soon.	**2.** *decrease, reduce, compress, condense, consolidate, contract*
extent		*n.*	**size, amount, scope, magnitude, range, limit, degree** We have not assessed the extent of the damage caused by the flood.	

Word			Synonyms	Antonyms
exterior	1.	*n.*	**outside, surface, skin** The exterior of the building was covered in ivy.	1. *inside, interior*
	2.	*adj.*	**external, outside, outer** Exterior walls need to be painted frequently.	2. *interior, internal, inner*
exterminate		*v.*	**destroy, kill, abolish, stamp out, wipe out, annihilate, eradicate** Chemical sprays were used to exterminate the cockroaches. *n.* Cockroaches are controlled by extermination.	*preserve, keep, protect, maintain, save*
external	1.	*adj.*	**exterior, outward, outer, outside** Some cars have thermometers that indicate the external temperature.	1. *internal, interior, inward, inner, inside*
	2.	*adj.*	**foreign** Who is responsible for external affairs in our government?	2. *native, home, national*
extinct		*adj.*	**obsolete, defunct, dead, annihilated** Dinosaurs are extinct. *n.* No one is sure what caused the extinction of the dinosaurs.	*existent, existing, current, alive*
extinguish		*v.*	**put out, quench, choke, smother, douse, suffocate, stifle, wipe out** Tzen extinguished the blaze with the fire extinguisher.	*fan, instigate, set, promote, initiate, incite, cause*
extort		*v.*	**extract, force, wrench, steal, exact** Blackmailers use threats to extort money from their victims. *n.* The blackmailer was charged with extortion.	*restore, give back, return*
extra		*adj.*	**additional, added, further, supplementary** Extra supplies were shipped to the famine victims.	*less, limited, insufficient, deficient*
extract	1.	*n.*	**quotation, selection, excerpt, passage** Read your favourite extract from the book.	1. *entirety, whole*
	2.	*v.*	**take out, remove, draw out** The dentist extracted the loose tooth.	2. *insert, add, put in*

Word			Synonyms	Antonyms
extraordinary		*adj.*	**remarkable, amazing, unusual, uncommon** Helen Keller was an extraordinary woman.	*usual, normal, ordinary, common*
extraterrestrial		*adj.*	**unearthly, alien, inhuman** Will astronauts see extraterrestrial beings in space?	*earthly, worldly, terrestrial*
extravagance		*n.*	**waste, excess, lavishness, indulgence** The couple's extravagances led to their bankruptcy. *adj.* Their extravagant lifestyle was the talk of the town.	*economy, thrift, frugality*
extreme	1.	*n.*	**height, limit, apex, end, climax, top, apogee** The music brought the audience to the extreme of pleasure.	
	2.	*adj.*	**farthest, most remote, outermost** Navigation is difficult in the extreme areas of the Arctic.	**2.** *nearest, closest*
	3.	*adj.*	**radical, immoderate, excessive** Some people have extreme political views.	**3.** *cautious, restrained, moderate*
extricate		*v.*	**free, liberate, loosen, dislodge, disengage, release, disentangle** The rescuers extricated the driver from the badly wrecked car.	*restrain, keep, hold, capture, seize, entangle*
eye		*v.*	**watch, view, observe, scrutinize, inspect, look at, examine, regard** The new students eyed their classmates carefully.	*ignore, neglect, overlook, disregard*

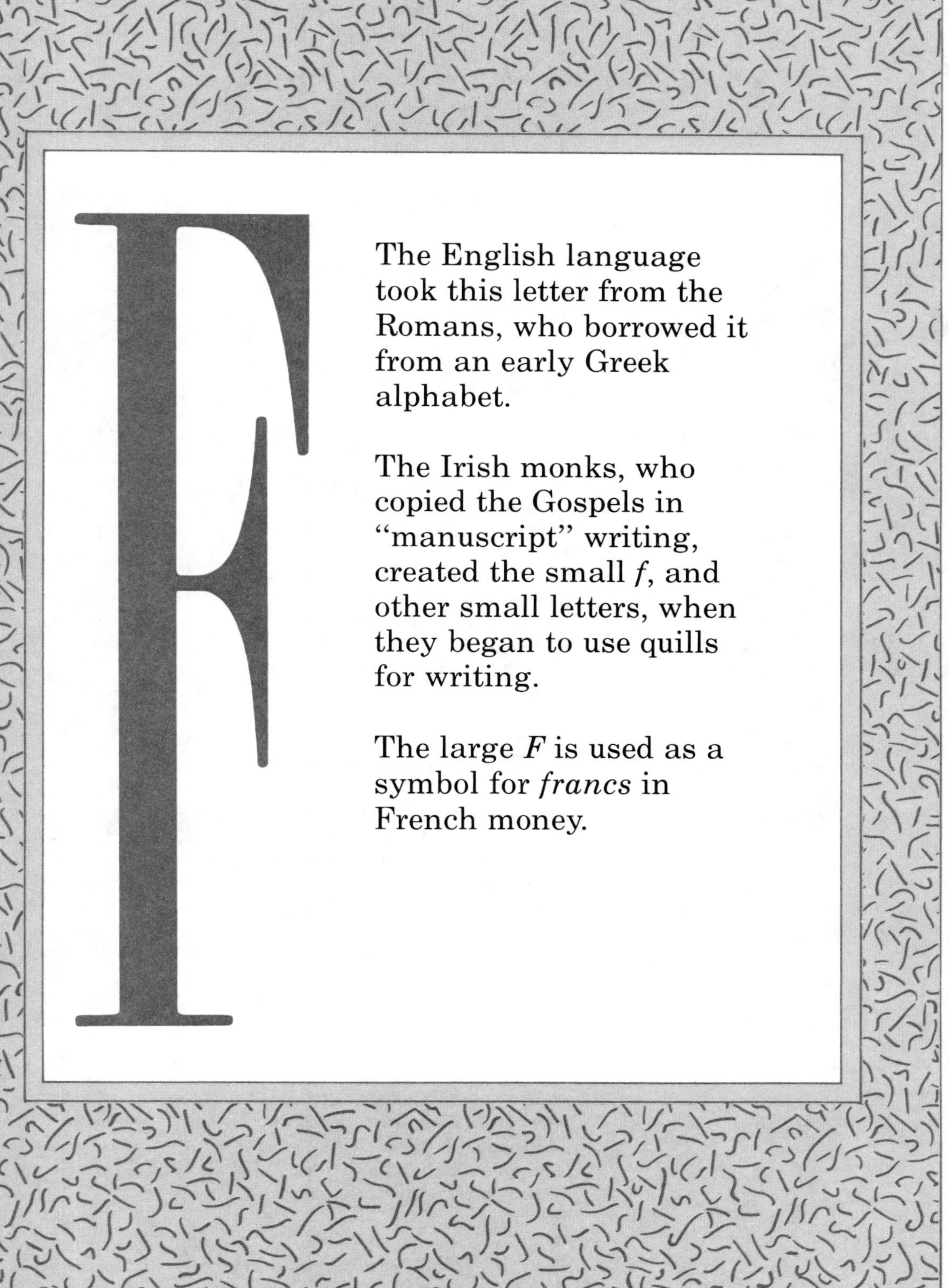

The English language took this letter from the Romans, who borrowed it from an early Greek alphabet.

The Irish monks, who copied the Gospels in "manuscript" writing, created the small *f*, and other small letters, when they began to use quills for writing.

The large *F* is used as a symbol for *francs* in French money.

Word			Synonyms	Antonyms
fabric		*n.*	**cloth, textile, material** Synthetic fabrics are popular because of their easy care.	
fabulous	1.	*adj.*	**incredible, astonishing, amazing, astounding, marvellous, wonderful, extraordinary** A trip to Tibet would be a fabulous adventure.	1. *simple, usual, normal, routine*
	2.	*adj.*	**mythical, legendary, fictitious** The unicorn is a fabulous animal.	2. *historical, real, authentic, genuine*
façade		*n.*	**front, exterior, appearance** Many old buildings have ornate façades.	
face	1.	*n.*	**countenance, visage, expression** Christine protected her face from the sun.	
	2.	*n.*	**outside, front, surface, exterior, façade** The face of the building was covered with marble from Italy.	2. *interior, inside, rear, back*
	3.	*v.*	**front, be opposite to, be turned toward** The window faced the lake so we were able to watch the boat race.	
	4.	*v.*	**brave, defy, meet, confront, encounter** The white water canoeists will face many dangers.	4. *avoid, withdraw evade*
facet		*n.*	**aspect, face, side** Cut diamonds have many facets.	
facility	1.	*n.*	**dexterity, adroitness, ease, skill, ability, skilfulness, capability** The gymnast shows great facility on the parallel bars.	1. *awkwardness, difficulty, inability*
	2.	*n.*	**equipment, tools, buildings, machinery** The school has excellent sports facilities.	
	3.	*n.*	**agency, bureau, company, office, establishment** In case of an emergency call the nearest medical facility.	
facsimile		*n.*	**duplicate, copy, reproduction, imitation, likeness** The contest directions said to send two box tops or their facsimiles with the entry.	*original*
fact	1.	*n.*	**certainty, truth, reality, actuality** Aging is a fact of life.	1. *fancy, fiction, imagination*

	2.	*n.*	**event, detail, action, act, episode, occurrence, circumstance** During the trial many facts were revealed to the jury.	2. *error, lie, falsehood, untruth*
factor		*n.*	**part, portion, component, determinant, element, condition** Many factors contribute to the success of a business.	*whole*
factual		*adj.*	**exact, precise, accurate, true** Factual reports of the accident will be required.	*inaccurate, untrue, contrived*
faculty	1.	*n.*	**ability, skill, talent, gift, capacity, genius, flair** Do you have a faculty for remembering names?	1. *inability, weakness, failing*
	2.	*n.*	**teaching staff, teachers, department** Dr. Ho is a member of the Dental faculty of the university.	
fad		*n.*	**craze, rage, whim** Skateboards were a fad last summer.	*tradition, custom, habit*
fade	1.	*v.*	**droop, wither, lose colour** The flowers faded quickly in the intense heat.	1. *flourish, revive, endure, last*
	2.	*v.*	**grow faint, die away** The picture faded from the television screen.	2. *become distinct, become clear, become sharp*
fail	1.	*v.*	**be unsuccessful, miss, flunk** Many pupils failed the college entrance examination. *n.* The failure upset their future plans.	1. *pass, succeed*
	2.	*v.*	**decline, deteriorate, weaken** Grandmother's health failed gradually after her fall.	2. *improve, strengthen*
faint	1.	*v.*	**collapse, black out, swoon** During the rock concert, many fans fainted in the crowded stadium. *n.* Sue crumpled in a faint when she heard the bad news.	
	2.	*adj.*	**indistinct, vague, unclear, faded, dim** The faint outline of a ship could be seen on the horizon.	2. *sharp, clear, distinct*
	3.	*adj.*	**weak, feeble, faltering, languid, frail** The survivor spoke in a faint whisper.	3. *strong, hearty, energetic, sturdy*

Word	No.	Part	Synonyms and Example	Antonyms
fair	1.	*adj.*	**beautiful, pleasing, attractive, pretty, lovely** Helen of Troy was said to be the fairest woman in Greece.	1. *unattractive, ugly, displeasing*
	2.	*adj.*	**clear, sunny, dry, pleasant, fine** It will be a fair day for the hike on Saturday.	2. *wet, cloudy, showery, inclement, dark, stormy*
	3.	*adj.*	**just, impartial, honest, proper** The judge's fair decision pleased everyone.	3. *unfair, dishonest, partial*
	4.	*adj.*	**passable, tolerable, reasonable** Your writing is fair but can be improved with practice.	
faith		*n.*	**belief, trust, confidence, reliance** Have faith in your ability to overcome this difficulty.	*doubt, disbelief, distrust, suspicion*
faithful		*adj.*	**true, loyal, dependable, constant, honest, sure, devoted, reliable** A faithful employee is a great asset to a company.	*fickle, unreliable, disloyal, false, unfaithful, faithless, undependable*
fake	1.	*n.*	**fraud, phony, imitation, counterfeit** Experts proved that the famous painting was a fake.	1. *original*
	2.	*v.*	**counterfeit, falsify, forge, simulate** The spy faked his papers.	
	3.	*adj.*	**phony, counterfeit, bogus, false** The fake money taken by the police will be destroyed.	3. *authentic, real, genuine*
fall	1.	*n.*	**tumble, spill, collapse** Lee suffered a bad fall while skiing. *v.* Ian slipped and fell on the icy road.	
	2.	*v.*	**lessen, decline, drop, go down, sink, plunge** Stock prices fell when war broke out in the Middle East. *n.* We were happy to hear about the fall in the price of airplane tickets.	2. *climb, ascend, rise, increase*
	3.	*v.*	**happen, occur, take place** On what day does your birthday fall this year?	
fallacy		*n.*	**error, untruth, blunder, misconception** "There are many fallacies in that argument," said the opposing debater.	*truth, verity*

fallow		*adj.*	**untilled, unused, uncultivated, unsowed, unseeded, unplanted** Fields need to lie fallow every few years to remain fertile.	*tilled, used, cultivated, seeded, planted*
false	1.	*adj.*	**untrue, incorrect, erroneous, mistaken, wrong** They had a false notion of the cause of the accident.	**1.** *right, true, correct, accurate, exact*
	2.	*adj.*	**bogus, counterfeit, fake, phony, imitation** A false jewel was substituted for the real one.	**2.** *authentic, real, genuine, natural, actual*
	3.	*adj.*	**disloyal, unfaithful, faithless** When she lost all her money her many false friends deserted her.	**3.** *loyal, faithful, true, sincere*
falter	1.	*v.*	**totter, waver, stagger, stumble** The boxer's punch caused his opponent to falter and fall to the floor.	
	2.	*v.*	**stutter, stammer, hesitate** The shy child faltered as she tried to ask for help.	
fame		*n.*	**distinction, renown, notoriety, glory, reputation, prestige** Madame Curie achieved fame as the discoverer of radium.	*discredit, shame, disrepute*
familiar	1.	*adj.*	**well-known, customary, usual** It was nice to see my friend's familiar face again when I returned.	**1.** *unfamiliar, strange, unknown, new*
	2.	*adj.*	**friendly, informal, close** The group members became quite familiar after working together on the project.	**2.** *formal, aloof*
famished		*adj.*	**starving, hungry** The lost child was famished after three days without food.	*well-fed, filled, satisfied*
famous		*adj.*	**well-known, renowned, celebrated, distinguished** Ann Murray is a famous Canadian singer.	*unknown, obscure*
fan	1.	*n.*	**follower, supporter, devotee, enthusiast** Fans cheered wildly during the team's victory parade.	**1.** *non-supporter, opponent*
	2.	*v.*	**stir up, incite, arouse** The union leader's speech fanned the workers' anger.	**2.** *douse, dampen, discourage, kill*

Word			Synonyms / Example	Antonyms
fanatic		*n.*	**zealot, devotee, enthusiast** Fanatics can speak with intense emotion about their beliefs. *adj.* Everyone avoids them because of their fanatical beliefs.	
fancy	**1.**	*n.*	**fantasy, imagination, illusion** Are flying saucers objects of fancy?	**1.** *reality, fact*
	2.	*n.*	**liking, fondness, preference** Nancy took a fancy to the white poodle in the kennels.	**2.** *dislike, distaste, aversion*
	3.	*v.*	**imagine, picture** Fancy that! What a story!	
	4.	*adj.*	**decorated, fussy, ornamental, elaborate** Sue Ling wore a fancy dress to the party.	**4.** *plain, unadorned, simple, ordinary*
fantastic		*adj.*	**fanciful, weird, strange, queer, imaginary, wonderful, peculiar, whimsical** I wonder what fantastic creatures live on other planets?	*common, ordinary, regular*
fantasy		*n.*	**imagination, illusion, fiction, reverie, dreams** Walt Disney's cartoons appeal to our fantasies.	*reality, actuality*
far		*adj.*	**distant, remote** Our new home is very far from town.	*near, close, handy*
farewell	**1.**	*n.*	**good-bye, adieu** The astronaut waved farewell before boarding the spacecraft.	**1.** *hello*
	2.	*adj.*	**parting, last** The actor's farewell performance was well attended.	**2.** *initial, first, opening*
fascinate		*v.*	**charm, enchant, delight** The magician's tricks fascinated the audience. *adj.* Watching the rope trick was a fascinating experience.	*disgust, repel, displease, bore*
fashion	**1.**	*n.*	**manner, way** Mario told the same story in a different fashion.	
	2.	*n.*	**style, trend** Movie stars often dress in the latest fashions. *adj.* They like to wear fashionable clothes. *adv.* They dress fashionably.	

	3.	*v.*	**shape, make, mould, form, create, design** The artist fashioned the statue out of clay.	
fast	1.	*adj.*	**quick, rapid, fleet, swift, speedy** Ben was a fast runner.	***1.*** *slow, sluggish*
	2.	*adv.*	**securely, tightly, firmly** Be sure the boat is tied fast to the dock. *adj.* The police had a fast hold of the suspect.	***2.*** *loosely, insecurely*
	3.	*adv.*	**thoroughly, soundly, completely, fully** Jay was still fast asleep when the alarm sounded.	***3.*** *hardy, barely*
fasten		*v.*	**tie, connect, link, attach, hook, bind, clasp, clamp** The sailor fastened the yacht to its mooring. *n.* "I can do up the fasteners myself," said Billy.	*untie, disconnect*
fat		*adj.*	**stout, plump, portly, obese, fleshy** The fat pigs were shipped to the market.	*skinny, lean, thin, slim, slight*
fatal		*adj.*	**deadly, killing, mortal, lethal** Many fatal accidents are caused by drunk drivers. *n.* With care and courtesy, many traffic fatalities could be prevented.	*harmless, slight*
fate		*n.*	**destiny, lot, fortune, doom** Captain Cook met his fate on Cebu island. *v.* Captain Cook seemed fated to die there.	
fatigue	1.	*n.*	**weariness, tiredness, exhaustion** The mountain climber was suffering from fatigue and lack of oxygen.	***1.*** *vim, vigour, energy*
	2.	*v.*	**tire, exhaust, weary** The difficult climb in heavy snow fatigued him.	***2.*** *revive, renew, strengthen*
fault	1.	*n.*	**mistake, error, slip, blunder** Several faults in the skater's performance cost her the medal.	
	2.	*n.*	**failing, weakness, disadvantage, defect, flaw** Bill's one fault was that he was always late.	***2.*** *strength, advantage, virtue*

Word	#	Part of speech	Synonyms and example	Antonyms
faultless		*adj.*	**perfect, ideal, correct, accurate, flawless** The concert pianist gave a faultless performance.	*imperfect, faulty, defective*
faulty		*adj.*	**imperfect, unsatisfactory, defective, flawed, blemished** Faulty brakes in a car can cause an accident.	*satisfactory, correct, perfect, faultless*
favour (also spelled favor)	1.	*n.*	**kindness, service, courtesy** Can you please do me a favour and drive me to school tomorrow?	1. *rebuff, unkindness, discourtesy*
	2.	*v.*	**prefer, like, approve, sanction, choose, lean toward, be partial to, back, promote** Which candidate do you favour?	2. *dislike, mistreat, deny, refuse*
favourable (also spelled favorable)	1.	*adj.*	**approving, positive, kind, kindly, friendly** The principal speaks of you in a favourable way. *adv.* Our proposal was favourably received by the committee.	1. *disapproving, negative, unkindly, unfriendly*
	2.	*adj.*	**helpful, useful, beneficial** Captains of the sailing ships always hoped for favourable winds.	2. *harmful, unfavourable*
	3.	*adj.*	**promising, hopeful** The weather looks favourable for the picnic tomorrow.	3. *threatening*
favourite (also spelled favorite)	1.	*n.*	**choice, pet, preferred one, best-liked one** The smallest puppy was the children's favourite.	1. *least-liked one*
	2.	*adj.*	**choice, special, best-liked, preferred** Yun's favourite dessert is chocolate cake.	2. *least-liked*
fear		*n.*	**fright, dread, terror, horror, alarm, anxiety** We tried to overcome his fear of the dark. *adj.* Sam is fearful of the dark. *v.* Children often fear the dark.	*bravery, boldness, courage*
fearless		*adj.*	**bold, brave, courageous, daring, gallant, heroic** The crowd cheered their fearless leader. *adv.* The leader told the people to face the enemy fearlessly.	*timid, scared, cowardly, fearful, afraid, frightened*

Entry	#	POS	Synonyms / Example	Antonyms
feast	1.	*n.*	**banquet, festival** There was a grand feast to celebrate the team's victory.	1. *famine, fast*
	2.	*v.*	**dine, gorge** The team feasted on the restaurant's fine food.	2. *starve, fast*
feat		*n.*	**achievement, deed, act, exploit, accomplishment, attainment** It was quite a feat for Marilyn Bell to swim across Lake Ontario.	
feature	1.	*n.*	**highlight, attraction, main item, prominent part** What is the feature at the sports show? *v.* Which soloist will be featured at the concert?	
	2.	*n.*	**characteristic, point, trait, peculiarity** His fiery red hair is his most distinctive feature.	
fee		*n.*	**remuneration, pay, salary, charge, compensation** How much is the lawyer's fee?	*donation*
feeble		*adj.*	**weak, puny, frail, ailing** The refugees were feeble from hunger. *adv.* The trapped boy cried feebly for help.	*healthy, strong, firm, hearty, robust*
feel	1.	*n.*	**touch, sensation, texture** I like the feel of materials like velour and velvet.	
	2.	*v.*	**touch, handle** The doctor gently felt my twisted ankle.	
	3.	*v.*	**grope, make one's way** Di felt her way in the darkness to find the light switch.	
	4.	*v.*	**seem, appear** The crocuses make it feel like spring has arrived.	
	5.	*v.*	**sense, be aware of, experience** I feel cold with the window open.	5. *be unaware of*
	6.	*v.*	**think, believe, consider** How do you feel about the new president?	
feeling	1.	*n.*	**sensation** I get a funny feeling in my stomach when I fly.	

	2.	*n.*	**emotion, reaction** Cat hurt Andy's feelings with her harsh remarks.	
	3.	*n.*	**opinion, belief, thought** What are your feelings about freedom of the press?	
feign		*v.*	**pretend, invent, simulate, fabricate, sham, falsify, affect, imitate, assume** The student feigned illness to avoid the examination.	
fence		*n.*	**barrier, railing, wall** The horse jumped over the fence and galloped off.	
ferocious		*adj.*	**fierce, savage, wild, ruthless, brutal, cruel, merciless, barbarous, violent** The tiger can be a ferocious beast when it is attacked. *n.* Its ferocity is terrifying. *adv.* The tiger charged ferociously at the hunter.	*mild, meek, gentle, tame, delicate*
fertile		*adj.*	**fruitful, productive, rich** Land along the Nile River is fertile. *v.* The farmer fertilized the land to produce better crops.	*barren, useless, unproductive*
fervent		*adj.*	**eager, ardent, zealous, devoted, passionate** Fervent prayers were offered to save the endangered town. *adv.* The people prayed fervently for help.	*indifferent, apathetic, dispassionate*
festival		*n.*	**holiday, fete, celebration** The Christmas festival is a busy time of the year.	
festive		*adj.*	**gay, merry, happy, joyful, jolly** Everyone was in a festive mood on New Year's Eve.	*sad, mournful, tragic*
fetch		*v.*	**bring, get, obtain, carry** Fetch the book from the library, please.	
feud		*n.*	**quarrel, row, dispute, strife** The feud between the families lasted for generations. *v.* The two families feuded for many years.	*peace, harmony*

Word			Synonyms	Antonyms
few		*adj.*	**not many, scarcely any** Few people attended the meeting.	*many, numerous, innumerable*
fib	**1.**	*n.*	**lie, falsehood, untruth, fiction** Don't believe those fibs about how much money he makes.	**1.** *truth*
	2.	*v.*	**lie** They fibbed about not being involved in the prank.	**2.** *tell the truth*
fidget		*v.*	**squirm, wriggle, twitch** The applicant fidgeted nervously during the interview.	*relax, sit still*
fidgety		*adj.*	**restless, uneasy, jittery, nervous** The storm has made the class fidgety today.	*calm, quiet, relaxed*
fierce	**1.**	*adj.*	**wild, savage, furious, cruel, ferocious, brutal** The gangs fought a fierce battle for the territory. *adv.* They fought fiercely for weeks.	**1.** *tame, gentle, mild, calm, peaceful*
	2.	*adj.*	**strong, powerful, intense, extreme** Many travellers were marooned in the fierce storm yesterday.	**2.** *weak, faint*
fiery	**1.**	*adj.*	**fierce, ardent, passionate, unrestrained, impetuous** A fiery debate took place between the two candidates running for mayor.	**1.** *indifferent, mild, passionless*
	2.	*adj.*	**hot, blazing, glowing** No one escaped from the fiery inferno.	
fight		*n.*	**struggle, battle, combat, contest, conflict, quarrel, brawl** Which boxer won the fight? *v.* The soldiers fought bravely till the end.	*peace, harmony*
figure	**1.**	*n.*	**outline, shape, form, design, pattern** The skater traced the figure eight on the ice.	
	2.	*n.*	**cost, amount, value, sum** The figure asked for the painting was beyond our means.	
	3.	*v.*	**compute, calculate, solve** Can you figure out the answer to the math problem?	

file 1. *n.* **list, dossier, record, catalogue, inventory**
Keep the information in the files.
2. *n.* **row, queue, string, line**
The soldiers marched in single file.
3. *v.* **classify, index, arrange, store, categorize, list**
The clerk filed the documents.
3. disorder, disarrange, disorganize
4. *v.* **scrape, rub down, pulverize, grind, smooth**
Manicurists file nails with emery boards.

fill 1. *v.* **pack, stuff, pour in, put in**
Have you filled the suitcase?
n. The lemon pie filling is delicious.
1. empty, drain, draw off
2. *v.* **occupy, serve**
Bob filled the position of secretary for the club.
2. leave, vacate

filter 1. *v.* **seep, penetrate, ooze, trickle, permeate, soak through, leak, drain**
Water from the spring run-off filtered through the rocks.
2. *v.* **clean, purify, strain, sieve, filtrate, separate**
Water is filtered to make it safe for drinking.
2. pollute, putrefy, contaminate

filth *n.* **dirt, impurity, contamination, pollution, corruption, uncleanness, foul matter**
We were disgusted with the filth in the cabin.
adj. Everyone helped to clean up the filthy mess.
cleanliness, spotlessness, purity

filtrate *v.* **separate, sterilize, pass through, filter**
Water is filtrated to make it pure.
n. The filtration is done in a plant.

final *adj.* **last, concluding, ultimate**
The final game of the basketball season will be played tomorrow.
first, initial, opening

finance 1. *n.* **money matters, banking, investment**
Lim is trained in finance.
adj. She handles the financial matters of the company.

	2.	*v.*	**fund, pay for, provide funds for, underwrite, subsidize, endow** Many students finance their education by working during holidays.	
find	1.	*n.*	**discovery** Tutankhamen's tomb was a real find.	1. *loss*
	2.	*v.*	**discover, detect, recover** Mel found her lost ring in her glove.	2. *lose, mislay, misplace*
fine	1.	*n.*	**penalty, forfeit** The driver received a fine for speeding. *v.* He was fined fifty dollars.	1. *reward, award*
	2.	*adj.*	**small, delicate, thin** Watchmakers are required to do fine work.	2. *coarse, thick, crude*
	3.	*adj.*	**very good, excellent, superior** Ken has proved to be a fine pupil.	3. *poor*
	4.	*adj.*	**clear, bright, sunny, pleasant** They had a fine day for their wedding.	4. *dull, dreary, dark, cloudy*
	5.	*adj.*	**attractive, handsome** Isn't this a fine looking car?	5. *unattractive, ugly*
finish	1.	*n.*	**end, completion, close, conclusion** He fought gamely to the finish of the match.	1. *beginning, start, commencement, opening*
	2.	*n.*	**surface, exterior, coating, veneer** This stain gives furniture a shiny finish.	
	3.	*v.*	**end, complete, conclude** Haven't you finished the essay yet?	3. *start, begin, commence*
fire	1.	*n.*	**flame, blaze, conflagration, holocaust** Forest fires endanger wildlife.	
	2.	*n.*	**verve, dash, sparkle, vim, enthusiasm** "Show more fire when you deliver that speech," urged the advisor.	2. *dullness, boredom, weariness*
	3.	*v.*	**kindle, ignite, inflame, light, set burning** The president's speech fired everyone's enthusiasm for the cause.	3. *extinguish, quench, smother*
	4.	*v.*	**shoot** The police recruits fired at the target.	
firm	1.	*n.*	**business establishment, company, organization, concern** Biz works for a publishing firm.	

	2.	*adj.*	**solid, sturdy, hard, tight** The opponents shook hands with a firm grip.	**2.** *weak, shaky*
	3.	*adj.*	**immovable, secure, rigid, steady** Make sure the tent poles are firm. *adv.* We hammered them in firmly.	**3.** *wobbly, unstable, unsteady*
	4.	*adv.*	**determined, decided, resolved, fearless, unshaken** Anton stood firm in his resolve not to reveal the secret.	
first	1.	*adj.*	**initial, original, earliest, opening, introductory, inaugural** Marconi received the first transatlantic wireless message from St. John's, Newfoundland.	**1.** *last, final, ultimate*
	2.	*adj.*	**foremost, chief, prime, principal, highest, leading, primary** Personal safety is our first concern on this expedition.	**2.** *secondary, lesser*
fishy		*adj.*	**suspicious, doubtful, strange, misleading, peculiar** The scheme to invest in that gold mine seems fishy.	*trustworthy, aboveboard, honest*
fit	1.	*n.*	**size, shape** "Your suit is a good fit," she remarked.	
	2.	*v.*	**agree, match, coincide** The views of the partners fitted well.	
	3.	*adj.*	**suitable, appropriate, apt, proper, right, becoming** This movie has too much violence in it and is not fit for children.	**3.** *inappropriate, improper, unfit*
	4.	*adj.*	**healthy, strong** It took Matt a long time to become fit after the accident.	**4.** *unhealthy, unfit, weak*
fitness		*n.*	**health, vigour, strength** Dad is a fitness enthusiast and jogs daily.	*weakness*
fix	1.	*v.*	**adjust, repair, correct, mend** Jan fixed the television set.	**1.** *damage, spoil, ruin*
	2.	*v.*	**settle on, decide, determine, establish** We will fix the date of the next meeting now.	
	3.	*v.*	**connect, fasten, secure, attach** The light was fixed to the ceiling.	**3.** *detach, loosen*

Word	No.	Part of speech	Synonyms and example	Antonyms
flabbergasted		*adj.*	**astonished, amazed, dumbfounded** We were flabbergasted when we saw our test results.	*unmoved*
flamboyant		*adj.*	**showy, flashy, ornate, gaudy, extravagant** Flamboyant colours were used for the costumes in the parade.	*drab, dull, sombre, bland, conservative*
flame	1.	*n.*	**blaze, fire, flare** Flames shot out from the burning house.	
	2.	*v.*	**burn, blaze, flare** The logs flamed brightly in the fireplace.	
flare	1.	*n.*	**flash, spark, flame** Flares warned oncoming motorists of the accident.	
	2.	*v.*	**flash, blaze, burn, glow** Warning lights flared in the dark.	
	3.	*v.*	**erupt, explode, go off, burst, blow up, break out** Fighting flared up suddenly at the border.	**3.** *remain dormant, stay quiet*
flash		*v.*	**flare, glitter, twinkle, sparkle, shimmer, glow** The meteor flashed across the sky. *n.* A sudden flash of lightning startled us. *adj.* The flashing lights on the police car warned us of the detour.	
flashy	1.	*adj.*	**showy, gaudy, loud, garish** The actor always wears flashy clothes. *adv.* He dresses flashily.	**1.** *simple, quiet, plain, conservative*
	2.	*adj.*	**glittering, shiny, dazzling** The fireworks exploded in flashy patterns across the sky.	
flat	1.	*adj.*	**level, even, horizontal** The prairies are flat stretches of land.	**1.** *uneven, hilly, mountainous, rolling*
	2.	*adj.*	**tasteless, dull, unpleasing, stale** The food in the hospital was flat.	**2.** *sharp, bubbling, tasty, sparkling*
flaunt		*v.*	**display, boast, parade** Some people flaunt their wealth in a vulgar way.	*conceal, hide, be modest*

Word		Part	Synonyms / Example	Antonyms
flavour (also spelled flavor)	1.	*n.*	**taste, savour, tang, relish, seasoning** Barbecued meat has a unique flavour. *v.* Pin flavoured the meat with lots of spices.	1. *flatness*
	2.	*n.*	**character, mark, quality, feeling, characteristic, trait, feature, attribute, distinction, identity** His stories all have the flavour of the Orient.	2. *generality*
flaw		*n.*	**defect, imperfection, fault, blemish** Some pieces of pottery are on sale because they have flaws. *adj.* The flawed pieces have been reduced in price.	*perfection*
flawless		*adj.*	**perfect, sound, faultless** The skater gave a flawless performance to win the medal.	*imperfect, damaged, defective, flawed*
flee		*v.*	**run away, take flight** The wanted man fled from the police.	*remain, stay, stand firm*
fleece	1.	*n.*	**hair, wool** High prices are paid for quality fleece from sheep.	
	2.	*v.*	**strip, rob, swindle, steal, deceive** Swindlers fleece innocent people of their money.	2. *reimburse, repay, pay, pay back*
fleecy		*adj.*	**downy, fuzzy, fluffy, woolly, soft, feathery** Yang snuggled under his fleecy wool blanket.	*hard, rough, coarse*
flex		*v.*	**bend, tighten, contract** Trevor flexed his leg muscles before he made the jump.	*relax*
flexible	1.	*adj.*	**pliable, supple, limber, springy** An athlete must have flexible muscles.	1. *rigid, unbending, inflexible, stiff*
	2.	*adj.*	**adaptable, variable, adjustable** We keep flexible working hours in this office. *n.* There is a certain amount of flexibility in the training program.	2. *inflexible, rigid, constrained*

Word		Synonyms and example	Antonyms
flicker	*v.*	**waver, shimmer, quiver, flare, fluctuate** The candle flickered and finally went out. *adj.* The flickering light cast eerie shadows in the room.	*remain steady*
flimsy	1. *adj.*	**sheer, thin, gauzy, fragile** The flimsy chiffon dress was ruined in the wash.	**1.** *thick, heavy, substantial, weighty, sturdy*
	2. *adj.*	**poor, weak, feeble** That's a flimsy excuse for not helping your friend.	**2.** *real, good, sound*
fling	*v.*	**throw, heave, toss, pitch, hurl, sling** The pitcher flung the ball to third base.	*catch, receive*
flip	1. *n.*	**flick, toss, tap, throw, snap** He removed the crumb from his jacket with a flip of his finger.	
	2. *v.*	**thumb, turn over, turn, leaf** She flipped through the book to find her favourite story.	
flippant	*adj.*	**impudent, rude, smart, saucy, pert, bold, forward, impertinent, disrespectful** Pam was told to leave for disrupting the class with her flippant remarks.	*polite, courteous, shy, well-mannered*
float	*v.*	**drift, hover, glide, sail** The canoe floated on the calm lake.	*sink, settle*
flock	1. *n.*	**group, herd, brood, pack, swarm, set, lot, collection, company, throng, gathering** A flock of sheep was grazing peacefully on the hillside.	
	2. *v.*	**troop, congregate, go in great numbers, crowd** People flock to the parks and pools on hot days.	
flop	*v.*	**tumble, slump, drop, fall, topple** The exhausted runner flopped to the ground.	*rise, ascend, climb*
flounder	*v.*	**struggle, toss, wallow, blunder, grope, fumble, stagger** The child floundered in the water before being rescued.	

Word	No.	Part	Synonyms and examples	Antonyms
flourish	1.	*v.*	**thrive, prosper, succeed** His business is really flourishing this year.	**1.** *lessen, decline, wither, fade, fail*
	2.	*v.*	**wave, twirl, brandish, flaunt** The drum major flourished her baton before marching on.	
flout		*v.*	**mock, ridicule, deride, scorn, taunt, sneer** He was punished for flouting the school rules.	*respect, revere, honour, venerate*
flow	1.	*n.*	**stream, course** The flow of water over the dam was constant.	
	2.	*v.*	**glide, stream, gush, move, run, pass** The St. Lawrence River flows eastward to the Atlantic Ocean.	**2.** *stagnate, stop*
fluid		*n.*	**liquid, solution** Water is a fluid. *adj.* This patient is on a fluid diet.	*solid*
flurry	1.	*n.*	**gust, light snowfall, squall** The sudden flurry of snow soon turned the ground white.	
	2.	*n.*	**fluster, disturbance, agitation, panic, alarm** There was a flurry of activity in the school before the science fair. *v.* The students were flurried when they realized they were running out of time to complete their projects.	**2.** *quiet, calm*
fluster	1.	*n.*	**turmoil, flurry, flutter, confusion, ferment** What a fluster when the band did not arrive for the party.	**1.** *quiet, calm*
	2.	*v.*	**confuse, agitate, excite, upset, bother, disturb, startle** The arrival of unexpected guests flustered us. *adj.* Sharon became flustered during the interview.	**2.** *calm, quieten*
fly	1.	*v.*	**soar, wing, glide** Great flocks of birds fly south every fall.	**1.** *alight, settle*
	2.	*v.*	**flutter, flap, float, wave** The flag flew above the Parliament Buildings.	

Word		Part	Synonyms	Antonyms
focus	1.	*n.*	**centre, focal point, core, heart, nucleus, hub, middle** The new baby was the focus of everyone's attention.	1. *periphery, border, outside, perimeter*
	2.	*v.*	**direct, centre, aim, fix, concentrate** Focus the camera on the leader of the parade.	
foe		*n.*	**enemy, rival, adversary, opponent** Sometimes foes make peace and become friends.	*friend, companion, ally, comrade, associate, helper*
foggy	1.	*adj.*	**misty, murky, hazy, clouded** The Atlantic Provinces often get foggy weather.	1. *fine, bright, clear, sunny*
	2.	*adj.*	**confused, puzzled, unclear, vague, obscure, blurred** Pedro has only a foggy idea of how to get to the beach.	2. *clear, lucid, thorough, accurate*
foil		*v.*	**frustrate, balk, circumvent, disappoint, hinder, thwart, check** Anti-missile devices foiled the enemy attack.	*aid, assist, help, oblige, expedite*
folk	1.	*n.*	**people, persons, individuals** It is good for older folk to keep busy and active.	
	2.	*n.*	**relatives, kin, family** Karl's folks are all coming to the wedding.	
follow	1.	*v.*	**go after, chase, pursue, track** The sheriff followed the cattle rustlers into the hills.	1. *lead, direct, guide*
	2.	*v.*	**come after, go behind** "H" follows "G" in our alphabet.	2. *precede, come before*
	3.	*v.*	**obey, adhere to, observe** Students have to follow the rules of the school.	3. *ignore, disregard, neglect*
	4.	*v.*	**imitate, copy, mimic** The children followed the dance instructor's steps.	
	5.	*v.*	**understand** I cannot follow what you're saying.	
	6.	*v.*	**trace, observe, track** The scientists followed the orbit of the space shuttle.	6. *lose track of*
follower		*n.*	**disciple, supporter, admirer** Mahatma Gandhi had many followers.	*leader*

Word			Synonyms	Antonyms
folly		*n.*	**silliness, madness, absurdity, rashness, foolishness** It is folly to go canoeing during a violent storm.	*wisdom, good sense good judgment, prudence*
fond		*adj.*	**attached to, loving, affectionate, kind, sentimental** Pat was very fond of her cousin Pierre. *adv.* She thought of him fondly.	*distant, cold, disinterested, unconcerned*
fondness		*n.*	**affection, concern, liking, tenderness, preference** Pat had a fondness for Pierre.	*dislike, aversion*
food		*n.*	**provisions, rations, fare, nourishment, edibles** The purchase of food takes a big portion of a family's income.	
fool	**1.**	*n.*	**dunce, idiot, simpleton, nitwit, ninny, clown** Hugo made a fool of himself at the party.	**1.** *wise person, genius, sage*
	2.	*v.*	**play, joke, clown** Two boys were fooling around in the library.	**2.** *to be serious*
	3.	*v.*	**trick, deceive, dupe, outwit** You didn't fool me with that disguise!	**3.** *be truthful, be straightforward*
foolhardy		*adj.*	**reckless, thoughtless, careless, foolish, rash** Jumping from the top of the tower was a foolhardy stunt.	*cautious, careful, thoughtful, wary, prudent*
foolish		*adj.*	**silly, crazy, absurd, ridiculous, daft, simple, brainless** It is foolish to pay so much for those boots. *n.* You might regret your foolishness.	*wise, thoughtful, intelligent, clever*
forbid		*v.*	**prohibit, prevent, refuse** Many restaurants forbid smoking in some areas.	*allow, approve, permit, let*
force	**1.**	*n.*	**power, strength, might, energy** The force of the blow knocked the man down.	**1.** *weakness, feebleness*
	2.	*n.*	**troops, company, body, group, organization, unit** That factory's work force numbers one hundred.	

	3.	*v.*	**require, make, compel, drive, oblige** Bad weather forced us to postpone the game.	
forecast	1.	*n.*	**prediction, prophecy, outlook** The weather forecast was accurate.	
	2.	*v.*	**predict, foretell, anticipate** The company forecasts great sales for next year.	
foregoing		*adj.*	**previous, preceding, former** The foregoing announcement was previously recorded for this broadcast.	*following, succeeding*
foreign		*adj.*	**strange, unfamiliar, unknown** Would you enjoy a trip to a foreign land?	*native, known, domestic*
foreigner		*n.*	**stranger, alien, outsider** Canadians are foreigners in other countries.	*native*
forever	1.	*adv.*	**permanently, everlastingly, eternally, ever, endlessly, forevermore, lastingly, perpetually, always** Atlantis is a city said to be lost forever.	**1.** *temporarily, now, at the moment, at present, for a time*
	2.	*adv.*	**continuously, ceaselessly, regularly, constantly** This child is forever whining for attention.	**2.** *sporadically, erratically, irregularly*
forfeit		*v.*	**give up, hand over, give over, relinquish, abandon, lose** The team forfeited the game because they were late. *n.* What a forfeit to pay for tardiness!	*maintain, keep, preserve*
forget		*v.*	**overlook, disregard** Nan was sad when everyone forgot her birthday.	*remember, recall, recollect*
forgive		*v.*	**pardon, excuse, overlook** "Please forgive me, I won't cheat again," he said. *adj.* The forgiving teacher let him off with just a detention. *n.* She showed him forgiveness.	*accuse, blame, condemn*

forlorn		*adj.*	**dejected, woebegone, forgotten, neglected, lonely, downcast, forsaken, deserted, unhappy, miserable, wretched** We felt sorry for the forlorn child weeping in the corner.	*merry, happy, content, satisfied, cheerful*
form	1.	*n.*	**shape, figure, outline** A strange form showed against the lighted window.	
	2.	*v.*	**make, shape, mould, design, construct, plan** The class formed many interesting objects with clay.	**2.** *destroy, ruin, wreck*
format		*n.*	**arrangement, mold, makeup, form, construction, pattern** Most television talk shows have a similar format.	
former		*adj.*	**previous, preceding, prior, earlier** Who was your former teacher?	*succeeding, following*
formula		*n.*	**rule, principle, recipe, prescription** The formula for the new vaccine is still a secret.	
formulate		*v.*	**devise, concoct, frame, make, produce, express, form, prepare** Scientists formulated plans for the peaceful uses of nuclear energy.	*destroy, blot out, erase*
forsake		*v.*	**abandon, desert, leave, disown, abdicate, give up** The guard had forsaken his post outside the prison.	*keep, cling to, maintain*
forsaken		*adj.*	**abandoned, forlorn, deserted, neglected, desolate** The forsaken puppies were found by the children.	*cared for, cherished, remembered*
fortunate		*adj.*	**lucky, blessed, timely** It was fortunate they were away when their house blew up. *adv.* Fortunately no one was killed or injured.	*unlucky, unfortunate*
fortune	1.	*n.*	**treasure, wealth, riches, prosperity** She made a fortune on the stock market.	**1.** *poverty, penury*

	2.	*n.*	**luck, chance, lot, fate** Her success was the result of skill and good fortune.	2. *misfortune*
foul	1.	*adj.*	**dirty, filthy, unclean, nasty, polluted, impure** Foul air can lead to acid rain over our country. *v.* The oil spill fouled the water.	1. *clean, sweet, pure*
	2.	*adj.*	**unfair** Foul play is not encouraged in sports.	2. *fair*
	3.	*adj.*	**unfavourable, stormy** The foul weather delayed the flight for several hours.	3. *fair, good*
found	1.	*v.*	**set up, establish, organize, originate, institute, produce** Who founded the first school in New France? *n.* Was the founder a missionary?	1. *end, uproot*
	2.	*adj.*	**discovered, unearthed, detected** Found items are to be returned to their owners.	2. *lost, missing, irretrievable*
foundation	1.	*n.*	**organization, institution, establishment, endowment** They set up a charitable foundation to help poor students.	
	2.	*n.*	**base, bottom, groundwork, basis, support** The foundation for the new stadium was laid last month.	2. *top, roof, covering*
foxy		*adj.*	**cunning, sly, tricky, crafty, shrewd, sharp, wily, shifty** The foxy agent sold that rundown farm.	*artless, open, frank, straightforward*
fraction		*n.*	**part, section, piece, bit, portion, division, segment** A quarter is a fraction of a dollar.	*whole, total*
fracture		*n.*	**break, split, crack** Ruth's fracture healed slowly after her bad fall. *v.* She fractured her arm in a hockey mishap.	
fragile		*adj.*	**frail, delicate, weak, brittle, breakable** This crystal is too fragile to put in the dishwasher.	*strong, tough, sturdy, durable*

Word			Synonyms	Antonyms
fragment		*n.*	**piece, part, fraction, scrap, chip, bit, shred, section** Fragments of ancient pottery were found in the tomb.	*whole, total*
fragrance		*n.*	**aroma, scent, sweet smell, perfume** This perfume has a light fragrance.	
fragrant		*adj.*	**sweet-smelling, perfumed, scented** Lilacs are fragrant after the rain.	*stinking, foul*
frail	1.	*adj.*	**fragile, delicate, brittle, breakable** Fine crystal is frail.	**1.** *strong, sturdy, unbreakable*
	2.	*adj.*	**weak, infirm, delicate, feeble** Grandpa was frail from his long illness.	**2.** *strong, sturdy, powerful, tough*
frank		*adj.*	**candid, open, sincere, direct, forthright, straightforward, aboveboard, honest, blunt** The people demanded frank answers from the government about the new tax.	*deceitful, secretive, insincere, dishonest, reserved*
frantic		*adj.*	**frenzied, excited, agitated, crazy** The travellers were frantic when they lost their airline tickets.	*calm, composed, docile, cool*
fraud	1.	*n.*	**deceit, trickery, deception, swindle, duplicity, guile** The bank teller was accused of fraud.	**1.** *fairness, openness, honesty*
	2.	*n.*	**imposter, quack, pretender, cheat, charlatan** The people were shocked to discover that their doctor was a fraud.	
free	1.	*v.*	**release, let go, discharge, liberate** The slaves in the United States were freed after the Civil War.	**1.** *imprison*
	2.	*adj.*	**unhindered, unfettered, unrestrained** In this country we are free to speak our minds.	**2.** *restrained, fettered, hindered*
	3.	*adj.*	**without cost, without fee** The restaurant gave the children a free meal on its opening day.	
	4.	*adj.*	**generous, liberal, lavish** The wealthy man is free with his money.	**4.** *miserly, stingy*
	5.	*adj.*	**unfastened, loose** He grabbed the free end of the rope.	**5.** *bound, fastened, tied*

Word		Synonyms	Antonyms
freedom	*n.*	**liberty, independence** Freedom of the press is guaranteed in a democratic society.	*slavery, subjection, bondage*
freeze	1. *v.*	**turn to ice, congeal, harden, solidify** Water freezes at 32 degrees Fahrenheit or 0 degrees Celsius.	**1.** *liquefy, turn to liquid, melt, thaw*
	2. *v.*	**chill, refrigerate, cool, make cold** Freeze the dessert before serving.	**2.** *heat, bake, cook*
frequent	*adj.*	**many, numerous, repeated, regular** Mom makes frequent business trips to Toronto.	*rare, infrequent, few, occasional*
frequently	*adv.*	**often, regularly, usually, repeatedly** Susan goes swimming frequently.	*rarely, seldom, infrequently*
fresh	1. *adj.*	**new, novel, recent, modern, innovative** The family immigrated to Canada and made a fresh start in life.	**1.** *stale, hackneyed, old, old-fashioned*
	2. *adj.*	**impudent, saucy, bold** The child was scolded for giving a fresh reply.	**2.** *polite, courteous*
	3. *adj.*	**unspoiled, newly grown** The market sells fresh fruits and vegetables.	**3.** *stale, spoiled*
	4. *adj.*	**young, vigorous, healthy, glowing, wholesome** Most children have fresh complexions.	**4.** *unhealthy*
	5. *adj.*	**bracing, pure, refreshing** "I'm longing for some fresh air," she said.	
fret	1. *v.*	**fuss, complain, fume, be vexed, be irritated** The children fretted all day because of the heat. *adj.* The fever made the baby fretful.	**1.** *soothe, calm, pacify*
	2. *v.*	**worry, grieve, agonize, be concerned** Why fret over something that cannot be changed?	**2.** *be content*
friction	1. *n.*	**abrasion, grinding, resistance, counteraction, rubbing** Friction in the car's brake drum caused the wheel to overheat.	**1.** *lubrication*

Word		Synonyms	Antonyms
	2. *n.*	**animosity, hatred, discontent, trouble, disagreement** Friction between the neighbouring countries eventually led to war.	**2.** *friendliness, compatibility, cooperation*
friend	*n.*	**chum, pal, buddy, companion, comrade, crony, ally** Shen and Matt have been good friends for a long time. *n.* They value each other's friendship.	*enemy, foe, rival, opponent*
friendly	*adj.*	**kind, helpful, neighbourly, agreeable** Several friendly neighbours welcomed the newcomers.	*unfriendly, hostile*
fright	*n.*	**scare, shock, terror** We had a fright when the burglar alarm went off.	
frighten	*v.*	**scare, terrify, intimidate, alarm, shock, startle** Lightning frightens me.	*comfort, calm*
frightened	*adj.*	**scared, fearful, alarmed, terrified, startled** The frightened deer bounded quickly away.	*brave, daring, courageous, heroic*
frightful	*adj.*	**dreadful, terrible, shocking, fearful, ghastly, horrible, horrid** The sinking of the *Titanic* was a frightful event.	*pleasing, inviting, appealing*
frigid	1. *adj.*	**very cold, freezing, glacial** Antarctica has a frigid climate.	**1.** *hot, sizzling, torrid*
	2. *adj.*	**unfriendly, cool** The girl gave him a frigid stare when he bumped into her.	**2.** *friendly, warm, cordial*
fringe	1. *n.*	**edge, border, outskirts, boundary** They live on the fringe of the city. *v.* The garden is fringed with tall trees.	**1.** *centre, heart, core*
	2. *n.*	**edging, border, hem, trimming** The bride's gown had an elaborate embroidered fringe.	
frivolous	*adj.*	**trivial, trifling, petty, superficial, unimportant, silly** Pupils cannot skip classes for frivolous reasons.	*serious, grave, important, earnest*

Word	No.	Part	Synonyms and example	Antonyms
frolic		*v.*	**sport, romp, frisk, play** The children frolicked in the water. *n.* They enjoyed their frolic in the pool.	*sulk*
front	1.	*n.*	**forward part** The bus waited at the front of the school.	1. *back, rear*
	2.	*v.*	**cover, façade** The hostel was a front for hiding illegal immigrants.	
frown		*n.*	**scowl, glare** The frown told us that she was displeased. *v.* Tom frowned as he tried to solve the puzzle.	*smile, grin*
frugal		*adj.*	**thrifty, prudent, careful, saving, parsimonious, economical** People with limited incomes must be frugal. *adv.* They lived frugally while they saved for a house.	*wasteful, lavish, extravagant, self-indulgent*
fruitful	1.	*adj.*	**productive, rich, abundant** The orchard had a fruitful harvest.	1. *poor, sparse, meagre*
	2.	*adj.*	**successful, profitable, productive** The meeting was a fruitful one that generated many good ideas.	2. *fruitless, useless, unproductive*
frustrate		*v.*	**foil, balk, disappoint, defeat, prevent, thwart, hinder, circumvent, deter, discourage** Bitter weather frustrated the mountain climbers. *n.* They cancelled the expedition in frustration.	*aid, help, encourage, assist, support, promote*
fuel	1.	*n.*	**combustible material** Gas and oil are fuels.	
	2.	*v.*	**take on fuel, feed, fill up, stoke** The family fuelled the fire upon entering the cold cottage.	
fugitive		*n.*	**deserter, runaway, escapee** The police caught the fugitives after a wild chase.	*pursuer*
fulfil (also spelled fulfill)		*v.*	**accomplish, complete, achieve, realize** I fulfilled my ambition when I graduated with honours.	*fail, give up, neglect, overlook*

Word	No.	Part	Synonyms and example	Antonyms
full	1.	*adj.*	**filled, brimming with, packed, stuffed** The bottle is full of milk.	1. *empty, void*
	2.	*adj.*	**complete, whole, entire** The full orchestra will perform tonight. *adv.* The carton is fully packed.	2. *partial*
fumble	1.	*v.*	**mishandle, bungle, botch, mismanage** The quarterback fumbled the ball. *n.* It was a costly fumble.	1. *handle, manage, control*
	2.	*v.*	**grope, search** Lu fumbled in her purse for her keys.	
fun		*n.*	**amusement, entertainment, merriment, enjoyment** We had fun at the beach party.	*drudgery*
function	1.	*n.*	**duty, role, part, use, capacity** What is the function of the Supreme Court?	
	2.	*n.*	**meeting, party, reception, get-together, social gathering, celebration** Many functions are held at hotels.	
	3.	*v.*	**perform, run, work, operate, serve, act** Certain people function best under stress.	3. *be inoperative, be inactive*
fundamental		*adj.*	**rudimentary, basic, elementary, essential, underlying, primary, important, indispensable, cardinal, necessary** Freedom is a fundamental right in any democracy.	*secondary, nonessential, unimportant, incidental, superficial*
funny	1.	*adj.*	**comical, humorous, amusing, laughable** Rae read a funny poem to the class.	1. *serious, sober, solemn*
	2.	*adj.*	**strange, peculiar, odd, unusual, uncommon** I have a funny feeling in my stomach.	2. *regular, usual, normal, common*
furious	1.	*adj.*	**angry, mad, infuriated, irate** Dad was furious when I was fined for speeding.	1. *calm, serene*
	2.	*adj.*	**violent, fierce, raging, ferocious, wild** The ocean liner survived the furious storm. *adv.* The wind blew furiously for three days.	2. *gentle, smooth, placid, calm*

Word	No.	Part	Synonyms / Example	Antonyms
furnish	1.	*v.*	**provide, give, supply** My friend furnished me with the answer.	**1.** *keep, withhold, retain*
	2.	*v.*	**equip, outfit, stock** Their house is furnished with modern furniture.	
furtive		*adj.*	**sly, stealthy, secretive, deceitful, shifty** The fugitive had a furtive look as he slipped out the back door. *adv.* He crept furtively upstairs at midnight.	*open, aboveboard, straightforward*
fury	1.	*n.*	**anger, frenzy, wrath, rage, furor** The people were in a fury when they learnt that a garbage dump was to be located in their town.	**1.** *calmness*
	2.	*n.*	**violence, force, might, fierceness** The coastal towns felt the full fury of the hurricane.	
fuse		*v.*	**merge, unite, combine, blend, amalgamate** The voices of the choirs fused in unison at the finale.	*divide, separate, part*
fusion		*n.*	**union, coalition, blending** The reaction caused by nuclear fusion produces great energy.	
fuss	1.	*n.*	**trouble, bother, disturbance, complaint** The tenants raised a fuss when the landlord raised their rent.	
	2.	*n.*	**ado, stir, bustle, confusion, agitation, hubbub, flurry** There was a big fuss in the house on the day of the wedding.	**2.** *tranquillity, quiet, peace, calm*
	3.	*v.*	**fret, fidget, worry, complain, whine, whimper, object** The passenger fussed about the delay in the flight.	**3.** *be content, approve, favour, sanction*
fussy	1.	*adj.*	**exacting, critical, particular, demanding, hard to please** Our family is fussy about buying fresh vegetables.	**1.** *easygoing*
	2.	*adj.*	**ornate, elaborate, cluttered, showy** That fussy dress would not be suitable for this affair.	**2.** *plain, simple*

Word			Synonyms	Antonyms
futile		*adj.*	**useless, worthless, ineffective, fruitless, vain, unsuccessful** The efforts to save the wrecked trawler were futile.	*successful, effective, fruitful, worthy*
future	**1.**	*n.*	**tomorrow, hereafter, time to come** She has a bright future ahead of her.	**1.** *past*
	2.	*adj.*	**eventual, projected, coming, later, following, anticipated** Karl's future plans include a trip to Austria.	**2.** *past, former, previous*
fuzzy	**1.**	*adj.*	**downy, woolly, furry** Peaches have a fuzzy skin. *n.* I don't enjoy eating the fuzz.	**1.** *smooth, silken*
	2.	*adj.*	**hazy, blurred, unclear, out of focus** Unless you focus the camera properly, the picture will be fuzzy.	**2.** *clear, sharp*

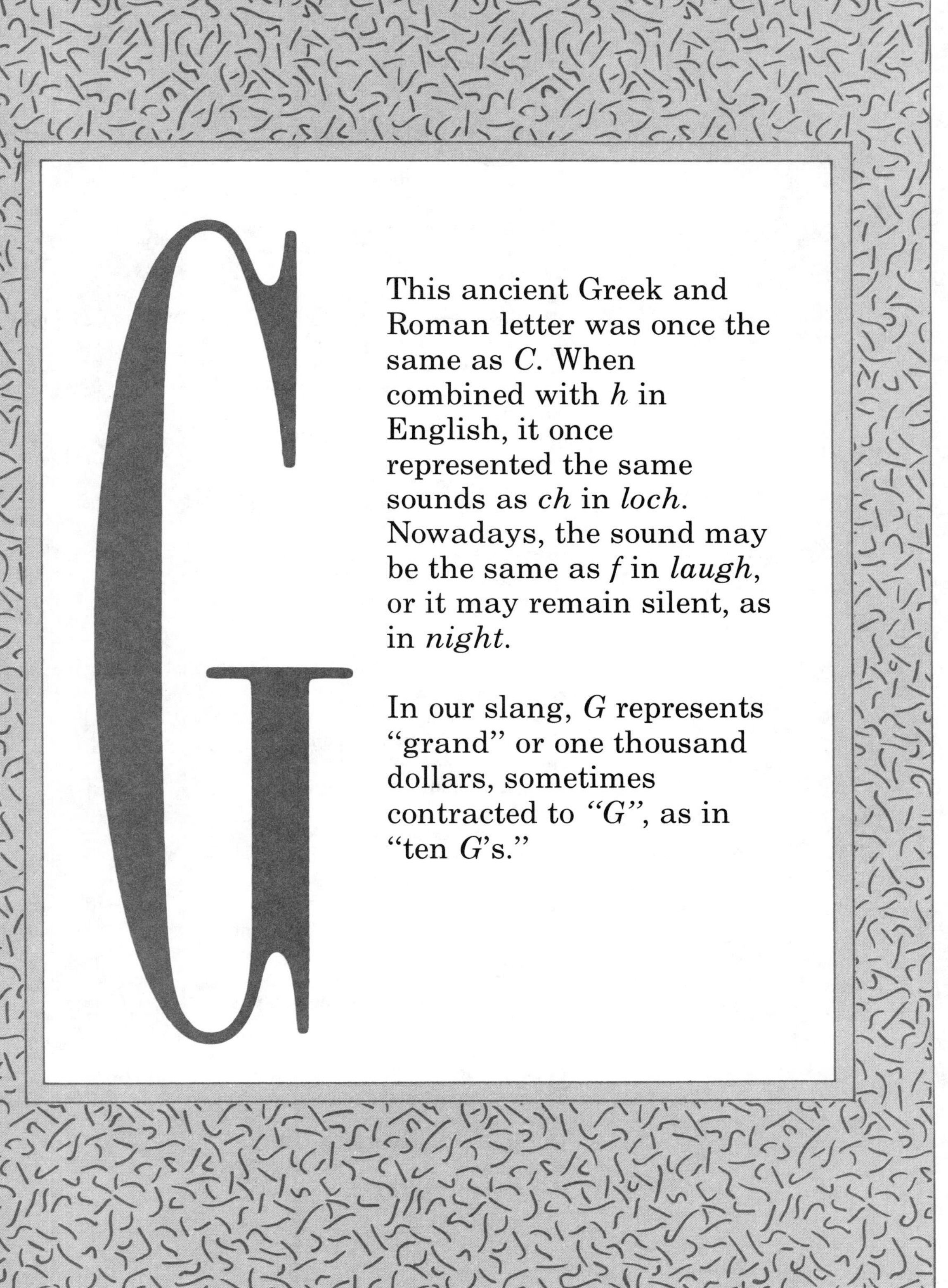

This ancient Greek and Roman letter was once the same as *C*. When combined with *h* in English, it once represented the same sounds as *ch* in *loch*. Nowadays, the sound may be the same as *f* in *laugh*, or it may remain silent, as in *night*.

In our slang, *G* represents "grand" or one thousand dollars, sometimes contracted to *"G"*, as in "ten *G*'s."

Word	No.	Part of speech	Synonyms and example	Antonyms
gag	**1.**	*v.*	**silence, muffle, repress** The kidnappers gagged their victim so he was unable to call for help.	
	2.	*v.*	**choke, retch, be nauseated** The baby gagged on the food.	
gain	**1.**	*n.*	**profit, increase, earnings, winnings** The company made a gain on the sale.	**1.** *loss, decrease*
	2.	*v.*	**profit, earn** The company gained $1 million on the deal.	**2.** *lose*
	3.	*v.*	**increase, grow, expand, enlarge** The baby gained weight rapidly.	**3.** *decrease, shrink, lessen, diminish*
	4.	*v.*	**advance, overtake, progress, move forward** The challenger is gaining on the leader in the race.	**4.** *move backward, retreat, halt, stop, stand still*
	5.	*v.*	**achieve, get, obtain, secure, realize, attain** Thomas Edison gained world recognition for his inventions.	**5.** *lose, forfeit*
gallant		*adj.*	**brave, bold, courageous, valiant, daring, heroic, fearless** Dave enjoys reading tales of gallant knights of old.	*cowardly, timid, fearful*
game	**1.**	*n.*	**amusement, fun, play, recreation, diversion, entertainment** The children's favourite game is checkers.	**1.** *work, labour, toi*
	2.	*n.*	**wild fowl, fish, wild animals, quarry, prey** No one can hunt game on a nature reserve.	**2.** *domestic animals, farm animals*
	3.	*adj.*	**sporting, plucky, spirited, brave, resolute, determined** Terry Fox was admired for his game spirit.	**3.** *uncertain, half-hearted, irresolute, indecisive, hesitant*
	4.	*adj.*	**lame, crippled** The horse with the game leg was put to sleep.	**4.** *sound, fit*
gang		*n.*	**group, clan, band, mob, horde** The entire gang went to the beach.	*individual*
gangster		*n.*	**mobster, criminal, ruffian, thug, racketeer** Gangsters cause a lot of crime in big cities.	*law-abiding person*

Word			Synonyms	Antonyms
garbage		*n.*	**waste, refuse, trash, rubbish, scraps** We are running out of space to dump garbage.	
gather	1.	*v.*	**infer, conclude, deduce, assume** I gather from your remarks that you approve of our plans.	1. *doubt, question, wonder*
	2.	*v.*	**pick up, collect, take in** After the class, the monitors gathered up the books.	2. *scatter, spread, distribute*
	3.	*v.*	**collect, assemble, group, meet, congregate, converge, convene, come together** The children gathered around the teacher for a story. *n.* We have a family gathering at Thanksgiving.	3. *scatter, disperse, part, break up, disband*
gaudy		*adj.*	**flashy, showy, garish, glaring, ornate** Students are not allowed to wear gaudy jewellery to school.	*dull, drab, simple, plain*
gauge	1.	*n.*	**measure, mark, scale, standard, check, criterion** The gas gauge registered full.	
	2.	*v.*	**weigh, measure, check, estimate, judge** Joe gauged the distance from the house to the lake to be 2 km.	
gaunt		*adj.*	**lean, skinny, bony, thin, underfed, emaciated, haggard** Mei looked gaunt after her diet.	*well-fed, fleshy, plump*
gaze		*v.*	**stare, watch, gape, look, observe, peer** Astronomers gaze at the stars. *n.* Are you a star gazer?	*glance, peek, glimpse*
general	1.	*adj.*	**common, usual, customary, normal, prevailing** The general opinion is that the school should become coeducational. *adv.* Do you generally vote on these matters?	1. *rare, unusual*
	2.	*adj.*	**public, extensive, widespread, universal** The unions organized a general strike of workers across the nation.	2. *confined, restricted, limited*
	3.	*adj.*	**broad, not specific** Give me a general outline of your proposal.	3. *detailed, specific*

Word		Part of speech	Synonyms and example	Antonyms
generate		*v.*	**form, make, produce, supply, furnish, originate** Huge turbines at Niagara Falls generate hydroelectricity.	*destroy, squash, squelch, dismantle, tear down*
generous	1.	*adj.*	**liberal, unselfish, magnanimous, philanthropic, free** She made a generous donation to her school.	**1.** *close, stingy, mean, miserly, petty, tightfisted*
	2.	*adj.*	**ample, plentiful, abundant, large, bountiful, overflowing** Dad heaped a generous helping of dessert on my plate.	**2.** *small, meagre, insufficient*
genial		*adj.*	**pleasant, warm, friendly, cheerful, kind, cordial, affable, sociable, courteous, congenial, approachable** The genial TV talk show host soon put everyone at ease.	*unfriendly, hostile, antagonistic, discourteous, unapproachable*
gentle	1.	*adj.*	**soft, balmy, light, calm, pleasant, mild, moderate** Gentle breezes are common in summer.	**1.** *rough, fierce, violent, strong, savage*
	2.	*adj.*	**tender, kind, delicate, careful, soft, considerate** Biz gave the kitten a gentle pat. *adv.* Marie gently picked up the injured bird.	**2.** *harsh, cruel, unkind, rough*
	3.	*adj.*	**tamed, broken, docile, disciplined, domesticated** The riding instructor gave the beginner rider a gentle horse.	**3.** *wild, untamed, savage*
genuine	1.	*adj.*	**real, true, honest, valid, trustworthy, actual, sincere, unquestionable, frank** Most people have a genuine concern for the environment.	**1.** *insincere, dishonest, hypocritical, simulated, affected*
	2.	*adj.*	**authentic, real, true** The vase proved to be a genuine antique.	**2.** *bogus, fake, counterfeit, sham*
get		*v.*	**obtain, acquire, receive, earn, secure, procure, win, achieve, gain, attain** Which candidate got the most votes in the last election?	*lose, surrender, forgo, forfeit, abandon*
ghastly	1.	*adj.*	**awful, terrible, horrible, dreadful** The accident scene was a ghastly sight.	**1.** *pleasing, attractive*

	2.	*adj.*	**pale, wan, ashen, pallid, macabre, deathlike, ghostlike** The ghastly faces of the earthquake survivors touched everyone.	2. *rosy*
ghost		*n.*	**spirit, vision, apparition, phantom, spectre** Do you believe in ghosts? *adj.* The storyteller told tales of seeing ghostly figures in the night.	
giant		*adj.*	**huge, enormous, immense, stupendous, gigantic, great, whopping, tremendous, jumbo, massive, colossal** The giant dinosaurs are extinct.	*tiny, petite, little, miniature, wee, minute, dwarf, diminutive, scant*
giddy	1.	*adj.*	**dizzy, unsteady** A person can get a giddy feeling from turning in circles.	1. *stable, steady*
	2.	*adj.*	**silly, flighty, frivolous, capricious, heedless** Lou was told to forget his giddy ideas and concentrate on his studies.	2. *serious, thoughtful*
gift	1.	*n.*	**present, offering** Did you receive many gifts on your birthday?	1. *loan, purchase*
	2.	*n.*	**talent, skill, aptitude, ability** The teacher recognized Min's musical gift. *adj.* The gifted violinist appeared on nationwide television.	2. *hindrance, disadvantage, block, obstacle*
gigantic		*adj.*	**huge, immense, enormous, massive, stupendous, colossal, great, monstrous, giant** During the hurricane, the coast was battered by gigantic waves.	*tiny, petite, little, small, wee, miniature, minute, dwarf, diminutive*
gist		*n.*	**essence, point, substance, basis** Just tell me the gist of your proposal.	
give	1.	*v.*	**provide, furnish, supply, grant** The principal gave the students permission to hold a science fair.	1. *deny, refuse, take away, remove*
	2.	*v.*	**transfer, bestow, present, endow, award, donate, dole out, bequeath** They are giving the money raised at the fair to charity.	2. *maintain, keep, withhold*

Word			Synonyms	Antonyms
glad		*adj.*	**happy, pleased, delighted, content** Yu Hua is glad to be in Canada. *adv.* The Hua family gladly moved to Canada.	*sad, gloomy, unhappy, discontent*
glamour		*n.*	**charm, allure, attraction, appeal, allurement, magnetism, romance** Large cities have a glamour all their own. *adj.* Paris is a glamourous city.	
glare	**1.**	*n.*	**shine, shimmer, bright light** Oncoming headlights caused a glare on the windshield.	**1.** *dullness*
	2.	*v.*	**stare angrily, scowl, frown, glower** The opponents glared at each other before the match.	**2.** *smile, laugh*
glaring	**1.**	*adj.*	**brilliant, dazzling, bright, glowing, showy, blinding, blazing** Wear sunglasses to protect your eyes from the glaring sun.	**1.** *dull, dim*
	2.	*adj.*	**obvious, conspicuous, evident** Ken lost marks for the glaring spelling errors in his essay.	**2.** *obscure, hidden, inconspicuous, concealed*
gleam	**1.**	*n.*	**glimmer, ray, beam, glow, flash** The search plane saw the gleam of light between the trees.	
	2	*n.*	**measure, small amount** There's not a gleam of truth in what he says.	
	3.	*v.*	**shine, sparkle, glimmer, glitter** Nadia's eyes gleamed with pleasure when she heard the good news.	
glee		*n.*	**joy, cheer, fun, gaiety, mirth, delight** At the puppet show, the children laughed in glee. *adj.* The gleeful audience shouted for an encore.	*dejection, grief, unhappiness, sorrow*
glimpse		*n.*	**flash, sight, flicker, brief look, glance, peek** They caught a glimpse of the deer before it bounded off. *v.* Hong glimpsed at his notes just before the test.	

Word		Part of speech	Synonyms / Example	Antonyms
glitter		*n.*	**sparkle, glisten, shine, twinkle** We saw the glitter of the city lights from the plane. *v.* The city lights glittered.	
global		*adj.*	**worldwide, universal** We watch global news on television every night.	*local, individual*
gloomy	1.	*adj.*	**sad, downhearted, depressed, unhappy, dejected, glum, miserable, melancholy** Yun is gloomy because her friend Tanya is moving away. *n.* An air of gloom hung over her after she heard the bad news.	**1.** *happy, cheerful, pleasant, jolly, content, pleased*
	2.	*adj.*	**dark, dismal, depressing, dim, cloudy** Rooms with a northern exposure can be gloomy.	**2.** *bright, pleasant, cheerful, attractive, sunny*
glorious		*adj.*	**wonderful, marvellous, splendid, magnificent, renowned, famous, distinguished, grand, celebrated** The skaters gave glorious performances.	*unimportant, insignificant, average, mediocre, uneventful, ordinary*
glory		*n.*	**honour, fame, renown, praise** The athletes returned in glory from the Olympic Games.	*disgrace, shame, ignominy*
glossy		*adj.*	**shiny, lustrous, polished, smooth** Print the photograph on glossy paper. *n.* She put some gloss on her lips to prevent them from chapping.	*dull, unpolished*
glow		*n.*	**gleam, shine, sheen, radiance** Northern lights cause a glow in the sky. *v.* Fires glow.	*blackness, darkness*
glum		*adj.*	**morose, moody, sullen, sad** The loser of the game has such a glum face!	*happy, cheerful, sunny, jaunty*
glut		*n.*	**excess, oversupply, overload, profusion, abundance, surplus** The oil glut caused prices to fall drastically.	*scarcity, lack, deficiency*
goal		*n.*	**aim, ambition, object, end, purpose, intention** Jie-Sing's goal is to become a lawyer.	

Word	No.	Part of speech	Synonyms and example	Antonyms
good	1.	*n.*	**benefit, advantage, interest, welfare** Laws are for the good of all citizens.	1. *harm, impediment, drawback, handicap*
	2.	*adj.*	**excellent, first-rate, great** The book was so good that I couldn't put it down till the end.	2. *bad, terrible, poor*
	3.	*adj.*	**honest, true, just, kind, worthy** That person has a good reputation.	3. *dishonest, bad, sneaky, fraudulent*
	4.	*adj.*	**well-behaved, mannerly, proper, fit, becoming** Good manners are learned.	4. *rude, improper, ill-mannered, unbecoming*
	5.	*adj.*	**clever, skilful, expert, able, qualified** She is a good skier.	5. *poor, inept, inexperienced*
	6.	*adj.*	**reliable, safe, dependable, sound, stable, healthy** Be sure that used car is in good condition before you buy it.	6. *bad, defective, unsafe, unreliable, unhealthy*
goods	1.	*n.*	**materials, merchandise, commodities, wares** Some imported goods are taxed.	
	2.	*n.*	**property, belongings, possessions** Personal goods can be insured.	
gorge	1.	*n.*	**chasm, abyss, ravine, gully** The lamb fell into the gorge.	
	2.	*v.*	**stuff, fill, cram, overeat, satiate** Sam was sick after gorging himself with spaghetti.	2. *empty, void, disgorge*
gorgeous		*adj.*	**splendid, magnificent, beautiful, superb, breathtaking** The tourists gaped in amazement at the gorgeous sunset.	*unimpressive, unattractive, ugly*
gory		*adj.*	**bloody, bloodsoaked, bloodstained, offensive, revolting** Bullfights can be gory events.	*pleasant, agreeable, likable*
govern		*v.*	**rule, control, direct, manage, command, administer, lead, conduct** The school is governed by a board of directors.	*obey, follow*
grab		*v.*	**snatch, seize, clutch, take** The thief grabbed the woman's purse and dashed off.	*return, give back, restore, reimburse*
grace	1.	*n.*	**dexterity, agility, nimbleness, smoothness** The ballerinas danced with grace. *adv.* They danced gracefully.	1. *awkwardness, stiffness, clumsiness*

2. *n.* **blessing, prayer, thanksgiving**
Many people say grace before meals.

3. *n.* **charm, allure, elegance**
She is much admired for her grace.
3. coarseness, awkwardness

4. *n.* **favour, good will**
Shane was in the teacher's good graces for helping the new students.
4. disfavour

5. *v.* **honour, favour**
The mayor graced the graduation ceremony with her presence.

gracious

1. *adj.* **courteous, charming**
The governor's gracious greeting put everyone at ease.
1. rude, vulgar, crude

2. *adj.* **elegant, refined, tasteful**
The guests were full of admiration for the governor's gracious mansion.
2. crude, coarse

grade

1. *n.* **rank, classification, level, rating**
Rob's school grades have improved this term.

2. *v.* **rank, rate, measure, classify**
He is graded as an A student.

gradual

adj. **slow, step by step, little by little, regular, progressive**
It is a gradual climb to the top of the hill.
adv. They gradually made it to the top of the hill.
sudden, abrupt, instantaneous

graft

1. *n.* **corruption, swindle, thievery, fraud**
The manager was found guilty of graft and fired from his job.
1. purity, goodness

2. *v.* **join, splice, unite**
Surgeons grafted new skin over the burn patient's wounds.
2. sever, separate, sunder

grand

1. *adj.* **splendid, superb, elegant, stately, magnificent, gorgeous, fine, impressive, majestic, imposing, sumptuous**
Grand ballrooms are found in European palaces.
1. plain, ordinary, commonplace, unimposing

2. *adj.* **lofty, stately, dignified, elevated, high, noble, great, illustrious**
Royalty occupies a grand position in some societies.
2. low, mediocre, ordinary, simple, unassuming, modest

3. *adj.* **good, first-class, excellent**
That job is a grand opportunity for one so young.
3. poor, inferior, imperfect

Word			Synonyms	Antonyms
grant	1.	*n.*	**award, gift, donation, present, endowment, bequest, reward** The museum received a substantial grant from the millionaire.	1. *deduction, deprivation, loss*
	2.	*v.*	**allow, permit, give, confer** Air traffic controllers granted the pilot permission for takeoff.	2. *refuse, prohibit, reject, decline*
graphic	1.	*adj.*	**pictorial, visual, illustrated, diagrammatic** Computers can produce incredible graphic designs.	
	2.	*adj.*	**vivid, explicit, striking, clear, realistic, lucid, definite, precise, exact, concrete** Ted's graphic descriptions of war horrified everyone.	2. *obscure, abstract, ambiguous*
grasp	1.	*n.*	**reach, hold, clutch, grip** The mountain climber lost her grasp and plunged into the ravine. *v.* The rescuers grasped her arms and hauled her up.	
	2.	*v.*	**comprehend, understand, apprehend, follow** Did you grasp what the teacher was saying? *n.* He has a good grasp of astronomy.	2. *misunderstand, ignore, be ignorant of, have no idea of*
grate		*v.*	**scrape, grind, scratch, rub** Grate the cheese for the pizza.	*massage, knead, smooth*
grateful		*adj.*	**thankful, appreciative, obliged, beholden** Hungry people are grateful to receive food. *adv.* Donations will be gratefully received.	*thankless, ungrateful*
grave	1.	*adj.*	**sombre, sober, solemn, serious** We were concerned when we saw the doctor's grave face.	1. *joyous, merrry, happy, cheerful*
	2.	*adj.*	**important, momentous, weighty, consequential** Grave decisions are made in the legislature.	2. *trivial, unimportant, insignificant, mundane*
	3.	*adj.*	**hazardous, precarious, dangerous, critical, serious, ominous, threatening** That accident victim is in grave condition.	3. *good, excellent, secure*

Word			Synonyms	Antonyms
gravitate		*v.*	**be attracted to, incline toward, drift toward** Most metals gravitate to magnets.	*be repulsed by, drift away*
great	**1.**	*adj.*	**big, large, huge, vast, immense** The Great Wall of China is an awesome sight.	**1.** *small, little, puny*
	2.	*adj.*	**eminent, noted, renowned, prominent, celebrated, famous, well-known, important, remarkable** Sir Winston Churchill was a great person.	**2.** *unknown, obscure*
greedy	**1.**	*adj.*	**gluttonous, piggish, ravenous** The greedy cat left no food for the kittens.	**1.** *satiated, satisfied, surfeited, filled*
	2.	*adj.*	**grasping, avaricious, selfish, miserly, stingy, covetous, acquisitive, mercenary** The greedy landlord raised the rent again.	**2.** *generous, giving, unselfish, charitable*
grief		*n.*	**sorrow, woe, sadness, misfortune, misery, trouble, anguish, heartache** Survivors of the hurricane saw grief and destruction everywhere. *v.* They grieved over the loss of their loved ones.	*happiness, joy gladness*
grim	**1.**	*adj.*	**severe, harsh, hard, stern, forbidding, austere** There were many grim faces when the bad news was announced.	**1.** *smiling, happy, cheerful, pleasant*
	2.	*adj.*	**awful, horrible, ghastly, grisly, hideous** The grim stories about the war depressed us.	**2.** *funny, pleasant, humorous*
grind	**1.**	*n.*	**hard work, drudgery, tediousness** The grind of college life soon wore him out. *v.* Jeff grinds away at his books all day.	**1.** *pleasure*
	2.	*v.*	**grate, crush** Mike ground the coffee beans in the grinder.	
grip		*v.*	**seize, hold, clasp, clutch, grasp, grab** The child gripped his father's hand. *n.* The police officer held the suspect in a firm grip.	*release, drop, let go, relinquish*

Word			Synonyms / Example	Antonyms
groan		*n.*	**moan, cry, sob, lament, whimper** There were groans of agony from the injured. *v.* The injured person groaned in pain.	*laugh, chuckle, giggle*
groom	1.	*v.*	**curry, tend, rub down** Horses are groomed regularly.	
	2.	*v.*	**make attractive, ready, prepare** Sal groomed himself for the interview. *n.* Good grooming is important on the job.	
grope		*v.*	**feel, fumble, hunt, search** They groped their way in the dark room.	
gross	1.	*adj.*	**whole, entire, total** What is your gross annual income?	**1.** *net, remaining*
	2.	*adj.*	**coarse, bad, vulgar** The student was expelled from school for gross misconduct.	
grotesque		*adj.*	**malformed, ugly, deformed, distorted, twisted, misshapen** Grotesque masks are often seen on Halloween.	*beautiful, lovely, appealing, well-formed, handsome*
grouchy		*adj*	**ill-tempered, crusty, surly, irritable, sullen** Everyone avoids the grouchy sales clerk. *n.* Are you ever a grouch?	*pleasant, affable, friendly*
ground	1.	*n.*	**earth, soil, land, terra firma, dirt** Fertile ground is needed for farming.	**1.** *water, air, space*
	2.	*n.*	**reason, basis** She filed for divorce on the grounds of desertion.	
group	1.	*n.*	**set, association, collection, assembly, company, cluster, bunch** The children huddled in a group at recess.	**1.** *individual*
	2.	*v.*	**classify, file, arrange, sort, assort, collect, gather, cluster, combine** We grouped the children into classes of 20.	

Word			Synonyms	Antonyms
grow	1.	*v.*	**swell, enlarge, expand, increase, stretch, spread, amplify, get bigger, flourish, develop** Plants need water to grow. *n.* Water is needed for plant growth.	**1.** *dwindle, shrink, lessen, decrease, get smaller, wither*
	2.	*v.*	**cultivate, plant, raise, tend, produce** Farmers grow crops annually.	**2.** *harm, impede, restrict*
growl		*n.*	**snarl, groan** The dog's growl frightened off the intruder. *v.* The dog growled at the postal worker.	
grudge		*n.*	**spite, rancour, animosity, malice, ill feeling** He holds no grudge against you for his loss.	*good will, kindness, benevolence*
gruesome		*adj.*	**ghastly, horrible, hideous, grisly, grim, frightening, ugly, revolting, offensive** There were some gruesome sights in the disaster area.	*likable, pleasant, agreeable, attractive, appealing, acceptable*
gruff	1.	*adj.*	**abrupt, brusque, blunt, impolite, rude, unfriendly, cross, surly, harsh** We were not frightened by the guard's gruff manner. *adv.* The guard gruffly told us to leave.	**1.** *polite, courteous, civil, gracious, refined, affable*
	2.	*adj.*	**hoarse, rough, grating, throaty, rasping, husky, jarring, harsh, guttural** I dislike the announcer's gruff voice. *adv.* Which announcer speaks gruffly?	**2.** *mild, sweet, smooth, harmonious, resonant*
grumble		*v.*	**complain, protest, fuss, whine, fret, object, criticize, mutter, carp, find fault** Customers grumbled about the high prices.	*approve, accept, sanction, praise*
guard	1.	*n.*	**protector, sentry, sentinel, defender** The guards stood erect at the entrance to the palace.	**1.** *attacker, intruder, trespasser*
	2.	*n.*	**covering, cover, protection, shield** She carefully removed the skate-guards and stepped onto the ice.	

Word	Sense	Synonyms and example	Antonyms
	3. *v.*	**defend, protect, watch, shield** Soldiers guard the borders.	**3.** *neglect, disregard, forsake*
guess	*v.*	**suppose, imagine, estimate, conjecture** Pam correctly guessed the number of beans in the jar. *n.* What a lucky guess!	*deduce, prove, establish, know*
guide	1. *n*	**leader, pilot, conductor, pathfinder** Sherpa guides led the mountain climbers to the summit.	**1.** *follower, imitator*
	2. *n*	**map, manual, chart, handbook, guidebook, instructions** Each new car owner is given a guide about the vehicle.	
	3. *n*	**model, example, pattern, design** Dressmakers use a guide to cut out the material.	
	4. *v.*	**lead, escort, conduct, show the way, pilot** Visitors are guided through the Parliament Buildings. *adj.* Planes follow guiding beams.	**4.** *follow, pursue, come after, accompany*
	5. *v.*	**direct, supervise, oversee, control, manage** The counsellor guided the students with their choice of university. *n.* They appreciated his guidance.	**5.** *mislead, obey, take orders, follow*
guilty	*adj.*	**at fault, in error, culpable** Those found guilty will be sentenced.	*innocent, blameless*
gullible	*adj.*	**naive, innocent, unsuspicious, credulous, unsuspecting, trusting** Cunning cheats prey on gullible people.	*incredulous, sceptical, suspicious, dubious, doubtful*
gush	*v.*	**burst, stream, pour out, flow out, flow, spout, rush, surge, spew** Blood gushed from the wound.	*drip, trickle, drop, dribble*
gyp	*v.*	**cheat, swindle, defraud, dupe, bamboozle, trick, deceive, mislead** Has the buyer been gypped on the deal?	*deal honourably, be fair*
gyrate	*v.*	**spin, rotate, whirl, revolve, turn, spiral, twirl** The blades of the helicopter gyrated rapidly.	*be inactive, be still*

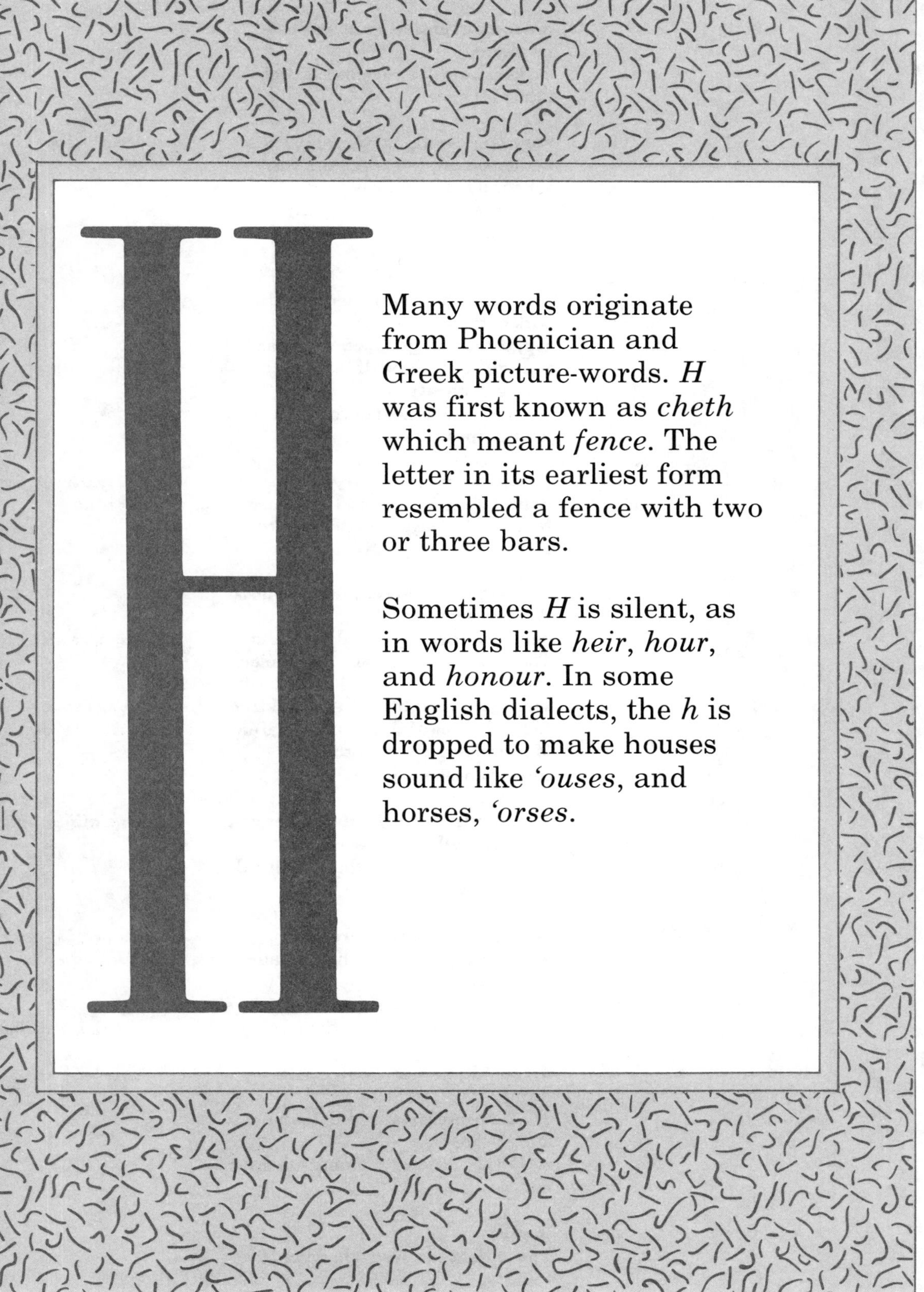

Many words originate from Phoenician and Greek picture-words. *H* was first known as *cheth* which meant *fence*. The letter in its earliest form resembled a fence with two or three bars.

Sometimes *H* is silent, as in words like *heir*, *hour*, and *honour*. In some English dialects, the *h* is dropped to make houses sound like *'ouses*, and horses, *'orses*.

Word	No.	Part	Synonyms and example	Antonyms
habit		*n.*	**custom, practice, rule, routine, tendency** Todd is trying to stop his habit of biting his nails.	
habitual		*adj.*	**regular, usual, customary, accustomed, normal, constant** Rose is a habitual early riser. *adv.* She habitually rises early to exercise.	*rare, infrequent, unusual*
hack	1.	*n.*	**cut, wound, gash** The axe made several hacks in the bark of the tree.	
	2.	*v.*	**rip, tear, cut, gash, chop, slash, mangle, split, mutilate, chip, break, lacerate** The marines hacked at the thick jungle vines.	
haggard		*adj.*	**gaunt, worried, weary, exhausted, worn-out, careworn** Marie looks haggard after her long illness.	*hearty, lively, fresh, vigorous*
hail	1.	*v.*	**call, signal to, signal for, shout to** We hailed a taxi.	
	2.	*v.*	**salute, cheer, applaud, acclaim** The citizens hailed their new leader.	**2.** *ignore, disregard, boo*
hair-raising		*adj.*	**terrifying, frightening, shocking, fearful, dreadful, awful, terrible** Mario frightened us with a hair-raising ghost story.	*comfortable, relaxing, soothing*
hale		*adj.*	**sound, vigorous, healthy, hearty, strong, well** At eighty, my grandfather is still hale and hearty.	*weak, ailing, frail*
halt	1.	*n.*	**stop, recess, pause, break** The traffic ground to a halt because of an accident.	**1.** *start, beginning, continuation*
	2.	*v.*	**end, check, suspend, arrest** Is is possible to halt inflation?	**2.** *proceed, advance, continue*
hammer		*v.*	**drive, hit, pound, beat, strike, bang** The carpenter hammered the nails into the boards. *n.* Carpenters use a hammer to drive in nails.	*yank, pull, extract*
hamper	1.	*n.*	**basket** The patient received a hamper of fruit.	

	2.	*v.*	**hinder, obstruct, impede, hold back** The runner was hampered by a sore toe.	2. *aid, help, assist, hasten*
hand	1.	*n.*	**palm and fingers, fist, paw** Tim cut his hand on the window.	
	2.	*n.*	**support, help, assistance, aid** Ross will give us a hand with the painting.	2. *hindrance*
	3.	*v.*	**pass, give, deliver** The clerk handed me the parcel.	
handicap	1.	*n.*	**difficulty, hindrance, burden, drawback, disadvantage, limitation** Lack of formal education can be a handicap in job hunting.	1. *assistance, advantage, help, asset*
	2.	*v.*	**limit, hinder, put at a disadvantage, impede** Lack of practice will handicap the team.	2. *assist, help, aid, benefit, promote*
handle	1.	*n.*	**knob, pull, hold** The door handle is quite loose.	
	2.	*v.*	**touch, feel, finger, stroke, hold** They handled the china carefully.	
	3.	*v.*	**manipulate, operate, manage** She handles her job very efficiently.	
handsome	1.	*adj.*	**good-looking, beautiful, attractive** In fairy tales, the princess usually marries the handsome prince.	1. *ugly, revolting, unattractive*
	2.	*adj.*	**generous, large, considerable** Hans made a handsome donation to the school's building fund.	2. *small, puny, insignificant*
handy	1.	*adj.*	**useful, convenient, helpful** A microwave oven is a handy appliance.	1. *useless, inconvenient*
	2.	*adj.*	**clever, skilled, skilful, resourceful** Our uncle is handy at making garden furniture.	2. *awkward, clumsy, unskilled*
	3.	*adv.*	**available, nearby, within reach** Keep the first aid kit handy during the trip.	
hang		*v.*	**suspend, dangle, drape, fasten** Hang your coat in the closet.	
happen		*v.*	**occur, take place, come to pass** A terrible accident happened on the expressway this morning.	

Word			Synonyms	Antonyms
happily	**1.**	*adv.*	**fortunately, luckily** Happily, no one was killed in the fire.	**1.** *unfortunately, unluckily*
	2.	*adv.*	**contentedly, joyfully** The family lived happily in their new home.	**2.** *unhappily, discontentedly*
happiness		*n.*	**joy, delight, gladness, contentment, pleasure** Carla was filled with happiness at the thought of going to the prom.	*sorrow, misery, gloom, grief, sadness, unhappiness*
happy		*adj.*	**joyful, merry, glad, delighted, cheerful, gay, jolly, jovial, sunny, cheery, pleased** Judy is happy because she won first prize.	*sad, sorrowful, dejected, moody, miserable, troubled, forlorn*
harass		*v.*	**disturb, annoy, bother, plague, vex, distress, torment** The merchant was harassed by his creditors. *n.* He closed his store to avoid the harassment.	
harbour (also spelled harbor)	**1.**	*n.*	**dock, port, quay, inlet** Many freighters sail into the harbour at Halifax.	
	2.	*v.*	**shield, conceal, protect, shelter, house** The family was accused of harbouring the escaped prisoner.	
hard	**1.**	*adj.*	**firm, solid, rigid, stiff** The new concrete is hard now.	**1.** *soft, yielding, pliable*
	2.	*adj.*	**difficult, exacting** "That was a hard test," moaned Tim.	**2.** *easy, simple*
	3.	*adj.*	**stern, severe, pitiless, strict, unfeeling, harsh** The judge handed down a hard sentence on the drunk driver.	**3.** *gentle, kind, tenderhearted*
	4.	*adj.*	**willing, eager, diligent, industrious** The new helper is a hard worker. *adv.* He works hard every day.	**4.** *lazy, unwilling*
hardhearted		*adj.*	**unsympathetic, cruel, unfeeling, heartless** The hardhearted owner evicted the tenants for not paying the rent.	*sympathetic, considerate, kind, warmhearted*
hardship		*n.*	**burden, trial, misfortune** People lived through terrible hardships during the war.	*pleasure, advantage, happiness*

Word	#	Part of speech	Synonyms and example	Antonyms
hardy		*adj.*	**strong, vigorous, robust, fit, hearty, sturdy** Mountain climbers are hardy people.	*weak, delicate, feeble, frail*
harm	1.	*n.*	**hardship, injury, wrong, hurt, damage** Humans have brought harm to the environment.	1. *good, benefit, improvement, aid, assistance*
	2.	*v.*	**hurt, damage, injure** The hail harmed the crops. *adj.* Many pesticides are harmful to human beings.	2. *help, benefit, improve, assist, aid*
harmless		*adj.*	**safe, inoffensive** Only harmless pesticides should be used.	*harmful, injurious, hurtful, unsafe*
harmony		*n.*	**cooperation, understanding, agreement, accord, friendship** These two groups work in complete harmony.	*conflict, discord*
harness	1.	*n.*	**lines, reins, traces, halter, bridle** Let's put the harness on the horse.	
	2.	*v.*	**utilize, make useful** The new dam will harness great energy from the falls.	
harsh	1.	*adj.*	**rough, grating, sharp, jarring, cutting, piercing, unpleasant** The sailors shielded their faces against the harsh wind.	1. *pleasing, mild, agreeable, gentle*
	2.	*adj.*	**mean, stern, cruel, severe, unkind** The children were terrified of their harsh guardian. *adv.* He treated them harshly.	2. *kind, merciful, gentle, considerate, loving*
harvest	1.	*n.*	**reaping, crop gathering** The farm neighbours helped each other with the harvest.	1. *sowing, planting*
	2.	*n.*	**yield, crop** The grape harvest this year was plentiful.	
	3.	*v.*	**reap, gather, cut, mow, pick, collect** The fruit crop was harvested before the frost came.	3. *seed, plant, sow*
hassle		*n.*	**struggle, argument, quarrel, squabble, conflict, trouble** What a hassle over who would pay for the meal!	

Entry	No.	Part	Synonyms / Example	Antonyms
haste		*n.*	**speed, quickness, swiftness, hurry, rush** The doctor went in haste to help the patient. *v.* Yen hastened to answer the phone.	*slowness, tardiness, delay*
hasty	1.	*adj.*	**swift, rushed, hurried, quick, fast, speedy** We had a hasty lunch between classes.	**1.** *slow, leisurely*
	2.	*adj.*	**rash, thoughtless, reckless** Don't make a hasty decision when you buy a house or a car.	**2.** *careful, cautious, thoughtful*
hate		*v.*	**dislike, detest, despise, abhor** The baby hated the taste of the medicine.	*like, regard, respect, love*
hateful		*adj.*	**obnoxious, distasteful, nasty, revolting, sickening, nauseating, unpleasant** Most people feel that hunting is a hateful pastime.	*lovable, pleasing, delightful, agreeable, desirable*
hatred		*n.*	**ill will, dislike, aversion, hostility** Hatred sometimes leads to violence.	*love, kindness, fondness, affection*
haughty		*adj.*	**proud, disdainful, arrogant, stuck-up, snobbish** The haughty girl refused to make friends with the new students. *adv.* She haughtily stomped off when we approached her for help. *n.* Someday she will pay for her haughtiness.	*unassuming, unpretentious, humble, modest*
haul	1.	*n.*	**amount, catch, take** The fishing crew pulled in a good haul of cod.	
	2.	*n.*	**pull, drag** The train needed extra diesels for the long haul.	
	3.	*v.*	**pull, drag, carry, draw, transport, move** Lumberjacks hauled logs from the bush all winter.	**3.** *shove, push*
have	1.	*v.*	**own, possess, hold** Do you have a car?	
	2.	*v.*	**take, get, obtain** Please have a seat.	**2.** *give up, forfeit, relinquish*
	3.	*v.*	**allow, permit** My parents won't have a dog in the house.	**3.** *disallow, forbid, refuse*

Word	No.	Part	Synonyms / Example	Antonyms
	4.	*v.*	**must, be compelled, be obliged** I have to do my homework tonight.	
haven		*n.*	**refuge, shelter, retreat, harbour** The travellers tried to find a haven from the storm.	
havoc		*n.*	**destruction, disaster, calamity, ruin, damage** The hurricane wreaked havoc over a wide area.	
hazard	1.	*n.*	**threat, risk, danger, peril, chance** The travellers faced many hazards on the icy highways. *adj.* The ice storm created hazardous driving conditions.	**1.** *safeguard, protection*
	2.	*v.*	**risk, venture, take a chance on** Hazard a guess about my age.	
haze		*n.*	**fog, smoke, vapour, mist** Forest fires created a haze over the whole valley.	
hazy	1.	*adj.*	**cloudy, foggy, misty, murky, smoky** On humid days the atmosphere can become quite hazy.	**1.** *clear, bright, sunny*
	2.	*adj.*	**uncertain, obscure, vague, confused** She has only a hazy idea of how the accident happened.	**2.** *clear, certain, clear-cut, positive, definite, sure*
head	1.	*n.*	**leader, boss, chief, ruler** His aunt is head of the company. *v.* She has headed the company for many years.	**1.** *follower, worker*
	2.	*n.*	**mind, brain, intellect, intelligence** Reta has a good head for mathematics.	
	3.	*v.*	**guide, direct, steer, proceed** Everyone headed home after the party.	
head-first		*adv.*	**headlong** Shawn toppled head-first into the river.	*feet-first*
headlong	1.	*adv.*	**head-first** Tom fell headlong down the stairs.	**1.** *feet-first*
	2.	*adv.*	**thoughtlessly, recklessly, rashly, hastily** Susan ran headlong into the path of the car.	**2.** *carefully, cautiously, warily*

Word	No.	Part	Synonyms / Example	Antonyms
headstrong		*adj.*	**stubborn, bullheaded, rash, reckless, hotheaded, obstinate** The headstrong hockey player was penalized for fighting.	*obliging, obedient, careful*
headway	1.	*n.*	**headroom, space** We had to crouch to enter the cave as there was not enough headway.	
	2.	*n.*	**progress, advancement** Scientists have made some headway in their search for a cure for AIDS.	
heal		*v.*	**cure, repair, remedy, mend, fix** Time is said to heal all wounds.	*injure, damage*
healthy		*adj.*	**well, vigorous, robust, sound, wholesome** She gave birth to a healthy girl. *n.* The baby is in good health.	*ill, sickly, unhealthy, ailing, frail, delicate*
heap	1.	*n.*	**pile, load, mass, stack, accumulation** There were heaps of gravel in the yard.	1. *bit*
	2.	*v.*	**pile, collect, gather, stack** We heaped the fallen leaves in piles.	2. *scatter, spread*
hearsay		*n.*	**rumour, gossip, idle talk** It is only hearsay that the company is in trouble.	
heartless		*adj.*	**hardhearted, cruel, pitiless, merciless, unkind** It would be heartless not to help the needy.	*gentle, kind, merciful, humane*
hearty	1.	*adj.*	**warm, sincere, cheerful, cheery, enthusiastic** We received a hearty welcome from our friends.	1. *insincere, unenthusiastic*
	2.	*adj.*	**healthy, strong, well, hardy, vigorous, robust** My grandmother is hale and hearty.	2. *sickly, weak, ill, ailing, frail, delicate*
heat	1.	*n.*	**hot weather, warmth, high temperature** Many people find the heat in July unbearable.	1. *cold, coldness*
	2.	*n.*	**passion, ardour, excitement** He slammed the table in the heat of the argument. *adj.* It was a heated argument.	2. *calm*

Word	No.	Part	Synonyms and example	Antonyms
	3.	*v.*	**make hot, bring to a boil, cook** Heat the leftovers in the microwave. *adj.* I burnt my hand on the heated pot.	3. *cool, let cool*
heave		*v.*	**hoist, raise, lift, elevate, toss, fling, throw** The workers heaved the bales of cotton onto the truck.	
heavy	1.	*adj.*	**weighty, burdensome, massive** That parcel is too heavy to carry.	1. *light*
	2.	*adj.*	**sad, gloomy, sorrowful** With a heavy heart, he told them the sad news.	2. *happy, cheerful, joyful*
heckle		*v.*	**pester, badger, taunt, harass, boo** The crowd heckled the speaker at the rally. *n.* The hecklers were thrown out of the meeting.	*applaud, agree with, appreciate*
hectic		*adj.*	**wild, frantic, busy** The opening day of school can be hectic.	*calm, restful, serene, peaceful, relaxing*
hedge	1.	*n.*	**row of bushes, border, barrier** The garden is surrounded by a thick hedge.	
	2.	*v.*	**surround, edge, fence, border, enclose** Our neighbour's garden is hedged with rosebushes.	
heed	1.	*n.*	**attention, notice, care, regard** The patient paid no heed to the doctor's advice.	1. *inattention, neglect*
	2.	*v.*	**observe, pay attention to, take notice of, follow** They heeded their parents' advice.	2. *ignore, neglect, disobey*
help	1.	*n.*	**aid, assistance, support** Thank you for your help with moving the furniture.	1. *hindrance*
	2.	*v.*	**aid, assist, befriend, support** We helped all those in need.	2. *hamper, hinder, obstruct*
hermit		*n.*	**recluse, solitary, loner** Many religious hermits live in the deserts of the Middle East.	

Word		Part of speech	Synonyms and example	Antonyms
heroic		*adj.*	**valiant, brave, fearless, bold, courageous, gallant, daring** Have you read about Don Quixote's heroic deeds? *n.* People admire heroism.	*cowardly, timid, fearful, afraid*
hesitate		*v.*	**falter, pause, waver, delay** The student hesitated before entering the principal's office. *n.* She agreed to help without any hesitation.	*advance, hurry, hasten*
hide	1.	*n.*	**skin, pelt** People tan the hides of some animals.	
	2.	*v.*	**conceal, cover** The boy hid the frog in his pocket. *adj.* The hidden frog began to croak.	**2.** *uncover, expose, exhibit, reveal, show*
hideous		*adj.*	**horrible, ugly, revolting, ghastly, frightful, terrible, awful** The actor wore a hideous mask.	*beautiful, lovely, handsome, pleasing*
high	1.	*adj.*	**tall, lofty, towering** The high mountains are always snow-capped.	**1.** *low, short*
	2.	*adj.*	**leading, eminent, exalted, senior, important** The Prime Minister has a high position in the government.	**2.** *unimportant, inferior, secondary*
	3.	*adj.*	**great, extreme** The police are working to lower the high crime rate.	**3.** *low, average*
highlight	1.	*n.*	**peak, climax, high point** The highlight of our trip was the launch of the space shuttle.	**1.** *low point, disappointment*
	2.	*v.*	**stress, emphasize, underline, accent** The minister's speech highlighted the need to conserve energy.	**2.** *neglect, overlook, slight*
hike		*n.*	**march, walk, tramp** After the long hike everyone was tired and hungry. *v.* The Scouts hiked ten kilometres.	
hilarious		*adj.*	**funny, merry, lively** Everyone laughed at Peng's hilarious stories.	*sad, miserable, unhappy, gloomy*
hinder		*v.*	**obstruct, delay, block, hamper, curb, thwart** The research project was hindered by a lack of funds.	*help, aid, assist, support*

Word			Synonyms / Example	Antonyms
hindrance		*n.*	**obstruction, obstacle, handicap** The thick smoke was a hindrance to the firefighters' rescue efforts.	*aid, support, help*
hint	1.	*n.*	**suggestion, inkling, clue, idea** There was not a hint of cloud in the sky.	
	2.	*v.*	**imply, suggest, intimate** Mom hinted that I might receive a gift.	**2.** *conceal, keep quiet*
hire	1.	*v.*	**employ, appoint, get, engage** The new factory will hire at least fifty people.	**1.** *dismiss, fire, let go, discharge*
	2.	*v.*	**lease, rent, charter, engage** Marge hired a car for the trip.	
historic		*adj.*	**memorable, important, significant, famous** The historic moon landing took place in 1969.	*unimportant, insignificant*
hit	1.	*n.*	**blow, bump, knock, strike** He suffered a direct hit to his head.	
	2.	*n.*	**success** The play was a big hit.	**2.** *failure, flop*
	3.	*v.*	**strike, rap, beat, slap, punch** The batter hit a home run.	
hitch	1.	*n.*	**problem, delay, mishap, mistake, difficulty** The wedding ceremony went off without a hitch.	
	2.	*v.*	**couple, attach, fasten, connect, secure** The trailer was hitched securely to the car. *n.* A new hitch was installed to pull the trailer.	**2.** *unfasten, untie, unhook, disconnect, loosen*
hoard		*v.*	**collect, stockpile, save, accumulate, store away** Squirrels hoard nuts for the winter. *n.* We found a hoard of acorns in a hollow tree.	*spend, distribute*
hoarse		*adj.*	**husky, rough, harsh, cracked** His cold gave him a hoarse voice.	*sweet, mellow, pleasant*
hoax		*n.*	**trick, deception, fraud, fake, spoof** The story of the flying saucer was a hoax.	*truth, fact, reality*

hobo *n.* **drifter, tramp, vagabond, bum, vagrant**
Two dogs barked at the hobo sleeping under the tree.

hoist
1. *n.* **lift, elevator**
A large hoist was used to lift the grand piano.
2. *v.* **raise, lift, heave, elevate, take up** — 2. *lower, take down*
The movers hoisted the piano to the third floor.

hold
1. *n.* **grasp, clutch, grip**
The police officer kept a firm hold on the suspect.
2. *v.* **keep, guard, reserve, set aside** — 2. *give up, cancel*
The airline will hold the tickets until Thursday.
3. *v.* **contain, enclose, accommodate**
That suitcase holds a lot of clothes.
4. *v.* **clutch, grip, grasp, clasp** — 4. *drop, let go, release*
The child held tightly to his mother's hand.
5. *v.* **bind, stick, cling, adhere** — 5. *loosen, come undone*
Will the glue hold a hook to the wall?
6. *v.* **have, conduct, execute** — 6. *cancel, postpone*
The committee will hold a meeting on Tuesday.
7. *v.* **restrain, keep, restrict, detain** — 7. *release, free, let go*
The suspect will be held without bail.
8. *v.* **keep, have, possess, occupy** — 8. *give up, leave*
Prime Minister Pierre Trudeau held office for a long time.

hole *n.* **cavity, opening, gap, pit, cave, excavation, hollow**
The gardener dug a hole to plant the bush.

holler *v.* **shout, call, yell, scream, bellow** — *whisper*
The letter carrier hollered when the dog attacked him.

hollow *adj.* **empty, vacant, unfilled** — *solid, filled, full*
The chocolate egg is hollow.

holy *adj.* **religious, godly, devout, sacred, blessed, divine** — *unholy, sacrilegious*
A church is a holy place.

homeland *n.* **birthplace, native land**
The refugee longed to return to her homeland.

Word		POS	Synonyms and example	Antonyms
homely		*adj.*	**plain, ordinary, simple** The dog's homely face is beautiful to its owner.	*beautiful, attractive, lovely*
honest		*adj.*	**reliable, sincere, trustworthy, honourable, fair, aboveboard** The honest man turned in the wallet that he found.	*dishonest, deceitful, devious, unreliable, insincere*
honesty		*n.*	**fairness, truthfulness, openness** Honesty is to be admired.	*dishonesty, deceit, deception*
honour (also spelled honor)		*n.*	**respect, esteem, glory, fame, renown, tribute** A scholarship was established in Terry Fox's honour.	*dishonour, disgrace, disrepute*
hope	1.	*n.*	**anticipation, expectation** May all your hopes come true.	1. *despair, fear*
	2.	*v.*	**wish, desire, trust** We hoped that you would come.	2. *dread, fear, doubt*
horrible		*adj.*	**dreadful, awful, horrid, terrible, frightful, repulsive, loathsome** Smallpox is a horrible disease.	*pleasant, attractive, good, pleasing*
horrid		*adj.*	**terrible, dreadful, awful, frightful, horrible, repulsive** What a horrid taste this medicine has!	*pleasant, pleasing, appealing*
horror		*n.*	**fear, panic, dismay, terror, dread, alarm** The face at the window filled me with horror.	*bravery, hope, courage, comfort, delight*
hospitable		*adj.*	**friendly, sociable, kind, neighbourly** The Yuens are hospitable hosts. *n.* Their friends always enjoy their hospitality.	*hostile, unfriendly, unkind, unsociable*
hostile		*adj.*	**unfriendly, antagonistic** The police had to control the hostile demonstrators.	*friendly, devoted, loyal, hospitable*
hot		*adj.*	**fiery, flaming, blazing, glowing, heated, burning, torrid** The campers cooked potatoes over the hot coals.	*cold, frigid, freezing, chilly, frosty*
hotheaded		*adj.*	**headstrong, rash, bad-tempered** Hotheaded people are difficult to live with.	*easygoing, even-tempered*

Word	No.	Part of speech	Synonyms and example	Antonyms
house	**1.**	*n.*	**residence, home, abode, dwelling, habitation** They expect to move into their new house in June.	
	2.	*n.*	**line, royal family, clan, dynasty, ancestry** Queen Elizabeth II is of the House of Windsor.	
	3.	*n.*	**store, shop, café, business** There is a pancake house on Main Street.	
	4.	*v.*	**shelter, accommodate, lodge** The flood victims were housed in temporary quarters.	**4.** *evict, expel*
howl		*n.*	**cry, yelp, whine, wail** The dog's howls kept us awake. *v.* The dog howled all night long.	
hug		*v.*	**cuddle, squeeze, embrace, hold** Jane hugged her dog.	
huge		*adj.*	**immense, great, gigantic, vast, enormous, monstrous, giant** The family laughed at Shen's story of the huge fish that got away.	*tiny, wee, miniature, little, small*
humane		*adj.*	**gentle, kind, tenderhearted, merciful** Treat animals in a humane way.	*cruel, brutal, pitiless, inhumane*
humble	**1.**	*adj.*	**modest, unassuming, shy, meek** The humble woman shyly acknowledged the applause.	**1.** *haughty, vain, boastful, arrogant, proud, conceited*
	2.	*adj.*	**plain, lowly, not grand** The shepherd lives in a humble hut.	**2.** *grand, elegant, pretentious*
humid		*adj.*	**damp, moist, muggy, clammy, sultry, sticky** We perspired on the humid day. *n.* The humidity was unbearable.	*dry, arid*
humiliate		*v.*	**shame, embarrass, disgrace, humble** The athletes were humiliated when they were caught cheating. *n.* Their humiliation was complete.	*please, honour, elate*
hunch		*n.*	**idea, premonition, feeling, suspicion** I've got a hunch that it will rain.	
hunger	**1.**	*n.*	**famine, starvation, lack of food** Hunger is a continuing problem in Africa.	**1.** *fullness*

Word			Synonyms	Antonyms
	2.	*v.*	**desire, wish, want, yearn for** The sailors hungered for the sight of land.	
hungry		*adj.*	**famished, starved, ravenous** Growing children are always hungry.	*well-fed, satisfied*
hunt	1.	*n.*	**search, pursuit, chase, quest** The hunt is on for the escaped convict.	**1.** *capture, discovery*
	2.	*v.*	**seek, pursue, chase, search, follow, track, trace** The ranch hands hunted for the lost cattle.	**2.** *find*
hurl		*v.*	**throw, pitch, cast, toss, fling** The young athlete hurled the discus sixty metres.	*catch, grasp*
hurry	1.	*n.*	**rush** I'm in a hurry to catch my bus.	
	2.	*v.*	**rush, speed, hasten, scurry, dash** Shoppers hurried through the store.	**2.** *slow down, dawdle*
hurt	1.	*n.*	**injury, wound** The doctor treated the boy's hurt in the hospital.	
	2.	*v.*	**harm, damage, wound, injure** I hurt my knee while skiing.	**2.** *cure, heal, benefit, help, assist*
	3.	*v.*	**ache, sting, pain** The knee still hurts from the injury.	
husky	1.	*adj.*	**hoarse, rough** A cold may cause a husky voice.	**1.** *smooth, soft*
	2.	*adj.*	**strong, hefty, solid, well-built, powerful** The husky boy easily carried the heavy box.	**2.** *weak, frail, puny, sickly*
hustle		*n.*	**hurry, scurry, bustle, stir, fuss, rush, scramble** What a hustle to get to the theatre on time! *v.* We hustled all the way down the street.	*peace, quiet, calm*
hyperactive		*adj.*	**overactive, overanimated** The hyperactive child had trouble sleeping.	*sluggish, dull, slow*

hypocrite	*n.*	**insincere person, two-faced person, deceitful person** I would be a hypocrite if I said I liked that outfit. *adj.* It would be hypocritical of me to say that I like it when I don't.	*sincere person, genuine person, honest person*
hypothesis	*n.*	**theory, proposal, thesis, assumption** The scientists stated their hypothesis before the experiment. *v.* The detective hypothesized about the motive for the crime.	*fact, certainty, proof*
hypothetical	*adj.*	**supposed, imaginary, possible** The lawyer spoke of a hypothetical situation.	*real, actual, true, proven*
hysteria	*n.*	**frenzy, emotional outburst, uncontrolled emotion, delirium** The passengers were close to hysteria when the plane was hijacked. *adj.* The plane's crew calmed the hysterical passengers.	*calm*

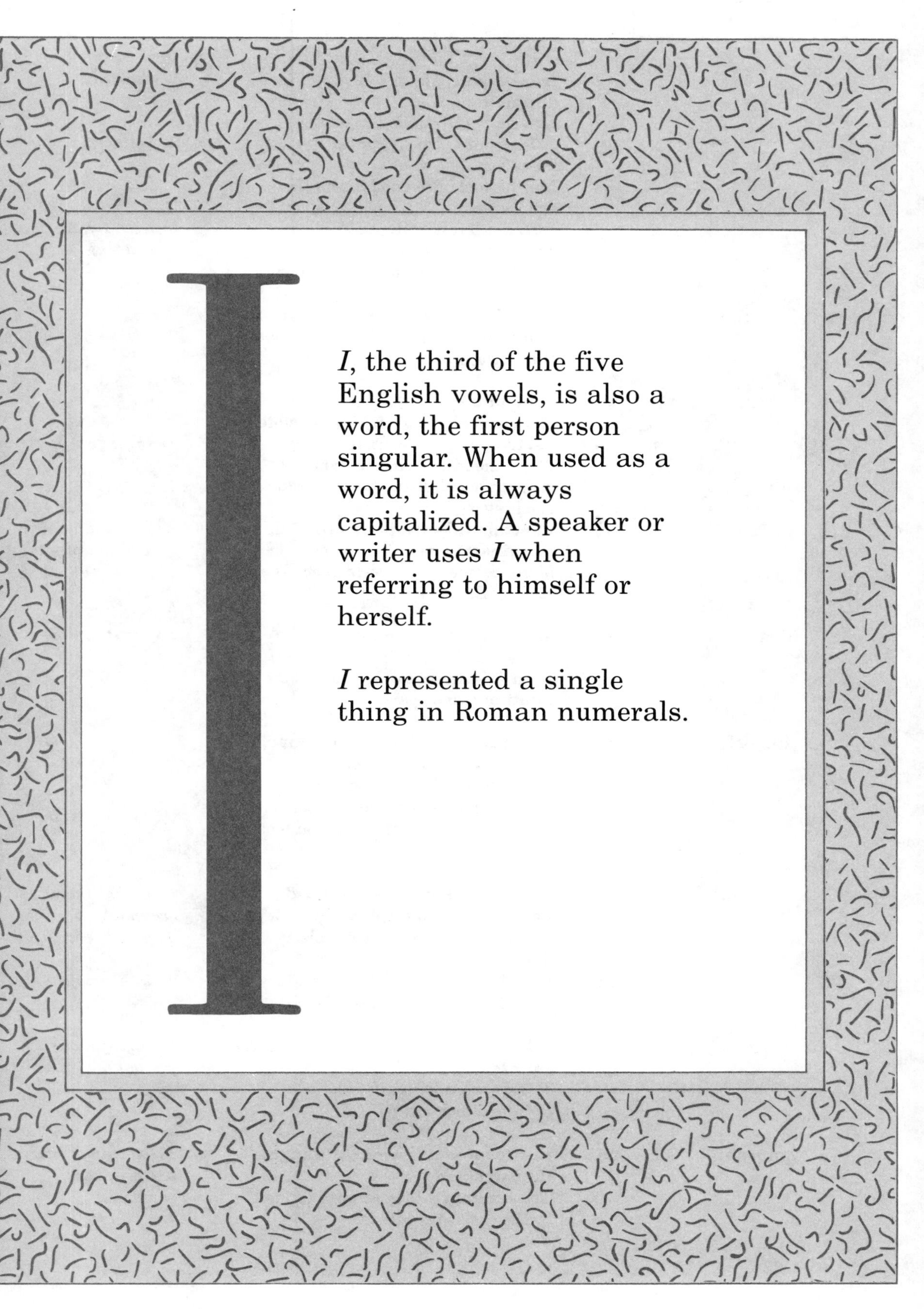

I, the third of the five English vowels, is also a word, the first person singular. When used as a word, it is always capitalized. A speaker or writer uses *I* when referring to himself or herself.

I represented a single thing in Roman numerals.

Word			Synonyms	Antonyms
icy	1.	*adj.*	**frozen over, glazed, frosted, iced, slippery** Drive carefully on icy streets.	**1.** *thawed*
	2.	*adj.*	**cold, frigid, frosty, polar, freezing** Many people drowned in the icy waters when the *Titanic* sank.	**2.** *hot, torrid, warm*
	3.	*adj.*	**unfriendly, hostile, cold** The rowdy students were silenced with an icy stare from the teacher.	**3.** *friendly, warm, welcoming*
idea		*n.*	**thought, notion, opinion, concept** Columbus had the brilliant idea that the world was round.	
ideal	1.	*n.*	**goal, aim** She has set herself lofty ideals in life.	
	2.	*adj.*	**perfect, supreme, exemplary** She is the ideal size for a gymnast. *n.* With her skill and her dedication, she is every coach's ideal.	**2.** *imperfect, faulty*
	3.	*adj.*	**unattainable, utopian, fanciful, imaginary, unreal, abstract** Many people think world peace is an ideal goal.	**3.** *practical, down-to-earth, attainable*
identical		*adj.*	**alike, like, twin, same, indistinguishable** Even close friends could not tell the identical twins apart.	*different, unlike*
identify		*v.*	**recognize, label, classify, name, catalogue, analyse, describe** The witness identified the robber from the pictures in the police files. *n.* The process of identification took a long time.	
idle	1.	*adj.*	**unoccupied, inactive, unused, unengaged, unemployed** The printing presses stood idle during the strike.	**1.** *active, busy, occupied, used, engaged, employed*
	2.	*adj.*	**lazy, indolent, shiftless** The idle worker soon lost his job.	**2.** *industrious, diligent, busy*
ignite		*v.*	**set on fire, burn, incinerate, light, set off** The scout leader ignited the campfire with a torch.	*extinguish, quench, put out*
ignorant	1.	*adj.*	**uneducated, illiterate, untaught, uninstructed** The ignorant villagers were conned by the slick salesperson.	**1.** *educated, literate, learned, wise, informed*

	2.	*adj.*	**unaware, uninformed** Many people are ignorant of the benefits of a healthy diet. *n.* Ignorance of the law is not excused by the court.	2. *aware , informed*
ignore		*v.*	**disregard, pass over, overlook, scorn** Swimmers unwisely ignored the sign warning of polluted water.	*heed, pay attention to*
ill	1.	*adj.*	**sick, unwell, ailing, indisposed, unhealthy** The school was closed because many students were ill with influenza. *n.* The students' serious illness caused concern.	1. *well, healthy, hale*
	2.	*adj.*	**unfortunate, bad, evil, unfavourable** The project was plagued with ill luck from the beginning. *adv.* You shouldn't speak ill of others.	2. *good, favourable*
	3.	*adv.*	**barely, scarcely, hardly** Anton bought a car even though he could ill afford it.	3. *amply, well, comfortably*
illegal		*adj.*	**unlawful, illicit, illegitimate, unauthorized, banned, prohibited, forbidden** The driver was fined for making an illegal turn. *adv.* The driver was fined for turning illegally.	*lawful, legal, legitimate, permissible, authorized*
illegible		*adj.*	**obscure, unintelligible, indistinct, unreadable** The teacher refused to read the essay because the writing was illegible.	*legible, distinct, clear, intelligible, easy to read*
illuminate	1.	*v.*	**brighten, lighten** Street lights illuminate the roads.	1. *darken, obscure*
	2.	*v.*	**explain, clarify, interpret, elucidate** Illuminate your answer with a diagram.	2. *confuse, puzzle, confound*
	3.	*v.*	**embellish, emboss, decorate, illustrate, ornament, trim** Some ancient scholars illuminated their manuscripts with gold leaf. *n.* These illuminations can be seen in museums.	

Word		Part	Synonyms	Antonyms
illusion	1.	*n.*	**mirage, fancy, ghost, vision, hallucination, apparition** Many magic tricks are merely optical illusions.	**1.** *form, reality, body, substance*
	2.	*n.*	**misconception, mistake, misunderstanding, delusion, false notion** The dictator was under the illusion that he would rule forever.	**2.** *fact, knowledge, understanding*
illustration	1.	*n.*	**example, instance, case, sample, model, specimen** That statue is an illustration of the sculptor's style.	
	2.	*n.*	**picture, photo, photograph, drawing, etching, cartoon** The illustrations in the book were by a famous artist.	
illustrious		*adj.*	**renowned, famous, eminent, important, distinguished, celebrated, famed** Pavarotti is an illustrious opera singer.	*unknown, obscure, hidden*
imaginary		*adj.*	**hypothetical, fancied, fanciful, whimsical, theoretical, unreal, illusory** The equator is an imaginary line around the centre of the Earth.	*real, factual, actual, existing*
imagination		*n.*	**fantasy, fancy** Writers of science fiction stories have vivid imaginations.	*reality*
imagine		*v.*	**visualize, picture, conceive, fancy, think of** Can you imagine living on the moon?	
imitate	1.	*v.*	**emulate, do likewise, follow, follow suit** People often imitate those whom they admire. *n.* Imitation is the sincerest form of flattery.	**1.** *neglect, disregard, depart from*
	2.	*v.*	**copy, mimic, duplicate, match, mirror, echo, simulate** The parrot imitated its owner's voice. *n.* Parrots are good imitators. *n.* The pearl necklace turned out to be a cheap imitation.	**2.** *change, alter, misrepresent*

immaculate	1.	*adj.*	**spotless, clean, stainless, unsullied** The house is in immaculate condition.	1. *dirty, soiled, filthy, unclean*
	2.	*adj.*	**sinless, pure, innocent, undefiled** Some people lead immaculate lives.	2. *sinful, defiled*
immature		*adj.*	**youthful, naive, childish, young, inexperienced, callow** Immature behaviour was the cause of the student's difficulty. *n.* His immaturity showed in his essay.	*mature, adult, experienced, sophisticated*
immediately		*adv.*	**instantly, now, right away, directly, at once, without delay, quickly, promptly, rapidly** "Come here immediately!" *adj.* There was an immediate reply to our request for help.	*later, in a while, presently*
immense	1.	*adj.*	**huge, great, big, large, vast, enormous, gigantic, mighty, colossal, tremendous, extensive** She inherited an immense fortune from her aunt.	1. *small, tiny, miniature, wee*
	2.	*adj.*	**boundless, eternal, limitless, endless, infinite** Outer space is immense.	2. *finite, limited, restricted*
immerse	1.	*v.*	**submerge, dip, douse, plunge, soak, drench, dunk** Electrical outlets should not be immersed in water.	1. *uncover, draw out, raise up*
	2.	*v.*	**engross, engage, involve, interest, absorb** The students immersed themselves in their discussion.	
imminent		*adj.*	**impending, near, at hand, destined, approaching, expected** The boats returned to shore when the radio reported that a storm was imminent.	*remote, distant, future, afar, possible*
immortal		*adj.*	**undying, perpetual, everlasting, endless, constant, interminable, unfading, abiding, enduring, permanent, never-ending** Shakespeare's plays have immortal appeal.	*temporary, fleeting, mortal, perishable*
immovable		*adj.*	**fixed, firm, immobile, stationary, stable, fastened** Train tracks are immovable.	*portable, mobile, movable, loose, free, removable*

Word			Synonyms and examples	Antonyms
immune	1.	*adj.*	**unaffected by, protected against, impervious, safe** They are immune to the disease as they have been immunized against it. *n.* Babies have a natural immunity to certain diseases.	1. *affected by*
	2.	*adj.*	**not liable, exempt** No one is immune from the law.	2. *liable, answerable*
impact	1.	*n.*	**collision, contact, clash, slam, shock** The driver got the full force of the impact when he hit the tree.	
	2.	*n.*	**influence, effect** The computer has had a tremendous impact on our lives.	
impair	1.	*v.*	**spoil, hurt, damage, injure** Smoking impairs health to a considerable degree.	1. *improve, repair, enhance*
	2.	*v.*	**weaken, lessen, diminish, handicap** Drinking impairs a person's concentration powers. *adj.* The drunk driver was charged with impaired driving.	2. *augment, enhance, strengthe*
impart		*v.*	**give, inform, tell, convey, disclose, divulge, reveal** A teacher imparts knowledge.	*conceal, hide, suppress, withhold*
impartial		*adj.*	**unbiassed, fair, just, unprejudiced, nonpartisan, equitable** Umpires have to make impartial decisions in a game.	*partial, biassed, one sided*
impassable		*adj.*	**closed, blocked, obstructed, impenetrable** Snow drifts make the expressway impassable.	*open, unobstructed, passable*
impatient	1.	*adj.*	**restless, anxious, eager** The children were impatient to set off on their holidays. *n.* In their impatience, they dashed outside to wait for their parents. *adv.* They called impatiently to their parents to hurry up.	1. *patient, calm*
	2.	*adj.*	**fretful, irritable, bothered, intolerant** The impatient man tooted his horn at the car in front of him.	2. *patient, relaxed, content*

Word			Synonyms	Antonyms
impeccable		*adj.*	**perfect, faultless, immaculate, flawless** Impeccable grooming is a must for television journalists. *adv.* They must be impeccably groomed when they are on the air.	*imperfect, deficient, defective*
impede		*v.*	**thwart, block, hinder, deter, obstruct, hamper** The strong current impeded the swimmer's progress.	*help, assist, aid, expedite*
impediment		*n.*	**hindrance, obstruction, obstacle, restriction, encumbrance, restraint, disadvantage** Heavy luggage is an impediment to a traveller.	*assistance, aid, benefit, advantage*
impel	1.	*v.*	**urge, drive, excite, induce** Curiosity impelled the explorers to continue with their quest.	1. *inhibit, repress*
	2.	*v.*	**move, push, prod, propel, shove, drive, press** The crash impelled the passengers into the windshield.	2. *restrain, hold back*
imperative	1.	*adj.*	**urgent, necessary, essential, crucial, compulsory** It is imperative that everyone be vaccinated at once.	1. *optional, useless, unessential, unnecessary*
	2.	*adj.*	**authoritative, masterful, commanding** The children quietened when they heard the principal's imperative tones.	2. *unauthoritative, supplicatory*
imperfection		*n.*	**fault, flaw, stain, blemish, defect, weakness** Imperfections in jewels lower their value.	*perfection*
impertinent	1.	*adj.*	**irrelevant, pointless, inappropriate, inapplicable** The paper contained too much impertinent information.	1. *pertinent, applicable, appropriate, relevant*
	2.	*adj.*	**impudent, rude, saucy, bold, insolent, brazen, impolite** Such impertinent behaviour requires an apology. *n.* Such impertinence cannot be tolerated.	2. *respectful, polite, courteous*

Word	No.	Part of speech	Synonyms / Example	Antonyms
impetuous		*adj.*	**rash, hasty, headstrong, impulsive** Mei's impetuous temper often gets her into trouble.	*thoughtful, careful, cautious*
implant		*v.*	**insert, root, stick in, embed** The surgical team implanted a donor's heart in the patient.	*remove, take out*
implement	1.	*n.*	**utensil, device, tool, instrument** Hardware stores sell garden implements.	
	2.	*v.*	**realize, achieve, fulfil, complete, effect, carry out** The schools implemented the revised science course.	**2.** *abandon, give up*
implicate	1.	*v.*	**imply, hint, insinuate, suggest** The accused implicated that others were involved.	**1.** *state, declare*
	2.	*v.*	**accuse, associate, entangle, involve, incriminate** The witness implicated a neighbour in the crime.	**2.** *acquit, extricate, dissociate*
imply		*v.*	**suggest, infer, hint, intimate** The students' frowns implied they were having trouble with the test.	*declare, state, express*
impolite		*adj.*	**rude, discourteous, impertinent, saucy, bold, forward, disrespectful** It is impolite to interrupt when someone is speaking.	*courteous, polite, respectful*
import		*v.*	**bring in, buy abroad** Canada imports many goods from the United States.	*export, sell abroad, send away*
important	1.	*adj.*	**significant, essential, pressing** Important decisions are made by parliament.	**1.** *trivial, inconsequential, unimportant*
	2.	*adj.*	**well-known, illustrious, prominent, notable, eminent** Prime ministers are important persons.	**2.** *obscure, unknown, unrecognized*
impose		*v.*	**force upon, inflict, place on** A fine will be imposed on jaywalkers.	
imposing		*adj.*	**impressive, striking, stirring, exciting, grand, majestic** The Eiffel Tower in Paris is an imposing sight.	*unimpressive, commonplace, uninteresting*

Word		Part of speech	Synonyms and example	Antonyms
impossible	1.	*adj.*	**unattainable, unworkable, futile, hopeless, unachievable** It is impossible to travel faster than the speed of light.	1. *possible*
	2.	*adj.*	**improbable, unlikely, doubtful, uncertain** The trip is impossible at this time.	2. *probable, likely*
impostor		*n.*	**pretender, charlatan, quack** The impostor carried fake documents.	
impractical		*adj.*	**unrealistic, unworkable, unfeasible, illogical** The electric car is considered impractical at present.	*practical, logical, reasonable*
impressive	1.	*adj.*	**striking, moving, exciting, thrilling, stirring, notable** The actor gave an impressive performance.	1. *dull, common, uninspiring*
	2.	*adj.*	**grand, noble, stately, majestic** The Taj Mahal is an impressive structure.	2. *simple, modest, unassuming, ordinary*
impromptu		*adj.*	**unprepared, spontaneous, unrehearsed** Most people find it difficult to make impromptu speeches.	*prepared, studied, premeditated, rehearsed*
improper	1.	*adj.*	**unsuitable, unbecoming, incorrect, inappropriate** It is improper to wear a bathing suit to an office.	1. *proper, correct, fitting, suitable, appropriate*
	2.	*adj.*	**wrong, indecent, immoral, shameful, wicked, vulgar** It used to be considered improper for women to expose their ankles in public.	2. *decent, proper, right*
impudent		*adj.*	**forward, brazen, rude, impertinent, brash, insolent** Impudent behaviour angers most parents. *n.* Parents don't like impudence.	*shy, polite, courteous*
impulsive	1.	*adj.*	**rash, hasty, thoughtless, impetuous** Vani regretted his impulsive remarks as soon as he said them.	1. *cautious, wary, careful*
	2.	*adj.*	**spontaneous, automatic, involuntary, instinctive** That outburst of anger was an impulsive act.	2. *premeditated, prepared*

Word		Synonyms	Antonyms
impure	*adj.*	**dirty, contaminated, polluted, tainted** We shouldn't drink impure water. *n.* Impurities in drinking water can be harmful to our health.	*clean, pure, uncontaminated*
inadequate	*adj.*	**insufficient, not enough, deficient** Inadequate ventilation made the workers drowsy.	*enough, adequate, sufficient*
inappropriate	*adj.*	**unsuitable, improper, out of place, unbecoming, incorrect** Slang is considered inappropriate language in formal reports.	*suitable, fitting, appropriate, proper*
inaugurate	*v.*	**begin, originate, introduce, initiate, start, install in office** The president-elect will be inaugurated in the new year. *adj.* President Kennedy's inaugural address touched many people.	*end, terminate, conclude, finish*
incense	*v.*	**anger, enrage, cross, infuriate, annoy, provoke** The baseball fans were incensed at the umpire's unfair call.	*calm down, soothe, pacify*
incentive	*n.*	**stimulus, inducement, impetus, enticement, spur** The salespeople were offered a bonus as an incentive for more sales.	*restraint, curb, constraint, check, deterrent, limitation*
incessant	*adj.*	**ceaseless, endless, continuous, unending, constant, continual, uninterrupted, perpetual** The dog's incessant barking annoyed the neighbours. *adv.* The dog barked incessantly because it was cold.	*occasional, rare, periodic, random, sporadic, infrequent irregular*
incident	*n.*	**event, occasion, episode, affair, happening, occurrence** The nasty incident took place yesterday.	
incidental	*adj.*	**minor, casual, secondary, subordinate** Winning is incidental to the thrill of participation.	*major, main, significant, principa*

incite		*v.*	**rouse, excite, stimulate, provoke, induce, stir up, prompt, inspire, foment** The leader's speech incited the people to rebel.	*calm, discourage, check, restrain, allay, soothe, abate, pacify*
inclement		*adj.*	**harsh, bitter, cruel, severe, raw, foul** The game was postponed because of inclement weather.	*calm, mild, benign, pleasant*
incline	**1.**	*n.*	**slope, grade, inclination, hill** The incline was used as a toboggan run in the winter.	**1.** *plain, flat*
	2.	*v.*	**lean, bend, bow, turn, slope, slant, tilt** Plants incline towards the sun.	**2.** *straighten*
	3.	*v.*	**prefer, favour, dispose** Looking at the evidence I am inclined to think he is guilty.	**3.** *disincline*
include	**1.**	*v.*	**contain, embrace, consist of, incorporate, be composed of, be comprise of, cover** The package price includes air travel and hotel.	**1.** *exclude, omit*
	2.	*v.*	**enter, incorporate, insert, combine, add, append** This report is to be included in the file.	**2.** *discard, reject, exclude*
incompetent		*adj.*	**incapable, unfit, inefficient, inexpert, unable, bungling, ineffectual** The incompetent worker was fired.	*able, fit, capable, qualified, expert, competent, proficient, skilful*
inconvenient		*adj.*	**bothersome, disturbing, awkward, troublesome, inopportune, unsuitable** Would it be inconvenient for you to drive me home? *n.* It is a great inconvenience to drive you home as you live so far away.	*convenient, timely, suitable, opportune*
incorporate		*v.*	**include, combine, consolidate, unite, join, embody, merge** The students' suggestions were incorporated into the plan.	*exclude, eliminate*
incorrect		*adj.*	**false, mistaken, inaccurate, unreliable, wrong, unprecise, erroneous, fallacious** Incorrect information is misleading. *adv.* The patient was incorrectly given the wrong medicine.	*true, accurate, reliable, correct, precise*

Word			Synonyms	Antonyms
increase	1.	*n.*	**growth, development, extension, enlargement, escalation, expansion** The increase in the cost of living is a concern.	1. *reduction, decrease, decline*
	2.	*n.*	**addition, gain, increment, boost** An increase in salary is always appreciated.	2. *decrease, cut, reduction, loss*
	3.	*v.*	**extend, enlarge, expand, magnify, improve, strengthen, grow, swell** The company's profits increased by 30 percent last year.	3. *decrease, lessen, reduce, shrink*
incredible		*adj.*	**unbelievable, improbable, extraordinary** Sean performed an incredible feat of bravery when he rescued the baby from the burning room. *adv.* It was incredibly brave of him.	*credible, believable, ordinary*
incur		*v.*	**obtain, get, acquire, bring on, meet with** The company incurred heavy losses during the strike.	
indecent		*adj.*	**improper, wrong, immoral, wicked, shameful** Swearing is considered by many to be indecent language. *n.* The book was banned because of its gross indecency.	*proper, decent, right, moral*
indefinite	1.	*adj.*	**vague, uncertain, unsure, unspecified, unclear, undefined, blurred, ambiguous** Our plans for the trip are still indefinite.	1. *certain, clear, definite, specified, defined, precise*
	2.	*adj.*	**unlimited, infinite** Outer space has indefinite dimensions.	2. *limited, finite*
independence		*n.*	**autonomy, self-reliance** Many British colonies achieved independence after World War II.	*dependence, subordination*
independent		*adj.*	**autonomous, self-reliant, self-sufficient** She is an independent thinker and cannot be easily swayed.	*subordinate, dependent*

Word			Synonyms and examples	Antonyms
indicate		*v.*	**show, designate, denote, register, point out, specify, signify** Their smiles indicate that they were successful in the competition. *n.* A person's facial expression is a good indicator of his or her mood.	
indifference		*n.*	**unconcern, disinterest, disregard, apathy, detachment** The team's indifference led to its defeat. *adj.* The indifferent players were defeated.	*concern, interest, regard, attention*
indigenous		*adj.*	**native, natural** Penguins are indigenous to the Antarctic region.	*alien, foreign*
indignant		*adj.*	**angry, piqued, upset, displeased, irritated, offended, resentful** The indignant customer stomped out of the store.	*pleased, content, flattered, satisfied*
indirect		*adj.*	**roundabout, circuitous, oblique, crooked, twisting, devious, rambling, zigzag** The indirect route to the hotel was the more scenic one.	*direct, straight, straightforward, immediate*
indispensable		*adj.*	**essential, vital, necessary, required, needed** Oxygen is indispensable to human life.	*dispensable, useless, unnecessary, unimportant*
indistinct		*adj.*	**vague, indefinite, obscure, blurred, dim, faint, inaudible** Her voice was indistinct as the telephone connection was very bad.	*clear, distinct, definite, sharp*
individual	1.	*n.*	**person, human being** Most individuals enjoy holidays.	
	2.	*adj.*	**singular, peculiar, unique, special, distinctive** Each student has an individual approach to research.	**2.** *ordinary, commonplace, everyday, general*
	3.	*adj.*	**separate, single, sole, solitary** Each candy bar had an individual wrapper. *adv.* Each candy bar was wrapped individually.	**3.** *collective, public, common, multiple*
induce	1.	*v.*	**urge, convince, persuade, prompt, influence** Advertisers induce consumers to buy their products.	**1.** *dissuade, discourage, deter, restrain*

Word	No.	Part	Synonyms and example	Antonyms
	2.	*v.*	**cause, bring about, effect, produce** The medicine induced sleep.	**2.** *restrain, cancel, nullify, stop*
indulge		*v.*	**revel, gratify, pamper** Holiday resorts encourage people to indulge their whims. *n.* Self-indulgence should not be carried too far.	*thwart, deny, be severe*
industrious		*adj.*	**diligent, busy, active, hardworking** The industrious students completed their project ahead of time.	*idle, inactive, unoccupied*
ineffective		*adj.*	**useless, weak, worthless, inadequate** The medicine proved ineffective as a painkiller.	*effective, useful*
inefficient	1.	*adj.*	**wasteful, extravagant** High horsepower engines are inefficient.	**1.** *economical, saving*
	2.	*adj.*	**incompetent, incapable, ineffective** Inefficient planning caused the project to fail. *n.* The workers were fired for their inefficiency.	**2.** *competent, fit, able, capable, adept, expert, effective*
inevitable		*adj.*	**unavoidable, sure, certain, inescapable, unpreventable, destined, assured, determined** Death is inevitable.	*doubtful, contingent, avoidable, escapable, preventable*
inexpensive		*adj.*	**cheap, thrifty, low-priced, modest, economical** On their budget they can only afford an inexpensive car.	*costly, expensive, high-priced, uneconomical*
infallible		*adj.*	**unerring, exact, unquestionable, perfect, true, authoritative, right, reliable, certain, dependable** The research is so thorough that the findings should be infallible.	*erroneous, false, questionable, doubtful*
infer	1.	*v.*	**conclude, deduce, reason, gather, understand** I inferred from her frown that I was not welcome.	
	2.	*v.*	**imply, insinuate, suggest, hint** The letter inferred that I was lazy. *n.* The inference was not a fair one.	

Word	No.	Part of speech	Synonyms / Example	Antonyms
inferior	1.	*adj.*	**secondary, minor, subordinate, junior, lesser, lower** In the army, all ranks are inferior to that of general.	**1.** *superior, senior, higher*
	2.	*adj.*	**second-rate, mediocre, poor** I was warned to avoid that store because it sells inferior products.	**2.** *first-rate, top, superior*
infiltrate	1.	*v.*	**seep, trickle, permeate, filter, penetrate** Shafts of sunlight infiltrated the thick forests.	**1.** *flood, flow, ooze, stream*
	2.	*v.*	**enter, penetrate** Spies infiltrated the company and stole valuable information.	
infinite	1.	*adj.*	**unlimited, boundless, incalculable, measureless, untold, immeasurable** The universe is infinite.	**1.** *limited, restricted, definite*
	2.	*adj.*	**endless, eternal, perpetual, incessant, constant** Many people take advantage of their infinite kindness.	**2.** *fleeting, short, temporary*
inflate	1.	*v.*	**blow up, pump up, expand, swell, fill** The cyclist inflated the tires before the race.	**1.** *deflate, empty*
	2.	*v.*	**exaggerate, magnify, enlarge, amplify** The media inflated the news event beyond the facts.	**2.** *minimize, underestimate, reduce*
influence		*n.*	**control, power, sway, effect** The media has a strong influence on how people think. *v.* The media influences people's opinions.	*impotence*
inform		*v.*	**instruct, teach, tell, notify, relate, mention** They informed us that they were moving.	*conceal, withhold*
information		*n.*	**facts, data, knowledge, news** A computer is able to store and process a great deal of information.	
infrequent		*adj.*	**rare, occasional, sparse, scarce, few** Healthy people make infrequent visits to the doctor.	*frequent, usual, regular, customary*

Word		Synonyms	Antonyms
infuriate	*v.*	**provoke, enrage, aggravate, vex, anger, arouse, incense** The matador infuriated the bull.	*calm, soothe, quiet*
ingenious	*adj.*	**creative, imaginative, inventive, resourceful, clever** He escaped punishment with an ingenious excuse.	*unresourceful, dull, unimaginative*
ingredient	*n.*	**component, element, constituent** This recipe calls for many ingredients.	*whole*
inhabit	*v.*	**occupy, stay, live in, dwell, reside, lodge** Polar bears inhabit the North Pole. *n.* The inhabitants of the village were shocked by the earthquake.	*vacate, desert, abandon*
initial	*adj.*	**first, primary, introductory, beginning** "A" is the initial letter of the English alphabet.	*last, terminal, final, concluding*
initially	*adv.*	**at first, in the beginning, at the beginning, originally** Initially, the world was thought to be flat.	*finally, in the end, at the end, in conclusion*
initiate	*v.*	**open, start, begin, commence, inaugurate, introduce** Singing of the anthem initiated the ceremonies.	*close, end, finish, complete, conclude*
injure	*v.*	**hurt, harm, wound, abuse, damage, impair** The cat pounced on the bird and injured it. *n.* The bird's injuries were severe.	*heal, repair*
injurious	*adj.*	**harmful, damaging, bad, detrimental, dangerous** Smoking is injurious to health.	*beneficial, helpful, advantageous*
injustice	*n.*	**unfairness, unjustness, prejudice, bias, partiality, inequity, inequality** Laws are made to prevent injustice.	*justice, justness, fairness, equity, equality*
innocent	1. *adj.*	**guiltless, blameless, upright, faultless** Laws are made to protect innocent citizens.	1. *guilty*

	2.	*adj.*	**inexperienced, raw, naive, callow** Innocent youths can be easily influenced. *n.* Many people exploit the innocence of youth.	**2.** *experienced*
	3.	*adj.*	**harmless, safe, inoffensive, innocuous** The teenagers had a day of innocent fun at the beach.	**3.** *dangerous, harmful*
innovation		*n.*	**change, alteration, variation, transformation** Henry Ford made innovations in the car industry. *n.* Ford was an innovator in the automobile industry. *adj.* He was an innovative man.	
input		*n*	**data, information, knowledge, facts** Computers can store large amounts of input.	
inquire	1.	*v.*	**ask, question** We inquired if the dogs were for sale. *n.* The answer to our inquiry was yes!	**1.** *answer, reply, respond*
	2.	*v.*	**investigate, probe, study, examine, analyse, delve into, look into, inspect, review** The detective inquired into the matter of the missing children.	**2.** *ignore, overlook*
inquisitive		*adj.*	**curious, inquiring, questioning, searching, prying** Young children are naturally inquisitive.	*indifferent, unconcerned*
insane	1.	*adj.*	**unbalanced, deranged, mad** The accused was declared insane. *n.* The accused was found not guilty because of insanity.	**1.** *sane, rational*
	2.	*adj.*	**foolish, idiotic, daft, stupid, ridiculous** Everyone scoffed at the insane plan.	**2.** *sensible, thoughtful, reasonable*
insert	1.	*n.*	**addition, inclusion** The entry form is an insert in the magazine.	
	2.	*v.*	**put in, embed, inject, include** Jane inserted the key into the lock.	**2.** *take out, extract, remove, exclude*
inside	1.	*adj.*	**inner, inward, innermost** It is an advantage to draw the inside track in a race.	**1.** *outer, peripheral*

Word			Synonyms	Antonyms
	2.	*adv.*	**indoors, within** We dashed inside when it rained.	*2. outside, in the open, outdoors*
	3.	*prep.*	**within, surrounded by, bounded by** The pupils are inside the schoolyard.	*3. beyond, outside of*
insight		*n.*	**perceptiveness, understanding, discernment, intuition, awareness** Anne Frank's diary provided deep insights into her life in hiding.	*misunderstanding, ignorance*
insignificant		*adj.*	**trivial, petty, unimportant, irrelevant, trifling** Their contribution to the research was insignificant.	*important, meaningful, significant*
insipid	1.	*adj.*	**tasteless, flat** The soup was so thin it was insipid.	*1. piquant, zesty, flavourful, tasty*
	2.	*adj.*	**weak, lifeless, dull, uninteresting** That play has too many insipid characters.	*2. interesting, exciting, dynamic, stimulating*
insist		*v.*	**require, order, command, expect** The teacher insisted on punctuality. *n.* We arrived punctually at his insistence.	*waive, forgo, defer*
insolent		*adj.*	**rude, offensive, arrogant, contemptuous, impertinent, impudent** The students were suspended for their insolent behaviour. *n.* Insolence is not tolerated in this school.	*polite, courteous, servile, meek, well-mannered*
inspect		*v.*	**investigate, study, probe, examine, scrutinize, check** All produce is inspected to determine its quality.	*ignore, overlook*
install	1.	*v.*	**establish, inaugurate** A new director will be installed at the meeting.	*1. remove, withdraw*
	2.	*v.*	**set up, put in, place** Traffic lights were installed at the busy crossroad.	
instant	1.	*n.*	**moment, second, flash, minute, jiffy, twinkling** In an instant the squirrel was up the tree.	

Entry	No.	Part	Synonyms / Example	Antonyms
	2.	*adj.*	**immediate, rapid, prompt, fast, quick, sudden, direct, speedy, instantaneous** Instant replays are part of modern sports telecasts. *adv.* Some pain can be relieved instantly.	**2.** *delayed, slow, later*
instantaneous		*adj.*	**instant, rapid, speedy, immediate, quick, fast, prompt** This pill claims to provide instantaneous relief for headaches.	*delayed, later*
instruct	1.	*v.*	**teach, guide, educate, direct, coach** The flight attendant instructed the passengers about safety procedures. *n.* She was a good instructor.	**1.** *learn*
	2.	*v.*	**order, tell, command, direct, bid** The captain instructed the crew to abandon ship. *n.* The crew obeyed the captain's instructions.	**2.** *ask, request*
insufferable		*adj.*	**unbearable, intolerable, painful, unendurable, agonizing, excrutiating** Many diseases cause insufferable pain.	*bearable, tolerable, endurable*
insufficient		*adj.*	**inadequate, meagre, skimpy** The trip was cancelled because of insufficient funds.	*sufficient, ample, enough, surplus, excess*
insulate		*v.*	**protect, line, coat, cover, shield** Buildings can be insulated against heat, cold, or sound.	*expose, uncover*
insure		*v.*	**guarantee, protect** Insure the car against theft. *n.* Car insurance is mandatory in some areas.	
intact		*adj.*	**together, whole, complete, sound, untouched, uninjured** Amazingly, the car remained intact after going over the cliff.	*damaged, in pieces, broken, dismantled*
intangible	1.	*adj.*	**indefinite, uncertain, unsure, vague, unspecific, abstract, hypothetical** The suspect was released because of intangible evidence.	**1.** *definite, sure, tangible, certain, specific*
	2.	*adj.*	**immaterial, untouchable** Shadows are intangible.	**2.** *material, real, physical*

Word	No.	Part	Synonyms and example	Antonyms
integrate		*v.*	**combine, join, unify, connect, blend** The immigrants tried to integrate into the new country. *adj.* An integrated school accepts students of all races and religions.	*separate*
intelligence	1.	*n.*	**intellect, acumen, mental ability, discernment, cleverness** The child's remarkable intelligence was obvious during the debate.	
	2.	*n.*	**vital information, secret information** The spy was jailed for selling military intelligence.	
intelligent	1.	*adj.*	**clever, bright, astute, smart, perceptive, quick, shrewd** The intelligent girl was always top of her class.	**1.** *stupid, dull, unintelligent*
	2.	*adj.*	**sensible, rational** Is there intelligent life on other planets?	**2.** *irrational*
intend	1.	*v.*	**aim, plan, propose, hope to, aspire to, resolve** I intend to do well in the examinations. *n.* It is my intention to do well.	
	2.	*v.*	**reserve, set apart, assign, mean, designate** Which gift did you intend for me?	
intense		*adj.*	**violent, strong, acute, keen, deep, extreme, exceptional, heightened** Intense heat drove back the firefighters.	*weak, dull, shallow*
intentional		*adj.*	**deliberate, prearranged, intended, premeditated, contemplated, planned** The cruel remarks were intentional. *adv.* The remarks were made intentionally to hurt you.	*accidental, unintentional, undesigned, unplanned, casual*
interfere	1.	*v.*	**meddle, pry, intervene** Don't interfere in my affairs! *n.* Such interference is not wanted.	**1.** *neglect, ignore, leave alone*
	2.	*v.*	**prevent, stop, conflict, hinder, obstruct, hamper** The rain interfered with our plans for a picnic.	**2.** *assist, aid, support*

Word		Part of speech	Synonyms and examples	Antonyms
interior		*adj.*	**inner, inward, inside, internal, indoor** The interior walls were painted pink. *n.* The interior of the house is decorated opulently.	*exterior, outward, outside, outdoor*
intermediate		*adj.*	**middle, neutral, compromising, moderate, central, halfway** The intermediate grades fall between the junior and senior grades.	*extreme, uncompromising, immoderate*
intermittent		*adj.*	**periodic, broken, on and off, occasional, irregular, discontinuous, interrupted** The foghorn sounded on an intermittent basis. *adv.* It sounded intermittently.	*constant, lasting, incessant, regular*
interrogate		*v.*	**examine, question, ask, probe, cross-examine** The lawyer interrogated the witness. *n.* The interrogation was stressful for the witness.	
interval		*n.*	**period, interlude, interim** We started exercising again after a short interval.	*continuity*
intervene		*v.*	**intercede, mediate** The referee intervened in the dispute.	
intimidate		*v.*	**scare, frighten, threaten** The guard dog intimidated the intruder.	*help, placate, encourage, reassure*
intolerant		*adj.*	**prejudiced, biassed, bigoted, narrow-minded** Some children are raised in intolerant families. *n.* Intolerance of people of different races should be discouraged.	*tolerant, receptive, open-minded*
intrepid		*adj.*	**courageous, bold, dauntless, brave, fearless** The champion is an intrepid fighter.	*cowardly, timid, cowering, fearful*
intricate		*adj.*	**involved, complicated, complex, tricky, difficult, elaborate** A spider spins an intricate web. *n.* Intricacies of the law confuse us.	*simple, plain, uncomplicated, uninvolved, easy*
intrigue	1.	*n.*	**plot, scheme, conspiracy** Spies are involved in intrigue.	

Word	No.	Part	Synonyms and examples	Antonyms
	2.	*v.*	**interest, fascinate** The plot of the novel intrigued most readers.	2. *bore, repel*
intrude		*v.*	**interfere, meddle, interrupt** Don't intrude on our meeting. *n.* Intruders will be thrown out of the meeting.	*neglect, ignore, leave alone*
invade	1.	*v.*	**attack, assail** The troops invaded the enemy camp at sunrise. *n.* The invaders attacked at sunrise. *n.* The invasion took the enemy completely by surprise.	1. *retreat, withdraw, surrender*
	2.	*v.*	**trespass, interfere with, meddle, encroach upon, violate** Do not invade my privacy. *n.* Reading someone's diary is an invasion of the person's privacy.	2. *ignore, leave alone*
invalid		*n.*	**patient, sick person, disabled person** He has been an invalid since his heart attack.	
invalid		*adj.*	**unusable, void, null, worthless, valueless** The cheque was invalid because it had no signature.	*valid, usable*
invent	1.	*v.*	**devise, conceive, design, create, discover, compose, plan, fashion** Who invented the steam engine? *n.* The invention is patented.	1. *imitate, copy*
	2.	*v.*	**fabricate, falsify, misrepresent** They invent the most fantastic excuses for not doing homework.	
invert	1.	*v.*	**upset, overturn, tip, topple, turn over** The strong wave inverted the canoe.	1. *put upright, straighten, stand up*
	2.	*v.*	**reverse, transpose, exchange** To divide by a fraction, invert the fraction and multiply.	2. *maintain, keep*
investigation		*n.*	**inquiry, search, study, examination, probe** There will be an investigation into the cause of the accident. *v.* The police will investigate the incident thoroughly.	

Word			Synonyms	Antonyms
invigorating		*adj.*	**bracing, exhilarating, refreshing, stimulating** The campers had an invigorating swim before breakfast.	*soft, mild, gentle*
invincible		*adj.*	**unconquerable, unbeatable, unyielding, impregnable, insurmountable** No team is invincible.	*conquerable, weak, surmountable*
involve	1.	*v.*	**implicate, incriminate, entangle** How many people were involved in the crime?	1. *exclude, disconnect, eliminate, separate*
	2.	*v.*	**include, encompass** This event involves both students and parents.	
irate		*adj.*	**furious, angry, incensed, enraged, annoyed, irritated** Irate fans booed when the concert was cancelled.	*calm, peaceful, quiet, appeased, serene, composed, soothed*
ire		*n.*	**wrath, fury, rage, anger** Public ire was aroused over the increase in taxes.	*patience, calmness, gentleness*
irk		*v.*	**annoy, bother, pester, irritate, harass, perturb** Constant sarcasm irks people. *adj.* Please stop your irksome whining.	*soothe, relax, calm, please, satisfy*
irregular	1.	*adj.*	**uneven, occasional, infrequent, sporadic, variable** The alarm sounded at irregular intervals.	1. *regular, even*
	2.	*adj.*	**unusual, extraordinary, abnormal, different** It is irregular for the guard to be absent.	2. *usual, normal, customary*
	3.	*adj.*	**uneven, broken, jagged, crooked, zigzag, lopsided** The brook followed an irregular course.	3. *straight, even, uniform, equal, symmetrical, regular*
irrelevant		*adj.*	**inappropriate, unrelated, unconnected** Irrelevant information is often given in court cases.	*relevant, related, appropriate, fitting, connected, apropos*
irritable		*adj.*	**bad-tempered, touchy, testy, peevish, cross, grouchy, fretful, fidgety, irascible** People can become irritable in hot weather.	*pleasant, calm, agreeable, good-natured, even-tempered*

Word	No.	Part	Synonyms and example	Antonyms
irritate	1.	*v.*	**provoke, irk, annoy, agitate, bother, pester, exasperate, disturb, nettle** The umpire's decision irritated the pitcher. *n.* The umpire is a constant irritation to the pitcher.	**1.** *soothe, calm, quiet, comfort*
	2.	*v.*	**inflame, redden, chafe** Constant coughing irritates the throat.	**2.** *soothe, comfort*
isolate		*v.*	**confine, detach, seclude, separate, withdraw, segregate, quarantine** The hospital isolates persons with contagious diseases. *n.* These patients are kept in isolation.	*desegregate, include*
isolated		*adj.*	**secluded, lonely, remote, solitary, out-of-the-way, unfrequented** Garbage dumps should be located in isolated areas.	*populated, crowded, populous*
issue	1.	*n.*	**question, dispute, concern, problem** Equality is an issue of the day.	**1.** *solution, answer, remedy*
	2.	*v.*	**emerge, appear, flow out, spurt** Blood issued from the wound.	**2.** *remain*
	3.	*v.*	**circulate, announce, declare, publish, send out, broadcast** The government issued the report.	**3.** *retain, keep, withhold*

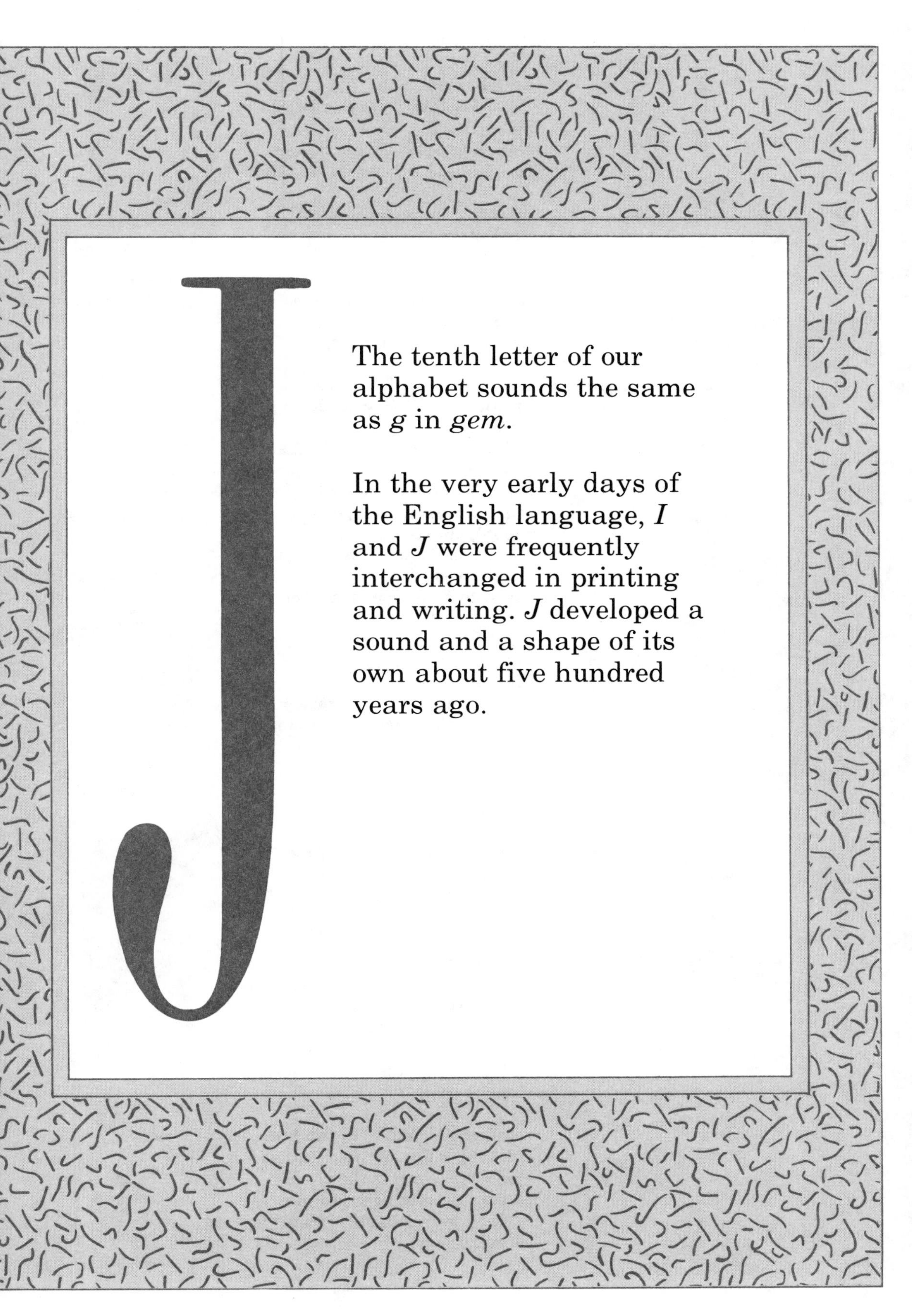

The tenth letter of our alphabet sounds the same as *g* in *gem*.

In the very early days of the English language, *I* and *J* were frequently interchanged in printing and writing. *J* developed a sound and a shape of its own about five hundred years ago.

Word			Synonyms	Antonyms
jab	**1.**	*n.*	**punch, blow, poke, hit** The boxer threw many quick jabs at his opponent.	
	2.	*v.*	**stab, dig, poke, thrust, pierce** Ling jabbed her fork into her steak.	
jail	**1.**	*n.*	**prison, penitentiary, penal institution** The robber was sentenced to one year in jail.	
	2.	*v.*	**imprison, confine, lock up, arrest, capture** He was jailed for robbery.	**2.** *release, let go*
jam	**1.**	*n.*	**tie-up, crush, block, press** Traffic jams often occur during rush hours.	
	2.	*n.*	**difficulty, mess, trouble, fix** The company has been in a jam since the president retired.	
	3.	*v.*	**stuff, squeeze, pack, cram, crowd, shove** He jammed his notes into his binder.	**3.** *ease, slip*
	4.	*v.*	**crush, wedge** The baby's finger was jammed in the door.	**4.** *release, let go*
jar	**1.**	*n.*	**bottle, container, jug** The jam jars were empty.	
	2.	*v.*	**jolt, bump, shake, vibrate, joggle** The vibrations from the passing train jarred the dishes.	
	3.	*v.*	**scrape, grate** Ali's whistle jars my nerves. *adj.* She has a jarring voice.	**3.** *calm, quiet, soothe, settle*
jargon		*n.*	**argot, specialized language, dialect** It is hard to understand the medical jargon of physicians.	
jealous	**1.**	*adj.*	**envious, resentful** Paul was jealous of Marco's success.	**1.** *loyal*
	2.	*adj.*	**suspicious, possessive** The jealous man was unhappy when his wife danced with another man. *n.* His jealousy turned him into a bitter person.	**2.** *trusting*
jeer		*v.*	**scoff, sneer, mock, taunt, boo, ridicule, laugh at, poke fun at** The crowd jeered at the tennis player's unsporting behaviour. *n.* Their jeers caused the player to leave the game.	*cheer, applaud*

Word	No.	Part	Synonyms and examples	Antonyms
jeopardize		*v.*	**endanger, imperil, risk** The refugees jeopardized their lives by escaping in crowded boats. *n.* Their lives were in jeopardy until they were picked up by a ship.	*assure*
jerk		*n.*	**tug, pull, twist** The sailor gave the rope a jerk to loosen the knot. *v.* He jerked the door open and ran outside. *adj.* The jerky movements of the bus made me feel ill.	*push, shove*
jiggle		*v.*	**joggle, shake, jerk, move, jostle** Muriel jiggled the desk when I was trying to write.	*steady, hold firm*
jittery		*adj.*	**nervous, jumpy** Susan was jittery before giving her speech.	*calm, relaxed*
jog	1.	*n.*	**push, shake, jerk, nudge** Kim gave me a jog with her elbow when I fell asleep during the show.	
	2.	*v.*	**trot, run** Helen and Vic jog daily. *n.* Jogging is a popular form of exercise. *n.* We often see joggers in our neighbourhood.	
joggle		*v.*	**jostle, shake, jerk, knock, jiggle, push** The train's motion joggled the passengers.	*steady, hold firm*
join	1.	*v.*	**link, couple, fasten** Join hands to form a circle.	**1.** *separate, uncouple, unfasten*
	2.	*v.*	**meet, connect, combine, unite** The highways joined outside the city.	**2.** *divide, disconnect*
	3.	*v.*	**sign up, enter, enrol in, become a member, associate with, enlist** Have you joined the debating club?	**3.** *resign, withdraw*
jolly		*adj.*	**merry, cheerful, gay, jovial, happy** Christmas is a jolly season.	*solemn, sober, grave, serious*
jostle		*v.*	**push, shove, jiggle, joggle, shake, prod, jab, poke, bump** The children jostled each other as they went to class.	

Word	No.	Part	Synonyms and example	Antonyms
journal	1.	*n.*	**record, diary, notebook, log** Do you keep a journal of your travels?	
	2.	*n.*	**magazine, periodical, publication, newspaper** Ken enjoys reading scientific journals.	
journey		*n.*	**trip, excursion, voyage, trek, expedition, tour, passage** Do you study the journeys of the explorers? *v.* They journeyed to the far corners of the Earth.	
jovial		*adj.*	**merry, happy, gay, cheerful, good-natured** The jovial man is well-liked by all his customers.	*sad, downcast, serious, gloomy*
joy		*n.*	**pleasure, gladness, delight, happiness** Children bring joy to their parents. *adj.* Birthdays are joyous occasions. *adj.* Students are joyful when they do well.	*sorrow, sadness, misery, gloom, unhappiness, despair*
jubilant		*adj.*	**joyful, elated, happy, pleased, delighted, excited, glad, in high spirits, overjoyed** The team was jubilant after winning the Cup for the third time.	*sorrowful, sad, despondent*
judge	1.	*n.*	**official, referee, umpire, critic, adjudicator** Mr. Brown was one of the judges at the flower show.	
	2.	*n.*	**legal official, public official, court justice, government official, justice of the peace, magistrate** It is an honour to be appointed a judge in the Supreme Court.	
	3.	*v.*	**settle, determine, try, rule on, hear, decide, find, pass sentence** Her Honour has judged many difficult cases in this court. *n.* Her judgments are always fair.	
	4.	*v.*	**guess, estimate, determine, suppose, believe, assume, imagine, conclude, surmise** I judge her age to be about thirty.	**4.** *know, be certain*
jumble	1.	*n.*	**clutter, muddle, hodgepodge, mess** The papers are in a jumble.	**1.** *order, system, arrangement*

Word	No.	Part	Synonyms	Antonyms
	2.	*v.*	**mix, confuse** The children jumbled the cards.	**2.** *put in order, arrange*
jumbo		*adj.*	**huge, very large, enormous, immense, mammoth** Have you ever flown on a jumbo jet? *n.* Elephants are called jumbos because of their size.	*small, tiny, little, wee, miniature*
junction		*n.*	**intersection, crossroads, joining, connecting point, meeting** There is always heavy traffic at the junction of those two highways.	
junk	1.	*n.*	**rubbish, trash, scrap, clutter, litter, waste, debris, rummage, garbage** All that junk in the basement needs to be cleared out.	
	2.	*v.*	**scrap, discard, dump, throw away, throw out** Mark junked his old bicycle.	**2.** *save, keep, retain, hold*
just	1.	*adj.*	**honest, fair, fitting, impartial, righteous** We believe our laws are just.	**1.** *unjust, unfair, one-sided*
	2.	*adv.*	**barely, hardly, scarcely** He was just in time to catch the bus.	
	3.	*adv.*	**exactly, precisely** The apples weigh just two kilograms.	**3.** *approximately, about*
justice		*n.*	**fairness, honesty, right** Justice was served when the criminal was sent to jail.	*injustice, dishonesty, unfairness*
jut		*v.*	**project, stick out, extend, protrude, overhang** Cape Tormentine juts far out into the Northumberland Strait.	
juvenile	1.	*n.*	**minor, youth, child** Some movies are not suitable for juveniles.	**1.** *adult, grown-up*
	2.	*adj.*	**young, immature, childish** "Farmer in the Dell" is a juvenile game.	**2.** *mature, adult, grown-up*

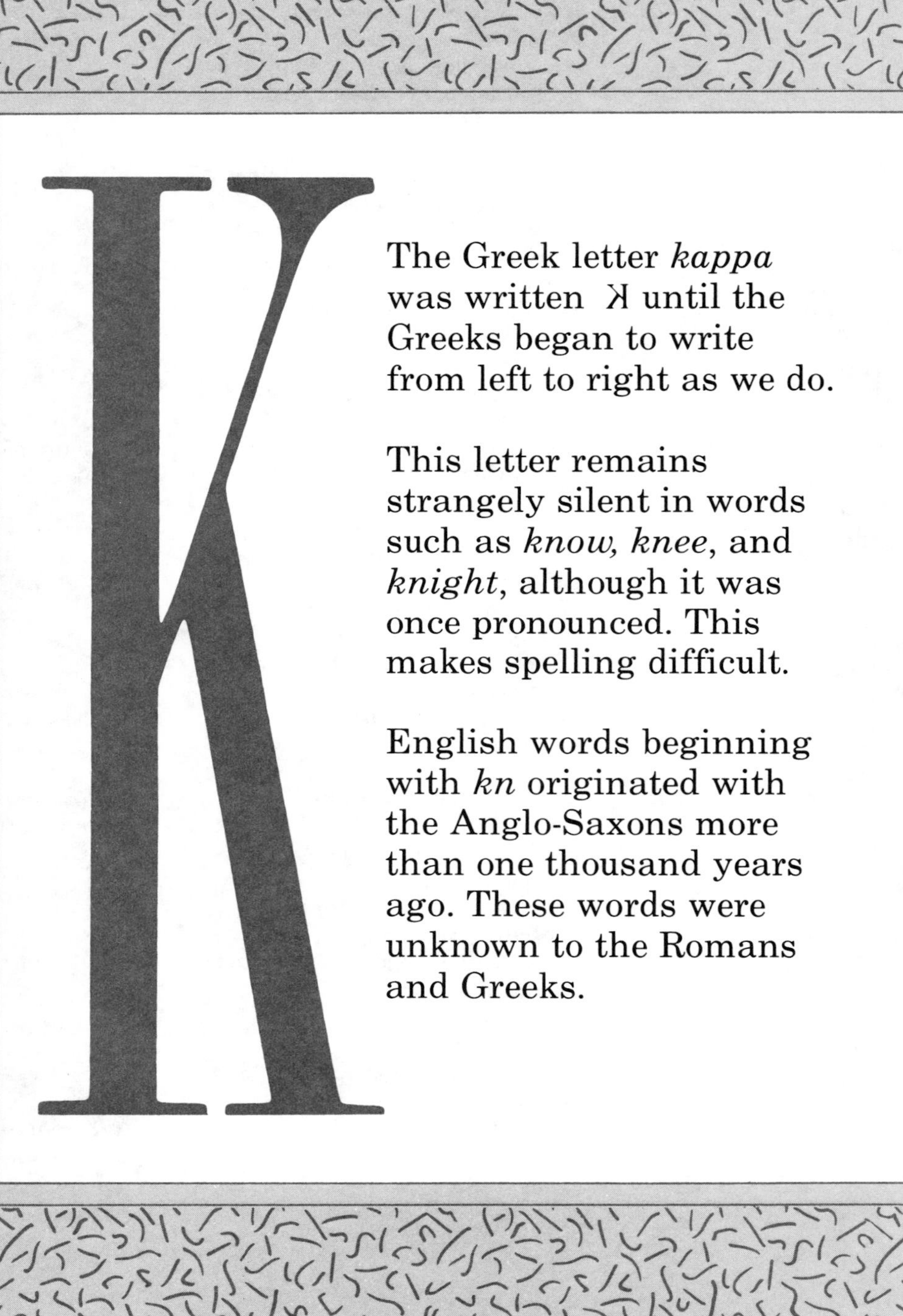

The Greek letter *kappa* was written ꓘ until the Greeks began to write from left to right as we do.

This letter remains strangely silent in words such as *know, knee*, and *knight*, although it was once pronounced. This makes spelling difficult.

English words beginning with *kn* originated with the Anglo-Saxons more than one thousand years ago. These words were unknown to the Romans and Greeks.

Word	#	Part	Synonyms / Example	Antonyms
keen	1.	*adj.*	**sharp, bitter, biting, piercing, cutting, extreme, penetrating, nippy** Keen winds swept across the Antarctic.	**1.** *gentle, mild, soft*
	2.	*adj.*	**sharp, razor-like, pointed** The cook accidentally cut his finger on the keen edge of the knife.	**2.** *dull, blunt, unsharpened*
	3.	*adj.*	**enthusiastic, energetic, interested, eager, ardent, intent** These students are keen athletes.	**3.** *lazy, disinterested*
	4.	*adj.*	**shrewd, clever, bright, astute, intelligent, judicious, quick** The students enjoy their teacher's keen wit.	**4.** *unintelligent, stupid, dull*
	5.	*adj.*	**sensitive, sharp, perceptive, penetrating** Animals have a keen sense of hearing.	**5.** *unobservant, inattentive, dull*
keep	1.	*v.*	**retain, hold, possess, save, guard, preserve** The school has kept records of all its students.	**1.** *give away, relinquish, release, give up, throw away*
	2.	*v.*	**care for, run, maintain, operate, administer, direct, manage** Gardeners were hired to keep the grounds.	**2.** *neglect, ignore*
	3.	*v.*	**continue, carry on, sustain** Who keeps that business going?	**3.** *end, discontinue*
	4.	*v.*	**prevent, stop, restrain, detain** What's keeping you from coming on this trip with us?	**4.** *encourage, help*
keepsake		*n.*	**souvenir, token, reminder, memento, remembrance** This ring is a keepsake of our friendship.	
kid	1.	*n.*	**youngster, child, young person, juvenile, adolescent** The kids really enjoy the video games. *adj.* Tim introduced us to his kid brother.	**1.** *adult, grown-up*
	2.	*n.*	**young goat, yearling** The kids were chasing around the pasture.	
	3.	*v.*	**tease, jest, ridicule, rib, trick, bluff** We kidded Yuriko about her new hairdo.	

Word			Synonyms	Antonyms
kidnap		*v.*	**abduct, seize, carry off, take, steal** The child was kidnapped and held for ransom.	*free, rescue*
kill		*v.*	**slay, murder, assassinate, destroy, slaughter** Hunters killed the animals for their fur. *n.* The police are looking for the killer of the security guard. *n.* The killing of the villagers in the war zone shocked everyone.	*preserve, protect, guard*
kin		*n.*	**family, relatives, relations** Fritz has no kin in this country.	
kind	1.	*n.*	**sort, type, variety, class, brand, style** What kind of apple is this?	
	2.	*adj.*	**friendly, gentle, good, tender, considerate, courteous, affectionate, loving** The kind woman stopped to help the accident victims. *adv.* She treated everyone kindly.	**2.** *cruel, harsh, brutal, unkind*
kindle		*v.*	**light, ignite, set fire to** The guide kindled the campfire. *adj.* The kindling wood burned rapidly.	*douse, quench, smother, stifle*
kindness		*n.*	**goodness, generosity, help, friendliness, understanding** Thank you for your kindness during our trouble.	*harshness, cruelty, unkindness*
kingdom		*n.*	**dominion, domain, realm, empire, country, land** The news of the prince's birth spread throughout the kingdom.	
knack		*n.*	**flair, gift, skill, ability, faculty, talent** Amos has a knack for carpentry.	*inability*
know	1.	*v.*	**understand, comprehend, realize, be sure of** The teacher knows the answer to this problem.	**1.** *misunderstand*
	2.	*v.*	**be acquainted with, be close to, be friends with** Alex knows several people in his new school.	

	3.	*v.*	**be aware of, be informed** Karen's friends knew she was in trouble and offered to help.	**3.** *be ignorant of, be unaware of*
knowing		*adj.*	**shrewd, sharp, cunning, intelligent, clever, understanding** The coach gave the team a knowing smile before the game began.	*ignorant, unintelligent*
knowledge	1.	*n.*	**learning, information, wisdom** Sue has a good knowledge of Canadian history. *adj.* She is knowledgeable about famous people.	**1.** *ignorance, misinformation*
	2.	*n.*	**sense, memory, comprehension, awareness, realization** The victim had no knowledge of what had happened.	

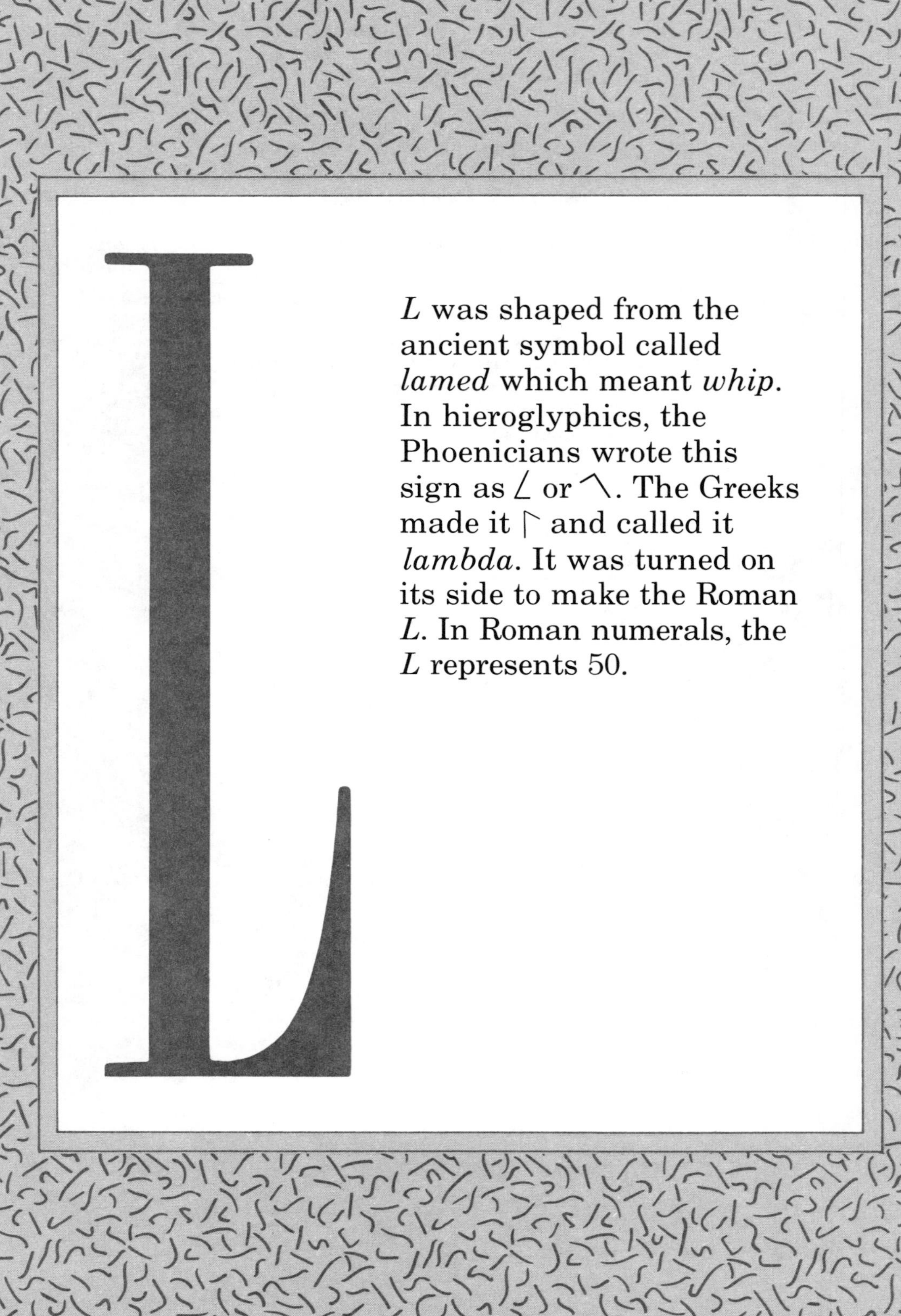

L was shaped from the ancient symbol called *lamed* which meant *whip*. In hieroglyphics, the Phoenicians wrote this sign as ∠ or ᄀ. The Greeks made it Γ and called it *lambda*. It was turned on its side to make the Roman *L*. In Roman numerals, the *L* represents 50.

laborious
1. *adj.* **hard, difficult, tough**
The research project proved to be a laborious task.
Antonyms: 1. *easy, light, simple, trivial*
2. *adj.* **hard-working, industrious, diligent**
The student was rewarded for his laborious effort.
Antonyms: 2. *lazy, indifferent*

labour (also spelled labor)
1. *n.* **work, toil, task, employment, effort**
The workers were well paid for their labour.
Antonyms: 1. *idleness, ease, relaxation, rest*
2. *n.* **workers, employees**
The country suffers from a shortage of skilled labour.
3. *v.* **work, toil**
The crew laboured for ten hours a day to finish the project.
n. The crew consisted of twenty labourers.
Antonyms: 3. *rest, relax*

lack
1. *n.* **absence, scarcity, shortage, deficiency**
There is a lack of medical services in some Third World countries.
Antonyms: 1. *plenty, excess, abundance, surplus*
2. *v.* **need, be short of, fail to have, be without**
The team lacked the dedication required to win.
Antonyms: 2. *have, hold, possess*

lag
v. **loiter, linger, straggle, drag**
The exhausted child lagged behind the rest of the family.
Antonyms: *hasten, hurry, hustle*

lame
1. *adj.* **handicapped, crippled, disabled**
The lame horse was put to sleep.
2. *adj.* **weak, poor, unsatisfactory**
Everyone saw through their lame excuse for not completing the job.
Antonyms: 2. *strong, excellent*

lament
1. *n.* **cry, sob, wail, moan, outcry**
Loud laments were heard at the funeral of the assassinated president.
Antonyms: 1. *laughter, joy, celebration*
2. *v.* **mourn, weep over, cry over, regret, deplore**
Alice lamented the loss of her dog.
adj. It was a lamentable event.
Antonyms: 2. *be joyful, laugh, rejoice*

land
1. *n.* **real estate, property, terrain, realty, grounds**
Land near the city is very expensive.
2. *n.* **dirt, soil, loam, earth, ground**
The land in Saskatchewan grows excellent wheat.

	3.	*n.*	**country, nation, region, state, homeland, realm, domain** Anna came here from the land of the Ukraine.	
	4.	*v.*	**alight, descend, come down** Our plane landed at Mirabelle Airport.	4. *ascend, go up, take off*
	5.	*v.*	**catch, capture, get, secure, take** Glenn landed several large salmon yesterday.	5. *lose, release*
languid		*adj.*	**listless, lifeless, slow, weak, feeble, weary, exhausted** The patient felt languid after a long illness.	*lively, tireless, energetic, vigorous, strong*
lanky		*adj.*	**tall and lean** The lanky basketball player is the star of the team.	*husky, brawny, stocky*
large		*adj.*	**big, great, huge, enormous, vast, grand, towering, massive, spacious, bulky, plentiful, mighty** The family made a large donation to the university.	*small, tiny, petite, miniature, little, insignificant, meagre,wee*
last	1.	*v.*	**endure, stay, remain, persist** The storm lasted several hours.	1. *cease, stop, end*
	2.	*adj.*	**final, latest** Our family was the last group to arrive. *adv.* We arrived last because of heavy traffic.	2. *first, foremost, initial*
lasting		*adj.*	**enduring, permanent, stable, durable** This chair has a lasting finish on it.	*temporary, short-lived, fleeting*
late	1.	*adj.*	**past, dead, deceased, departed** The late J. F. Kennedy was President of the United States.	
	2.	*adj.*	**tardy, slow, delayed** Yasmin was late for school. *adv.* She arrived late.	2. *early, prompt, on time, punctual*
lately		*adv.*	**recently** Have you seen Brenda lately?	
latent		*adj.*	**passive, dormant, sleeping, inactive, hidden, concealed** Mario has a latent desire to visit his homeland.	*active, developed, expressed*

Word			Synonyms	Antonyms
lateral		*adj.*	**sideways, sidelong, from the side, oblique** Will that lateral pass benefit our team? *adv.* That quarterback often passes laterally.	*forward, backward*
laugh		*v.*	**chuckle, giggle, guffaw, titter** The children laughed at the clown's jokes. *n.* Their laughter filled the circus tent.	*cry, weep*
laughable		*adj.*	**funny, comical, humorous, ridiculous, absurd, amusing** That masquerade costume is laughable.	*serious, morbid, solemn, sad, melancholy*
lavish	**1.**	*v.*	**waste, squander, pour out** The millionaire lavished his money on expensive yachts.	**1.** *save, hoard, stint*
	2.	*adj.*	**spendthrift, extravagant, wasteful, excessive** The movie star leads a lavish life. *adv.* He spends his money lavishly on clothes and parties.	**2.** *thrifty, stingy*
	3.	*adj.*	**generous, bountiful, abundant liberal, profuse** Her lavish praise told us she was pleased with our work.	**3.** *meagre, stingy, skimpy*
lawful		*adj.*	**legal, legitimate, permissible, allowable** It is lawful to drive at 80 kilometres per hour on some highways. *adv.* They were lawfully married.	*illegal, prohibited, unlawful*
lawless		*adj.*	**defiant, uncontrolled, unruly, rebellious** Lawless mobs can cause much trouble.	*law-abiding, obedient, orderly*
lax		*adj.*	**loose, slack, careless, indifferent** Discipline is lax in this school.	*firm, reliable, strict, careful, exact*
lazy	**1.**	*adj.*	**idle, shiftless, indolent** The lazy workers did not complete their work on time. *n.* The workers lost their jobs because of their laziiness.	**1.** *industrious, energetic, active*
	2.	*adj.*	**sleepy, languid, sluggish, slow-moving, drowsy** We all feel lazy on hot, humid days. *adv.* The cows grazed lazily in the fields.	**2.** *brisk, active, wide-awake*

Word	No.	Part	Synonyms / Example	Antonyms
lead	1.	*n.*	**main role, principal part, star** Roy has been chosen to play the lead in the play.	1. *supporting role, minor role*
	2.	*n.*	**clue, hint** Police are asking for leads on the robbery.	
	3.	*v.*	**guide, conduct, direct, command, pilot, steer** The guide led the tourists to the river's edge.	3. *follow*
	4.	*v.*	**excel, surpass, come first** Reg leads the company in sales. *n.* He is in the lead in sales.	4. *trail*
leader		*n.*	**chief, head, director, master, conductor, commander** Police are looking for the leader of this gang.	*follower*
lean	1.	*v.*	**bend, slope, slant, incline, tilt** The fence leans to the right.	
	2.	*adj.*	**skinny, thin, slender, slim, wiry, sinewy** Paul's lean build makes him an excellent athlete.	2. *stout, fat, obese, overweight*
	3.	*adj.*	**not fatty, fatfree** Our family only eats lean meat.	3. *fatty*
leap		*n.*	**jump, spring, bound, vault** The skater made several leaps into the air. *v.* The frog leapt into the pond.	
learn		*v.*	**acquire knowledge, understand, be educated** The child is learning to read. *n.* She is a fast learner.	*teach, instruct*
learned		*adj.*	**educated, well-informed, scholarly, wise** Professor Smythe is a learned woman.	*ignorant, illiterate, uneducated*
leave	1.	*n.*	**permission, consent, approval** The class was given leave to go on the trip.	1. *refusal, denial*
	2.	*n.*	**holiday, furlough, vacation, absence** The soldier has a four day leave.	
	3.	*v.*	**depart, go away, set out** Has Sue left for her holidays?	3. *stay, remain, arrive*
legal		*adj.*	**permitted, permissible, lawful, allowed, legitimate** Ravi is the children's legal guardian.	*illegal, unlawful*

Word			Synonyms	Antonyms
legend		*n.*	**myth, tale** I enjoy reading the Greek legends.	
legendary		*adj.*	**fictitious, mythical** Paul Bunyan is a legendary hero.	*actual, true, factual*
legible		*adj.*	**plain, distinct, clear, neat, readable** Your writing is legible, but mine is illegible. *adv.* We all should write legibly.	*illegible, unreadable*
legitimate	1.	*adj.*	**lawful, legal, rightful** The family made a legitimate claim to the property.	1. *unlawful, illegal, invalid*
	2.	*adj.*	**true, real, genuine, authentic, valid** Illness is a legitimate reason for absence.	2. *false, counterfeit*
leisure	1.	*n.*	**rest, ease, relaxation, recreation** We have more time for leisure in the summer.	1. *work, toil, employment*
	2.	*adj.*	**free, idle, unoccupied, unemployed** How many leisure hours do you have in a day? *adv.* We strolled leisurely through the park.	2. *busy, employed, occupied*
lengthen		*v.*	**extend, increase, stretch** The days lengthened as spring approached.	*shorten, reduce, lessen*
lenient		*adj.*	**tolerant, gentle, merciful, compassionate, forgiving** The owner was lenient when the tenant was late with the rent.	*strict, harsh, severe, stern, merciless*
lessen		*v.*	**decrease, shorten, reduce, ease** Modern appliances lessen the amount of housework.	*increase, extend, stretch*
let		*v.*	**allow, permit, tolerate** "Please let me help you," she said.	*forbid, prohibit*
level	1.	*n.*	**depth, height** The water level rose quickly in the flood.	
	2.	*v.*	**aim, point, direct** The pilot levelled the missiles at the army camp.	
	3.	*v.*	**destroy, demolish, knock down** Wreckers levelled the old building.	3. *restore, build, erect, construct*

	4.	*adj.*	**flat, smooth, horizontal, regular** An airplane runway must be level.	**4.** *uneven, rough, vertical, irregular*
liable	**1.**	*adj.*	**prone, inclined, likely, apt** People are liable to fall on this icy sidewalk.	**1.** *unlikely*
	2.	*adj.*	**responsible, accountable** The court found him liable for the accident.	**2.** *innocent, unaccountable*
liberal	**1.**	*adj.*	**ample, generous, lavish, abundant** Alex receives a liberal allowance.	**1.** *stingy, frugal, miserly, small*
	2.	*adj.*	**broad-minded, tolerant** Unlike his conservative brother, Andrew is a liberal thinker.	**2.** *prejudiced, narrow-minded, intolerant*
liberate		*v.*	**free, release, discharge** The prisoners were liberated when the war ended.	*hold, keep, confine, detain*
liberty		*n.*	**freedom, right, privilege, independence** The people fought for liberty and equality in the French Revolution.	*tyranny, restraint*
lie	**1.**	*n.*	**fib, untruth, falsehood** They finally confessed that they had been telling lies. *v.* They lied about the stolen money. *n.* They admitted to being liars.	**1.** *truth*
	2.	*v.*	**rest, recline** Dad lay on the couch to take a nap.	**2.** *sit up, stand up, rise*
life	**1.**	*n.*	**human, person, soul, individual, being** How many lives were lost in that plane crash?	
	2.	*n.*	**existence, way of living** They lead busy lives in the city.	
	3.	*n.*	**energy, spirit, vigour** There was little life left in her at the end of a long day's work.	
lift	**1.**	*v.*	**raise, hoist, boost, elevate** Who lifted that heavy box for you?	**1.** *lower*
	2.	*v.*	**cancel, remove, rescind, withdraw** Will the government lift the ban on foreign imports?	**2.** *impose, establish*
light	**1.**	*n.*	**brightness, illumination, glow, glare, shine** The light of the moon turned the lake to silver.	**1.** *dark, shadow, darkness, shade*

	2.	*n.*	**lamp, source of light** We switched on the lights when it got dark.	
	3.	*v.*	**kindle, set fire to, ignite, spark** Rae lit the fire before we arrived at the cottage.	**3.** *put out, extinguish*
	4.	*v.*	**illuminate, turn on, switch on** Have you lighted all the lamps in the living room?	**4.** *turn off, switch off, dim, darken*
	5.	*adj.*	**bright, illuminated, well-lit** It was still light enough to see the path.	**5.** *dark, dim, gloomy, dull*
	6.	*adj.*	**not heavy, lightweight** Let the child carry a light parcel.	**6.** *heavy*
	7.	*adj.*	**small, scanty, sparse, meagre, not rich, simple, spare** We asked the waiter to suggest a light meal.	**7.** *heavy, rich, large, substantial*
lighten	1.	*v.*	**ease, relieve, lessen** We lightened the load on the wagon before going up the hill.	**1.** *increase, enlarge*
	2.	*v.*	**brighten, clear** The sky lightened after the storm.	**2.** *darken*
likelihood		*n.*	**probability, chance** There is a likelihood of snow tomorrow. *adj.* It's likely to snow tomorrow.	
likeness		*n.*	**similarity, resemblance** There was no likeness between the brother and the sister.	*difference*
limit	1.	*n.*	**maximum, restriction, ceiling** What is the speed limit on this highway?	
	2.	*n.*	**boundary, border, edge, end** Small towns have sprung up just beyond the city limits.	
	3.	*v.*	**restrict, confine, restrain, check** Hans is limited to three phone calls a day.	**3.** *extend, increase*
limp	1.	*n.*	**lameness** The injured football player walks with a painful limp. *v.* He limped to the bench after he injured his ankle.	
	2.	*adj.*	**slack, lax, drooping, flabby, soft** Limp vegetables don't make an appetizing salad.	**2.** *stiff, rigid, firm*

Word		Part of speech	Synonyms / Example	Antonyms
limpid		*adj.*	**clear, transparent, lucid** We threw pennies into the limpid pool in the park.	*murky, muddy, dark, cloudy*
linger		*v.*	**loiter, lag, tarry, dawdle, dally** Zane lingered on her way to school.	*hurry, speed, hasten, rush*
link	1.	*n.*	**connection, tie, bond** Champlain's statue is a link with the past.	
	2.	*v.*	**join, connect, tie, bind, unite, couple** The children linked hands and formed a circle.	**2.** *disconnect, untie, uncouple*
liquefy		*v.*	**dissolve, melt, make fluid, make liquid** Oxygen can be liquefied at extremely low temperatures.	*solidify, harden, congeal, freeze*
liquid	1.	*n.*	**fluid, drink, beverage** The patient was allowed only liquids after surgery.	**1.** *solid, vapour, gas*
	2.	*adj.*	**fluid, molten, thawed, melted** An active volcano sends out liquid rock called lava.	**2.** *solid, gaseous, hard, frozen*
list	1.	*n.*	**record, roll, schedule, account, file, tally, inventory** The list of names seemed endless.	
	2.	*v.*	**record, arrange, set down, catalogue** The teacher listed our names on the first day of school.	**2.** *delete, cancel, erase*
	3.	*v.*	**tilt, lean, tip** The boat listed to one side in the strong winds.	
listless		*adj.*	**lazy, inactive, dull, indolent, languid** I feel listless on hot, humid days.	*active, lively, alert, energetic*
literal		*adj.*	**exact, accurate, precise, factual, correct, true, actual** The English newspapers requested a literal translation of the French minister's speech.	*free, liberal, inexact*
literate	1.	*adj.*	**able to read and write** A majority of the people in this country is literate.	**1.** *illiterate*
	2.	*adj.*	**educated, well-informed, learned, well-read, scholarly** Our English professor was a literate person.	**2.** *unlearned, uninformed*

Word			Synonyms	Antonyms
lithe		*adj.*	**agile, supple, nimble, flexible** The track and field contestants seemed lithe and strong.	*stiff, rigid, awkward*
litter	**1.**	*n.*	**rubbish, trash, junk, refuse, clutter, mess** There is a fine for throwing litter on the highway.	
	2.	*n.*	**offspring, young, group of animals** Ben's cocker spaniel had a litter of six pups.	
	3.	*v.*	**scatter, strew, clutter, heap, pile** The beach was littered with debris after the big storm.	
little		*adj.*	**small, minute, wee, tiny** Is this little puppy lost?	*big, great, mighty, large*
live	**1.**	*v.*	**reside, dwell, inhabit, stay, lodge, remain** The Turners live on Maple Avenue.	
	2.	*v.*	**exist, subsist, survive** Will they be able to live on that pension?	**2.** *die*
lively	**1.**	*adj.*	**vigorous, spirited, active** The party was a lively affair.	**1.** *inactive, listless, dull, boring*
	2.	*adj.*	**bright, vivid, cheerful, gay** Red is a lively colour.	**2.** *drab, dull, dreary*
livid	**1.**	*adj.*	**discoloured, bruised, black-and-blue, purple** The boxer's skin was livid from the many blows he received.	
	2.	*adj.*	**furious, angry, vexed, indignant, fuming** Ying was livid over the salesperson's dishonesty.	**2.** *pleased, happy, content, forgiving*
load	**1.**	*n.*	**cargo, shipment, truckload, carload, planeload, freight** How many loads of topsoil did you put on the garden?	
	2.	*n.*	**burden, pressure, trouble, worry, weight** "That's a real load off my mind!" she exclaimed.	**2.** *support, help, consolation*
	3.	*v.*	**fill, pile, heap, pack, stack, stow** The movers loaded the van with the furniture.	**3.** *unload, empty, unpack*
loaf	**1.**	*n.*	**shaped mass of dough, meat, etc.** The chef baked two loaves of bread and a meat loaf.	

	2.	*v.*	**take it easy, do nothing, laze, waste time, idle** Some of the repair crew were loafing on the job. *n.* Some people are born loafers.	2. *labour, work, toil*
loan	1.	*n.*	**advance, credit** The bank arranged a loan for Owen's new car.	
	2.	*v.*	**lend, permit to borrow** We loaned the neighbours our ladder.	2. *borrow, return, give back*
local		*adj.*	**neighbourhood, regional, district** The local theatre shows many good movies. *adv.* People are pleased that these movies can be seen locally.	*worldwide, international*
locate	1.	*v.*	**place, put, situate, establish, fix** The library is located on Main Street. *n.* The location is handy for everyone.	1. *remove*
	2.	*v.*	**find, discover, detect, uncover, track down** The divers located the remains of the *Titanic* in the Atlantic Ocean.	2. *lose, hide, conceal, displace*
lofty	1.	*adj.*	**high, elevated, tall** Mountaineers scaled the lofty peak.	1. *low*
	2.	*adj.*	**haughty, conceited, inflated, proud** Some people have lofty ideas of themselves.	2. *meek, humble, lowly*
log	1.	*n.*	**lumber, timber, stump, block** The trucks hauled the logs to the sawmill.	
	2.	*n.*	**diary, account, schedule, journal, calendar** The captain made a daily entry in the ship's log. *v.* He carefully logged all events.	
logic		*n.*	**reasoning, deduction, organized thinking** Mathematicians are usually skilled in logic. *adj.* They are logical thinkers.	
loiter		*v.*	**linger, dawdle, lag, dally, tarry, delay** Several students loitered in the schoolyard after school was over.	*hasten, hurry, hustle*

Word			Synonyms	Antonyms
lonely	1.	*adj.*	**lonesome, forlorn, friendless, forsaken** People living alone are often lonely.	
	2.	*adj.*	**remote, secluded, isolated, deserted** The children were warned against loitering in the lonely areas of town.	**2.** *crowded, populated*
lonesome		*adj.*	**lonely, alone, forlorn** Keith's pup is lonesome when his master is at school.	
long	1.	*v.*	**yearn, crave, wish, hope** Everyone is longing for some warm weather.	
	2.	*adj.*	**lengthy, prolonged, extended** The audience listened politely to the long speech.	**2.** *short, brief, concise*
look	1.	*n.*	**appearance, manner, air, expression** The tired worker has a weary look.	
	2.	*v.*	**appear, seem** She looks tired after a long day's work.	
	3.	*v.*	**see, view, observe, gaze, stare** Tourists looked around the museum with interest. *n.* They only had time for a quick look at the displays.	**3.** *overlook, omit, pass over*
loose	1.	*v.*	**untie, free, release, unfasten, let go, undo, set free** The hunters loosed the hounds to track the deer. *adv.* They let the dogs run loose.	**1.** *tie, fasten, secure*
	2.	*adj.*	**untied, unfastened** Your shoelace is loose.	**2.** *tied, fastened*
	3.	*adj.*	**not tight, unrestricted, slack** You should wear loose clothes when it is hot.	**3.** *tight*
lopsided		*adj.*	**uneven, unbalanced** The lopsided table has one leg shorter than the others.	*balanced, even, upright*
lose	1.	*v.*	**mislay, misplace, drop** Marie lost her watch at the park.	**1.** *find, get, obtain*
	2.	*v.*	**be defeated, succumb** They lost the game after a tough match.	**2.** *win, triumph*
lot	1.	*n.*	**property, plot, tract, field, piece of land** My aunt sold the lot she owned on Shadow Lake.	

	2. *n.*	**great deal, abundance, large amount** "What a lot of food!" they exclaimed.	2. *scarcity*
loud	1. *adj.*	**noisy, blaring, boisterous** Loud music can be annoying.	1. *soft, quiet, faint*
	2. *adj.*	**flashy, garish, gaudy, showy** The rock star's loud clothes drew much attention.	2. *conservative*
love	*n.*	**affection, tenderness, fondness, devotion** The trainer treated the animals with much love. *v.* He loved them all.	*hatred, aversion, dislike, loathing*
lovely	*adj.*	**beautiful, attractive, pleasing, charming, handsome** Our neighbour has a lovely baby.	*ugly, plain, unattractive*
low	1. *adj.*	**short, squat, not high** There is a low hedge around the backyard.	1. *high*
	2. *adj.*	**sunken, depressed, below sea level** Many of the low areas were flooded in the recent storm.	2. *high, elevated*
	3. *adj.*	**mean, cruel, vile, base, cowardly** That was a low trick to pull on a friend.	3. *fine, good, courteous, kind, honourable*
	4. *adj.*	**quiet, soft, whispered, gentle, hushed** We spoke in low voices so we wouldn't wake the baby. *v.* Lower your voices, please.	4. *loud, noisy*
	5. *adj.*	**depressed, downcast, unhappy, dejected, down, gloomy** The team felt low when they lost the final game.	5. *cheerful, happy, elated*
	6. *adj.*	**small, little, paltry, trifling** The salary for a beginner is often low.	6. *high, above average, big*
loyal	*adj.*	**faithful, true, devoted, constant** Dogs are loyal to their masters. *n.* Workers are often rewarded for their loyalty to the company.	*disloyal, untrue, faithless*
lucid	*adj.*	**clear, precise, direct, accurate, straightforward** A lucid account of the event was given by the witness.	*vague, inaccurate, muddled*
luck	1. *n.*	**good fortune, success** We wished Rudy luck before the job interview.	1. *misfortune*

Word	No.	Part	Synonyms / Example	Antonyms
	2.	*n.*	**fortune, chance, fate** They have had a run of bad luck recently.	
lucky		*adj.*	**fortunate** The lucky couple won $1 million in the lottery.	*unlucky, unfortunate*
ludicrous		*adj.*	**ridiculous, crazy, absurd, preposterous** We laughed at the ludicrous stories about the aliens.	*sensible, serious*
lurch		*v.*	**swerve, stumble, sway, stagger, reel, totter** The wounded man lurched forward and fell.	
lure	1.	*n.*	**bait, decoy** They used plastic lures instead of worms to fish.	
	2.	*n.*	**attraction, pull** We couldn't resist the lure of the countryside.	**2.** *repulsion*
	3.	*v.*	**entice, bait, trap, persuade, coax, trick, tempt, attract** These decoys will lure the ducks to the marsh.	**3.** *repel, repulse, deter*
lurk		*v.*	**prowl, slink, sneak, skulk, hide** A prowler lurked among the bushes.	
luscious		*adj.*	**delicious, tasty, savoury, delectable, exquisite, appetizing** I couldn't resist eating one of the luscious apples.	*unsavoury, unappetizing, tasteless*
lustre (also spelled luster)		*n.*	**shine, glow, sparkle, brightness, gloss, glare, sheen** This silver dish has lost its lustre.	*dimness, tarnish, dullness*
luxuriant		*adj.*	**abundant, profuse, lush, dense, thick** We couldn't get through the luxuriant undergrowth of the jungle.	*sparse, meagre, thin, scanty*
luxury		*n.*	**extreme comfort, wealth, riches, extravagance, material abundance** The wealthy live in great luxury. *adj.* We stayed at a luxurious hotel on our holiday.	*poverty, need, want*

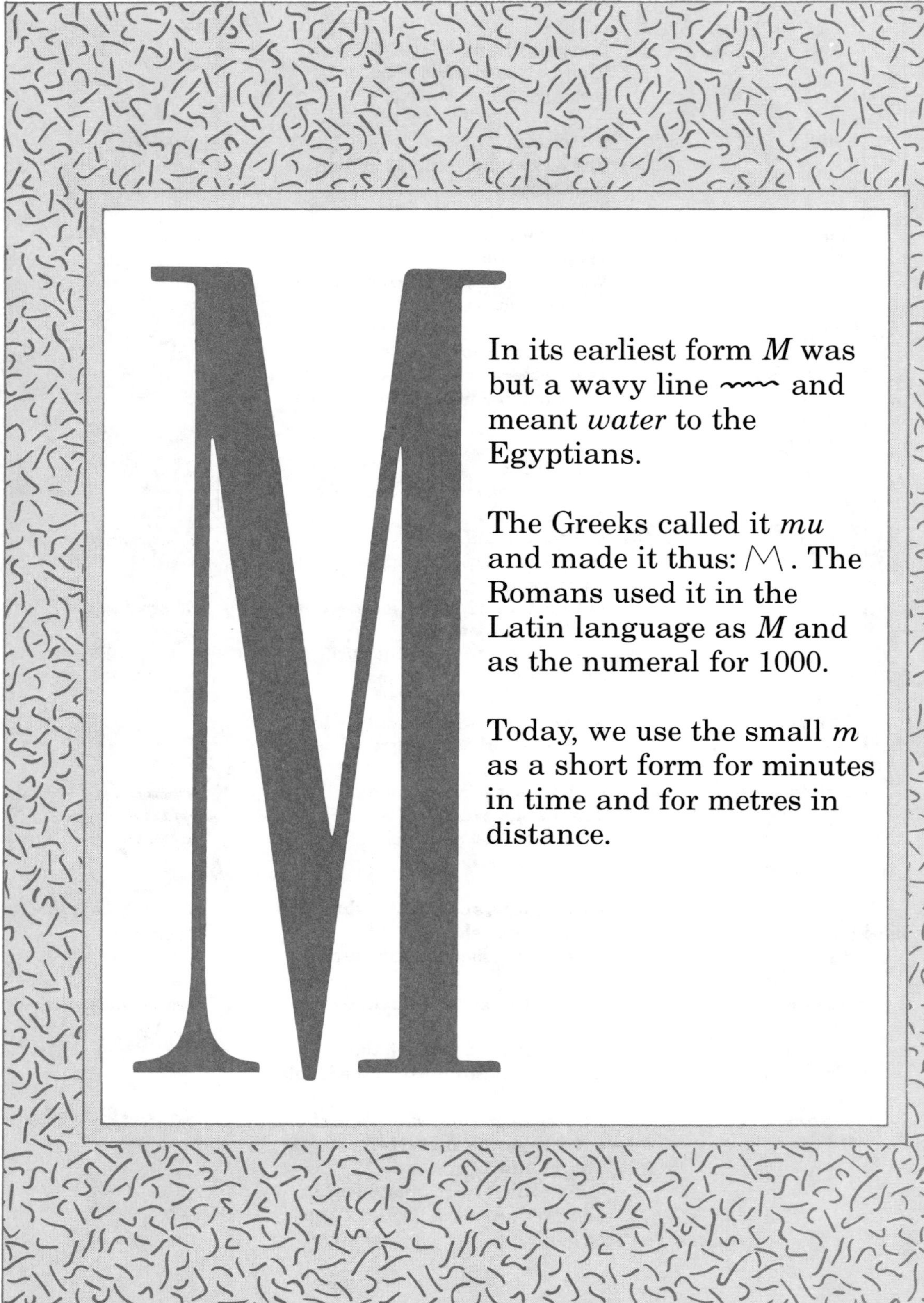

In its earliest form *M* was but a wavy line ~~~ and meant *water* to the Egyptians.

The Greeks called it *mu* and made it thus: /V\ . The Romans used it in the Latin language as *M* and as the numeral for 1000.

Today, we use the small *m* as a short form for minutes in time and for metres in distance.

Entry			Synonyms	Antonyms
mad	1.	*adj.*	**crazy, unbalanced, insane, deranged, demented** The dog was mad from rabies.	**1.** *sane, normal, rational*
	2.	*adj.*	**angry, furious, irate, provoked** The traveller was mad when he missed the train.	**2.** *glad, happy, pleased*
magic	1.	*n.*	**sleight of hand, illusion, trickery** Magicians thrill audiences with their magic.	
	2.	*n.*	**witchcraft, sorcery** The casting of spells is associated with black magic.	
magnetic		*adj.*	**inviting, attractive, fascinating, irresistible, captivating** No one can resist her magnetic personality.	*repulsive, repelling, unattractive*
magnificent		*adj.*	**imposing, splendid, fine, superb, grand, glorious** There are many magnificent old churches in Rome. *n.* Many tourists come to view the magnificence of the Sistine Chapel.	*ordinary, poor, unimposing*
magnify	1.	*v.*	**enlarge, increase, expand, amplify, blow up** Scientists use a microscope to magnify minute objects for study.	**1.** *reduce, minimize, lessen, condense*
	2.	*v.*	**exaggerate, overstate** Jim magnified his problems to gain sympathy.	**2.** *understate, minimize*
magnitude		*n.*	**measure, greatness, extent, size, consequence, significance** The San Francisco earthquake of 1989 was of great magnitude.	*insignificance*
maim		*v.*	**cripple, disable, damage, hurt, mangle, mutilate** Dave was maimed in an industrial accident.	*restore, repair, reconstruct, heal, cure*
main		*adj.*	**primary, essential, chief, central, principal** State the main idea of your story.	*subordinate, lesser, secondary*
maintain	1.	*v.*	**assert, contend, claim, insist, declare, state, attest, affirm** The suspect maintained that she was innocent.	**1.** *deny, reject*
	2.	*v.*	**uphold, preserve, keep** The police do a tremendous job in maintaining law and order.	**2.** *ignore*

	3.	*v.*	**provide for, support, sustain** It is expensive to maintain a large family.	3. *abandon, neglect*
majestic		*adj.*	**grand, noble, dignified, stately, magnificent, splendid, imposing** The Rockies are truly majestic mountains. *n.* Her Majesty Queen Elizabeth II is a British monarch.	*lowly, common, ordinary*
major	1.	*n.*	**military officer** The major ordered the troops to rest.	
	2.	*adj.*	**senior, superior, more important, leading, chief** John had the major part in the play.	2. *minor, lesser, junior*
make	1.	*n.*	**kind, brand, form** What make of computer do you prefer?	
	2.	*v.*	**manufacture, produce, create, build, erect** This company makes a good brand of shoes.	2. *destroy, wreck*
	3.	*v.*	**force, press, compel, require** His parents made him work hard before the final examination.	3. *ask, beg*
	4.	*v.*	**arrive at, reach, catch, attain** Can we make the 9:30 train?	4. *miss*
malady		*n.*	**illness, complaint, sickness, ailment, disease** Kim suffers from an unusual malady.	*strength, vigour, health*
malice		*n.*	**spite, grudge, hate, resentment, ill will, enmity** Although he walked out on her, Sim bears him no malice.	*good will, kindness, benevolence*
malicious		*adj.*	**hateful, spiteful** Someone has been spreading malicious rumours about our new neighbours.	*kind*
malnourished		*adj.*	**undernourished, starved, emaciated** Many children in the Third World are malnourished. *n.* They suffer from malnutrition.	*overfed, well-nourished*
mammoth		*adj.*	**giant, colossal, gigantic, enormous, huge** The school is in the middle of a mammoth fundraising project.	*tiny, little, small, minute, miniature*

Word	No.	Part	Synonyms / Example	Antonyms
man	1.	*n.*	**male, fellow, chap, guy** Many men stayed home today because of the strike.	1. *woman, female*
	2.	*v.*	**staff, attend, operate, maintain** The spacecraft will be manned by three astronauts.	
manage		*v.*	**direct, govern, administer, regulate, control, cope** Can you manage the job alone? *adj.* It is a manageable job. *n.* Who is the manager here?	*mismanage, misdirect*
management	1.	*n.*	**supervision, operation, guidance, conduct, command, control** The success of this company is due to good management.	1. *mismanagement*
	2.	*n.*	**executive board, board of directors, administrators** The management turned down the union's request for more pay.	2. *labour, staff, employees, workers*
mandate		*n.*	**order, command, directive, approval, authorization** The county committee issued a mandate for immediate road repairs.	*request, appeal, petition*
mandatory		*adj.*	**compulsory, obligatory, necessary, required** It is mandatory to wear seatbelts in the car.	
manipulate	1.	*v.*	**operate, use, handle, control, manage** Have you learned how to manipulate a computer?	
	2.	*v.*	**deceive, defraud, control, influence** The cult leader manipulated the group into obeying him blindly.	
manner	1.	*n.*	**style, form, way, method** Her manner of speaking is clear and concise.	
	2.	*n.*	**kind, type, sort, variety** What manner of book is this?	
manners		*n.*	**conduct, behaviour, deportment, bearing** It pays to watch your manners.	
manual	1.	*n.*	**handbook, book of instruction, guide, reference** They read the manual to find out how to assemble the furniture.	

	2.	*adj.*	**physical, hand-operated** The car is equipped with a manual transmission. *adv.* The machine was operated manually.	**2.** *mechanical, automatic*
manufacture		*v.*	**make, build, construct, produce, assemble, form** In Canada, cars are manufactured in Oshawa and Windsor. *n.* Japan and the United States are major manufacturers of cars.	*destroy, demolish, scrap*
many		*adj.*	**numerous, ample, abundant** My brother and I have gone swimming many times in the ocean.	*few*
map	1.	*n.*	**chart, plan, diagram** The road map was most helpful when we drove across Europe.	
	2.	*v.*	**draw, illustrate, describe, plot, plan, chart** "Map a new route," ordered the leader.	
mar		*v.*	**blemish, mark, damage, spoil, harm, stain** The hockey game was marred by violence.	*beautify, decorate, adorn*
margin	1.	*n.*	**edge, border, boundary, limit** Keep inside the margins of your page.	**1.** *centre, middle*
	2.	*n.*	**allowance, leeway** There is no margin for error in the space flights.	
marine		*adj.*	**of the sea, nautical, oceanic** Scuba divers examine marine life in the ocean depths.	*terrestrial, of the land*
mark	1.	*n.*	**stamp, brand, proof, symbol, sign, impression, hallmark** The artist put her mark on her work. *v.* She marked her name on her work.	
	2.	*n.*	**spot, stain, blotch, streak, blemish** The spilt soup left a mark on the tablecloth. *v.* Her face is marked by acne.	
	3.	*n.*	**target, goal** The president is the mark of kidnappers.	
	4.	*n.*	**grade, score, rating** Yuni got a good mark on the test.	

Word	No.	Part	Synonyms / Example	Antonyms
	5.	*v.*	**take notice, watch, note** "Mark my words," said the teacher, "all those who don't work will fail."	5. *ignore, disregard*
marked		*adj.*	**definite, notable, outstanding, significant, prominent** There is a marked improvement in Tracie's grades this year.	*insignificant, slight*
market	1.	*n.*	**bazaar, store, shop, fair** There are always fresh vegetables at the market.	
	2.	*n.*	**demand, buyers, consumers** There is a large market for home videos.	
	3.	*v.*	**sell, exchange, trade, offer for sale, vend** The farmers market their produce at the fair.	3. *buy*
maroon		*v.*	**abandon, leave helpless, desert, strand** The shipwreck victims were marooned on the island.	*rescue*
martial		*adj.*	**military, warlike** The army imposed martial law after the coup.	*civil, civilian*
marvellous (also spelled marvelous)		*adj.*	**wonderful, fabulous, splendid, superb, amazing, remarkable** The world watched in awe as Neil Armstrong made his marvellous journey to the moon.	*ordinary, plain, common, terrible*
mask	1.	*n.*	**false face, face guard, face cover** The children wore ghostly masks on Halloween.	
	2.	*v.*	**hide, disguise, cover, conceal** The bank robbers masked their faces with nylon stockings.	2. *unmask, uncover, show, reveal*
mass	1.	*n.*	**crowd, mob, great number** The mass of people prevented us from entering the building.	1. *small number*
	2.	*n.*	**size, bulk, extent** Please determine the mass of this shipment of books.	
	3.	*v.*	**collect, gather, assemble, congregate** The protesters massed in front of the Prime Minister's office.	3. *scatter, spread, disperse*

Word		Synonyms	Antonyms
massacre	*n.*	**mass slaughter, killing, carnage, butchery** The massacre of six million Jews took place in Nazi death camps. *v.* They were massacred under Hitler's orders during World War II.	
massive	1. *adj.*	**large, big, bulky, heavy** Massive rocks were hurled down the mountain during the landslide.	**1.** *tiny, small, minute, miniature*
	2. *adj.*	**vast, widespread, immense** The police launched a massive search for the escaped convict.	**2.** *small scale*
mass media	*n.*	**information means, communications means** The mass media keep people abreast of events around the world.	
master	1. *n.*	**leader, employer, director, boss, expert, teacher** The judo master demonstrated the steps to the students.	**1.** *employee, novice, disciple, beginner*
	2. *v.*	**tame, subdue, overpower, conquer, triumph over** Susan finally mastered her fear of heights.	**2.** *be defeated, be overcome by*
	3. *v.*	**become expert at, become skilled at, learn** She mastered the art of public speaking at school.	
	4. *adj.*	**expert, skilled, able, gifted** A master artisan carved that beautiful statue.	**4.** *amateur*
	5. *adj.*	**main, chief, best, principal** The master bedroom has its own bathroom.	
match	1. *n.*	**contest, competition, game** The tennis match drew a large crowd of spectators.	
	2. *n.*	**equal, equivalent, peer** Ray admitted he had met his match in Lim when they tied in the race.	
	3. *v.*	**fit together, join, pair** We matched the pieces of the puzzle.	**3.** *take apart, scatter*
	4. *v.*	**be similar to, resemble** Your taste in clothes matches mine.	**4.** *differ*
	5. *v.*	**harmonize with, suit** The shoes match the outfit perfectly.	**5.** *clash with*
material	1. *n.*	**data, facts, notes, resources** Have you enough material for a good story?	

	2.	*n.*	**fabric, goods, cloth** Quality materials wear better and last longer.	
	3.	*adj.*	**physical, tangible, real** They place too much importance on the material comforts of life.	**3.** *spiritual, intangible*
	4.	*adj.*	**substantial, important, valuable** The company made a material gain in its sales of computers.	**4.** *unimportant, slight, small*
matter	1.	*n.*	**object, thing, material, substance** There is some foreign matter in the patient's eye.	
	2.	*n.*	**event, episode, affair, topic, question, situation, subject** This matter does not concern you.	
	3.	*n.*	**trouble, difficulty, cause of distress** What is the matter with the car?	
	4.	*v.*	**signify, count, be important** Losing the job mattered a great deal to Carlo.	**4.** *be unimportant*
mature	1.	*v.*	**ripen, bring to perfection, develop, mellow, age** Fruit matures in the sun.	
	2.	*adj.*	**adult, full-grown, developed** She has very mature views for one so young. *n.* She displayed her maturity in the way she handled the crisis.	**2.** *immature, young*
maxim		*n.*	**proverb, motto, rule, adage, axiom** Have you heard this maxim: "Many hands make light work"?	
maximize		*v.*	**increase, intensify, amplify** The workers were asked to maximize their efforts to increase productivity.	*minimize, lessen*
maximum		*adj.*	**greatest, supreme, highest, utmost, top** The ambulance rushed off at maximum speed.	*least, smallest, minimum, lowest*
maybe		*adv.*	**possibly, perchance, perhaps** Maybe we can go with you.	*definitely, positively*
meagre (also spelled meager)	1.	*adj.*	**sparse, scant, slight** The campers had only a meagre supply of food.	**1.** *ample, plentiful, abundant, sufficient*

	2.	*adj.*	**lean, slim, thin, spare** Mei's meagre face caused us concern.	**2.** *full*
meal	**1.**	*n.*	**repast, food, nourishment, refreshment** Our evening meal is usually at six o'clock.	
	2.	*n.*	**flour, oatmeal, bran, cornmeal, ground grain** The bakery sells muffins made from different meals.	
mean	**1.**	*v.*	**intend, plan, propose** He means to win this competition.	
	2.	*v.*	**signify, convey, suggest** Your kindness meant a lot to me.	
	3.	*adj.*	**nasty, miserable, unkind, cruel, rude, disagreeable** The circus trainer is mean to animals. *n.* Meanness to animals is not to be tolerated.	**3.** *generous, kind, noble, warm, good, humane*
	4.	*adj.*	**median, average, norm, middle, centre** The mean temperature in winter is five degrees celsius.	
meander		*v.*	**wander, ramble, roam** The tourists meandered through the narrow, old streets of Quebec City.	*go straight*
meaning		*n.*	**point, substance, sense, aim, intention, significance** The meaning of the secret message was unclear.	
measure	**1.**	*n.*	**share, quota, allowance, portion, quantity** A full measure of aid was given to the flood victims.	
	2.	*n.*	**law, act, bill, proposal, plan** The House of Commons will be debating that measure tomorrow.	
	3.	*n.*	**step, method, procedure, resort, course, means** What measures have been taken to prevent further flooding?	
	4.	*n.*	**size, extent, dimension, quantity** A kilometre is a standard measure of distance.	

	5.	*v.*	**size, gauge, judge, assess** The decorator measured the windows for the new drapes. *n.* He gave us their measurements in metres.	
meddle		*v.*	**interfere, intervene, tamper with** The neighbours are constantly meddling in our affairs. *adj.* Meddlesome people cause trouble.	*avoid, shun, ignore, stay away from*
mediocre		*adj.*	**passable, fair, common, ordinary** The lazy student handed in a mediocre essay.	*excellent, superior, extraordinary*
meditate		*v.*	**think, contemplate, ponder, concentrate, reflect** Sue meditated on her dilemma for many months. *n.* She arrived at a decision after careful meditation.	
meek		*adj.*	**mild, gentle, humble, yielding, submissive** The meek worker was bullied by his supervisor. *adv.* He meekly did whatever he was told to do.	*bold, forward, domineering, bossy*
meet	1.	*v.*	**join, converge, intersect** An intersection is a point where roads meet.	**1.** *separate, divide*
	2.	*v.*	**come together, convene, gather, assemble** The committee will be meeting to elect a chairperson. *n.* The athletic meet was cancelled because of the rain.	**2.** *disperse, scatter*
	3.	*v.*	**fulfil, satisfy, answer** His work meets the standards required to graduate.	**3.** *fail, fall short of*
	4.	*v.*	**encounter, run into** The friends met each other at the exhibition.	**4.** *avoid, ignore, shun, miss*
meeting		*n.*	**gathering, discussion, assembly, rally, conference** The school called a meeting to discuss the new rules.	
melancholy	1.	*n.*	**unhappiness, gloom, despair, dejection, sorrow, grief** The bad news filled all of us with melancholy.	**1.** *happiness, joy, cheer, gladness*

	2.	*adj.*	**sad, dismal, gloomy, sorrowful, glum, depressed, dispirited** Hamlet was known as the melancholy Dane.	**2.** *happy, bright, cheerful, joyous, jolly, merry*
mellow		*adj.*	**smooth, soft, sweet, delicate** Some fruits have a mellow taste when ripe.	*harsh, bitter*
melody		*n.*	**tune, music, theme** This song has a lively melody. *adj.* The singer had a melodious voice.	
melt	1.	*v.*	**thaw, dissolve, liquefy** The snow melted quickly in the warm sunshine.	**1.** *freeze, set, harden, congeal*
	2.	*v.*	**scatter, vanish, disappear, merge** His attackers melted into the night when they heard the police siren.	**2.** *gather, appear*
memento		*n.*	**souvenir, keepsake, token** Did you bring me a memento of your trip?	
memorable		*adj.*	**unforgettable, impressive, remarkable, outstanding, extraordinary, notable** The Browns often speak of their memorable holiday in China.	*ordinary, dull, mediocre, commonplace*
menace	1.	*n.*	**threat, danger, hazard, peril, risk** Hurricanes are a menace in the Caribbean.	**1.** *aid, blessing, benefit, advantage*
	2.	*v.*	**threaten, scare, terrify** The bully menaced the small boys into giving him their pocket money.	**2.** *aid, defend, help, support, protect*
mend	1.	*v.*	**repair, fix, overhaul, restore** Will the cobbler mend your shoes?	**1.** *break, damage, mar, tear*
	2.	*v.*	**sew, darn, patch** Chris can mend his own clothes.	**2.** *rip*
	3.	*v.*	**get well, heal, cure, recover** My cut is mending quickly. *n.* Ken is on the mend after a prolonged illness.	**3.** *deteriorate, get sick*
mention	1.	*n.*	**report, notice, reference, citation** The art display received little mention in the newspapers.	
	2.	*v.*	**declare, name, tell, state, speak of, refer to, cite** Nan mentioned that you are interested in a job.	**2.** *conceal, withhold, disregard*

Word		POS	Synonyms / Example	Antonyms
merciful		*adj.*	**compassionate, humane, kind, lenient, sparing** The merciful villagers offered the starving man some food.	*unmerciful, pitiless, cruel, merciless, unforgiving, ruthless, inhumane*
mercy		*n.*	**kindness, tolerance, pity, compassion, sympathy** The guerrillas showed no mercy to their captives.	*severity, harshness, cruelty*
mere		*adj.*	**minor, paltry, insignificant** The bracelet was a mere trinket and of no real value.	*considerable, significant*
merely		*adv.*	**only, solely, simply** This car is not merely good, it is also affordable.	
merge		*v.*	**mix, mingle, blend, join, unite** Traffic merges into one lane here.	*separate, divide, part*
merit	1.	*n.*	**value, worth, advantage, benefit, credit** Amos feels there is great merit in studying hard.	1. *weakness, fault, discredit*
	2.	*v.*	**deserve, earn, rate, warrant** He merited the high marks he received in every subject.	2. *be unworthy of*
merry		*adj.*	**gay, jolly, festive, jovial, lively, vivacious, cheerful, happy** The children sang a merry tune.	*sad, unhappy, dejected, miserable, melancholy*
mess	1.	*n.*	**confusion, muddle, jumble, disorder, clutter** The house was in a mess after the party. *adj.* The living room was especially messy after the party.	1. *order*
	2.	*v.*	**dirty, soil, disorder** Try not to mess your clean clothes.	2. *clean, tidy*
meteoric		*adj.*	**brilliant, rapid, speedy, sudden, blazing, swift, flashing** The Beatles had a meteoric rise to fame.	*slow, gradual*
method		*n.*	**way, process, means, manner, procedure** What is the best method of cooking potatoes?	

Word			Synonyms / Example	Antonyms
mettle		*n.*	**courage, nerve, spirit, pluck, bravery, boldness, grit** Henry Hudson showed great mettle in his Arctic exploration.	*cowardice, timidity*
microscopic		*adj.*	**minute, atomic, infinitesimal, miniature, tiny** Because many viruses are microscopic, they can only be seen under a microscope.	*large, huge, immense, colossal, gigantic*
middle	1.	*n.*	**centre, midpoint, main part, hub** The middle of our town is always busy.	1. *edge, outskirts, periphery, border*
	2.	*adj.*	**central, midway, intermediate** Merv took the middle position on the issue.	
might		*n.*	**strength, power, force, energy** The people fought with all their might to overthrow the dictator.	*weakness*
mighty		*adj.*	**powerful, strong, intense, great, forceful, vigorous** A mighty shove released the stone.	*weak, ineffective, gentle*
migrant		*adj.*	**nomadic, itinerant, roving** Migrant farm workers are hired during the harvest.	
migrate		*v.*	**move, relocate** People from the countryside migrate to the cities to look for jobs. *n.* The migration of people to the cities has left farms with no workers.	
mild	1.	*adj.*	**gentle, easy, calm, placid, kind, serene, agreeable** The children like the mild manners of their babysitter.	1. *rough, cross, unkind, harsh, severe, disagreeable*
	2.	*adj.*	**temperate, warm, moderate** Everyone was out enjoying the mild spring day.	2. *cold, unpleasant, chilly, stormy*
milestone		*n.*	**turning point, significant event** Winning the scholarship was a milestone in Shannon's career.	
militant		*adj.*	**uncompromising, defiant, assertive, martial, resolute, warlike, aggressive** The speaker's militant views drew much criticism from the audience.	*moderate, peaceable, submissive*

Word		Part of speech	Synonyms and example	Antonyms
mimic		*v.*	**imitate, impersonate** The parrot mimicked my laugh. *n.* Parrots are good mimics.	
mind	**1.**	*n.*	**brain, intellect, intelligence** Alexander Graham Bell used his mind well.	
	2.	*v.*	**look after, tend, take care of** Who will mind the baby?	***2.*** *ignore, neglect*
	3.	*v.*	**heed, attend to, obey** Competitors were told to mind the rules of the game.	***3.*** *disobey, forget, neglect*
	4.	*v.*	**object, resent, detest** Do you mind the noise?	***4.*** *approve of*
mingle		*v.*	**blend, mix, combine, merge, socialize, circulate, associate** The movie star mingled with his fans at the party.	*part, separate, divide*
miniature		*adj.*	**small, tiny, petite, toy, minute** Yun collects miniature crystal animals.	*colossal, giant, huge, mammoth, large*
minimize		*v.*	**reduce, lessen, decrease** The carpenter added insulation to minimize the noise in the restaurant.	*maximize, increase, enlarge, expand*
minimum		*adj.*	**least, smallest, lowest, basic** He was offered the minimum wage.	*maximum, largest, greatest*
minor		*adj.*	**less, smaller, lower, junior** He had a minor part in the play.	*major, large, senior, main*
minute		*adj.*	**microscopic, insignificant, tiny, small, slight** A minute speck of dust irritated her eye.	*large, massive, huge, bulky, immense, great, colossal*
miracle		*n.*	**marvel, surprise, wonder** The rescue of the trapped miners was a miracle. *adj.* They made a miraculous escape.	
mirror	**1.**	*n.*	**glass, reflector, looking glass** Look in the mirror.	
	2.	*v.*	**reflect, show** The smooth lake mirrored the trees along the shore.	
mirth		*n.*	**merriment, festivity, gaiety, merrymaking, laughter** There was a great deal of fun and mirth at Jin's birthday party.	*misery, sadness, depression*

Word			Synonyms and examples	Antonyms
misbehaviour (also spelled misbehavior)		*n.*	**misconduct, disorder, impudence** Misbehaviour in class is not allowed. *v.* Some pupils deliberately misbehave.	*obedience, order, good conduct*
miscalculate		*v.*	**err, miscount, mistake** Joe miscalculated the time needed to drive to the airport. *n.* He missed his plane as a result of his miscalculation.	
miscellaneous		*adj.*	**various, mixed, diverse, assorted** A miscellaneous collection of old cards was in the box.	*uniform, identical*
mischief		*n.*	**prank, naughtiness, misbehaviour, vandalism** The gang was up to mischief as usual. *adj.* Some children are more mischievous than others.	*assistance, help, good conduct*
misconduct		*n.*	**misbehaviour, bad conduct, mismanagement, disorder** Jo was fired for professional misconduct.	*order, good conduct*
miserable	1.	*adj.*	**wretched, very poor, deplorable, mean, desperate** The refugees lived in miserable conditions.	1. *comfortable, good*
	2.	*adj.*	**unhappy, distressed, sad, sorrowful, forlorn** Doug was miserable until he found his dog.	2. *happy, merry, gay, glad, cheerful*
misery		*n.*	**sorrow, grief, suffering, agony, distress, trouble** A severe illness can cause much misery.	*joy, gladness, happiness, comfort, relief, contentment*
misfortune		*n.*	**disaster, calamity, hardship, trouble, mishap** Our holiday was marred by several misfortunes.	*fortune, good luck*
misgiving		*n.*	**anxiety, doubt, foreboding, fear, worry, apprehension** We had some misgivings about driving in the freezing rain.	*trust, confidence, assurance*
mishap		*n.*	**setback, disaster, misfortune, snag, upset, accident** An unfortunate mishap put that horse out of the race.	

Word			Synonyms	Antonyms
miss	1.	*n.*	**blunder, slip, oversight, mistake, failure, fault, error** I had too many misses to score well.	1. *success, hit*
	2.	*n.*	**girl, lass, young woman** The young miss won first prize in the competition.	2. *boy, lad, young man*
	3.	*v.*	**fail to hit, overlook, lose** Did you miss your chance to score?	3. *get, obtain, gain*
	4.	*v.*	**long for, yearn for, desire** The newcomers missed their family back home.	4. *forget*
mission	1.	*n.*	**errand, task, assignment** The soldiers were sent overseas on a special mission.	
	2.	*n.*	**calling, vocation** Her mission in life is to help the poor.	
mist		*n.*	**moisture, dew, fog, haze** Mist forms when air is chilled. *adj.* His eyes were misty with tears when he heard the good news.	
mistake	1.	*n.*	**error, slip, blunder, oversight** The cashier made a mistake on our bill.	1. *correction*
	2.	*v.*	**confuse, mix up, misunderstand** Vera mistook the salt for sugar when sweetening the raspberries!	
mistaken		*adj.*	**wrong, incorrect, erroneous, inaccurate** He has a mistaken idea about what happened.	*correct, right, accurate*
mix	1.	*v.*	**blend, combine, unite** Mix the ingredients in a bowl. *n.* This mixture makes a better drink.	1. *separate*
	2.	*v.*	**join, mingle, associate** John mixes well with everyone. *n.* He is a good mixer.	2. *segregate, separate, divide*
mob	1.	*n.*	**swarm, mass, crowd, rabble, throng, horde** The police were called to disperse the angry mob of demonstrators.	
	2.	*v.*	**crowd, jostle, surround, swarm** The singer was mobbed by her fans.	2. *ignore, overlook*
mobile		*adj.*	**movable, portable** The mobile library visits our centre every week.	*immobile, fixed, immovable*

Word			Synonyms	Antonyms
mock	**1.**	*v.*	**imitate, mimic, tease, laugh at, jeer, ridicule** The rude audience mocked her singing.	**1.** *applaud, cheer, compliment, praise*
	2.	*adj.*	**fake, counterfeit, sham, false, imitation** There was a mock fur coat in the store window.	**2.** *real, actual, genuine*
mode		*n.*	**style, manner, fashion, method, custom, way, means** What will be our mode of travel in the year 2500?	
model	**1.**	*n.*	**pattern, replica, dummy, copy, duplicate, representation** A model of the space shuttle was displayed at the science show.	
	2.	*n.*	**design, style, type, variety** What model is your new car?	
	3.	*n.*	**ideal, good example** The courageous and dedicated leader is a model for everyone. *adj.* She is a model citizen.	
	4.	*v.*	**shape, mould, form, design, build, fashion** Tim modelled a statue out of clay.	
moderate	**1.**	*v.*	**soothe, soften, quiet, quell, reduce, control, curb, check** The umpire's words moderated the tempers of the players. *adj.* His words had a moderating influence on the team.	**1.** *aggravate, excite, disturb, stir up, increase*
	2.	*adj.*	**reasonable, medium, average, ordinary** The Tangs are looking for a house with a moderate price.	**2.** *outrageous, extreme, severe*
modern		*adj.*	**new, up-to-date, recent** The modern hospital has the latest equipment.	*old, ancient, old-fashioned, antique, primitive*
modest		*adj.*	**humble, meek, quiet, unassuming** The modest girl never talks about her achievements. *n.* Her modesty is noticed by all.	*showy, immodest, conceited, gaudy, extravagant*
modify		*v.*	**change, alter, revise** Adjectives and adverbs modify the meaning of other words.	*keep, maintain, uphold*

Word		Synonyms	Antonyms
moist		*adj.* **damp, humid, wet, watery** The moist grass smelled sweet. *v.* She moistened her parched lips by licking them. *n.* Moisture in the carpet caused it to turn mouldy.	*dry, arid, parched, dehydrated*
moment		*n.* **second, jiffy, flash, minute, instant** Stay for a moment. *adj.* There was a momentary silence when the bad news was announced.	*eternity, age*
momentous		*adj.* **eventful, important, notable, memorable, outstanding** Canada's Centennial in 1967 was a momentous occasion.	*insignificant, unimportant, trivial, common, ordinary*
momentum		*n.* **force, energy, impetus, thrust, drive, push, velocity, speed** The bobsled gathered momentum as it sped down the icy slope.	
monarch		*n.* **sovereign, emperor, king, queen** Queen Elizabeth II is the monarch of the United Kingdom.	*subject, follower*
money	1.	*n.* **cash, funds, currency, coin, legal tender** The money was deposited in Paul's account at the bank.	
	2.	*n.* **wealth, riches, large income, affluence** She made her money in the stock market.	
monopolize		*v.* **control, corner, take over, appropriate, dominate** It is against the law to monopolize any commodity.	*share, divide*
monopoly		*n.* **control, cartel, exclusive right, exclusive possession** No one firm should have a monopoly on any kind of industry.	*open market*
monotonous		*adj.* **tedious, dull, boring, tiresome, wearisome, routine** Workers in monotonous jobs require frequent breaks. *n.* Some people find the monotony of the prairie scenery unbearable.	*stimulating interesting, pleasing*

Word	No.	Part	Synonyms / Example	Antonyms
mood		*n.*	**feeling, temper, frame of mind, disposition** The students were in a holiday mood on the last day of school.	
moody		*adj.*	**unhappy, dejected, melancholy, gloomy, sullen, brooding, despondent** Sheen is moody because she did not win the match.	*happy, cheerful, amiable*
morale		*n.*	**confidence, self-assurance, resolution, mental attitude, spirit** A win tomorrow would greatly improve the team's morale.	
morbid		*adj.*	**gruesome, sickening, unwholesome, grim, depressing** What a morbid movie that was!	*wholesome, pleasant, uplifting*
more	1.	*adj.*	**extra, additional, spare, reserve, other, supplementary** There are more sandwiches in the refrigerator. *n.* Can we have more of the same please?	**1.** *less, fewer*
	2.	*adv.*	**to a greater degree, to a greater extent** She reads more than anyone else.	**2.** *less than, fewer than*
morose		*adj.*	**sad, low, moody, depressed, melancholy, glum** What a morose ending to that story!	*cheerful, happy, pleasant*
mortal	1.	*n.*	**human being, person, creature, individual** Will mortals ever set foot on Mars?	
	2.	*adj.*	**human, temporal, earthly** There are mortal limitations to what we can do.	**2.** *immortal, eternal, everlasting, perpetual*
	3.	*adj.*	**fatal, lethal, deadly** The warrior dealt his enemy a mortal blow. *adv.* The soldier was mortally wounded in battle.	**3.** *lifesaving, lifegiving*
	4.	*adj.*	**intense, enormous, extreme** The escapee was in mortal fear of being captured.	
motion	1.	*n.*	**movement, passage, progress, action, flow** The motion of the ship made some passengers ill.	**1.** *stillness, calm, rest, repose*

2. *n.* **suggestion, recommendation, request, proposition**
Tina made a motion to adjourn the meeting.

3. *v.* **signal, gesture, wave, beckon, nod**
The police officer motioned us to proceed around the stalled vehicle.

motionless *adj.* **still, stationary, unmoving**
The motionless cat watched the mouse.
moving, shifting

motivate *v.* **induce, drive, prompt, stimulate, incite, impel**
The chance to win a scholarship motivated Yen to work hard.
n. Her motivation was strengthened by the competition she faced.

mount
1. *v.* **climb, rise, ascend, go up**
Mount the stairs slowly.
1. *descend, go down*

2. *v.* **swell, grow, multiply, increase, rise**
Unemployment figures mounted last year.
2. *lessen, decline, fall*

3. *v.* **get on, climb on**
The cowboy mounted his horse and rode away.
3. *dismount, get down*

4. *v.* **prepare, set, fix, place, install**
The photographer mounted our pictures in suitable frames.

mourn *v.* **grieve, sorrow, regret, lament**
We mourn the loss of a loved one.
adj. The funeral was a mournful occasion.
rejoice, be glad, cheer, delight in

move
1. *v.* **shift, go, proceed, travel**
The procession moved slowly through the city.
n. The movement of troops to the border worried everyone.
1. *remain, halt, stand, pause, stay*

2. *v.* **transfer, carry, shift**
The company moved our furniture to Vancouver.
n. Nothing was broken in the move!

3. *v.* **suggest, recommend, propose**
John moved that we adjourn the meeting.

4. *v.* **affect, touch, arouse, stir**
I was deeply moved by his letter.

Word			Synonyms / Example	Antonyms
movie		*n.*	**film, cinema, show, motion picture, picture** Do you often go to the movies?	
much	1.	*n.*	**great deal, lots, large amount** There's much to be done before a wedding.	1. *little*
	2.	*adj.*	**plentiful, ample, sufficient, a lot of, abundant** There was much food spread out on the long tables.	2. *little, scarce*
	3.	*adv.*	**greatly, decidedly, exceedingly, extremely** Terry Fox is much admired for his "Marathon of Hope."	3. *not much, scarcely, hardly*
	4.	*adv.*	**nearly, somewhat, almost, about, approximately** The old house looks much the same as it did five years ago.	4. *hardly, barely*
muddy		*adj.*	**cloudy, unclear, murky** We didn't want to swim in the muddy waters of the pond.	*clear, transparent, lucid*
muffle	1.	*v.*	**cover, wrap, enclose, swathe** We muffled our faces with scarves against the bitter cold.	1. *uncover*
	2.	*v.*	**silence, blot out, quieten, mute, stifle** The thick walls muffled the captive's cries for help.	2. *magnify, increase*
multiply		*v.*	**reproduce, increase, expand** The world population multiplies each year.	*decrease, lessen, diminish, reduce*
multitude		*n.*	**crowd, swarm, mass, horde, flock, throng, host** A multitude of gulls rested on the beach.	*small number*
mumble		*v.*	**whisper, murmur, mutter** Tim mumbled that he was sorry to be late.	*speak clearly, enunciate*
murky	1.	*adj.*	**gloomy, dim, cloudy, dreary, dismal, overcast** Murky weather is usual in the winter.	1. *sunny, bright, clear*
	2.	*adj.*	**muddy, cloudy, dirty** I refused to drink the murky water.	2. *clear, unclouded, clean*

Word		Part	Synonyms / Example	Antonyms
murmur		*n.*	**low sound, whisper, undertone, soft utterance** There was a murmur of agreement at the mayor's suggestion. *v.* We murmured our approval.	*shout, yell*
muse		*v.*	**ponder, meditate, reflect, deliberate, contemplate** "Shall I buy that stereo," he mused, "or save the money?"	
musty		*adj.*	**stale, damp, mildewed, mouldy** There was a box of musty old letters in the attic.	*fresh, new*
mutiny		*n.*	**rebellion, revolt, riot, insurrection** There was a mutiny on the ship. *v.* The sailors mutinied against their violent captain. *adj.* The mutinous sailors took over control of the ship.	
mutter		*v.*	**mumble, growl, grumble** No one can hear you if you mutter.	*speak clearly, enunciate*
mutual		*adj.*	**common, shared, joint** Sylvia is a mutual friend of ours.	*exclusive*
myriad		*adj.*	**countless, infinite, endless, limitless, untold, immeasurable** Myriad stars are found in the Milky Way.	*few, limited*
mysterious		*adj.*	**weird, puzzling, secretive, strange, unnatural** The mysterious disappearance of the scientist caused much concern.	*obvious, definite, evident, clear*
mystery		*n.*	**riddle, puzzle, secret** Sherlock Holmes solved many mysteries.	*answer*
mystify		*v.*	**perplex, puzzle, bewilder, baffle, confuse** We were mystified by the neighbour's sudden disappearance.	*clarify, explain*
myth	1.	*n.*	**story, tale, fable, parable, legend** The ancient Greeks invented myths to explain natural occurrences. *adj.* A unicorn is a mythical creature.	**1.** *fact, real life, happening*
	2.	*n.*	**error, illusion, delusion, false belief** Tales of his riches turned out to be mere myth.	**2.** *truth, fact, actuality*

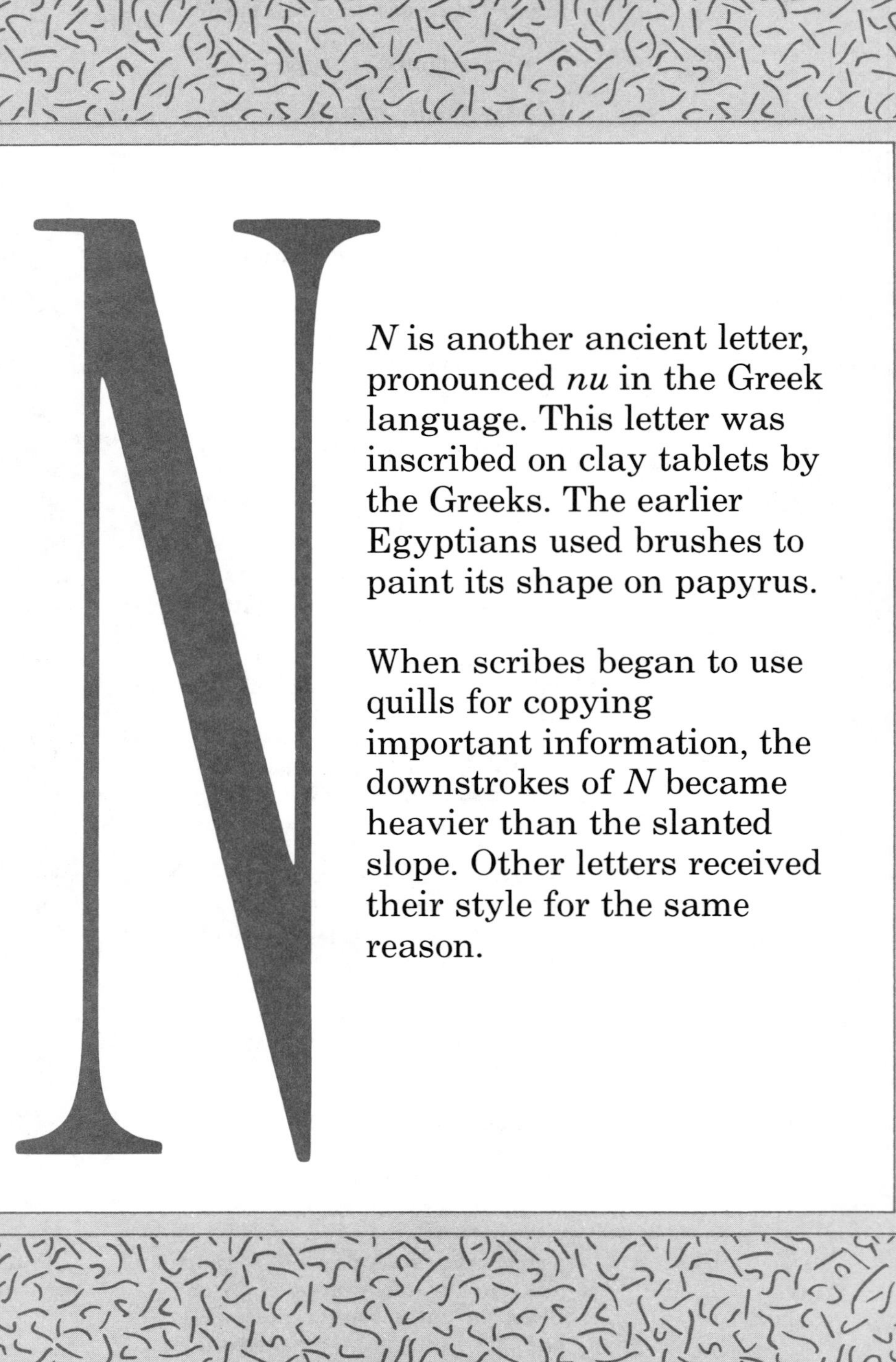

N is another ancient letter, pronounced *nu* in the Greek language. This letter was inscribed on clay tablets by the Greeks. The earlier Egyptians used brushes to paint its shape on papyrus.

When scribes began to use quills for copying important information, the downstrokes of *N* became heavier than the slanted slope. Other letters received their style for the same reason.

Entry			Synonyms	Antonyms
nab		*v.*	**seize, grab, snatch, catch** The police nabbed the robber in the alley.	*release, set free*
naked		*adj.*	**nude, bare, uncovered, exposed, unclothed, undressed** The child ran out of his bath stark naked.	*covered, clothed, dressed*
name	1.	*n.*	**title, term** What is your name, age, and address? *v.* They named the baby after her grandmother.	
	2.	*n.*	**reputation** A good name is earned by good deeds.	
	3.	*v.*	**mention, speak of** The author named our family in his book.	
	4.	*v.*	**choose, appoint, select, nominate** Has the school named a new principal yet?	
nap	1.	*n.*	**short sleep, siesta, snooze, catnap** The baby takes a nap each afternoon.	
	2.	*v.*	**doze, slumber, drowse** Mike was napping in front of the television.	
narrate		*v.*	**tell, describe, recite, state, make known, reveal** Norman narrated his own story to the audience. *n.* He is a good narrator. *n.* His powerful narration kept the audience spellbound.	*conceal, withhold*
narrow	1.	*v.*	**restrict, contract, limit** We narrowed the distance between us and the group ahead.	**1.** *broaden, widen, enlarge*
	2.	*adj.*	**small in width, compressed, cramped, slender, tight** We couldn't crawl through the narrow space in the cave.	**2.** *wide, broad, spacious*
nasty	1.	*adj.*	**offensive, mean, vicious** Everyone was shocked at his nasty remarks.	**1.** *pleasant, kind*
	2.	*adj.*	**foul, dirty, offensive, disagreeable, unpleasant** Nasty odours came from the chemical plant.	**2.** *agreeable, clean, pleasant*

native

1. *n.* **original inhabitant, aborigine**
The Beothuks were the natives who once inhabited Newfoundland.
Antonyms: 1. *invader, intrude*

2. *n.* **citizen, lifetime inhabitant, longtime resident, one born there**
William Shakespeare was a native of England.
Antonyms: 2. *foreigner, alien*

3. *adj.* **of birth, natal, home**
Stavro's native land is Greece.
Antonyms: 3. *adopted*

4. *adj.* **inborn, innate, natural, ingrained, instinctive, inherent**
The pianist Glenn Gould had native music ability.
Antonyms: 4. *acquired, learne*

5. *adj.* **homegrown, local, domestic, national**
To help the economy, we should buy native products.
Antonyms: 5. *imported, foreig*

natural

1. *adj.* **original, close to nature**
Many poets have praised the natural beauty of England's Lake District.
Antonyms: 1. *artificial, unnatural, created, manufactured*

2. *adj.* **unforced, unaffected**
Sally is a natural actress.
adv. She acts quite naturally.
Antonyms: 2. *affected, unnatural*

3. *adj.* **normal, usual, typical**
It's natural to feel depressed when things go wrong.
Antonyms: 3. *abnormal*

4. *adj.* **inborn, innate, native, instinctive**
She should be encouraged to develop her natural artistic ability.
Antonyms: 4. *acquired, learne*

nature

1. *n.* **natural world**
Human beings have destroyed much of nature through industrialization.

2. *n.* **personality, disposition, character**
Simone is a pleasure to be with because of her sunny nature.

3. *n.* **instinct, spirit**
He is by nature a hard worker.

4. *n.* **sort, kind, variety, type**
What is the nature of your problem?

naughty

adj. **mischievous, bad, ill-behaved, unruly, disobedient**
The naughty child was not allowed to watch television.
Antonyms: *good, well-behaved, obedient*

navigate

v. **steer, direct, guide, pilot, cruise, sail**
The contestants navigated their bikes through the obstacle course.
n. Sandy was the best navigator.
n. Her expert navigation earned her first prize.

Word	#	Part	Synonyms / Examples	Antonyms
near	1.	*v.*	**approach, come up to, come toward** We were happy as we neared home.	
	2.	*adj.*	**close, approaching, impending, imminent** Those dark clouds mean a storm is near. *adv.* Tension rises as examinations draw near.	
	3.	*adj.*	**close, next door, close by, alongside** I walk to school as it is quite near.	**3.** *distant, far, remote*
	4.	*prep.*	**close to, not far from, in sight of** Herb lives near the school.	
nearly		*adv.*	**almost, just about, about, practically, approximately** The work on the new house is nearly finished.	
neat		*adj.*	**tidy, groomed, well-kept, trim, orderly** Mei always has a neat appearance. *n.* Neatness is a desirable habit. *adv.* Mark writes neatly.	*unkempt, messy, untidy*
necessary		*adj.*	**essential, needed, indispensable, required** She was hired as she had all the necessary skills for the job. *n.* Water is a necessity for survival.	*unnecessary, needless, useless*
need	1.	*n.*	**hardship, poverty, distress** Some families live in great need. *adj.* The needy ones must be helped.	**1.** *plenty, comfort, luxury*
	2.	*n.*	**necessity, requirement, want** Bev is in need of medical help.	
	3.	*v.*	**require, want** What credits do you need to graduate?	**3.** *possess, own*
negative	1.	*adj.*	**antagonistic, contrary** Sam's negative attitude dampened the team's morale.	**1.** *positive, helpful, encouraging*
	2.	*adj.*	**opposing, dissenting, opposed** The vote was altogether negative.	**2.** *affirmative, positive, assenting*
neglect	1.	*n.*	**lack of care, disregard, inattention** Years of neglect had left the house in ruins. *v.* The parents neglected their children because of their hectic jobs.	**1.** *care, attention*

	2.	*v.*	**miss, skip, omit, ignore, disregard** Who neglected his homework this time?	**2.** *attend to, take care of*
negligent		*adj.*	**careless, inattentive, thoughtless, heedless, neglectful** Sam was charged with negligent driving after the accident.	*careful, watchful, keen, alert, attentive*
negotiate		*v.*	**bargain, set terms, arrange for, discuss** The boys negotiated a better price for the equipment. *n.* Their negotiations saved them money.	
neighbourhood (also spelled neighborhood)		*n.*	**vicinity, district, locality, area** Is your home in the neighbourhood of the school?	
neighbouring (also spelled neighboring)		*adj.*	**nearby, adjacent, next, bordering** Our house is on a neighbouring street.	*distant, remote, far-off*
nerve		*n.*	**daring, vigour, courage, pluck** It takes a lot of nerve to perform on a high wire.	*cowardice, weakness*
nervous		*adj.*	**restless, uneasy, tense, jumpy, jittery, fearful, agitated** Loud noises make me nervous. *adv.* The suspect stuttered nervously when he was questioned by the police.	*calm, poised, at ease brave, courageous, steady*
net	1.	*n.*	**snare, mesh, web, trap** Pierre used a net to catch the butterfly.	
	2.	*v.*	**bag, capture, catch, seize** Jay netted three fish from the pond.	**2.** *release, set free*
	3.	*v.*	**earn, gain, acquire, take in** Their business netted a good profit last year.	
neutral		*adj.*	**nonpartisan, impartial, indifferent, unbiassed** Switzerland has been neutral in all foreign wars since 1815. *n.* The country practises a policy of neutrality.	*active, biassed, partisan*

Word	#	Part	Synonyms / Example	Antonyms
neutralize		*v.*	**offset, check, block, annul, cancel, stop, halt, impede, overcome** The doctor neutralized the effects of the poison with an antidote.	
nevertheless		*adv.*	**yet, but, regardless, anyhow, however, even so** The weather was terrible, nevertheless we set out for Halifax.	
new	1.	*adj.*	**recent, fresh, just out, novel, original** The Chinese wear new clothes to celebrate the Chinese New Year. *adv.* The house is newly painted.	1. *old, out-of-date old-fashioned*
	2.	*adj.*	**different** Todd will be going to a new school next fall.	2. *same*
	3.	*adj.*	**unaccustomed, strange** All this research and writing is new to me.	3. *familiar*
news		*n.*	**information, tidings, report, story, message, account** Did you watch the news on television?	
next		*adj.*	**following, succeeding, subsequent** Please turn to the next page. *adv.* Next, let's read chapter two.	*previous, preceding, prior*
nice	1.	*adj.*	**pleasant, agreeable, fine, wonderful** We had a nice time at Jose's birthday party. *adv.* The room was decorated very nicely with balloons and streamers.	1. *unpleasant, disagreeable, revolting, horrid, dreadful, awful*
	2.	*adj.*	**charming, lovely, delightful, friendly** Everyone likes him because he is such a nice person.	2. *rude, awful, unpleasant*
nimble		*adj.*	**active, spry, agile, lively, sprightly, supple** The nimble gymnast leapt gracefully onto the bar.	*slow, awkward, sluggish, clumsy*
noble	1.	*n.*	**nobleman, noblewoman, aristocrat** The group visited the castle of an ancient noble.	1. *commoner, plebeian*

	2.	*adj.*	**dignified, majestic, grand, magnificent, worthy, regal** The soldiers died for a noble cause.	**2.** *inferior, lowly, mean*
noise		*n.*	**din, clatter, discord, sound, tumult, racket** The baby was awakened by a loud noise. *adj.* The students had a noisy argument over homework.	*silence, stillness, hush, peace, quiet*
nominate		*v.*	**propose, name, recommend, appoint, suggest** Shaila was nominated to run for class president. *n.* She accepted the nomination.	
nonrenewable		*adj.*	**irreplaceable, irrecoverable** Oil and coal are nonrenewable sources of energy.	*renewable, replaceable*
nonsense		*n.*	**drivel, folly, absurdity, foolishness** Their claims about seeing a Martian were dismissed as utter nonsense. *adj.* At parties we play nonsensical games.	*common sense, wisdom, sense, reality*
normal		*adj.*	**usual, typical, regular, natural, ordinary, customary, average** Our normal work hours are 9 to 5. *adv.* The letter carrier normally comes in the morning.	*unusual, odd, peculiar, irregular, uncommon, abnormal*
notable		*adj.*	**great, outstanding, momentous, remarkable, important** Neil Armstrong's walk on the moon was a notable event.	*insignificant, unimportant, obscure, unknown*
note	1.	*n.*	**letter, message, communication** Leave a note for us.	
	2.	*v.*	**write, put down** The monitor noted our names on the board.	
	3.	*v.*	**observe, notice, regard** Note the colours of that bird.	**3.** *disregard, ignore, overlook*
noted		*adj.*	**outstanding, famous, celebrated, renowned** Winston Churchill was a noted leader.	*unknown, obscure*
notice	1.	*n.*	**announcement, poster, circular, advertisement** Where did you see the notice for the game?	

2. *v.* **note, observe**
Did you notice my new shoes?
Antonyms: **2.** *disregard, ignore*

notify *v.* **inform, let know, acquaint, tell**
The university notified Yang-Yi that he had been accepted.
n. The notification of his acceptance came in the mail.
conceal, keep silent, withhold

notion *n.* **opinion, impression, idea, view, thought**
Where did he get the notion that he had won the scholarship?

notorious *adj.* **infamous, outstanding, well-known**
Have you read about the notorious Jack the Ripper?
unknown

nourish *v.* **feed, sustain, nurture, support**
Birds nourish their young.
n. All living things require nourishment.
adj. Have a nourishing meal before you set off on your trip.
starve, deprive, weaken

novel **1.** *n.* **fiction, tale, story**
Treasure Island is a famous novel.
2. *adj.* **fresh, new, original, unusual**
Designers have to introduce novel ideas in their clothes.
n. The novelty of the game made it a success.
2. *common, ordinary, hackneyed*

novice *n.* **beginner, learner, apprentice, amateur, newcomer**
I'm a novice when it comes to using the computer.
professional, master, old hand

numb *adj.* **dulled, insensible, deadened**
Ed's fingers were numb from the cold.
v. The anesthetic numbed his pain.
sensitive

number **1.** *n.* **amount, volume**
A large number of people attended our concert.
2. *n.* **figure, digit**
Pick a lucky number.
3. *n.* **song, tune**
All of us sang a merry number.
4. *v.* **count, calculate, enumerate**
Biz numbered the pages of the manuscript.

numerous	*adj.*	**many, abundant, various** Selene received numerous job offers after her outstanding performance.	*few, hardly any*
nutrient	*n.*	**nourishment, food, sustenance, nutriment** There are excellent nutrients in whole grain cereals. *adj.* Synthetic nutrient foods are sometimes used by the astronauts.	
nutritious	*adj.*	**nourishing, healthful, wholesome** Bread is a nutritious food. *n.* What other foods give us nutrition?	*harmful*

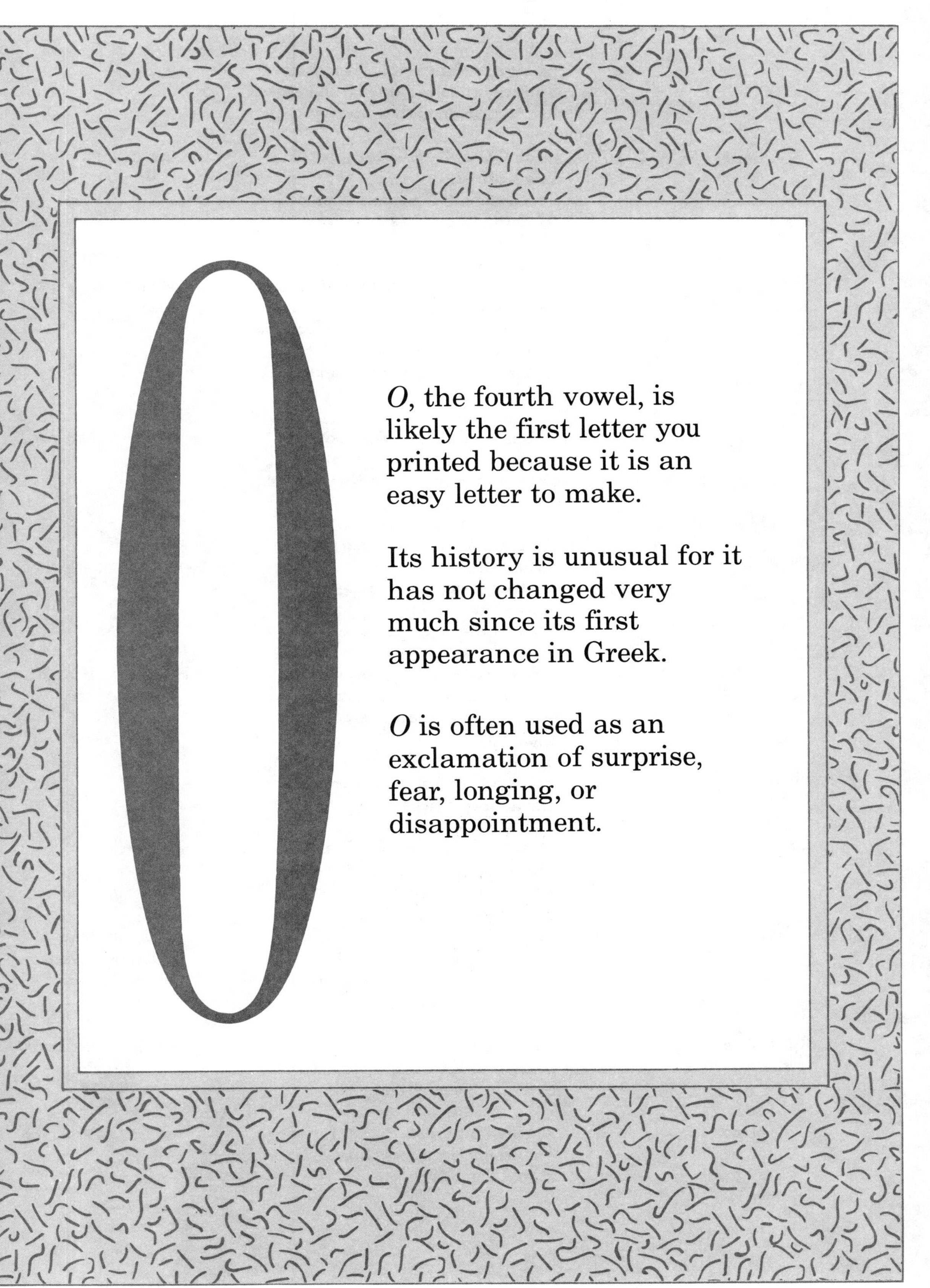

O, the fourth vowel, is likely the first letter you printed because it is an easy letter to make.

Its history is unusual for it has not changed very much since its first appearance in Greek.

O is often used as an exclamation of surprise, fear, longing, or disappointment.

oath *n.* **pledge, solemn promise, vow**
The scientists working on the project had to take an oath of secrecy.

obedient *adj.* **orderly, well-behaved, dutiful, law-abiding**
The obedient dog came when called.
n. Our new dog has been trained in obedience.
disobedient, unruly, defiant

obese *adj.* **fat, overweight, heavy, stout, plump, chubby**
Al became obese from too much food and too little exercise.
n. He is working hard to get rid of his obesity.
slim, thin, slender, lean

obey *v.* **submit to, agree with, comply with**
Soldiers are trained to obey orders.
disobey, disregard, defy

object
1. *n.* **device, article, thing**
People claim to have seen strange flying objects.
2. *n.* **motive, aim, purpose, goal, intent, use, point**
What is the object of these experiments?
3. *v.* **criticize, protest, disapprove, oppose, dislike, condemn**
Many people object to smoking in their homes or workplace.
n. The strong objection to smoking in the workplace has led to many smoke-free offices.
3. *agree, consent, approve, like, admire*

objective
1. *n.* **aim, purpose, intent, design, target, object, intention**
Kai's main objective in life is to become extremely rich.
2. *adj.* **impartial, fair, just, unbiassed, open-minded, detached**
The judge offered an objective opinion of the debate.
2. *subjective, prejudiced, biassed, unjust, unfair*

obligation *n.* **duty, task, responsibility**
Each of us has an obligation to help clean up the environment.
choice, freedom

oblige *v.* **require, compel, make, force**
The whole class was obliged to attend the lecture.
spare, exempt, free, release

Word	No.	Part of speech	Synonyms and example	Antonyms
obliterate		*v.*	**erase, wipe out, delete, rub out, abolish, cancel, blot out** Some important evidence had been obliterated from the tapes.	*keep, preserve, add*
oblivious		*adj.*	**unmindful, unaware, heedless, unconcerned, forgetful** The pianist was oblivious to everything except the music.	*aware, concerned, conscious, attentive, observant*
obnoxious		*adj.*	**offensive, repulsive, displeasing, distressing, disagreeable, unpleasant** Obnoxious odours came from the chemical plant.	*pleasing, inviting, pleasant, delightful, agreeable*
obscure	1.	*v.*	**block, hide, conceal, overshadow, cover** Clouds obscured the tops of the mountains.	1. *reveal, show, display*
	2.	*adj.*	**little-known, unknown** The book was written by some obscure person. *n.* She has since risen from obscurity to fame.	2. *famous, renowned*
	3.	*adj.*	**unclear, indefinite, hidden, vague, hazy** We were puzzled by the book's obscure ending.	3. *evident, plain, obvious, definite, clear*
observant		*adj.*	**attentive, alert, watchful, perceptive, careful** The observant guard stopped the shoplifter from leaving the store.	*unobservant, heedless, careless, inattentive*
observation		*n.*	**view, theory, opinion, comment, remark, finding** Write down your observations of the experiment.	
observe	1.	*v.*	**obey, keep, follow, respect, comply with, conform to** Our team observed all the rules of the game.	1. *violate, break, disobey, disregard*
	2.	*v.*	**notice, see, detect, watch, perceive** We observed two strangers loitering in the street.	2. *ignore, overlook, miss*
obsolete		*adj.*	**outdated, outmoded, old-fashioned, worn-out** The company replaced its obsolete equipment with the latest computers.	*recent, new, current, modern, avant-garde*

Word		Part of speech	Synonyms and example	Antonyms
obstacle		*n.*	**obstruction, barrier, hindrance** All traffic had to detour around the obstacles on the road.	*aid, assistance, help*
obstinate		*adj.*	**stubborn, determined, persistent, willful** The obstinate man refused to change his mind. *adv.* He obstinately refused to make way for us.	*willing, obliging, cooperative*
obstruct		*v.*	**hinder, bar, block, impede, retard, restrict, stop** The new building obstructed our view of the lake. *n.* The obstruction of traffic was caused by a stalled car.	*aid, help, speed, assist, clear, open*
obtain		*v.*	**get, secure, earn, acquire, procure, gain** How did you obtain this information?	*forfeit, lose, give*
obvious		*adj.*	**plain, clear, apparent** It was obvious from the start that our team was better. *adv.* The better team obviously won.	*doubtful, unclear*
occasion	1.	*n.*	**affair, event, episode, happening, circumstance, situation** The baby shower was a happy occasion.	
	2.	*n.*	**cause, reason, motive, grounds** We had occasion to celebrate after we heard the test results.	
occasional		*adj.*	**infrequent, irregular, rare, uncommon** Reg enjoys an occasional game of golf. *adv.* We play occasionally.	*regular, frequent*
occupant		*n.*	**householder, tenant, inhabitant, resident** Who is the occupant of the next apartment?	
occupation	1.	*n.*	**work, calling, job, business, craft, vocation, profession, trade, employment** He's been in the same occupation all his life.	

Word	No.	Part	Synonyms and example	Antonyms
	2.	*n.*	**ownership, possession** The new owners will take occupation of the house soon.	
occupy	1.	*v.*	**inhabit, own, possess, live in** Who occupied this house before you?	**1.** *abandon, desert, leave, move from*
	2.	*v.*	**fill, engage, employ, absorb** My aunt occupies her time with skiing.	
	3.	*v.*	**conquer, control, possess** Enemy troops occupied the territory.	**3.** *liberate, free*
occur		*v.*	**happen, befall, result, take place, transpire** A serious accident occurred yesterday at this intersection.	
occurrence		*n.*	**episode, event, experience, happening, incident, occasion** The sudden storm was an unusual occurrence in this region.	
odd	1.	*adj.*	**strange, queer, peculiar, irregular, unusual, abnormal** Peng has an odd habit of twitching his nose. *adv.* He has been behaving oddly lately.	**1.** *normal, usual, ordinary, common, customary*
	2.	*adj.*	**sundry, various, casual, occasional, extra** Our students do odd jobs for retired people.	**2.** *regular, steady, full-time*
odour (also spelled odor)		*n.*	**smell, scent, aroma, fragrance, stench** The lovely odour of roses filled the room.	
offence		*n.*	**crime, error, fault, wrong, violation** The suspect was accused of a serious offence.	
offend		*v.*	**insult, displease, anger, hurt, irritate** Hank offended his friend with his rude remarks.	*please, satisfy, help, calm*
offensive	1.	*adj.*	**impudent, impertinent, insulting, rude, obnoxious** The tennis player was disqualified for his offensive manners.	**1.** *courteous, polite, charming*
	2.	*adj.*	**foul, unpleasant, nasty, revolting** Rotten eggs produce offensive odours.	**2.** *agreeable, pleasant, pleasing, delightful*

Word			Synonyms	Antonyms
offer		*v.*	**suggest, present, give, advance, volunteer, propose** Our neighbours offered to help build the fence. *n.* We gladly accepted their offer.	*deny, refuse, decline, withhold*
official	1.	*n*	**officer, leader, executive, administrator** Government officials made the decisions regarding tax exemptions.	
	2.	*adj.*	**authorized, appointed, endorsed, sanctioned, approved** Canada has two official languages — English and French.	**2.** *unauthorized, unofficial*
often		*adv.*	**frequently, generally, regularly, constantly, habitually** We often stop at the restaurant on our way home.	*never, rarely, seldom, occasionally*
old	1.	*adj.*	**ancient, antique** This old piece of furniture belonged to my grandmother.	**1.** *modern, recent, new*
	2.	*adj.*	**aged, elderly** Old people like to keep active and interested.	**2.** *young, youthful*
	3.	*adj.*	**outdated, out-of-date** Who wants to read an old newspaper?	**3.** *current, up-to-date*
	4.	*adj.*	**worn, used, aged** We reupholstered our old sofa and it looks new again.	**4.** *new*
	5.	*adj.*	**former, previous** I visited my old school recently.	**5.** *current, present*
ominous		*adj.*	**threatening, sinister, menacing, unfavourable** The ominous rumours about nuclear war make people anxious.	*encouraging, promising, favourable*
omit		*v.*	**exclude, overlook, leave out, disregard** Omar omitted one question on the test. *n.* The omission cost him some marks.	*include, insert, put in*
onlooker		*n*	**spectator, witness, bystander** Curious onlookers crowded around the scene of the accident.	
only	1.	*adj.*	**sole, single, lone** Eugene is an only child.	**1.** *one of many*
	2.	*adv.*	**exclusively, just, solely, merely** He comes only on Saturdays.	

Word			Synonyms	Antonyms
open	1.	*v.*	**unfasten, release, unlock** Please open the door.	1. *close, fasten, lock, shut, seal*
	2.	*v.*	**commence, start, initiate, begin** The meeting opened with the singing of the national anthem.	2. *conclude, end, close, finish*
	3.	*adj*	**unlocked, unobstructed** We entered through the open door.	3. *closed, shut, fastened, locked*
opening	1.	*n.*	**opportunity, chance, occasion, possibility** He had a good opening to score in the last period.	
	2.	*n.*	**clearing, gap, hole, break** The snowmobile fell through the opening in the ice.	2. *barrier, block, blockade*
	3.	*n.*	**vacancy, space, place, job, position** The company has an opening for an editor.	
	4.	*adj.*	**beginning, starting, initial, first** The opening ceremony of the Olympic Games was most impressive.	4. *final, concluding, closing, ending*
operate		*v.*	**work, manage, drive, run, manipulate** Even a child can operate this machine. *n.* Telephone operators at the police station are trained to handle emergency calls.	
operation		*n.*	**action, performance, process, procedure** Liz is responsible for the smooth operation of the company.	
opinion		*n.*	**viewpoint, idea, impression, judgment, notion, conclusion** What's your opinion on this issue?	
opponent		*n.*	**antagonist, rival, competitor, enemy** The two opponents faced each other in a debate.	*ally, partner, friend, colleague, helper, supporter*
opportunity		*n.*	**chance, occasion, opening, time** Here is your opportunity to learn a new language.	
oppose		*v.*	**object to, dispute, disapprove of** We are opposed to the new taxes.	*support, agree with, approve, defend*

Word	No.	Part	Synonyms and examples	Antonyms
opposite	1.	*adj.*	**conflicting, contrary, opposed** We have entirely opposite political views. *n.* "Left" is the opposite of "right."	**1.** *same, similar, agreeable*
	2.	*prep.*	**facing, across from** Sit opposite me.	**2.** *beside, next to*
opposition		*n.*	**defiance, antagonism, resistance** There was strong opposition to the government's proposals.	*cooperation, support, approval, assistance*
oppressive	1.	*adj.*	**harsh, cruel, brutal, despotic** Oppressive leaders are often overthrown.	**1.** *just, kind, humane, benevolent*
	2.	*adj.*	**overwhelming, overpowering, unbearable** Many people fainted from the oppressive heat in the stadium.	**2.** *comfortable, soothing*
optimistic		*adj.*	**hopeful, confident, upbeat, encouraging** We are optimistic about our chance of winning the championship. *n.* The finance minister expressed optimism about the economy. *n.* She is an optimist.	*pessimistic, gloomy, cynical*
option		*n.*	**choice, selection, alternative** Weigh your options carefully.	
orbit	1.	*n.*	**path, circuit, course, trajectory, revolution** Many satellites have been put into orbit around the Earth.	
	2.	*v.*	**circle, revolve around, travel around** The Soviet satellite Mir orbited the Earth for 366 days.	
order	1.	*n.*	**quiet, calm, control, discipline** The police were called in to restore order among the rioters.	**1.** *disorder, chaos*
	2.	*n.*	**command, instruction, decree** The mayor gave orders to evacuate the town because of a chemical leak. *v.* The mayor ordered the evacuation of the town.	
	3.	*n.*	**system, form, arrangement, rank, sequence, progression** List the names in alphabetical order.	**3.** *disorder, chaos, confusion*
	4.	*v.*	**request, ask for, obtain, purchase** Let's order some dessert. *n.* We placed an order for a new car.	

Word	Sense	Part	Synonyms and example	Antonyms
orderly	1.	*adj.*	**well-behaved, calm** People left in an orderly fashion after the play.	1. *disorderly, unruly*
	2.	*adj.*	**tidy, neat, systematic, organized, methodical, regulated** The chairs were arranged in orderly rows.	2. *chaotic, confused*
ordinary		*adj.*	**common, usual, normal, customary, regular** We had another ordinary day at school. *adv.* We ordinarily leave for school by eight o'clock.	*extraordinary, unusual, exceptional*
organization	1.	*n.*	**company, firm, establishment, business** Mom works for a large organization.	
	2.	*n.*	**system, arrangement** The students were responsible for the organization of the dance.	
organize		*v.*	**arrange, establish, coordinate** Who organized the science fair? *n.* The organizer of the fair did a terrific job.	*disorganize, upset, disturb*
origin	1.	*n.*	**source, beginning, cause, base** Ideas, like rivers, often have hidden origins.	1. *end, finish*
	2.	*n.*	**descent, family, ancestry, lineage, race, stock, parentage** Maki's family is of Japanese origin.	
original	1.	*adj.*	**first, earliest, primary** Indians were the original inhabitants of North America.	1. *last, latest, final*
	2.	*adj.*	**unique, novel, creative, fresh, imaginative, unusual, inventive** John has an original idea for the poster. *n.* His idea shows originality.	2. *unoriginal, imitative*
originate		*v.*	**start, introduce, begin, create, invent** The idea for this book originated from a childhood experience.	
ornate		*adj.*	**showy, fancy, elaborate, lavish, adorned, ornamented** The ornate decorations were admired by the visitors.	*simple, plain, unadorned*
ought		*v.*	**should, be obliged, must** Helen ought to keep her promise to help us.	

Word			Synonyms / Example	Antonyms
oust		*v.*	**remove, expel, dismiss, eject, throw out, fire, discharge** The unethical director was ousted from the board.	*admit, welcome*
outbreak	1.	*n.*	**rebellion, uprising, mutiny, riot** The army is busy keeping down the outbreaks from the rebels.	1. *peace, harmony*
	2.	*n.*	**eruption, explosion, outburst** A sudden outbreak of laughter echoed down the hall.	
outcome		*n.*	**consequence, effect, end, result** The outcome of the game was surprising.	*cause, origin, beginning*
outfit	1.	*n.*	**supplies, equipment, apparatus, gear, provisions** Is your camping outfit ready?	
	2.	*n.*	**group, organization** He works for a large medical outfit.	
	3.	*n.*	**ensemble, clothes** Patti chose a stunning outfit for her wedding.	
	4.	*v.*	**equip, supply** The motorhome is outfitted with a fridge, stove, and a microwave oven.	4. *strip*
outlaw	1.	*n.*	**bandit, criminal, desperado, fugitive** The outlaw was arrested by the sheriff.	
	2.	*v.*	**ban, forbid, make illegal** Speeding is outlawed here.	2. *allow, make legal, permit*
outline	1.	*n.*	**plan, scheme, framework, draft** First, make an outline for your story.	
	2.	*n.*	**edge, frame, boundary** She drew a black outline around her picture.	
	3.	*v.*	**describe, summarize, draft** The teachers outlined their plans for the class trip.	
	4.	*v.*	**draw, sketch** George outlined a map on the board.	
outlook	1.	*n.*	**view, viewpoint, attitude, perspective, frame of mind** Her outlook on life has changed since she became ill.	
	2.	*n.*	**prospect, forecast, expectation, probability** The outlook for the economy is promising.	2. *retrospect*

Word	No.	Part	Synonyms / Example	Antonyms
	3.	*n.*	**view, vista, sight, scene, panorama** The outlook from the top of the tower is spectacular.	
outrageous		*adj.*	**awful, atrocious, indecent, offensive, shocking, shameful** We were embarrassed by their outrageous behaviour at the party.	*honourable, decent*
outset		*n.*	**beginning, start, origin, commencement, opening, inception** We had a flat tire at the very outset of our trip.	*end, finish, closing, conclusion, termination*
outspoken		*adj.*	**blunt, direct, frank, candid, forthright, straightforward** The coach was most outspoken in his criticism of the players.	*tactful, guarded, diplomatic*
outstanding	1.	*adj.*	**leading, notable, famous, great, prominent, celebrated** Marie Curie was an outstanding scientist.	**1.** *commonplace, ordinary*
	2.	*adj.*	**exceptional, superior, great, remarkable, excellent** Shi-Lan is an outstanding student.	**2.** *inferior*
	3.	*adj.*	**unpaid, due, payable, owing** All outstanding accounts are charged 20 percent interest.	**3.** *paid, settled*
over	1.	*adj.*	**finished, complete, done, ended** School is over by four o'clock.	**1.** *beginning*
	2.	*prep.*	**across, above** Jump over the fence.	**2.** *under, beneath, below*
	3.	*prep.*	**more than, beyond** The tickets cost over a dollar.	**3.** *less than, under*
overcast		*adj.*	**cloudy, dull, gloomy, sunless, gray** The skies have been overcast all day.	*cloudless, clear, sunny, bright*
overcome		*v.*	**conquer, overpower, subdue, vanquish, defeat** People can overcome many of their fears.	*yield, give in to, submit to*
overdue	1.	*adj.*	**unpaid, owing, outstanding** The account was long overdue.	**1.** *paid, settled*
	2.	*adj.*	**delayed, belated, late** Many people were worried about the overdue flight.	**2.** *early, prompt*

Word			Synonyms	Antonyms
overload	1.	*n.*	**excessive load, surplus, undue amount** The overload on the circuit blew the fuses.	
	2.	*v.*	**burden excessively, load excessively, weigh down** The workers overloaded the truck.	
overlook	1.	*v.*	**ignore, disregard, excuse, forgive** Please overlook my being late.	1. *heed, pay attention to, notice, criticize*
	2.	*v.*	**forget, neglect, miss, slight** The quiet worker is often overlooked by the supervisor.	2. *remember, heed, notice*
overt		*adj.*	**apparent, visible, plain, obvious, evident, easily seen** There was no overt evidence of fraud in the offer.	*hidden, secret, invisible, covert*
overthrow	1.	*n.*	**downfall, defeat, undoing, upset, destruction** The overthrow of the tyrant brought peace to the land.	1. *protection, preservation*
	2.	*v.*	**overcome, overpower, defeat, crush, abolish, topple** The rebels overthrew the dictator after a short battle with his troops.	2. *preserve, maintain, keep, support, guard, uphold, protect*
overwhelm	1.	*v.*	**vanquish, subdue, conquer, crush, defeat, beat, overcome** The other team overwhelmed us in spite of our best efforts.	1. *yield, submit to, surrender*
	2.	*v.*	**swamp, bury, engulf** Susan drowned when her canoe was overwhelmed by huge waves. *adj.* Her friends suffered overwhelming sorrow when they heard the news of her death.	
own	1.	*v.*	**possess, have, hold** Our family has owned this house for three generations.	
	2.	*adj.*	**personal, private, individual** Donna has her own car now.	2. *another's*

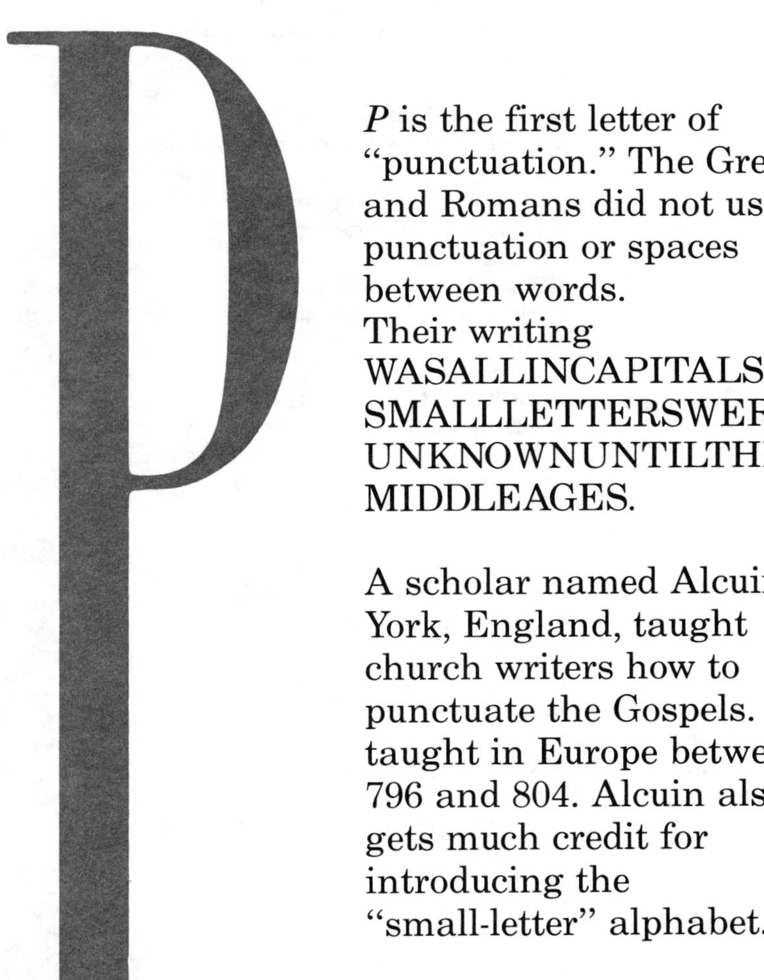

P is the first letter of "punctuation." The Greeks and Romans did not use punctuation or spaces between words. Their writing WASALLINCAPITALS SMALLLETTERSWERE UNKNOWNUNTILTHE MIDDLEAGES.

A scholar named Alcuin, of York, England, taught church writers how to punctuate the Gospels. He taught in Europe between 796 and 804. Alcuin also gets much credit for introducing the "small-letter" alphabet.

Word	#	Part	Synonyms / Example	Antonyms
pace	1.	*n.*	**speed, tempo, rate** Sam could not keep up the pace with the other runners.	
	2.	*n.*	**step, stride, footstep** Take three paces forward.	
	3.	*v.*	**walk, march, tread** The Tans paced up and down the hall during their son's operation.	
pacify		*v.*	**settle, appease, calm, quieten** No amount of rocking could pacify the screaming baby.	*antagonize, anger, stir up, enrage, provoke*
pack	1.	*n.*	**bundle, package, parcel, load** The hiker carried a large pack on her back.	
	2.	*n.*	**group, horde, gang, mob** A pack of wolves attacked the chicken farm.	
	3.	*v.*	**fill, load, cram, stuff** Pack your bags, we're going to Hawaii!	**3.** *empty, unload, unpack*
package	1.	*n.*	**bundle, crate, case, parcel** A large package was delivered next door.	
	2.	*v.*	**wrap, encase, pack, display** The wedding gift was beautifully packaged.	**2.** *unwrap, unpack*
pact		*n.*	**contract, agreement, bond, treaty, settlement, bargain, deal, understanding** Canada has signed a major trade pact with the United States.	
pain	1.	*n.*	**ache, twinge, pang, suffering, agony** The pain in his tooth kept him awake all night.	**1.** *pleasure, joy, enjoyment, delight*
	2.	*v.*	**hurt, distress, trouble** Dora was pained by Mei's hurtful remarks. *adj.* Losing our cat was a painful experience.	**2.** *relieve, comfort, ease*
pains		*n.*	**care, trouble, consideration, effort** The group took great pains to make sure the science fair was a success.	*neglect, indifference, negligence, carelessness*
painstaking		*adj.*	**thorough, careful, exacting, precise, meticulous** It took years of painstaking research to discover insulin.	*careless, uncaring, haphazard*

pal *n.* **chum, friend, companion, buddy, comrade**
Earl and I have been pals since kindergarten.
enemy, antagonist, opponent, rival, foe

pale 1. *adj.* **whitish, ashen, pasty, wan, pallid, colourless**
People are often pale after an illness.
v. Carol paled visibly when she heard the bad news.
1. *high-coloured, radiant, rosy*
2. *adj.* **light, faint, weak**
We painted the room a pale green.
2. *dark, deep, bright, strong*

pamper *v.* **spoil, coddle, humour, indulge**
The whole family pampered the baby.
mistreat, abuse

pandemonium *n.* **uproar, din, clatter, tumult, chaos, disorder**
There was pandemonium when our team won the game.
silence, quiet, order, calm, peace

panic *n.* **fright, alarm, terror, dread, fear, anxiety**
Everyone was in a panic when the fire alarm sounded.
v. The teachers panicked when they realized a child was missing.
adj. They could not think logically because they were panicky.
peace, calm, quiet, security, contentment

parade 1. *n.* **procession, display, show**
There were many beautiful floats in the parade.
2. *v.* **strut, swagger, show off, exhibit, flaunt**
The models paraded in front of the crowd.
2. *be shy*
3. *v.* **march**
The demonstrators paraded through the city.

paralyse (also spelled paralyze) 1. *v.* **cripple, disable**
Tim was paralysed after a diving accident.
2. *v.* **make powerless**
A heavy snowstorm paralysed the city.
2. *enliven, make active*

paramount *adj.* **utmost, greatest, main, chief, highest, supreme, leading**
The student's paramount concern is to get into a good university.
least, slight, trifling, minor, smallest

Word	No.	Part of speech	Synonyms and examples	Antonyms
pardon	**1.**	*n.*	**forgiveness** I beg your pardon for the trouble I caused.	**1.** *blame, conviction, condemnation*
	2.	*n.*	**discharge, acquittal, release, reprieve** The former minister was granted a full pardon by the government. *v.* The government pardoned the former minister.	**2.** *conviction, imprisonment, condemnation, punishment*
	3.	*v.*	**forgive, excuse, overlook** Please pardon my lateness.	**3.** *punish, accuse, sentence*
part	**1.**	*n.*	**share, piece, portion, fraction, fragment, section** They sold us a part of their business.	**1.** *whole, all, total*
	2.	*n.*	**function, role, capacity, share, task, duty** What was your part in preparing the dinner?	
	3.	*n.*	**role, character** Ed has a small part in the play.	
	4.	*v.*	**detach, separate, divide, split** The crowd parted to make way for the ambulance.	**4.** *join, unite*
	5.	*v.*	**take leave, say good-bye** We parted at the back door.	**5.** *meet, arrive, stay, remain*
partial	**1.**	*adj.*	**incomplete, unfinished** He suffered a partial paralysis after a stroke. *adv.* He was partially paralysed.	**1.** *whole, complete, entire*
	2.	*adj.*	**biassed, prejudiced** The umpire was partial to the other team.	**2.** *fair, impartial*
participate		*v.*	**take part, perform, join in, share, engage in** Only amateurs are allowed to participate in this tournament. *n.* Participation is limited to those under eighteen. *n.* Jean is a keen participant in these tournaments.	*be excluded, withdraw*
particular	**1.**	*adj.*	**special, distinct, exclusive** Your well-being is of particular concern to me.	
	2.	*adj.*	**choosy, careful, selective, fussy** It pays to be particular in making friends.	**2.** *careless, reckless, heedless*
particularly		*adv.*	**especially, exceptionally, unusually** My sister is particularly fond of science fiction.	

Word			Synonyms / Example	Antonyms
partner		*n.*	**co-worker, companion, mate, ally, colleague, associate** Ross and Tina are partners on this project.	*rival, competitor, opponent*
party	**1.**	*n.*	**gathering, affair, social function** We threw a surprise birthday party for Helen.	
	2.	*n.*	**group, force, band, company** Several search parties were out looking for the missing child.	
pass	**1.**	*n.*	**permit, ticket** Bill has a free pass to the movies.	
	2.	*n.*	**gap, passageway, path, opening** The railway uses the Crowsnest Pass through the Rockies.	**2.** *barrier, obstacle*
	3.	*v.*	**exceed, go beyond, go ahead** The truck passed us on the highway.	**3.** *follow, stay behind, trail*
	4.	*v.*	**transfer, hand over, throw, toss, deliver, give, present** Please pass the salt. *n.* The quarterback made an impressive pass.	**4.** *receive, get, catch, hold, retain*
	5.	*v.*	**approve, authorize, allow, sanction, legislate, confirm** The legislature passed the new Family Reform Act.	**5.** *disallow, reject, disapprove, deny, veto, defeat*
	6.	*v.*	**spend, use, occupy, fill, employ** My uncle passes his time reading.	
passage	**1.**	*n.*	**corridor, hall, route, access** We walked down the long passage to the rear of the museum.	
	2.	*n.*	**voyage, journey, trip** The ship had a rough passage crossing the Atlantic.	
	3.	*n.*	**portion, part, selection, excerpt** Read a passage from this essay.	**3.** *whole, entirety*
	4.	*n.*	**approval, enactment, legislation, acceptance** Passage of the new bill took a long time.	**4.** *veto, defeat*
	5.	*n.*	**passing, movement** His wounds healed with the passage of time.	
passionate	**1.**	*adj.*	**ardent, fervent, intense** He has a passionate interest in computers.	**1.** *calm, cool*
	2.	*adj.*	**fiery, inflamed, impassioned** The leader's passionate speech excited the crowd.	**2.** *dull, boring, listless*
past	**1.**	*n.*	**history, previous times** He is secretive about his past.	**1.** *future*

Word			Synonyms	Antonyms
	2.	*adj.*	**gone by, ended, elapsed** Archaeologists try to find out about times past.	2. *forthcoming*
	3.	*adj.*	**former, earlier, previous** She is the past president of the club.	3. *future, present*
paste	1.	*n.*	**glue, gum, cement, adhesive** Where do you keep the paste?	
	2.	*v.*	**stick, glue, fasten** Paste the labels on the parcel.	2. *peel off, remove*
pastime		*n.*	**recreation, amusement, hobby** Fishing is grandpa's favourite pastime.	*job, labour, occupation, work*
patch	1.	*n.*	**strip, piece, portion** Tom sewed patches on his jeans.	
	2.	*n.*	**plot, lot, piece, tract, area, spot** There is a patch of grass behind our shed.	
	3.	*v.*	**fix, mend, repair, sew, darn** Di patched the rip in her skirt.	3. *tear, rip, break, damage*
path		*n.*	**route, way, road, trail** We take the same path to school every day.	
pathetic		*adj.*	**miserable, sad, wretched, pitiful, melancholy, distressing** The thin, starving child was a pathetic sight.	*happy, cheerful*
patience		*n.*	**composure, calm, endurance** The man lost his patience when told that his suit was still not ready.	*impatience*
patient	1.	*n.*	**invalid, convalescent, sick person** The nurses took good care of the patient.	
	2.	*adj.*	**meek, tolerant, long-suffering, uncomplaining** Sam is very patient with children. *adv.* Tina waited patiently in line for her turn.	2. *impatient, hasty, restless, irritable*
patrol	1.	*n.*	**police, soldiers, scouts, guards, watchguards** The neighbourhood patrol was on guard for looters.	
	2.	*v.*	**watch, guard, protect, inspect** The police patrolled the streets after the riots.	2. *neglect, ignore*

Word	No.	Part	Synonyms / Example	Antonyms
patron	**1.**	*n.*	**helper, supporter, sponsor, promoter, benefactor** The patrons of the museum donated money for its renovation.	
	2.	*n.*	**customer, purchaser, buyer, client** The store keeps its patrons happy with excellent service.	**2.** *salesperson, seller, employee*
pause	**1.**	*n.*	**rest, recess, intermission, interruption, interlude, lapse** Television programs have many pauses for advertisements.	
	2.	*v.*	**stop, halt, rest, linger, delay** Let's pause for lunch.	**2.** *continue, advance, proceed*
pay	**1.**	*n.*	**salary, earnings, allowance, wages, remuneration, income** The workers asked for higher pay.	
	2.	*v.*	**award, remunerate, compensate** Many workers are paid every Friday.	
	3.	*v.*	**give, extend, grant, present** Pay attention to this announcement.	**3.** *withhold, retain*
peace	**1.**	*n.*	**calm, quiet, harmony, tranquillity, order** Let's stop quarrelling and have peace again.	**1.** *uproar, racket, pandemonium, chaos*
	2.	*n.*	**armistice, concord, amity** The signing of the treaty ended the war and brought peace to the two nations.	**2.** *war, warfare, battle*
peaceful	**1.**	*adj.*	**restful, calm, quiet, serene, tranquil** We spent a peaceful day by the lake.	**1.** *noisy, disturbed, restless*
	2.	*adj.*	**friendly, agreeable, harmonious** The strike was settled in a peaceful way. *adv.* It was settled peacefully.	**2.** *hostile, bitter, unfriendly*
peak	**1.**	*n.*	**tip, top, pinnacle, summit, crest** The mountain peak is snow-capped.	**1.** *base, bottom, foundation*
	2.	*n.*	**height, highest level, top, apex** She is at the peak of her career. *adj.* Airplanes are packed during the peak holiday season.	**2.** *bottom, lowest level*
peculiar	**1.**	*adj.*	**odd, unusual, curious, strange, queer** There is a peculiar smell in the zoo.	**1.** *usual, common, ordinary*
	2.	*adj.*	**special, particular, unique** The rare stamp is of peculiar interest to collectors.	**2.** *common, ordinary*

Word		Part	Synonyms / Example	Antonyms
peek		*v.*	**look, peep, peer, glance** Pino peeked around the corner.	
peer	1.	*n.*	**equal, companion** His peers in school encouraged him to work hard.	
	2.	*v.*	**stare, gaze, inspect, scrutinize** The scientist peered through the microscope to study the specimen.	
pelt	1.	*n.*	**skin, hide, fleece** The hunters sold their beaver pelts.	
	2.	*v.*	**beat, strike, hit, knock** Rain pelted against the windows.	
penalty		*n.*	**punishment, fine** He was given a penalty for foul play. *v.* The referee penalized the player.	*reward, payment*
penetrate	1.	*v.*	**puncture, enter, pierce** A nail penetrated the tire and caused it to go flat.	
	2.	*v.*	**seep, infiltrate** Cold air penetrated the room from a crack in the window.	
penetrating	1.	*adj.*	**sharp, piercing** A penetrating scream in the other room alarmed us.	**1.** *soft, gentle, soothing*
	2.	*adj.*	**keen, acute, insightful** Reiko's penetrating essay on racism inspired many students.	**2.** *insensitive, unaware*
pensive		*adj.*	**thoughtful, reflective, dreamy, serious** Jules was in a pensive mood after he received a letter from home. *adv.* He stared pensively out the window all day.	*frivolous, carefree*
people	1.	*n.*	**humans, human beings, mortals, persons, humanity** Will people ever learn to live in peace?	
	2.	*n.*	**inhabitants, citizens, populace, public** The people of the city elected a new mayor.	
	3.	*n.*	**family, relatives, ancestors, kin** Patrick's people came from Ireland.	
perennial	1.	*adj.*	**continuing, enduring, constant** For many people, music is a perennial source of joy.	**1.** *temporary, short-lived*

Word	No.	Part	Synonyms / Examples	Antonyms
	2.	*adj.*	**longlasting, durable, permanent** Perennial plants last for many years. *n.* Dandelions are perennials.	
perfect	1.	*adj.*	**faultless, flawless, impeccable** The student wrote a perfect test. *adv.* The coat fit perfectly. *v.* She perfected her skating skills through years of practice. *n.* She strives for perfection in everything she does.	*1. imperfect, incorrect*
	2.	*adj.*	**entire, absolute, complete** A good driver has perfect control of the car.	*2. inadequate, incomplete*
	3.	*adj.*	**exact, strict, precise** The soldiers marched in perfect order.	*3. imperfect, haphazard*
perform	1.	*v.*	**do, accomplish, execute** Surgeons perform operations.	
	2.	*v.*	**act, present, exhibit** The acrobats performed at the circus. *n.* Their performance held the audience spellbound. *n.* The other performers were magicians.	
perhaps		*adv.*	**maybe, possibly, probably** Perhaps we can go to a show tonight.	
peril		*n.*	**danger, risk, hazard, menace** They were warned of the perils of skating on thin ice. *adj.* The racers drove at a perilous speed.	*safety*
perish		*v.*	**die, wither, pass away** Thousands of people perished in the rebellion. *adj.* Perishable foods must be refrigerated.	*live, grow, thrive, flourish*
permanent		*adj.*	**endless, enduring, lasting, durable, abiding** The accident left a permanent scar on his arm. *adv.* The arm was scarred permanently.	*temporary, brief, short-lived*
permission		*n.*	**consent, approval, allowance, leave, authorization** The pilot was given permission to take off.	*refusal, denial*

Word			Synonyms	Antonyms
permit	1.	*n.*	**licence, warrant, sanction** We applied for a building permit to build an extension on the house.	1. *prohibition*
	2.	*v.*	**allow, let, authorize** I permitted him to use my car.	2. *deny, refuse, prevent, prohibit*
perpendicular		*adj.*	**upright, steep, sheer** It was difficult climbing up the perpendicular path. *adv.* The path runs perpendicularly to the top of the cliff.	*horizontal, level*
perpetual	1.	*adj.*	**everlasting, unceasing, eternal, endless** A perpetual flame burns at the grave of John F. Kennedy.	1. *momentary, brief, short-lived*
	2.	*adj.*	**constant, incessant, continual** The city is a perpetual hive of activity. *adv.* They are perpetually striving to help the poor.	2. *temporary, transitory*
perplex		*v.*	**puzzle, confuse, baffle, bewilder, mystify** We were perplexed by Carlo's strange behaviour. *adj.* The students' perplexed faces told us they had not understood the lesson.	
persecute		*v.*	**torment, plague, annoy, harass, oppress, abuse, molest** Some governments persecute people for their religious beliefs. *n.* Many people leave their homeland because of political or religious persecution.	*encourage, help, aid, support, uphold*
persevere		*v.*	**persist, endure, continue, hold on, keep on** All the runners persevered to the end of the race. *n.* They were applauded for their perseverance.	*yield, give up, quit, stop*
persist		*v.*	**stand fast, persevere, continue, hold on** Despite setbacks, she persisted in trying to enter medical school. *adj.* She was the most persistent student in the class. *n.* Her persistence was rewarded when she became a doctor.	*stop, cease, give up, change, falter, quit*

personal		*adj.*	**private, individual, intimate** The president warned reporters not to pry into her personal affairs.	*public*
persuade		*v.*	**convince, influence, urge, coax, induce, lure** They persuaded us to leave the party and go skiing instead. *n.* We agreed to go after much persuasion.	*dissuade, discourage, deter*
pervade		*v.*	**fill, penetrate, spread through, permeate** The aroma of baking bread pervaded the house.	
perverse		*adj.*	**contrary, stubborn, willful, headstrong, obstinate, dogged** She took a perverse delight in being rude.	*agreeable, amiable, obliging*
pessimistic		*adj.*	**gloomy, hopeless, downhearted, discouraging, glum** Some people take a pessimistic view of the future. *n.* The pessimist predicted that it would rain on our sports day. *n.* There was pessimism about our chances of winning the game.	*optimistic, cheerful, hopeful, confident, encouraging*
pest	1.	*n.*	**nuisance, annoyance, irritation** All his classmates avoid him because he is such a pest.	**1.** *help, assistance*
	2.	*n.*	**harmful insect** The gardener uses insecticides to control pests.	
pester		*v.*	**vex, bother, annoy, irk, aggravate, irritate, torment, disturb, harass** I have been pestered by this cough all winter.	*comfort, help, aid*
petite		*adj.*	**tiny, small, little, wee** The petite gymnast amazed everyone with her skill.	*large, huge, big, enormous, immense*
petrify	1.	*v.*	**harden, turn to stone, solidify** It took millenniums for the trees to petrify in Arizona's Petrified Forest.	
	2.	*v.*	**frighten, terrorize, alarm** The rioting mob petrified the tourists. *adj.* The petrified child stood frozen on the spot.	

petty 1. *adj.* **mean, narrow-minded, shabby**
His petty remarks upset the team.
n. Pettiness makes others unhappy.
2. *adj.* **small, trivial, unimportant, trifling, minor**
How could such a petty matter cause a quarrel?
1. generous, tolerant, broad-minded
2. significant, important, major

petulant *adj.* **cross, sulky, grumpy, irritable, sullen, huffy, peevish**
Gord was quite petulant when we didn't accept his idea.
adv. He argued petulantly all night.
n. His petulance got him nowhere with us.
agreeable, cheerful, good-natured, content

phantom *n.* **ghost, apparition, mirage, illusion, vision, spectre**
Was the figure that he saw in the drifting fog real, or was it a phantom?

phenomenal *adj.* **exceptional, outstanding, extraordinary, unusual, remarkable, marvellous, amazing, sensational**
Terry Fox had phenomenal courage.
ordinary, common, normal, usual, average

phony *adj.* **imitation, fake, false, bogus, counterfeit, forged**
The customer tried to pass a phony one hundred dollar bill.
n. It was difficult to detect that the bill was a phony.
legal, real, actual, honest, genuine

phrase 1. *n.* **saying, expression, proverb, maxim, cliché**
Who coined the phrase, "Might is right?"
2. *v.* **express, state, say, put, declare, utter, voice**
"Let me phrase the problem another way," she suggested.

pick 1. *v.* **select, choose**
The class picked Suki as president.
2. *v.* **gather, harvest, pluck, collect**
The workers picked the ripe peaches.
1. reject, refuse

picture 1. *n.* **painting, portrait, illustration**
The artist painted a picture of the school.
2. *n.* **photograph, snapshot, likeness**
This camera takes an excellent picture.

Word	No.	Part of speech	Synonyms and example	Antonyms
	3.	*v.*	**describe, illustrate, portray, depict, represent** The media pictured the dictator as a ruthless tyrant.	
	4.	*v.*	**visualize, fantasize, imagine** Yun pictured herself receiving the Nobel Prize.	
picturesque		*adj.*	**scenic, interesting, artistic, attractive, quaint** We drove through picturesque countryside in Victoria.	*unattractive, unsightly, uninteresting*
piece	1.	*n.*	**portion, fragment, lump, share, quantity, part, amount, fraction, segment** Did you get a piece of cake?	**1.** *entirety, whole*
	2.	*n.*	**selection, composition, work, study, creation, article** The orchestra played a piece by Mozart.	
	3.	*v.*	**put together, make complete or whole, assemble, combine** The detective pieced the evidence together and solved the mystery.	**3.** *break apart*
pierce		*v.*	**stab, penetrate, perforate, puncture** The tire was pierced by a nail.	
piercing		*adj.*	**shrill, keen, penetrating, strident** Sally's piercing shriek brought everyone running.	*soft, soothing, faint, muffled, calm*
pile	1.	*n.*	**heap, mass, quantity, stack, mound** The children romped in a pile of leaves.	
	2.	*v.*	**stack, collect, load, assemble** Pile the books on the shelf.	**2.** *spread, scatter*
pilfer		*v.*	**steal, embezzle** The cashier pilfered money from the cash register. *n.* She was arrested for the pilferage.	
pilot	1.	*n.*	**aviator** The pilot skilfully brought the plane to a safe landing.	
	2.	*v.*	**steer, direct, guide, lead, handle** Mag piloted the canoe safely through the rapids.	

Word	No.	Part of speech	Synonyms and example	Antonyms
pinnacle		*n.*	**top, crest, summit, crown, peak** The mountain climbers placed a flag on the pinnacle.	*bottom, foot, depth, base*
pinpoint	1.	*n.*	**dot, spot, speck** The giant plane was now only a pinpoint in the distance.	
	2.	*v.*	**locate exactly, zero in on, detect** Engineers are trying to pinpoint the cause of leaks in the spacecraft.	
pioneer	1.	*n.*	**settler, colonist, immigrant** Pioneers from around the world settled in North America.	
	2.	*v.*	**start, begin, lead** The Americans and the Russians pioneered space exploration.	
pitch	1.	*n.*	**tone, sound** The choir sang off pitch.	
	2.	*n.*	**tar, asphalt** Black pitch is very sticky.	
	3.	*v.*	**sling, hurl, throw, toss, fling, heave** Tom pitched the ball at the batter. *n.* Tom is a good pitcher.	
	4.	*v.*	**erect, set up, place, fix, raise, establish, locate** The Girl Guides pitched their tents near the lake.	**4.** *take down*
pitcher		*n.*	**container, jug, jar** Where is the milk pitcher?	
pitiful	1.	*adj.*	**sad, sorry, pathetic, wretched, miserable, piteous, moving** The wet puppy was a pitiful sight. *adv.* It howled pitifully.	**1.** *cheerful, happy, contented, noble, joyful*
	2.	*adj.*	**small, meagre, scanty, paltry** The appeal raised only a pitiful sum of money for the refugees.	**2.** *plentiful, abundant, large*
pity	1.	*n.*	**mercy, kindliness, compassion, sympathy** The starving children aroused everyone's pity.	**1.** *cruelty, harshness*
	2.	*v.*	**feel sorry for, sympathize with** We pitied the animals in the small cage.	**2.** *hurt, tease, molest, annoy*
place	1.	*n.*	**region, spot, location, site, space** Can't we find a better place for our tent?	

Entry	No.	Part	Synonyms / Example	Antonyms
	2.	*n.*	**shop, concern, store, business, restaurant** That place on Main Street has good food.	
	3.	*v.*	**lay, deposit, set, arrange, put** Who placed the dishes that way?	**3.** *remove, take away, disarrange*
placid		*adj.*	**peaceful, quiet, restful, serene, calm, tranquil** The boat drifted on the placid river.	*rough, restless, agitated, turbulent*
plague	1.	*n.*	**epidemic, contagion, disease, affliction** A cholera plague killed many people.	
	2.	*v.*	**bother, annoy, torment, worry, pester, trouble, irk** Leila plagued her parents until she got her own way.	**2.** *please, leave alone, satisfy*
plain	1.	*n.*	**level land, prairie, grassland** Buffalo used to live on the plains of North America.	
	2.	*adj.*	**obvious, clear, evident** It was plain to everyone that Ravi was very ill.	**2.** *obscure*
	3.	*adj.*	**simple, clear, distinct, direct** Please speak in plain English so everyone can understand. *adv.* Speak plainly, please.	**3.** *complicated, difficult, indistinct, obscure*
	4.	*adj.*	**ordinary, homely, simple, modest, unadorned** She wore plain but comfortable clothes.	**4.** *fancy, ornate, intricate, frilly*
plaintive		*adj.*	**mournful, sad, melancholy** The plaintive sound of a violin filled the air. *adv.* The puppy howled plaintively through the night.	*merry, cheerful, happy, bright*
plan	1.	*n.*	**program, course, design, scheme, arrangement, method** Our club meetings follow a regular plan.	
	2.	*n.*	**scheme, plot, project, design** The plan to overthrow the government was foiled. *v.* The army had planned the overthrow of the government.	
	3.	*v.*	**map, chart, plot, prepare** The tourist bureau planned our route to Alaska.	
	4.	*v.*	**intend, aim, propose** Do you plan to leave early?	

Word	No.	Part	Synonyms / Example	Antonyms
plant	**1.**	*n.*	**shrub, tree, bush, weed, seedling** Young plants need much water.	
	2.	*n.*	**factory, shop, mill, business** Dad works at an automobile plant.	
	3.	*v.*	**sow, deposit, seed** Who planted the pumpkin seeds?	**3.** *remove, uproot, dig out*
	4.	*v.*	**place, put, establish, infiltrate** The secret service planted a spy in the organization.	**4.** *remove, take away*
plaque		*n.*	**plate, disc, slab, tablet** A bronze plaque on the wall tells the history of the building.	
plastic	**1.**	*n.*	**synthetic compound, mouldable substance, pliable material** The car upholstery is not leather, it is plastic. *adj.* We'll use plastic plates and cutlery for the party.	
	2.	*adj.*	**pliable, easily moulded, yielding, soft, pliant** Clay, plasticine, and dough are plastic materials.	**2.** *hard, stiff, rigid*
plateau	**1.**	*n.*	**highland, level region, elevation, mesa, tableland** Our camp was on a small plateau overlooking the valley.	**1.** *valley, ravine, lowland*
	2.	*n.*	**stable level** House prices reached a plateau last year.	
plausible		*adj.*	**likely, probable, sound, valid, reasonable, logical, sensible, believable** That isn't a plausible explanation for your absence, Paul.	*unlikely, unreasonable, improbable*
play	**1.**	*n.*	**drama, show, theatrical production** Shakespeare wrote many plays.	
	2.	*v.*	**act, perform, take part** Peter played the piano at the school concert. *n.* He is a good player.	
	3.	*v.*	**frolic, make merry, romp** The children rushed out to play at recess.	**3.** *work, toil, labour*
playful		*adj.*	**frisky, frolicsome, jolly, lively, amusing** The playful child would not sit still. *adv.* The puppy playfully nipped Rani's ankles.	*serious, earnest, sad, sedate*

Word			Synonyms / Example	Antonyms
plea		*n.*	**appeal, request, entreaty, petition** The lawyer entered a plea of "not guilty" for his client. *v.* The accused pleaded his innocence in court.	
plead		*v.*	**beg, implore, beseech** Tanya pleaded for permission to go to the rock concert.	
pleasant		*adj.*	**agreeable, cheerful, delightful, lovely, enchanting, enjoyable** We spent a pleasant week at the cottage.	*unpleasant, disagreeable, sad, dreary*
please	1.	*v.*	**satisfy, suit, delight, enchant, cheer, gladden, content, gratify** It pleases me to help others.	**1.** *displease, offend, anger*
	2.	*v.*	**want, will, choose, wish, desire, like, prefer** You are free to do as you please.	
pleasing		*adj.*	**pleasant, agreeable, inviting** Pleasing aromas drifted from the kitchen.	*unpleasant, disagreeable, distasteful*
pleasure		*n.*	**joy, delight, thrill, satisfaction, enjoyment, happiness** Music gives many people deep pleasure.	*pain, sorrow, displeasure*
pledge	1.	*n.*	**promise, agreement, vow, oath, word** The new citizens made a pledge of allegiance to the country.	
	2.	*v.*	**promise, assure, vow, swear** I pledge my loyalty to this country.	
plentiful		*adj.*	**large, abundant, ample** The farmers were pleased with their plentiful harvest.	*insufficient, scarce, sparse, scant, small*
plenty		*n.*	**ample amount, abundance** We have plenty of packing to do before we leave.	*scarcity, lack, shortage*
pliable	1.	*adj.*	**plastic, flexible, supple, pliant** Soaking reed or cane will make it pliable for weaving.	**1.** *stiff, rigid*
	2.	*adj.*	**easily persuaded, easily influenced** The president is too pliable to be an effective leader.	**2.** *firm, obstinate*

Word	No.	Part	Synonyms and example	Antonyms
plight		*n.*	**condition, state, dilemma, distress, difficulty, predicament** The government is moving to improve the plight of the homeless.	
plot	1.	*n.*	**scheme, conspiracy, plan, stratagem** The police uncovered a plot to kidnap the prime minister. *v.* The suspects had carefully plotted the kidnapping.	
	2.	*n.*	**structure, design, development** This book has an interesting plot.	
	3.	*n.*	**land, lot, field, tract** Are they building on this plot?	
	4.	*v.*	**draw, map, chart, mark** The travellers plotted their route before setting off.	
ploy		*n.*	**manoeuvre, move, stratagem, trick** That clever ploy won him the chess game.	
plucky		*adj.*	**brave, daring, courageous** The plucky girl rescued the two children from the fire.	*cowardly, timid*
plump		*adj.*	**stout, chubby, fat, obese** The doctor told the plump child not to eat any more candies.	*lean, thin, scrawny, skinny*
plunder	1.	*n.*	**stolen goods, loot, booty** The pirate ship was loaded with plunder.	
	2.	*v.*	**rob, loot, steal, raid** Pirates plundered other ships.	
plunge	1.	*v.*	**thrust, drive, force** The cook plunged the knife into the roast.	**1.** *withdraw, remove*
	2.	*v.*	**dip, submerge, dive, leap into** The divers plunged into the pool.	**2.** *emerge*
plus	1.	*adj.*	**extra, additional, added, helpful, useful, supplementary, desirable** It is a plus factor for a politician to be bilingual. *n.* Being bilingual is a plus for anyone.	**1.** *minus, undesirable*
	2.	*prep.*	**added to** Three plus four equals seven.	**2.** *minus, less, subtracted from*

Word	#	Part	Synonyms / Example	Antonyms
plush		*adj.*	**luxurious, rich, opulent** The movie star lives in a plush house.	*poor, ordinary, mean*
poetry		*n.*	**verse, rhyme, poem, song** Good poetry can lift the spirits.	*prose*
point	1.	*n.*	**nib, tip, end** Who broke the point of your pen?	
	2.	*n.*	**spot, place, dot, location, position** Find the right point on the map for Moosonee.	
	3.	*n.*	**detail, feature, item, aspect** Don't overlook this important point in your answer.	
	4.	*n.*	**purpose, reason** What's the point of buying it if you don't need it?	
	5.	*v.*	**aim, level, direct** Bill pointed his gun at the target.	
	6.	*v.*	**show, indicate, steer, guide** The child pointed the way to the principal's office.	
pointed		*adj.*	**sharp, pronged, barbed** Use a pointed stick to hold the marshmallows over the fire.	*blunt, dull*
pointless		*adj.*	**meaningless, useless** It is pointless to attend school and not do your homework.	*meaningful, useful*
poise	1.	*n.*	**assurance, self-confidence, calm, composure** The child star showed poise during the press conference. *adv.* He remained poised throughout the interview.	1. *insecurity*
	2.	*v.*	**balance, brace** Steve poised himself on the diving board before diving.	
poison	1.	*n.*	**toxic chemical, toxin, venom, harmful drug** Poisons should be kept out of the reach of children. *adj.* Many insecticides and weed killers are poisonous to humans.	1. *antidote*
	2.	*v.*	**pollute, taint, contaminate** Industrial waste has poisoned our water supply.	
poke	1.	*n.*	**thrust, jab, punch, hit, push** Someone gave him a poke from behind and he fell over.	

	2.	*v.*	**jab, nudge, jostle, prod** The clumsy person poked me with an umbrella.	
pokey		*adj.*	**slow, dull** A pokey old horse pulled our wagon.	*speedy, agile*
polish	1.	*n.*	**gloss, shine, glaze, finish, wax** Apply the polish to your shoes.	
	2.	*v.*	**buff, rub, shine** Polish the silver before the party.	**2.** *tarnish, dull*
polite		*adj.*	**courteous, well-mannered, refined** The polite girl offered her seat to the old man. *n.* He appreciated her politeness.	*impolite, rude, boorish, insulting, discourteous*
poll	1.	*n.*	**census, count, public survey** A poll was taken to find out how many people supported the new bill.	
	2.	*n.*	**voting place, vote, tally, returns** The polls for the election open at eight o'clock.	
	3.	*v.*	**canvass, register the vote of, sample the opinion of, question** The company polled its employees about working on Sundays.	
pollute		*v.*	**contaminate, taint, infect, dirty, defile** The waste from the plant is polluting the lake. *adj.* Fish are dying in the polluted lakes. *n.* Laws are being passed to stop environmental pollution.	*cleanse, purify, refresh*
pomp		*n.*	**ceremony, splendour, grandeur, magnificence, pageantry, show** The opening of Parliament was conducted with great pomp.	
ponder		*v.*	**study, consider, reflect on, examine, think over, deliberate** We pondered over the problem all evening.	
poor	1.	*adj.*	**impoverished, destitute, needy, underprivileged** The scholarship is to help children from poor families. *n.* The Salvation Army does much to help the poor.	**1.** *rich, wealthy, affluent*

2. *adj.* **bad, inferior, deficient**
Su-min was told to work hard to improve his poor marks.
2. superior, fine, excellent

3. *adj.* **unfortunate, pitiful**
The poor children lost their parents in an automobile accident.

popular *adj.* **admired, well-liked, favourite, in demand**
Yun-Yi is a popular student.
n. Her popularity has not made her conceited.
unpopular, offensive, disliked

populate *v.* **inhabit, live in, settle**
The tropical jungles are populated by wild animals.
adj. The cities are usually the most heavily populated areas.
desert

population *n.* **inhabitants, dwellers, citizenry, residents**
The world population grows at a tremendous rate.

porous *adj.* **absorbent, permeable**
The spill was quickly absorbed by the porous paper towel.

portable *adj.* **transportable, handy, movable**
Mom takes her portable computer with her when she travels.
permanent, immovable, fixed, stationary

portion *n.* **piece, fragment, fraction, share, segment, section**
Save me a portion of the cake.
all, whole, total

position 1. *n.* **spot, site, location, place**
Are you in a good position to see the game?
v. We positioned ourselves in front of the window to watch the parade.

2. *n.* **job, situation, office, place, post**
What position do you hold in this company?

positive 1. *adj.* **absolute, confident, assured, definite, certain, firm, sure**
Are you positive you saw him?

2. *adj.* **optimistic, progressive, cooperative**
The coach encouraged us to be positive.
adv. "Think positively," he said.

1. doubtful, uncertain, unsure, vague, indefinite
2. negative, pessimistic

Entry	No.	Part of speech	Synonyms / Example	Antonyms
possess	**1.**	*v.*	**have, own** The family possesses great wealth. *n.* They lost all their possessions when their house burnt down.	**1.** *relinquish, give up, lose*
	2.	*v.*	**occupy, control** The area was possessed by the enemy during the war.	
possible		*adj.*	**likely, probable, conceivable** Three possible answers to the question were discussed. *n.* There is a possibility of rain today. *adv.* This possibly could be a good choice.	*impossible, unlikely, unthinkable*
post	**1.**	*n.*	**pole, support, beam, prop** Do not move the post.	
	2.	*n.*	**place, position, job, office** Rita was elected to the post of chairperson.	
	3.	*n.*	**mail, postal service** Please send this by priority post. *v.* I posted the letter yesterday.	
	4.	*v.*	**place, display, put** We posted the announcements on the bulletin board.	**4.** *conceal, remove*
poster		*n.*	**placard, bill, handbill** Election campaign posters were displayed around the school.	
postpone		*v.*	**delay, put off, defer, shelve** Campbell postponed the meeting until next week. *n.* He informed the committee members of the postponement.	*move ahead, hasten*
potent		*adj.*	**strong, forceful, powerful, influential, effective** Television is a potent force in our lives.	*impotent, weak, ineffective*
potential	**1.**	*n.*	**ability, possibility, capability** Min has potential for success in music.	
	2.	*adj.*	**possible, concealed, hidden, unrealized** There are many potential dangers in riding a motorcycle.	**2.** *actual, real*
pound	**1.**	*n.*	**trap, enclosure, cage, pen** The stray dog was put in the pound.	

Word			Synonyms / Example	Antonyms
	2.	*v.*	**strike, hammer, beat, thump, hit, batter** The worker pounded the metal into the required shape.	
poverty		*n.*	**want, destitution, need** Some people live in utter poverty.	*luxury, wealth, riches, affluence*
power	1.	*n.*	**force, energy** Some submarines use nuclear power.	
	2.	*n.*	**authority, control, influence, right** The government has the power to declare holidays.	
	3.	*n.*	**strength, might, vigour, brawn** He has amazing power in his hands. *adj.* The singer has a powerful voice.	**3.** *weakness*
practical		*adj.*	**efficient, sensible, workable, useful, effective** Harry has many practical ideas about helping the homeless.	*impractical, ineffective, unsound*
practically		*adv.*	**almost, nearly, essentially, just about, virtually** We were practically home when the car stalled.	
practice	1.	*n.*	**habit, custom, method, routine, procedure** It is the family's practice to eat out on Sundays.	
	2.	*n.*	**drill, preparation, rehearsal, training** Keep up your practice if you wish to excel.	
	3.	*n.*	**business, profession** Ethel's law practice is doing well.	
practise	1.	*v.*	**train, drill, rehearse** Musicians must practise daily to improve their skills.	
	2.	*v.*	**work at, employ oneself in** Ethel practises law.	
practised		*adj.*	**experienced, trained, skilled** Jill is a practised dancer.	*inexperienced, untrained, unskilled*
praise	1.	*n.*	**acclaim, respect, appreciation, applause, approval, esteem** Glenn received much praise for his performance.	**1.** *contempt, scorn, disapproval, blame*

	2. *v.*	**acclaim, glorify, applaud, compliment** The scientist was highly praised for her outstanding discovery.	**2.** *scold, blame, criticize*
precarious	*adj.*	**risky, uncertain, hazardous, insecure, dangerous** The worker was cleaning windows at a precarious height. *adv.* He was perched precariously on the ramp.	*safe, secure*
precaution	*n.*	**safeguard, protection, provision, security, safety, care, measure** Every precaution was taken to ensure the children's safety.	*carelessness*
precede	*v.*	**lead, go before** The band preceded the majorettes in the parade.	*follow, come after*
preceding	*adj.*	**previous, earlier, prior, former** Reread the preceding paragraph.	*following, later, succeeding*
precious	*adj.*	**valuable, costly, priceless, treasured** Precious gems should be insured against theft and loss.	*worthless, cheap, trashy, common*
precipitation	*n.*	**condensation, rain, snow, hail** The weather forecast calls for no precipitation today.	
precise	*adj.*	**accurate, exact, specific, correct, explicit** A scientist works with precise measurements. *n.* Everything is calculated with precision.	*inaccurate, erratic, incorrect, inexact, vague*
predict	*v.*	**anticipate, forecast, foretell, prophesy** I predict our team will win tomorrow.	
predominant	*adj.*	**major, chief, main, leading, supreme, principal, prevalent** The predominant reason for not going is lack of money.	*minor, unimportant, secondary*
preface	*n.*	**introduction, foreword, prelude** The preface of a book helps people to understand it. *v.* The principal prefaced her speech with a welcome to the parents.	*appendix*

Word			Synonyms	Antonyms
prefer		*v.*	**choose, select, fancy, favour** The boys prefer pizza to salad. *n.* The girl's preference was a salad. *adj.* Is steak preferable to a roast?	
prejudice	1.	*n.*	**unfairness, bias, intolerance** Avoid prejudice in judging others.	**1.** *impartiality, fairness, tolerance*
	2.	*v.*	**sway, bias, influence** His remarks prejudiced my opinion of her work.	
preliminary		*adj.*	**introductory, preparatory** The preliminary races will be run a day before the finals.	*final, concluding*
preoccupied		*adj.*	**engrossed, inattentive, absent-minded, lost in thought** Dad seemed preoccupied at supper.	*attentive, alert*
preparation		*n.*	**arrangement, precaution, groundwork, rehearsal** The crew underwent intensive preparations for the space voyage.	
preparatory		*adj.*	**introductory, preliminary** The council made a preparatory plan for the building.	*final, concluding*
prepare		*v.*	**arrange, provide, get ready, fix** Dan is preparing dinner.	
preposterous		*adj.*	**absurd, ridiculous, outrageous, unreasonable, silly** Do you expect me to believe that preposterous story about a talking dog?	*reasonable, believable, sensible*
prerequisite	1.	*n.*	**qualification, need, necessity, requirement, demand, condition** A pass in Level I is a prerequisite for the Level II course.	
	2.	*adj.*	**required, essential, necessary, called for, demanded** The prerequisite deposit for the purchase of the land has been paid.	
presence		*n.*	**attendance, existence, being** Is your presence at school checked every day?	*absence*
present	1.	*n.*	**gift, donation** How many presents did you get for your birthday?	
	2.	*n.*	**today, now, nowadays** We are too busy at present to take on another project.	**2.** *past, future*

Word	No.	Part	Synonyms and example	Antonyms
	3.	*adj.*	**current, contemporary, existing** The present generation is concerned about preserving the environment for future generations.	**3.** *past, future*
present	1.	*v.*	**give, offer, award, proffer** We presented flowers to the soloist after the concert.	**1.** *receive, obtain, get*
	2.	*v.*	**exhibit, display, act, perform** The group presented a concert for the public.	
presently	1.	*adv.*	**soon, shortly, before long** Be patient, the train will arrive presently.	
	2.	*adv.*	**currently, now** They are presently on holiday.	
preservation		*n.*	**protection, conservation, safekeeping, saving, defence** The preservation of our natural resources is of great importance.	*destruction, waste, deterioration, ruin*
preserve	1.	*n.*	**shelter, sanctuary, refuge** National parks are preserves for wildlife.	
	2.	*n.*	**jam, jelly, conserve** Doug makes delicious preserves with strawberries.	
	3.	*v.*	**protect, guard, keep, conserve, maintain, save** Measures have been taken to preserve wildlife.	**3.** *destroy, spoil, kill, exterminate*
press	1.	*n.*	**news media, journalists, reporters, newspapers** The scientists announced their discovery to the press.	
	2.	*v.*	**squeeze, crush, compress** We press fruit to get the juice.	
	3.	*v.*	**iron, smooth, flatten** Bill pressed his trousers for the dance.	**3.** *wrinkle, crease*
	4.	*v.*	**hurry, hasten, rush, push on** "Press on," said the leader.	**4.** *slow down, delay*
	5.	*v.*	**urge, encourage, implore, force** Tony's friends pressed him to stay a little longer.	**5.** *discourage, restrain, prevent, check*
pressing		*adj.*	**urgent, important, demanding** A pressing matter at work forced Mom to miss the party.	*unimportant, trivial*
pressure	1.	*n.*	**strain, tension, stress** Some athletes don't perform well under pressure.	

	2.	*v.*	**force, compel, press, coerce** The salesperson pressured the customer into buying the car.	**2.** *discourage*
prestige		*n.*	**fame, distinction, importance, note, reputation, esteem** Glenn Gould was a pianist of international prestige.	*obscurity*
presume		*v.*	**assume, suppose** The law presumes everyone is innocent until proven guilty. *n.* My presumption that Jordan would do well proved correct.	*doubt*
pretence		*n.*	**hoax, invention, make-believe, trick, deception, fabrication** The movie battle seemed real, but it was only pretence.	*reality, fact*
pretend	1.	*v.*	**imagine, fancy, suppose, make believe, playact** The children pretended they were astronauts.	
	2.	*v.*	**fake, sham, feign** She pretended not to see him when he came in.	
pretentious		*adj.*	**showy, ostentatious, ornate, garish, gaudy, overdone** All the furnishings in the castle are pretentious.	*modest, plain, simple*
pretty	1.	*adj.*	**attractive, lovely, beautiful, pleasing, handsome, fair** What a pretty child!	**1.** *homely, ugly, plain, unattractive*
	2.	*adv.*	**moderately, fairly, rather** The debate went pretty well.	**2.** *extremely, exceptionally*
prevalent		*adj.*	**frequent, common, general, abundant, usual, normal** Mosquitoes and black-flies are prevalent during the summer.	*rare, unusual, uncommon, infrequent*
prevent		*v.*	**obstruct, stop, hinder, prohibit** A storm prevented the plane from taking off.	*aid, assist, help, permit, allow*
prevention		*n.*	**restraint, hindrance, inhibition** Vaccination is a prevention against measles.	*assistance, encouragement*
previous		*adj.*	**earlier, prior, former, foregoing** I did much better on a previous test than on this one.	*later, subsequent, following*

Word			Synonyms	Antonyms
price		*n.*	**cost, expenditure, figure, rate, charge, value, expense, outlay** The price of the car is too high for me.	
priceless		*adj.*	**rare, prized, valuable, precious, costly** Priceless antiques are displayed at the museum.	*worthless, cheap, inexpensive, common*
primary	1.	*adj.*	**elementary, first, beginning, introductory** The primary school children leave first.	1. *secondary, later*
	2.	*adj.*	**basic, principal, main, chief, essential, most important** The primary aim here is to learn to speak French.	2. *lesser, unimportant*
prime	1.	*n.*	**peak, best time, best part** The athlete was in the prime of her career when she was injured.	1. *decline*
	2.	*adj.*	**superior, first-class, splendid, superb, first-rate, choice** The old car was in prime condition.	2. *poor, inferior, second-rate*
	3.	*adj.*	**chief, main, first** The prime reason for their success is hard work.	3. *secondary, unimportant*
primitive	1.	*adj.*	**beginning, early, first, original, primary, fundamental** Plans for regular space journeys are still in the primitive stage.	1. *advanced*
	2.	*adj.*	**crude, simple, rough, rude** Living conditions at the hunting camp are quite primitive.	2. *developed, sophisticated*
principal	1.	*n.*	**headmistress, headmaster, leader, chief, administrator** The school principal is admired for her leadership and understanding.	
	2.	*adj.*	**leading, main, foremost, most important, paramount** Who has the principal part in the play?	2. *minor, small, trivial*
principle		*n.*	**regulation, rule, law, truth** We follow certain principles in scientific research.	
prior		*adj.*	**earlier, previous, former** A prior engagement prevented the speaker from coming here.	*following, later*

Word			Synonyms	Antonyms
prisoner		*n.*	**captive, convict, hostage** The prisoner served his sentence.	
private	1.	*adj.*	**remote, isolated, secluded** Jan prefers to read in a private place.	**1.** *crowded, busy, populated*
	2.	*adj.*	**secret, confidential, personal** Please do not pry into my private diary.	**2.** *public, open*
privilege		*n.*	**advantage, right, freedom, liberty, benefit, favour** Club membership entitles you to many privileges.	
prize	1.	*n.*	**reward, award, trophy** Jon won first prize for public speaking.	**1.** *penalty, punishment*
	2.	*v.*	**value, cherish, treasure, love, appreciate** Tracie prizes her swimming awards.	**2.** *abhor, dislike*
probable		*adj.*	**likely, reasonable, possible** It is probable that there will be snow tonight. *n.* There is a probability of snow tonight. *adv.* The snowfall will probably be heavy.	*improbable, unlikely, impossible*
problem	1.	*n.*	**puzzle, riddle, question** The problem was easily solved.	**1.** *answer, solution*
	2.	*n.*	**difficulty, trouble** The child has had lots of problems in school. *adj.* The problem child is getting special assistance.	
procedure		*n.*	**method, process, plan, system** The procedure must be followed exactly if the experiment is to work.	
proceed		*v.*	**advance, progress, continue** Finish the first book before you proceed to the next one.	*retreat, retire*
proceeds		*n.*	**yield, income, returns, gain, profit** All proceeds from the candy sales will go to charity.	*expenses, costs*
process	1.	*n.*	**method, plan, scheme, practice, project, system** Building a house is a long, complicated process.	

Word			Synonyms	Antonyms
	2.	*v.*	**prepare, preserve, treat, dry, can, dehydrate** Many foods today are processed by freezing or dehydrating.	
	3.	*v.*	**deal with, fill, ship, handle, take care of** The order clerk promised to process our book order today.	
proclaim		*v.*	**announce, declare, inform, tell** The rebel leader proclaimed himself the new president of the republic. *n.* The proclamation was announced over television and radio.	*retract, cancel*
procure		*v.*	**secure, pick up, gather, win, gain, acquire, get, obtain** The candidate procured votes by making grand promises.	*lose, squander, waste, spend*
prod		*v.*	**stimulate, move, urge, drive, spur, prompt, encourage** The coach prodded the team to make a greater effort.	*discourage, hinder*
produce		*n.*	**yield, fruits and vegetables, goods for sale, products** The produce is sold at the market.	
produce		*v.*	**make, create, cause, originate** Leonardo da Vinci produced many great masterpieces.	*destroy, demolish*
producer	1.	*n.*	**creator, originator** The producer of the movie accepted the award for Best Film of the Year. *n.* The movie was an excellent production.	
	2.	*n.*	**grower, breeder** Orchards in British Columbia are the producers of fine apples.	
product		*n.*	**result, effect, consequence** Success is often the product of hard work.	*cause, origin*
productive		*adj.*	**rich, fruitful, luxuriant, prolific** Good climate has made this a productive area for farming.	*barren, poor*

profession		*n.*	**occupation, career, calling, business, field, vocation** She is a journalist by profession. *adj.* Previously, professional athletes were not allowed to compete in the Olympic Games.	
proficient		*adj.*	**confident, skilful, expert, able** Paul is a proficient pianist. *adv.* He plays the piano proficiently. *n.* Proficiency comes with much practice.	*incapable, incompetent, unskilled*
profile	1.	*n.*	**side view, silhouette, outline, form, shape** A profile of Queen Elizabeth II appears on British coins.	1. *full face*
	2.	*n.*	**biography, character sketch, summary** A profile of the student was included in her university application.	
profit		*n.*	**return, proceeds, gain, benefit, advantage** The profits from the dance were donated to charity. *adj.* Our club had a profitable skate exchange. *v.* We all profited by the deal.	*loss*
profound	1.	*adj.*	**deeply felt, great, intense** Sam sent his profound apologies for forgetting our date.	1. *light, shallow*
	2.	*adj.*	**wise, shrewd, penetrating, intellectual** Einstein was a profound thinker.	2. *simple, shallow, superficial*
profuse		*adj.*	**lavish, ample, generous, plentiful, abundant, bountiful** There is a profuse growth of ferns in the woods. *n.* It was difficult to walk through the profusion of ferns in the woods. *adv.* We thanked our hosts profusely for their kindness.	*scanty, sparse, meagre*
program (also spelled programme)	1.	*n.*	**outline, schedule, plan, agenda, design** The program for the concert looks most exciting.	
	2.	*n.*	**concert, performance, show** Acrobats were included in the program.	

Word	#	Part	Synonyms / Example	Antonyms
	3.	*v.*	**arrange, direct, control** The technician programed the computer for the job.	
progress	1.	*n.*	**advancement, development, improvement, growth, headway** Todd shows much progress in his writing.	**1.** *decline, decrease, recession*
	2.	*v.*	**advance, proceed, gain, develop** Su-Lin is progressing very well at school.	**2.** *retreat, regress*
progressive	1.	*adj.*	**mounting, increasing, rising, advancing** The chart showed progressive improvement in sales.	**1.** *decreasing, deteriorating, declining*
	2.	*adj.*	**modern, up-to-date, forward, advanced** Our leader has many progressive ideas.	**2.** *backward, old-fashioned, out-of-date*
prohibit		*v.*	**forbid, deny, ban, prevent** The law prohibits drinking and driving.	*permit, allow, let, tolerate*
project		*n.*	**plan, design, enterprise, task, scheme, undertaking** Our science projects are attractively displayed.	
project	1.	*v.*	**overhang, extend, jut out, protrude, stick out** The roof projects beyond the walls by one metre.	**1.** *withdraw*
	2.	*v.*	**throw, shoot, hurl, thrust, fire, discharge, fling, eject, propel, launch** Missiles are projected into space by jet propulsion. *n.* Projectiles may be fired from submarines.	**2.** *catch, receive*
prolific	1.	*adj.*	**fertile, fruitful, productive** Hamsters, guinea pigs, and rabbits are prolific animals.	**1.** *barren, unproductive*
	2.	*adj.*	**creative, very productive** Agatha Christie was a prolific writer.	**2.** *unproductive*
prolong		*v.*	**lengthen, stretch, continue, extend, increase** The debate on the dumpsite was prolonged into the night. *adj.* The councillors were exhausted after the prolonged debate.	*shorten, reduce, limit, lessen*

Word	No.	Part	Synonyms / Example	Antonyms
prominent	1.	*adj.*	**famous, outstanding, notable, distinguished, well-known** Several prominent writers were at the conference.	1. *unknown, obscure*
	2.	*adj.*	**conspicuous, noticeable** The award was displayed in a prominent place in the school. *adv.* It was prominently displayed.	2. *inconspicuous, obscure*
promise	1.	*n.*	**pledge, vow, guarantee, pact** Never break a promise. *v.* Dad promised to take us skiing this weekend.	1. *refusal, denial*
	2.	*n.*	**hope, expectation, indication** The child shows promise of being an outstanding musician.	
promising		*adj.*	**favourable, hopeful, likely, encouraging** She has a promising future in music.	*discouraging, unfavourable*
promote	1.	*v.*	**advance, upgrade** The sales representative was promoted to sales manager. *n.* Her promotion was well-deserved.	1. *demote, downgrade*
	2.	*v.*	**advance, encourage, help, assist, aid** The organization promotes the preservation of the environment.	2. *hinder, deter, discourage*
prompt	1.	*v.*	**encourage, prod, inspire, spur, motivate, provoke** What prompted him to quit school?	1. *discourage, deter*
	2.	*v.*	**help, assist, advise, aid, cue** The audience was told not to prompt the contestant. *n.* Prompters help actors who forget their lines during a performance.	2. *hinder*
	3.	*adj.*	**punctual, ready, swift, quick** Customers appreciate prompt service. *adv.* Answer this letter promptly.	3. *slow, late, negligent, lax*
prone	1.	*adj.*	**inclined, liable, apt, likely, predisposed** Alvin is prone to accidents.	1. *disinclined, unaccustomed*
	2.	*adj.*	**face down, horizontal, prostrate** The child was lying prone in bed, sound asleep.	2. *face up, erect, vertical, upright*
pronounce	1.	*v.*	**articulate, speak, say, utter, state, voice, vocalize** Actors have to pronounce their words clearly.	1. *mispronounce*

	2.	*v.*	**proclaim, declare** The judge pronounced the defendant guilty as charged.	
pronounced		*adj.*	**evident, obvious, noticeable, eye-catching, striking, decided** Everyone commented on Guy's pronounced weight loss.	*unnoticeable, slight, insignificant, indiscernible, imperceptible*
proof		*n.*	**evidence, verification, demonstration, confirmation** The car rental company asked Lin for her proof of identity.	
prop	1.	*n.*	**support, reinforcement, brace, buttress, stay** Many props were needed to keep the roof from collapsing. *v.* The workers propped the roof with beams and braces.	
	2.	*v.*	**stand, lean, rest, set, place** The roofers propped their ladders against the wall.	
propel		*v.*	**push, thrust forward, drive, force ahead, project** Steam propelled the tugboat. *n.* A propeller moves a boat.	*repel, hold*
proper	1.	*adj.*	**correct, suitable, fitting, right** Wear proper shoes when jogging. *adv.* Dress properly for the cold.	**1.** *improper, incorrect, unsuitable*
	2.	*adj.*	**customary, conventional, standard, accepted, respectable** Proper table manners are expected.	**2.** *improper, unconventional*
property	1.	*n.*	**land, lot, holdings, real estate, realty, grounds** Dad hired an agent to take care of the family property in Florida.	
	2.	*n.*	**possessions, assets, belongings, resources** Personal property can be insured against theft or fire.	
	3.	*n.*	**quality, characteristic, attribute, trait, earmark** The foal has all the properties of a champion.	
proportion		*n.*	**part, share, ration, dimension, size, measurement, extent** A large proportion of the students are planning to go on to university.	

Word			Synonyms / Example	Antonyms
proposal		*n.*	**suggestion, recommendation, proposition, offer** The town rejected a proposal to build a large nuclear plant in the area.	
propose		*v.*	**suggest, put forward, offer, present, submit, recommend** The students proposed a new system for choosing prefects. *n.* The proposition was voted on by the class.	*oppose, protest, reject*
prospect	1.	*n.*	**outlook, hope, chance, likelihood** What are the prospects for getting out early today?	
	2.	*n.*	**view, picture, spectacle, scene, sight, outlook** One gets a good prospect of the town from that hill.	
	3.	*n.*	**expectation, hope, proposal, anticipation** The children were excited at the prospect of visiting the zoo.	
prosper		*v.*	**succeed, thrive, grow, gain, flourish, progress** Japan prospered after World War II.	*fail, decline, deteriorate*
prosperity		*n.*	**abundance, good fortune, success** Dad's business has enjoyed prosperity for many years. *adj.* We hope for a prosperous future.	*failure, misfortune, adversity*
protect		*v.*	**shield, guard, preserve, care for, keep, defend, shelter** The bear protected its cub from the hunter.	*attack, expose, mistreat*
protection		*n.*	**care, shelter, defence, security** The frightened people asked for police protection. *adj.* Animals are protective of their young.	*exposure, danger*
protest		*v.*	**complain, object, disagree, oppose** The team captain protested the umpire's decision. *n.* He later wrote an official protest.	*agree, assent, consent*

Word	Sense	Part of speech	Synonyms and example	Antonyms
proud		*adj.*	**conceited, vain, arrogant, boastful, haughty, imperious** The proud Roman Caesars were finally defeated. *n.* Their pride was one cause of their downfall.	*humble, modest, meek*
prove		*v.*	**verify, confirm, justify, support, demonstrate, show, substantiate** Shen proved his skill in writing by winning the essay competition. *n.* His victory was proof of his ability.	*disprove, contradict, refute*
provide		*v.*	**supply, give, furnish** The people provided food and aid for the earthquake victims. *n.* The victims were grateful for the provision of aid.	*withhold, refuse, deprive, deny, take away*
provoke	1.	*v.*	**stir up, arouse, incite** Tina provoked a fight by being rude. *n.* Jo loses his temper at the slightest provocation.	*calm*
		v.	**irritate, enrage, anger, vex, infuriate, annoy** Vic provoked us by being late again.	*please, satisfy*
prowl		*v.*	**rove, roam, wander, slink** Wolves prowled through the forest.	
prudent		*adj.*	**thoughtful, shrewd, cautious, careful, wise, thrifty** He made a prudent decision when he bought a coat instead of skis.	*careless, wasteful, unwise, reckless, rash*
pry	1.	*v.*	**peer, spy, snoop, inquire, poke, investigate** Don't pry into other people's private affairs.	1. *ignore, neglect*
	2.	*v.*	**raise, lift, force, lever** Jim pried the lid off the can of paint.	2. *press, push*
public	1.	*n.*	**people, society, community** Let the public decide whether it wants Sunday shopping.	
	2.	*adj.*	**common, general, well-known, open to all** The museum is a public building.	2. *private, personal, restricted*
publish	1.	*v.*	**announce, make known, disclose, reveal, communicate, circulate** The results of the draw will be published next week.	1. *conceal, suppress, withhold*

Word	No.	Part	Synonyms and examples	Antonyms
	2.	*v.*	**print, issue, bring out** The company published a successful dictionary last year. *n.* The publisher was pleased with the success of the dictionary.	
pull	1.	*n.*	**attraction, magnetism** The pull of gravity makes things stay on the ground.	
	2.	*v.*	**haul, tow, drag** Tom pulled his chair to the front.	**2.** *push, shove*
pulsate		*v.*	**throb, beat, shake, tremble, shiver, shudder, pound, vibrate** The healthy heart pulsates with a steady, even beat. *n.* The pulsations of the heart can be felt in the neck and wrists.	
punch	1.	*n.*	**poke, blow, wallop, jab, hit** The boxer got a punch on the nose.	
	2.	*n.*	**beverage** There was a delicious fruit punch at the party.	
	3.	*v.*	**pierce, puncture, perforate** The train conductor checked and punched our tickets.	
punctual		*adj.*	**on time, prompt, on schedule, not late** We can rely on Sonia to be punctual. *adv.* She arrives punctually at school every day. *n.* The school is strict about punctuality.	*late, tardy, unpunctual*
punish		*v.*	**discipline, chastise, correct, rebuke, penalize** The children were punished for not doing their homework. *n.* They had to stay in after school as punishment.	*reward, excuse*
puny		*adj.*	**tiny, insignificant, undersized, feeble, inferior, delicate, weak** The boxer scoffed at his opponent's puny muscles.	*large, giant, oversized, great, strong*
purchase		*v.*	**buy, acquire, get, invest in** They purchased their house after years of saving. *n.* The purchase of a new house is an exciting event.	*sell, dispose of*

pure	1.	*adj.*	**clean, immaculate, untainted, spotless, uncontaminated** We should get pure water from the spring. *n.* The water is tested for purity.	***1.*** *impure, dirty, contaminated, tainted*
	2.	*adj.*	**absolute, complete** It is pure folly to drink and drive.	
purify		*v.*	**distil, cleanse, refine, filter** Water is purified to make it safe to drink.	*soil, spoil, dirty, contaminate*
purpose		*n.*	**function, aim, intention, ambition, object** The group's purpose is to entertain.	
purposely		*adv.*	**intentionally, deliberately, knowingly** The paragraph was left out purposely.	*accidentally, by chance*
pursue		*v.*	**follow, chase, seek, track, trail** Hounds pursued the fox. *n.* The hunters watched the pursuit.	*avoid, shun*
push	1.	*v.*	**press, nudge, shove** The runner pushed the pedestrian out of the way.	***1.*** *draw, pull*
	2.	*v.*	**encourage, prod, urge, drive, impel, force** The salesperson pushed them to buy a stereo.	***2.*** *discourage, hinder, prevent*
put	1.	*v.*	**place, deposit, rest, lay, set** Please put the dishes on the table.	***1.*** *remove, transfer*
	2.	*v.*	**state, express, word, phrase** Can you put the problem another way?	
	3.	*v.*	**present, pose, submit, propose, offer** The chairperson put the plan to the committee members.	***3.*** *withdraw, remove*
puzzle	1.	*n.*	**mystery, confusion, enigma, riddle** How the house caught fire is a puzzle to everyone.	
	2.	*v.*	**bewilder, confuse, baffle, confound, embarrass, perplex** His strange answer puzzled me.	***2.*** *make clear, enlighten*

Q is the only letter that has a constant partner. In English, Q is always followed by a *u*.

Q has two sounds. In *quote, equal*, and *quick*, it is like *kw*. In words like *conquer* or *antique* (which we borrowed from the French), the sound is the same as *k*.

Word	#	Part	Synonyms / Example	Antonyms
quack		*n.*	**charlatan, rogue, fake, cheat, imposter, fraud, pretender** The doctor turned out to be a quack. *adj.* The quack doctor was arrested.	
quaint	1.	*adj.*	**odd, unusual, queer, peculiar, extraordinary, strange, curious** Grandma's pendant has a quaint design.	**1.** *usual, common, customary, ordinary, typical*
	2.	*adj.*	**old, antique, old-fashioned** Tourists like to visit quaint places.	**2.** *up-to-date, modern, modish*
quake	1.	*n.*	**tremor, shock, earthquake** The severe quake ruined many buildings.	
	2.	*v.*	**tremble, shiver, shake, quiver, shudder, vibrate** The mouse quaked with fear at the sight of the cat.	**2.** *be stable, be firm*
qualified	1.	*adj.*	**capable, able, trained, competent** Qualified instructors will train the athletes at the camp.	**1.** *unqualified, incapable, inept, incompetent*
	2.	*adj.*	**limited, conditional, modified, restricted** In the interview, the mayor gave a qualified "yes" to the question.	**2.** *unlimited, unconditional*
qualify	1.	*v.*	**pass, meet the demands** Our team qualified for the finals.	**1.** *fail, be unsuited*
	2.	*v.*	**change, modify, alter, moderate, temper, limit, restrain, reduce** The driver qualified his statement when questioned by the police.	**2.** *retain, solidify*
qualm		*n.*	**doubt, anxiety, misgiving, indecision, uncertainty** The teenagers had qualms about staying out late.	*confidence*
quandary		*n.*	**plight, dilemma, predicament, puzzle, perplexity** The tourist was in a quandary when she lost her passport.	
quantity		*n.*	**amount, number, extent, portion, volume, measure, stock, supply** A large quantity of food is required for the party.	

Word			Synonyms	Antonyms
quarrel		*n.*	**disagreement, dispute, argument, misunderstanding, squabble, dissension, feud** Quarrels arose over sharing the money. *v.* The winners quarrelled over the prize money.	*agreement, harmony, understanding*
queer		*adj.*	**strange, unusual, odd, peculiar, curious, extraordinary** Queer sounds could be heard inside the empty house.	*usual, common, ordinary, familiar, customary*
quell	**1.**	*v.*	**subdue, defeat, stop, silence, vanquish** The army quelled the uprising.	**1.** *yield, give up, concede*
	2.	*v.*	**calm, check, allay, quiet, overcome** The singer quelled his stage fright and walked on stage.	**2.** *incite, excite, agitate, arouse*
quench	**1.**	*v.*	**satisfy, satiate** She quenched her thirst with a large glass of water.	**1.** *stimulate, promote*
	2.	*v.*	**suffocate, smother, stifle, douse, extinguish** Forest fires are difficult to quench.	**2.** *fan, replenish, renew, promote*
query		*n.*	**question, inquiry** Several queries were made about the accident at the factory. *v.* The police queried the witnesses about the accident.	*answer, reply, response*
quest		*n.*	**search, pursuit, hunt** Prospectors rushed to the West in quest of gold.	
question	**1.**	*n.*	**query, inquiry** Each contestant was asked one question.	**1.** *reply, response, answer, solution*
	2.	*v.*	**ask, inquire, interrogate, quiz, query, solicit** Lawyers question witnesses in court.	**2.** *answer, reply, respond*
	3.	*v.*	**dispute, doubt, suspect, distrust** I question your right to attend this meeting.	**3.** *trust, believe*
questionable		*adj.*	**doubtful, uncertain, dubious, debatable, disputable, unconfirmed, suspicious** Some works of art are of questionable value.	*certain, definite, proven, unquestionable*

Word	No.	Part	Synonyms and example	Antonyms
quick	**1.**	*adj.*	**fast, rapid, speedy, fleet, swift** Magicians make quick movements to trick the audiences. *adv.* They move quickly.	**1.** *sluggish, slow*
	2.	*adj.*	**prompt, immediate, sudden** The car came to a quick stop.	**2.** *slow, tardy*
	3.	*adj.*	**impatient, hasty, rash, irascible, impetuous** Her quick temper often lands her in trouble.	**3.** *easygoing, calm, cool, level-headed, patient*
quiet	**1.**	*adj.*	**noiseless, still, silent, hushed** Patients need quiet surroundings. *n.* The dog's howl broke the quiet of the night.	**1.** *noisy, loud*
	2.	*adj.*	**still, placid, motionless, calm, smooth, unruffled, level** The boat drifted on the quiet lake.	**2.** *turbulent, moving*
	3.	*v.*	**soothe, calm, relax, pacify, console, comfort, ease** Lullabies can quiet babies. *adv.* Lullabies are sung quietly.	**3.** *agitate, excite, disturb*
quit	**1.**	*v.*	**abandon, surrender, relinquish, renounce** Which soldier quit the battle?	**1.** *invade, attack*
	2.	*v.*	**end, cease, stop** Mike is trying to quit smoking.	**2.** *start, begin, commence, continue*
	3.	*v.*	**leave, cease work, resign, discontinue** Those workers quit their jobs.	**3.** *seek, apply for*
	4.	*v.*	**vacate, depart, leave** When do the tenants quit the apartment?	**4.** *get to, arrive, move in*
quite	**1.**	*adv.*	**entirely, wholly, totally, completely** You're quite right about the matter.	**1.** *partially, somewhat*
	2.	*adv.*	**really, truly, very, positively, genuinely, actually, indeed** I am quite astounded at your remarks!	**2.** *somewhat, barely, hardly*
quiver		*v.*	**tremble, shake, shudder, quaver, shiver, flutter, vibrate** The child's lips quivered as he bit back his tears.	*stay still, be stable, stay calm*
quiz		*n.*	**test, query, interrogation, probe, examination, review** The students sat through a rigorous mathematics quiz. *v.* The witnesses were quizzed on the events of the day.	

quota *n.* **share, allotment, proportion, part, percentage, apportionment, portion**
That company has exceeded its quota of imported textiles.

quotation

1. *n.* **selection, citing, citation, excerpt, passage, extract**
Many people begin a speech with a quotation from a famous person.
2. *n.* **market price, current price, published price, price**
Stock market quotations are published in the newspapers.

quote

1. *v.* **repeat, recite, extract, cite, echo**
She quoted some lines from Shakespeare.
2. *v.* **give a price, name a price**
The stockbroker quoted the price of the stock.
n. The carpenter gave us a low quote for the job.

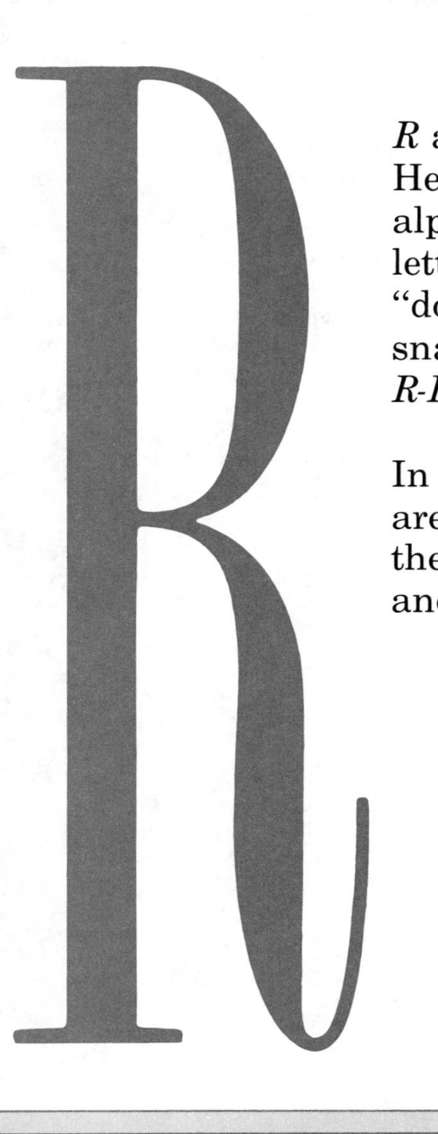

R appears in ancient Hebrew and Phoenician alphabets as the twentieth letter. *R* has been called the "dog letter" because of its snarling sound, *R-R-R-R-R-R*.

In addition, the three *R*'s are famous. Did you know these are "reading, 'riting, and 'rithmetic?"

rabid

1. *adj.* **mad, insane, frenzied, hydrophobic**
Rabid animals are dangerous to humans.
Antonyms: 1. *sane, normal, well*

2. *adj.* **fanatical, zealous, ardent, fervent, obsessed**
Rabid fans rushed onto the soccer field after the match.
Antonyms: 2. *indifferent, neutral, lukewarm, half-hearted*

race

1. *n.* **species, type, strain**
The human race is more developed than the other animal races.

2. *n.* **nationality, tribe, clan, people, ethnic group, cultural group**
Many races form the multicultural mosaic of Canadian society.

3. *n.* **competition, speed contest, run, meet, match**
Sena won the race on Sports Day.
v. How many drivers raced in the grand prix?

4. *v.* **run, hurry, hasten, speed, hustle, dash, sprint, bolt, scamper, rush**
People raced for cover when the storm hit.
Antonyms: 4. *delay, creep, crawl, plod, amble, stroll, saunter*

racket

n. **uproar, tumult, din, noise, disturbance, confusion**
The protestors made a racket during the meeting.
Antonyms: *quiet, peace, harmony, calmness, tranquillity*

radiant

1. *adj.* **luminous, shining, bright, glowing, brilliant, sparkling, resplendent**
The princess wore a radiant diamond tiara.
n. The travellers were blinded by the radiance of the sun.
Antonyms: 1. *dull, dim, drab, tarnished, lacklustre*

2. *adj.* **bright, happy**
The bride and groom had radiant smiles on their faces.
adv. They smiled radiantly all day.
Antonyms: 2. *solemn, glum, downcast, sad, miserable, dejected*

radiate

1. *v.* **shed, emit, give out, send out, transmit, disseminate, discharge**
The sun radiates heat and light.
n. Electric radiators give off heat.
Antonyms: 1. *absorb, take in, assimilate, consume, digest*

2. *v.* **spread out, diverge**
Many roads radiate from the centre of town.
Antonyms: 2. *converge, meet*

radical

1. *adj.* **fundamental, basic, original**
Ore is the radical form of metal.
Antonyms: 1. *derived, acquired*

	2.	*adj.*	**complete, extreme, entire, drastic, thorough** After his heart attack, Ken made a radical change in his lifestyle. *adv.* Ken radically changed his lifestyle.	**2.** *partial, superficial, extraneous*
	3.	*adj.*	**revolutionary, rebellious** The French Revolution was started by radical citizens. *n.* The radicals changed France from an imperial society to a democracy.	**3.** *patriotic, loyal, tempered*
	4.	*adj.*	**original, novel, advanced, forward, different, unusual, new, unconventional, progressive** Sigmund Freud was regarded as a radical thinker.	**4.** *imitative, ordinary, conservative, conventional, moderate*
rage	1.	*n.*	**anger, wrath, fury, frenzy** The coach flew into a rage when the team was late for practice.	**1.** *calmness, serenity, gentleness*
	2.	*n.*	**fashion, fad, vogue, style, trend** Which colour is the rage this season?	
	3.	*v.*	**rave, fume, rant, show anger** The crowd raged at the umpire's unfair call.	**3.** *be calm, remain quiet*
ragged	1.	*adj.*	**torn, tattered, shabby, worn, in shreds, frayed, threadbare** The refugees arrived in ragged clothing.	**1.** *untorn, new, well-kept, repaired*
	2.	*adj.*	**jagged, uneven** They stood in ragged rows outside waiting for help.	**2.** *smooth, even*
raid	1.	*n.*	**invasion, assault, attack, onset, incursion, foray** The army launched a surprise raid at dawn.	**1.** *retreat, withdrawal*
	2.	*v.*	**maraud, ransack, assault, loot, invade, plunder, assail, storm** Vikings raided the coastal towns.	**2.** *surrender, defend, protect*
raise	1.	*n.*	**increase** Cindy had a large raise in her salary when she was promoted.	**1.** *decrease, cutbac*
	2.	*v.*	**lift, hoist, heave, elevate, boost** The crane raised the girder to the top of the building.	**2.** *lower, bring down, take down, drop, lay down*
	3.	*v.*	**arouse, stir up** The wild applause after Jean's performance raised her hopes of winning the competition.	**3.** *quell, subdue, lul quiet, compose, cal*

	4.	*v.*	**grow, breed, cultivate, rear, produce, nurture, bring up** "What breed of cattle are raised on this range?"	**4.** *retard, destroy*
	5.	*v.*	**increase, advance, enlarge, appreciate** Why did the storekeeper raise the price of vegetables?	**5.** *lower, drop, reduce, diminish, depreciate*
	6.	*v.*	**collect, gather, procure, accumulate** The students are washing cars to raise money for computers.	**6.** *disperse, scatter*
	7.	*v.*	**erect, build, construct, put up** A monument was raised to honour the war veterans.	**7.** *tear down, demolish, destroy*
	8.	*v.*	**suggest, ask, bring up, propose** Opposition members in Parliament raised questions about the budget.	
	9.	*v.*	**exalt, promote, advance, further** The sergeant will be raised to the rank of lieutenant.	**9.** *demote, lower, downgrade, degrade*
ram		*v.*	**run into, butt, strike, bump, hit, pound, drive** The drunk driver rammed his car into the fence.	*avoid, dodge*
ramble	**1.**	*v.*	**stroll, walk, saunter, wander, roam, amble** It's fun to ramble through the park. *n.* We were tired after our ramble in the park.	**1.** *run, bound, dash, dart, rush*
	2.	*v.*	**digress, get off the point, babble, write or speak aimlessly** The speaker rambled on, unaware that the audience had fallen asleep.	**2.** *stick to the point*
	3.	*v.*	**twist, turn, spread, wind** Vines ramble in all directions.	
ramshackle		*adj.*	**dilapidated, neglected, shabby, rickety, decrepit, crumbling** The ramshackle cottage will be demolished.	*well-kept*
rancid		*adj.*	**stale, rank, sour, putrid, tainted, impure, contaminated, polluted** Rancid tuna should not be eaten.	*fresh, pure, untainted*
random		*adj.*	**haphazard, chance, aimless, irregular** Lottery numbers were chosen in random order.	*selective, specified, designated*
range	**1.**	*n.*	**extent, spread, distance, scope** The search covered a wide range that spread over ten kilometres.	

	2.	*n.*	**pasture, meadow, grassland, field, prairie, plain, grazing land** Cattle graze on the range.	**2.** *wasteland, tundra, forest, desert*
	3.	*v.*	**fluctuate, spread, vary** Temperatures range from very hot to very cold in desert regions.	**3.** *remain constant*
rank	1.	*n.*	**order, grade, position, standing, station, status** Colonel is a position of high rank in the armed forces.	
	2.	*v.*	**arrange, classify, order, grade, categorize** We ranked ourselves according to height.	**2.** *disarrange, disorder, disorganize*
ransack		*v.*	**plunder, raid, loot, pillage, ravage** Robbers ransacked the house while the owners were on vacation.	*protect, defend*
rap		*n.*	**knock, thump, blow, tap** There was a loud rap on the window. *v.* Someone rapped on the door in the middle of the night.	
rapid		*adj.*	**quick, fast, speedy, fleet, swift, accelerated** The sailors got into trouble in the rapid waters of the river.	*slow, sluggish, languid, tardy*
rare	1.	*adj.*	**unusual, uncommon, extraordinary** That pianist has a rare talent! *n.* Such talent is a rarity.	**1.** *usual, ordinary, common, typical*
	2.	*adj.*	**sparse, few, scanty, meagre, limited** Pandas are rare animals.	**2.** *abundant, plentiful*
	3.	*adj.*	**select, choice, superlative** Rare gems are among the crown jewels.	**3.** *inferior, mediocre*
	4.	*adj.*	**thin, light, tenuous** Rare air is found at high altitudes.	**4.** *dense, heavy*
	5.	*adj.*	**nearly uncooked, nearly raw, underdone** Many people enjoy eating rare steaks.	**5.** *well-done, overdone*
rarely		*adv.*	**seldom, not often, infrequently, occasionally** Robins are rarely seen in winter.	*frequently, often*

Word			Synonyms / Example	Antonyms
rascal		*n.*	**imp, rogue, scoundrel, scamp, scalawag, rapscallion** He was a rascal to pull that trick on me.	*model, paragon, saint*
rash		*adj.*	**reckless, hasty, impetuous, impulsive, unthinking, foolhardy, careless, madcap** Imra made a rash decision to quit school.	*level-headed, cautious, safe, wary*
rate	1.	*n.*	**speed, tempo, flow, motion, movement, pace** Some cities have seen a tremendous rate of growth in recent years.	
	2.	*n.*	**cost, price, value, amount** What is the monthly rate to park the car?	
	3.	*n.*	**ratio, percent, proportion** Interest rates rise and fall.	
	4.	*v.*	**rank, judge, evaluate, grade, assess, class** A panel of international judges rated the skaters' performances.	
rational		*adj.*	**level-headed, logical, sound, thoughtful, reasonable, sensible** The committee met to find a rational solution to the problem.	*irrational, rash, reckless, unsound, absurd*
rattle	1.	*n.*	**racket, noise, clatter, clack** The rattle of machine guns sent everyone dashing for safety.	**1.** *silence, quiet*
	2.	*v.*	**unnerve, confuse, fluster, bewilder, bother** The speaker was rattled by the hecklers in the audience.	**2.** *aid, help, assist, calm, soothe*
ravage		*v.*	**wreck, lay waste to, destroy, devastate, ruin** Hurricane Hugo ravaged the islands.	*build, improve, rehabilitate, restore*
rave	1.	*v.*	**babble, jabber, gabble** Delirious patients often rave.	**1.** *speak coherently*
	2.	*v.*	**bluster, storm, rant, rage, rail** The customer raved at the waiter for serving cold soup.	**2.** *remain calm*
ravenous		*adj.*	**starved, hungry, famished, voracious** We were ravenous after our hike. *adj.* We dug ravenously into our dinner.	*satisfied, full*

Word			Synonyms	Antonyms
ravine		*n.*	**gully, gorge, gap, chasm, gulch** There is a variety of wildlife in the ravine.	
ravish	**1.**	*v.*	**charm, delight, please, enchant, captivate, fascinate, enthral** The singer ravished the audience with a stunning performance. *adj.* The audience was bewitched by her ravishing beauty.	**1.** *repel, offend, disgust, displease*
	2.	*v.*	**violate, ravage, spoil** Fire ravished the forest.	**2.** *respect, protect, restore*
raw	**1.**	*adj.*	**uncooked, unprepared** Raw carrots are crunchy.	**1.** *cooked, prepared*
	2.	*adj.*	**unfinished, crude, natural** Canada exports raw materials like lumber and minerals.	**2.** *manufactured, processed, refined*
	3.	*adj.*	**undisciplined, inexperienced, new, untrained** The armed forces train raw recruits.	**3.** *experienced, trained, expert, seasoned*
	4.	*adj.*	**cold, biting, cutting, piercing** Raw winds forced the cancellation of the outdoor meet.	**4.** *balmy, pleasant, moderate, warm*
	5.	*adj.*	**chafed, scraped** The mountain climber's hands were raw from clutching the rope.	**5.** *healed*
reach	**1.**	*v.*	**arrive, get to** We finally reached home at midnight.	**1.** *set off, start, leave*
	2.	*v.*	**contact, get in touch with** You can reach me at this number.	**2.** *ignore, avoid, shun*
	3.	*v.*	**stretch, extend** Sheen reached for the cookie jar on the top shelf.	**3.** *crouch, shrink*
react		*v.*	**respond, reply, reciprocate** Most people react positively to kindness. *n.* There was a violent reaction from the fans when the rock concert was cancelled.	*ignore, shun*
ready	**1.**	*adj.*	**prepared, fit, equipped** I'm ready for the test.	**1.** *unprepared, unfi*
	2.	*adj.*	**complete, finished, available** Your wedding gown is ready.	**2.** *incomplete, unfinished*
	3.	*adj.*	**prompt, willing, quick, alert, fast, immediate, instant, swift** Ready help arrived at the scene of the plane crash. *adv.* The workers readily accepted the company's proposal.	**3.** *slow, hesitant*

real

1. *adj.* **actual, true, genuine, authentic**
Real diamonds are so hard they can cut glass.
2. *adj.* **actual, existent, concrete, tangible**
Nonfiction books deal with real life situations.
adv. Is that story really true?

1. false, fake, counterfeit, bogus, artificial, imitation
2. unreal, imaginary, hypothetical, fictitious, non-existent

realize

1. *v.* **comprehend, understand, recognize, see, appreciate, know**
Do you realize what you are doing?
2. *v.* **fulfil, achieve**
After years of struggle she realized her dream of success.
n. The realization of her dreams brought her much happiness.
3. *v.* **earn, obtain, receive**
We realized a good profit from the sale of our house.

1. misunderstand, not know, be ignorant of, ignore
2. fail, abandon, give up
3. lose

rear

1. *n.* **back, background**
Park at the rear of the building.
2. *v.* **raise, lift, elevate**
The bull reared its head and charged at the matador.
3. *v.* **bring up, raise, breed**
The farmer rears pigs.

1. front, foreground
2. lower, bow, drop

reason

1. *n.* **purpose, aim, objective, motive**
The reason for this meeting is to clear up some misunderstandings.
2. *n.* **logic, sense, thinking ability**
She is a person of reason and can be trusted to do the right thing.
3. *v.* **think, contemplate, reflect, consider, conclude, deduce**
The detective reasoned that the suspect was innocent.
n. His reasoning was based on the many clues he had examined.

reasonable

1. *adj.* **fair, moderate, just, sensible, inexpensive, fair, modest**
That's a reasonable price for a car.
2. *adj.* **feasible, sound, plausible**
Which candidate has the most reasonable arguments?

1. excessive, extreme, exorbitant, outlandish
2. implausible, unsound, unreasonable

rebel

1. *n.* **revolutionary, agitator, rioter, guerrilla, insurgent**
The rebels attacked the president's palace.

1. loyalist

	2.	*n.*	**individualist, independent, innovator** Picasso was considered to be a rebel in the art world.	2. *follower*
rebel		*v.*	**revolt, mutiny, rise up, resist** The army rebelled against the government. *n.* The rebellion was a success.	*submit, obey, follow*
rebuke		*n.*	**reprimand, reproach, reproof, disapproval, criticism** The coach's rebuke upset the skater. *v.* The coach rebuked the skater for his lack of concentration.	*compliment, praise, congratulations, applause, approval, encouragement*
recall	1.	*v.*	**recollect, remember, think of** Can you recall her name?	1. *forget*
	2.	*v.*	**call back, summon, reconvene** Auto manufacturers can recall their products for safety checks.	2. *send out, dispatch*
recede	1.	*v.*	**withdraw, retreat, go back** The troops receded under the heavy attack. *adj.* Dad has a receding hairline.	1. *go forward, go ahead, advance*
	2.	*v.*	**sink, fall, drop, lessen, abate, decline, ebb** The flood waters receded after a week.	2. *rise, increase*
receive	1.	*v.*	**get, accept, take, gain, acquire, procure, come by, secure, win** The swimmers received praise for their performance.	1. *give, donate, contribute, discard, abandon, refuse*
	2.	*v.*	**greet, welcome, admit, accept** Who received the guests at the door?	2. *reject, refuse, decline, oust, banish*
recess	1.	*n.*	**intermission, pause, break, interruption, respite, rest period** We have a short recess at school in the morning.	
	2.	*n.*	**opening, hole, indentation, alcove, niche, nook, hollow** The children hid in a recess in the rock.	
recite		*v.*	**relate, tell, repeat, deliver from memory** The student recited a comical poem. *n.* Everyone gave recitations of their favourite poem in class.	*ad lib*

Word			Synonyms	Antonyms
reckless		*adj.*	**rash, inconsiderate, careless, wild, thoughtless, foolhardy** Reckless drivers are a menace. *adv.* The child dashed recklessly across the road.	*careful, cautious, considerate*
reckon	**1.**	*v.*	**calculate, estimate, figure, count, compute, enumerate** The cashier reckoned the change correctly.	**1.** *guess, miscalculate, miscount*
	2.	*v.*	**think, consider, judge** She is reckoned to be the best tennis player of the century.	
reclaim		*v.*	**retrieve, renew, redeem, restore, regenerate, remodel, recondition** The Dutch have reclaimed much of their land from the sea. *adj.* Whole towns have been built on reclaimed land in Singapore.	*exhaust, waste, abandon*
recognize	**1.**	*v.*	**identify, know, distinguish** We recognized our relatives immediately, although we hadn't seen them in years.	**1.** *misidentify*
	2.	*v.*	**perceive, realize, see, admit, understand** Robert recognized that he had made a mistake in not working harder.	**2.** *miss, overlook*
	3.	*v.*	**acknowledge, take notice of, consider** She is recognized as the best swimmer on the team.	**3.** *ban, ignore, overlook*
recollect		*v.*	**recall, remember** I can't recollect what I did with my glasses. *n.* I have no recollection of where I left my glasses.	*forget*
recommend		*v.*	**suggest, approve, commend, favour, endorse** Kim recommended Amy for the job. *n.* Her recommendation helped Amy get the job.	*disapprove, censure, denounce*
record		*v.*	**write down, list, note, register, enter, chronicle, catalogue** Record the information in the notebook. *n.* Everything that happened during the meeting is on record.	*obliterate, delete, leave no trace*

Word	No.	Part	Synonyms and examples	Antonyms
records		*n.*	**documents, chronicles, registers, archives, accounts, diaries** Historical records are kept in museums.	
recover	1.	*v.*	**get well, regain health, rally, improve, recuperate** Atif is recovering from the accident.	1. *relapse, decline, become worse, fail*
	2.	*v.*	**restore, reclaim, regain, redeem, retrieve, rescue** Police recovered the stolen goods from a warehouse.	2. *lose, mislay, misplace*
recreation		*n.*	**amusement, sport, pastime, relaxation, diversion** The family's favourite recreation is sailing. *adj.* The town offers good recreational facilities.	*labour, work, toil*
rectify		*v.*	**correct, revise, amend, remedy, repair, redress** The cashier rectified the error on my bill.	*disregard, set aside, ignore, overlook*
recur		*v.*	**return, reappear, repeat, come back, reoccur** Measures must be taken to stop the floods from recurring. *adj.* Rani is plagued by a recurring nightmare about examinations.	*end, terminate, stop, cease*
reduce	1.	*v.*	**diminish, lessen, decrease, lower** The store reduced the prices during the sale. *n.* Watch for the price reductions.	1. *increase, magnify, enlarge, inflate, extend*
	2.	*v.*	**subdue, overcome, humiliate** The young offender was reduced to tears by the judge's comments.	
reflect		*v.*	**think, ponder, consider, study, contemplate** Grandpa enjoys reflecting on the past. *n.* He shares his reflections with us.	*disregard, neglect, ignore, overlook*
reform	1.	*v.*	**revise, amend, reconstruct, change, alter, remodel** Parliament voted to reform the existing tax laws.	1. *perpetuate, keep, maintain*
	2.	*v.*	**correct, improve** The young offender was warned to reform his ways.	

Word			Synonyms	Antonyms
refrain	1.	*n.*	**verse, song, theme, phrase, chorus** "Auld Lang Syne" is a refrain often heard on New Year's Eve.	
	2.	*v.*	**abstain, avoid, forgo** Dissenting club members refrained from voting.	**2.** *indulge, partake, join*
refresh		*v.*	**revive, restore, renew, invigorate, freshen** The runners refreshed themselves with cold drinks. *adj.* That was a refreshing shower!	*debilitate, tire, weary, enervate*
refrigerate		*v.*	**chill, cool, freeze, make cold** Refrigerate all dairy products. *n.* Keep milk in the refrigerator.	*heat, warm*
refuge		*n.*	**shelter, protection, sanctuary, haven, retreat** The millionaire built a refuge for homeless children.	*hazard, trap, peril*
refund		*v.*	**give back, pay back, rebate, return, repay, reimburse** The storekeeper refunded the customer's money. *n.* How much is the refund?	*take away, keep*
refuse		*n.*	**waste, garbage, rubbish, trash, debris, scrap** Much refuse can be recycled instead of discarded.	
refuse		*v.*	**decline, reject, turn down** The principal refused to give the students permission to hold a dance.	*allow, admit, consent, accept, agree*
regain		*v.*	**recover, retrieve, get back, recapture** The patient regained his health after months of convalescence.	*lose*
regard	1.	*n.*	**esteem, respect, admiration** Gandhi was held in high regard.	**1.** *disrespect, dishonour*
	2.	*v.*	**consider, view, look at, think of** I regard my teacher as a friend.	**2.** *dismiss, disregard*
region		*n.*	**area, district, territory, section, locality, sector, zone, vicinity** The Niagara region is noted for its orchards. *adj.* Regional elections will be held soon.	

register

1. *v.* **show, reveal, disclose, express, display**
The winner's face registered joy.
— *Antonyms:* 1. *hide, conceal*

2. *v.* **enrol, enlist, sign in, check in**
Sam registered for summer school.
n. Names are listed in the register.
— *Antonyms:* 2. *drop out, withdraw*

3. *v.* **indicate, point to, designate**
Thermometers register the temperature.

regret

1. *n.* **remorse, repentance, sorrow**
The driver expressed regret for the accident.
adv. The driver spoke regretfully of the accident.
— *Antonyms:* 1. *satisfaction, pleasure*

2. *v.* **be sorry for, rue, lament, mourn, grieve, repent, bemoan, deplore**
Everyone regretted the outcome of the accident.
— *Antonyms:* 2. *be satisfied with, celebrate, be glad, rejoice*

regular

1. *adj.* **customary, usual, normal, routine**
Our regular business hours are from nine to five.
adv. We eat regularly at six o'clock.
— *Antonyms:* 1. *irregular, unusual, odd*

2. *adj.* **consistent, methodical, steady, patterned, uniform, rhythmic**
We were hypnotized by the regular beat of the drums.
— *Antonyms:* 2. *sporadic, erratic, irregular, uneven, broken, interrupted*

regulate

1. *v.* **manage, direct, control, govern**
The council regulates the business of the city.

2. *v.* **adjust, set, standardize**
Can the electrician regulate the heat in the building?
— *Antonyms:* 2. *upset, confuse*

regulation

n. **rule, order, law, ordinance, statute, command**
Please observe all traffic regulations when driving.

rehearse

v. **practise, prepare**
The dancers rehearsed for the concert.
n. The dress rehearsal was a hectic affair.

reject

1. *v.* **discard, throw out, eliminate**
The sorters rejected all imperfect produce.
— *Antonyms:* 1. *choose, keep, maintain, accept*

2. *v.* **deny, refuse, decline**
The injured cyclist rejected all offers of help.
— *Antonyms:* 2. *accept*

rejoice		*v.*	**revel, enjoy, exult, celebrate** Entire nations rejoiced when peace was declared.	*lament, mourn, grieve, weep, sorrow*
relate	**1.**	*v.*	**tell, narrate, state, describe, report, recount** Pin related the events of his holiday to his friends.	**1.** *conceal, keep silent*
	2.	*v.*	**connect, link** The two families are related through marriage. *n.* People who are related are known as relatives or relations.	**2.** *estrange, separate*
relax	**1.**	*v.*	**loosen, slacken, let go** The doctor told me to relax my arm before she gave me the injection.	**1.** *tighten, strengthen*
	2.	*v.*	**rest, take it easy, lounge** Let's go home and relax. *n.* Everyone needs some relaxation after hard work.	**2.** *work, struggle*
release	**1.**	*n.*	**freedom, liberation, discharge** News of the hostage's release spread quickly.	**1.** *restraint, constraint, captivity*
	2.	*v.*	**let go, free, liberate** The kidnappers released the hostage after they were paid a ransom.	**2.** *confine, hold, constrain*
relentless		*adj.*	**merciless, ruthless, hard, pitiless, harsh, remorseless, unyielding** The suspect was subjected to relentless interrogation.	*merciful, kind, forgiving, compassionate*
relevant		*adj.*	**appropriate, pertinent, related, applicable, associated, connected** All relevant information will be considered in court.	*inapplicable, incongruous, inappropriate*
reliable		*adj.*	**dependable, staunch, steady, loyal, true, faithful, reputable, trustworthy, responsible** The news came from a reliable source.	*unreliable, insincere, false, irresponsible, undependable*
relieve	**1.**	*v.*	**assist, comfort, soothe, lessen, lighten, aid, allay, diminish, help** Cold compresses relieved the swelling. *n.* The rain was a relief from the heat.	**1.** *aggravate, worsen, increase*

	2.	*v.*	**replace, take over for, substitute for** New troops were sent in to relieve the tired soldiers. *adj.* How many relief pitchers were used during the game?	**2.** *reinstate, restore, put back*
relinquish		*v.*	**give up, surrender, yield, abandon, quit, cede** The prince relinquished all claims to the throne.	*keep, hold, retain, possess, maintain*
relish	1.	*n.*	**condiment, seasoning, sauce** Try some relish on the hot dog.	
	2.	*n.*	**liking, zest, gusto, enjoyment, appetite** The children dug into their food with relish. *v.* Certain people relish vegetarian meals.	**2.** *aversion, dislike, distaste*
reluctant		*adj.*	**unwilling, hesitant, averse** The scientist was reluctant to talk to the press about his discovery. *n.* His reluctance to discuss his discovery aroused much curiosity. *adv.* After much badgering he reluctantly agreed to come.	*anxious, keen, eager, willing*
rely		*v.*	**depend on, count on, trust** We rely on the mass media for accurate and up-to-date news. *adj.* Is television a reliable news source?	*be wary of, distrust*
remain		*v.*	**stay, linger, settle, continue on** The tourists remained on the island for another day.	*leave, go, depart*
remainder		*n.*	**leftover, balance, excess, rest** The remainder of the money was spent on food.	
remarkable		*adj.*	**exceptional, extraordinary, noteworthy, notable, striking** She is admired for her remarkable achievements in science.	*unremarkable, ordinary, common, undistinguished*
remedy		*n.*	**cure, treatment, relief, antidote** Many new remedies for illnesses are now available. *v.* Physiotherapy remedied Vern's back ailment.	

Word	No.	Part	Synonyms / Example	Antonyms
remember	1.	*v.*	**recall, recollect** Do you remember your former neighbours?	1. *forget*
	2.	*v.*	**keep in mind, call to mind** Remember to turn off the oven before you leave.	2. *overlook, forget*
remind	1.	*v.*	**prompt, call to mind** She reminded me that it was my turn to do the dishes.	
	2.	*v.*	**caution, warn, point out, prompt** Signs remind drivers to go slowly. *n.* Reminders are given on the radio.	
remorse		*n.*	**grief, regret, anguish, self-reproach** No remorse was shown by the murderer.	*complacency, self-satisfaction*
remote	1.	*adj.*	**distant, far away, far-off, removed, isolated, secluded** We holidayed on a remote island.	1. *near, close, accessible*
	2.	*adj.*	**unrelated, irrelevant** The suspect was released because all evidence proved to be remote.	2. *relevant, related*
	3.	*adj.*	**slight, faint** Our team only has a remote chance of winning as the other team is very strong.	3. *strong*
remove	1.	*v.*	**take away, carry off, clear, withdraw** Truckers removed the goods from the warehouse. *n.* Removal of the goods was quick.	1. *deposit, put in, install*
	2.	*v.*	**dismiss, discharge** The council removed the president from office.	2. *install, establish, reinstate*
render	1.	*v.*	**perform, deliver, play, present, give, do** The singer rendered a powerful performance.	
	2.	*v.*	**give, contribute, present, pay, hand over** To whom should I render my donation?	2. *keep, retain, withhold*
renew	1.	*v.*	**refresh, revive, restore, rebuild, regenerate, revive, rejuvenate** Has your city renewed its downtown core? *n.* Urban renewal is changing the appearance of many cities. *adj.* Some natural resources are renewable.	1. *deteriorate, exhaust, empty, spend, consume, weaken, debilitate, impair, kill, destroy*

Word			Synonyms	Antonyms
	2.	*v.*	**resume, repeat, continue** The committee renewed its efforts to raise funds for a health centre. *adj.* The committee's renewed efforts got some results.	**2.** *stop, discontinue, end*
renounce		*v.*	**forgo, relinquish, abandon, quit, forsake, give up, surrender** Jack renounced his successful career for a life of peace in the country.	*profess, hold, defend, retain, own, claim, assert*
renown		*n.*	**fame, distinction** Marie Curie was a scientist of great renown.	
renowned		*adj.*	**famous, noted, celebrated, distinguished, notable, illustrious, well-known** The world's most renowned authors were present at the conference.	*unknown, obscure, undistinguished*
repair		*v.*	**remedy, correct, fix, mend, overhaul, refurbish, renew, put in order** Mechanics repaired the car after the accident. *n.* The repairs were costly.	*break, destroy, wreck, damage, smash*
repay		*v.*	**refund, return, pay back, reimburse, give back** Who will repay the owner for the damages? *n.* Repayment must be made in full.	
repeat		*v.*	**do again, say again, duplicate** The witness repeated the answer. *n.* Work that requires repetition can be boring.	*discontinue, stop, d[illegible] once, say once*
repel	1.	*v.*	**rebuff, oppose, repulse, resist, force back** Invaders were repelled at the border by the troops.	**1.** *accept, surrende[illegible] yield, give in, withdraw, retire*
	2.	*v.*	**disgust, revolt, offend, nauseate** The smell of dead fish repelled us.	**2.** *attract, please, invite, entice, charm*
replace	1.	*v.*	**return, restore, reinstate** Mona replaced the library books that she had lost. *n.* Replacement of lost books is costly for libraries.	**1.** *remove, take away, take*
	2.	*v.*	**take the place of, substitute for** Robots have replaced humans on many assembly lines.	

Word	No.	Part	Synonyms and example	Antonyms
reply		*v.*	**answer, respond, retort** When asked to join us for dinner she replied that she was busy. *n.* We were disappointed with her reply.	*ask, question, query, ignore, be silent*
report	1.	*n.*	**record, account, statement** The treasurer's report is accurate.	
	2.	*n.*	**bang, blast, noise, detonation** Cannons give loud reports when fired.	2. *silence*
	3.	*v.*	**make known, publish, proclaim, announce, detail, disclose, tell** The scientists reported their astounding discovery at a press conference. *n.* The news reporters asked for more information.	3. *suppress, conceal, hide, withhold*
reproach	1.	*n.*	**blame, reproof, disgrace, discredit, dishonour, rebuke** Is your conduct beyond reproach?	1. *credit, honour, commendation, praise*
	2.	*v.*	**condemn, blame, censure, upbraid, reprove, rebuke** The judge reproached the jury for its inattention.	2. *laud, praise, commend, approve*
repulsive		*adj.*	**disgusting, odious, offensive, forbidding, disagreeable, revolting, ugly, unattractive** Rotten fish has a repulsive odour.	*agreeable, attractive, winning, alluring, seductive, pleasant, captivating*
request		*v.*	**ask, petition, solicit, appeal** People requested money for the disaster fund. *n.* Requests for aid poured in daily.	
require	1.	*v.*	**want, need** Animals require food and water.	1. *have*
	2.	*v.*	**demand, insist upon, command, expect** The company requires complete loyalty from its employees. *n.* Loyalty is a requirement.	
required		*adj.*	**compulsory, necessary, essential, imperative, mandatory** Which are the required subjects for the diploma?	*voluntary, optional, discretionary, elective*
rescue	1.	*v.*	**save, preserve, recover, retrieve, redeem, salvage** Divers rescued the cargo from the sunken hulk.	1. *lose, relinquish*

	2.	*v.*	**free, deliver, liberate, release, set free, extricate** Who rescued the hostages from the terrorists? *n.* The story of the daring rescue was in the news.	**2.** *capture, jail, imprison*
research		*v.*	**study, examine, investigate, inquire into, explore, analyse** Authors research their topics before writing stories. *n.* Research can take place in libraries.	
resemble		*v.*	**look like, be similar to, take after, approximate** Does the baby resemble her mother? *n.* The child bears a slight resemblance to her mother.	*differ from, be unlike*
resentment		*n.*	**anger, ill will, malice, displeasure, animosity, bitterness, indignation** The people have a deep resentment toward the cruel dictator. *v.* We resent cruelty to animals.	*friendship, affection, gratitude*
reserve	1.	*n.*	**provisions, store, supply, resources, stock** Squirrels have a reserve of nuts for the winter. *v.* Hibernating animals reserve food for winter.	
	2.	*n.*	**shyness, aloofness, restraint, caution, reticence** They spoke to the press with some reserve.	**2.** *boldness, confidence*
	3.	*v.*	**retain, keep, save, hold** Reserve seats for the performance.	**3.** *offer, use, relinquish, spend*
reside		*v.*	**live, dwell, occupy, inhabit, stay, abide, lodge** Millions of people reside in Toronto. *n.* They are residents of the city.	
residence		*n.*	**home, abode, address, dwelling, living quarters** The prime minister's official residence is in Ottawa.	
residue		*n.*	**remainder, leavings, remnant, leftover** Was there any residue in the glass of water?	

Word		Part	Synonyms and example	Antonyms
resign		*v.*	**quit, step down, leave, retire, give notice** The chairperson resigned after a disagreement with the committee. *n.* The resignation was accepted.	*retain, keep, remain*
resist		*v.*	**oppose, defy, withstand, strive against** The people resisted attempts by the new government to make changes. *n.* The government's proposals met with strong resistance.	*submit, give in, yield, surrender*
resistance		*n.*	**immunity, endurance** Overwork has worn down their resistance to illness.	*susceptibility*
resource		*n.*	**reserve, supply, source, stock** The Middle East has large resources of oil.	
resourceful		*adj.*	**ingenious, inventive, creative, imaginative** Resourceful leaders are needed in summer camps.	*unimaginative*
resources		*n.*	**riches, assets, wealth, reserves** Canada is rich in natural resources.	
respect		*n.*	**esteem, regard, admiration, honour** A person must earn the respect of others. *v.* Everyone should respect their elders.	*ridicule, scorn, disrespect*
respectable	1.	*adj.*	**decent, honourable, upright, proper, reputable** She comes from a respectable family.	1. *disreputable, dishonourable*
	2.	*adj.*	**good, impressive** She makes a respectable income.	2. *bad, poor*
respectful		*adj.*	**polite, considerate, courteous** The people stood in respectful silence during the funeral.	*rude, impolite, disrespectful, contemptuous*
respond		*v.*	**answer, reply, acknowledge** Has the university responded to your application? *n.* Was it a favourable response?	*ignore, overlook*

Word			Synonyms	Antonyms
responsible	**1.**	*adj.*	**dependable, reliable, trustworthy, competent** The jury is comprised of responsible citizens. *adv.* Members of the jury have to act responsibly.	**1.** *irresponsible, unreliable, flighty*
	2.	*adj.*	**liable, accountable, answerable** Wen-Li is responsible for the safety of the children. *n.* Taking care of the children is a big responsibility for her.	**2.** *not responsible, not accountable*
restful		*adj.*	**peaceful, quiet, placid, tranquil, soothing** What a restful place for a holiday!	*irritating, loud, agitating, disturbing, upsetting*
restless		*adj.*	**agitated, disturbed, unsettled, uneasy, fidgety, jumpy, flustered** The children became restless after the long wait.	*calm, relaxed, placid, contented, satisfied*
restore	**1.**	*v.*	**replace, put back, return** Restore the toys to the proper box.	**1.** *remove, take, take away*
	2.	*v.*	**repair, recondition, recover, renew, reconstruct** The old mansion has been restored to its former grandeur. *n.* The restoration of the old manor took two years to complete.	**2.** *destroy, ruin, spoil, wreck*
	3.	*v.*	**reinstate, reinstall, re-establish** The police quickly restored law and order after the riots.	**3.** *expel, remove, dismiss, discharge*
restrain		*v.*	**hold back, check, curb, bridle, repress, inhibit, confine, restrict** The police formed a human chain to restrain the rowdy crowd. *n.* They exercised restraint in dealing with their unpleasant neighbours.	*encourage, urge, incite, free, let loose*
restrict		*v.*	**restrain, curb, check, confine, limit, control** Bylaws restricted parking in the downtown core. *n.* There is a restriction on the watering of lawns during the drought.	*encourage, allow, permit, extend, expand, increase*
result		*n.*	**effect, consequence, conclusion, outcome, product** Earthquakes have devastating results. *v.* The storm resulted in serious damage to the town.	*cause, origin*

Word	No.	Part	Synonyms / Example	Antonyms
resume		*v.*	**continue, go on, proceed with, recommence** The postal workers resumed work after a long strike. *n.* The resumption of postal service was much welcomed.	*stop, cease*
retain	1.	*v.*	**hold, keep, maintain** The house is designed to retain heat.	**1.** *relinquish, let go, drop, yield, give up*
	2.	*v.*	**employ, engage, hire** The accused retained a lawyer.	**2.** *fire, let go, release*
	3.	*v.*	**remember, recall, recollect** Do you retain facts easily?	**3.** *forget*
retaliate		*v.*	**get even with, repay, pay back, avenge** Will that nation retaliate because of the raid? *n.* Retaliation is often swift.	*forgive, pardon*
retard		*v.*	**delay, slow down, check, hinder, impede, hold up** The heavy volume of mail retards the postal service at Christmas.	*expedite, promote, hasten, speed up*
retire	1.	*v.*	**withdraw, leave, depart, retreat, part, draw back** One of the contenders retired from the leadership race.	**1.** *join, take part in*
	2.	*v.*	**go to bed, lie down, rest, sleep** At what time did the guests retire?	**2.** *get up, rise, awaken*
	3.	*v.*	**resign, give up work** She retired at the age of sixty-five. *n.* She has been travelling since her retirement.	**3.** *work*
retort		*v.*	**reply, respond, rejoin, snap back** "No way!" the child retorted angrily when she was asked to go to bed. *n.* What a rude retort!	*remain silent, question, ask, listen, reply calmly*
retract	1.	*v.*	**remove, draw in, withdraw** The cat retracted its claws.	**1.** *extend, put forth*
	2.	*v.*	**take back, recant, deny, revoke, disclaim, rescind, disown, withdraw** The witness retracted the statement she had made to the police.	**2.** *reaffirm, proclaim, admit, insist, assert, repeat*
retreat	1.	*n.*	**shelter, refuge, haven, sanctuary, asylum** The camp was the explorer's retreat.	**1.** *trap, hazard, peril, danger*

2. *n.* **withdrawal, evacuation, flight**
Many prisoners were taken during the brigade's retreat.
v. Troops retreated from the front lines after a day of heavy fighting.
2. *advance, progress, front*

retrieve *v.* **regain, reclaim, bring back, recover**
The dog retrieved the bird shot down by the hunter.
lose, give up, relinquish

return **1.** *v.* **go back, come back**
The tourists returned to the cruise ship after a day of sightseeing.
1. *go forward, advance*

2. *v.* **restore, replace, put back, send back, give back**
I returned the damaged goods to the store.
2. *keep, hold back, retain*

3. *v.* **pay off, yield, produce, pay, show a profit of**
That investment returned thousands of dollars!
n. That was a handsome return on our investment.
3. *lose, show a deficit of*

reveal **1.** *v.* **expose, divulge, make known, disclose, tell, make public, publish**
The report revealed secret information.
n. The revelations in the report shocked the nation.
1. *hide, keep secret, withhold, be silent*

2. *v.* **expose, show, display, exhibit**
In the early 1900s bathing suits revealed little of the human body.
2. *conceal, hide, veil, cover*

revenue *n.* **income, returns, earnings, yield, receipts**
What is the annual revenue of the theatre?
expenses, expenditures

reverse **1.** *n.* **opposite**
Is the true story the reverse of what was described?

2. *v.* **invert, transpose, turn around, overturn**
The judge reversed the decision of the lower court.

review **1.** *n.* **critique, evaluation, appraisal**
The film received critical reviews.
n. Only one reviewer liked the film.

	2.	*n.*	**examination, study, analysis, inspection, survey** A review of the situation will be conducted. *v.* Who will review the situation?	
revise	1.	*v.*	**edit, correct, rewrite, improve** The writer revised her story before submitting it to a publisher. *n.* The revision process greatly improved the story. *adj.* A revised edition of our science textbook has just been published.	
	2.	*v.*	**change, alter, amend** The school revised its policy about Saturday classes.	
revive		*v.*	**enliven, renew, wake up, refresh, regenerate, invigorate, vivify, energize, restore** Water revives most plants.	*wither, weaken*
revolt		*n.*	**rebellion, revolution, uprising** The students stirred up a revolt against the government. *v.* They revolted against the harsh dictator.	*submission, obedience*
revolting		*adj.*	**disgusting, offensive, unpleasant** Revolting smells issued from the laboratory.	*appetizing, pleasant, pleasing, appealing*
revolution	1.	*n.*	**rebellion, revolt, uprising, mutiny, overthrow** The army put down a revolution by rebels.	**1.** *law, order, stability*
	2.	*n.*	**rotation, whirl, turning, spin, turn, reel, twirl, gyration** Wheels make many revolutions per minute.	
revolve		*v.*	**rotate, spin, whirl, twirl, turn** Car wheels revolve on axles. *adj.* Be careful with the revolving door.	
reward		*n.*	**payment, bonus, recompense, compensation, remuneration** A reward has been offered for information on the missing child. *v.* The police rewarded Simon for his help in finding the child.	*penalty, punishment*

Word			Synonyms	Antonyms
rhythm		*n.*	**tempo, beat, swing, cadence, metre, accent** This dance music has a fast rhythm.	
rich	1.	*adj.*	**wealthy, prosperous, moneyed** The rich countries should help the poorer nations. *n.* Some people are generous about sharing their riches. *n.* The rich live a life of luxury.	**1.** *poor, needy, destitute*
	2.	*adj.*	**fertile, luxuriant, fruitful, productive** This region is a rich farming area.	**2.** *sterile, barren, infertile, unproductive*
	3.	*adj.*	**abundant, lush, copious, plentiful, profuse, luxuriant** Rich undergrowth is found in equatorial regions.	**3.** *inadequate, deficient*
	4.	*adj.*	**opulent, luxurious, sumptuous, extravagant, lavish, magnificent** The windows were draped in rich velvet. *adv.* The house is richly furnished.	**4.** *dull, drab, bland, cheap, simple, plain*
	5.	*adj.*	**deep, resonant, sonorous, mellow, full** The singer has a rich voice.	**5.** *thin, weak*
rickety		*adj.*	**wobbly, shaky, unsteady, feeble, fragile, weak** Don't climb the rickety fence!	*stable, secure, steady, firm*
riddle		*n.*	**puzzle, mystery, secret, conundrum, enigma** It's a real riddle as to who stole the painting.	*explanation, answer, solution*
ridicule	1.	*n.*	**derision, scoffing, mockery, scorn, sarcasm, jeering** The critics heaped ridicule on the new play.	**1.** *respect, honour, praise, approval, commendation*
	2.	*v.*	**laugh at, jeer, mock, make fun of, deride, snigger at, lampoon** Hecklers ridiculed the candidate's speech.	**2.** *respect, honour, approve, praise, applaud, encourage*
ridiculous		*adj.*	**absurd, silly, unreasonable, foolish, odd, preposterous, ludicrous, funny** It's ridiculous to spend so much money on a wedding.	*sensible, proper, respectable, usual*
rig		*n.*	**apparatus, equipment, gear** Drilling rigs are used to find oil.	
right	1.	*n.*	**justice, truth, propriety** Children have to be taught right from wrong.	**1.** *wrong, injustice, impropriety*

	2.	*n.*	**claim, liberty, privilege, authority, prerogative** You had no right to drive my car without my permission.	
	3.	*v.*	**correct, repair, remedy, rectify, mend, set right** Hopefully, the new laws will right some injustices.	**3.** *wrong, hurt, harm*
	4.	*adj.*	**suitable, apt, appropriate, proper** Make sure you wear the right clothes for the occasion.	**4.** *unsuitable, inappropriate, improper*
	5.	*adj.*	**true, correct, valid, accurate, precise** That is the right answer!	**5.** *invalid, wrong, incorrect, imprecise, inaccurate*
	6.	*adj.*	**not left, dextral** Do you write with your right hand? *n.* Who is sitting on your right?	**6.** *left, sinistral*
	7.	*adj.*	**outward, outer, top, finished** The right side of the tablecloth should be seen.	**7.** *inner, bottom, unfinished*
	8.	*adj.*	**straighten, put upright, set upright, turn** Please right the garbage can.	**8.** *upset, spill, turn upside down*
rigid	**1.**	*adj.*	**solid, stiff, firm, hard, unyielding** The tent is held up by a rigid frame.	**1.** *flexible, soft, yielding, pliant*
	2.	*adj.*	**strict, severe, exacting, firm** Rigid rules were in place at the school.	**2.** *lax, lenient, accommodating*
	3.	*adj.*	**fixed, set, unmoving, definite, determined, stationary** World time zones are rigid.	**3.** *indefinite, undetermined, movable*
rigorous	**1.**	*adj.*	**severe, harsh, austere, rugged** Early settlers were exposed to rigorous conditions.	**1.** *soft, luxurious*
	2.	*adj.*	**exact, precise, accurate, meticulous, definite** Each recruit was given a rigorous examination.	**2.** *lax, slack, imprecise, inaccurate*
ring	**1.**	*n.*	**loop, circle, rim** Circus horses galloped around the ring.	**1.** *square, sphere, rectangle, oblong*
	2.	*n.*	**tinkle, chime, peal, jingle, jangle, clang** Everyone heard the ring of the doorbell. *v.* The telephone rang in the middle of the night. *adj.* What is that ringing sound?	
	3.	*n.*	**band, group, gang, crew** The police finally succeeded in breaking up the smuggling ring.	

Word	No.	Part of speech	Synonyms and examples	Antonyms
	4.	*v.*	**enclose, encircle, circle, surround, rim, gird, encompass** Tall trees ringed the garden.	
riot		*n.*	**revolt, uprising, tumult, disturbance, protest** Street riots resulted from a shortage of food. *v.* The citizens rioted in the streets. *adj.* The police quelled their riotous actions.	*peace, harmony*
ripe		*adj.*	**mature, well-developed, ready, fit, mellow** These apples are ripe enough to eat. *v.* Fruit ripens on the trees.	*green, unripe, unfit, undeveloped, immature*
rise	1.	*n.*	**growth, increase, climb, inflation, ascent, upsurge** What is causing the rise in prices? *v.* Prices rose last month.	**1.** *fall, drop, sinking, reduction, lessening, decrease*
	2.	*v.*	**get out of bed, arise, get up, wake up** At what time do you rise?	**2.** *retire, go to sleep, go to bed*
	3.	*v.*	**begin, spring, issue, emanate, originate, start** Rivers rise in the hills. *n.* The invention of machines contributed to the rise of the Industrial Revolution.	**3.** *end, terminate*
risk		*v.*	**venture, hazard, chance, gamble, jeopardize** She risked her life to save her child. *n.* The risks are high when one gambles.	*be safe, be secure*
rival	1.	*n.*	**opponent, competitor, enemy, antagonist, adversary** The champion met her arch rival in a gruelling match.	**1.** *partner, colleague, ally, friend, mate*
	2.	*v.*	**match, equal, vie with, approximate, compare with, approach, compete with** These fireworks rival those of last year. *n.* There is a strong rivalry between the two brothers.	**2.** *cooperate, be unequal to*
road		*n.*	**thoroughfare, route, way, path, track, passage, trail, roadway, highway, street** Which is the shortest road to your place?	

Word			Synonyms / Examples	Antonyms
rob		*v.*	**take from, plunder, steal, pilfer, pillage, burglarize** The bank was robbed in daylight. *n.* Security at the bank has been tightened since the robbery.	*give, donate, return*
robber		*n.*	**thief, burglar, bandit, pirate** The robbers were caught in the act.	
robe		*n.*	**gown, garment, outfit, costume, cloak, mantle, cape, wrap** The judge wore a black robe. *v.* She was robed in black.	
robust		*adj.*	**vigorous, sturdy, hardy, athletic, strong, healthy, hearty, hale** The robust athletes ran all day.	*weak, frail, puny, feeble*
rock	1.	*n.*	**stone, boulder, pebble** Move the rocks out of the way. *adj.* The rocky road is bad for my new car.	
	2.	*v.*	**sway, teeter, wobble, swing, oscillate, vibrate, reel, shake, move** The boat rocked back and forth in the choppy waters.	**2.** *remain still, be stationary, be fixed*
rogue		*n.*	**scoundrel, rascal, villain, scamp** The rogue was arrested by the police.	
roguish		*adj.*	**mischievous, playful, impish** We suspected he was up to no good when we saw his roguish grin.	*serious*
role	1.	*n.*	**task, function** My role is to help new students settle into the school.	
	2.	*n.*	**actor's part, character** Pina has the lead role in the play.	
roll	1.	*n.*	**record, list, register, catalogue, index, schedule, table** Names are recorded on the roll.	
	2.	*v.*	**rotate, spin, turn over, revolve** The golf ball rolled into the hole.	**2.** *stay still*
	3.	*v.*	**flatten, press, level** My brother rolled the lawn.	**3.** *fluff up*
romantic		*adj.*	**dreamy, fanciful, imaginative, sentimental, idealistic** Romantic novels are popular.	*realistic, unromantic, down-to-earth*

Word		Synonyms / Example	Antonyms
rookie	*n.*	**beginner, novice, recruit** Taka was chosen the best rookie in the hockey league this year.	*veteran*
root	1. *n.*	**reason, cause, origin, source** The mechanic found the root of the problem.	1. *consequence, result*
	2. *n.*	**bottom, base, lower part** Plants absorb water through their roots.	
rot	*v.*	**decay, spoil, decompose, putrefy** Vegetables rot in the heat. *adj.* Rotten food must be thrown out.	
rotate	*v.*	**revolve, turn, twirl, whirl, spin, circle** The Earth rotates on its axis. *n.* The rate of the Earth's rotation can be measured.	
rough	1. *adj.*	**uneven, bumpy, irregular, coarse, jagged, knobby** She cut her knee when she fell on the rough driveway.	1. *smooth, even, regular, polished, level, flat*
	2. *adj.*	**coarse, crude, disorderly, rude, vulgar, uncivil, boorish** The rough behaviour of the audience upset the performers.	2. *polite, courteous, orderly, civil, mannerly*
	3. *adj.*	**approximate, inexact, unprecise** A rough estimate of the cost was given by the plumber.	3. *exact, precise*
round	*adj.*	**circular, spherical, globular** The Earth is round.	*square, straight, flat, angular*
rouse	*v.*	**arouse, waken, stir up, excite** Loud noises roused the sleeping family.	*lull, soothe, calm*
route	*n.*	**path, road, track, course, way, direction** We marked our route on the map before setting off on our trip.	
routine	1. *n.*	**habit, practice, system, regimen, procedure** We have a busy routine at school.	
	2. *adj.*	**customary, usual, general, regular, habitual, scheduled** The children are due for their routine dental checkup.	2. *irregular, unusual*

Word			Synonyms	Antonyms
row		*n.*	**quarrel, disturbance, brawl, disagreement, fight, hassle, squabble, trouble** They had a row over who should cut the grass.	*harmony, agreement*
row	**1.**	*n.*	**line, queue** The children stood in a neat row.	
	2.	*v.*	**paddle** We rowed down the river in our canoe.	
rowdy		*adj.*	**noisy, loud, boisterous, disorderly, rebellious, unruly** Rowdy crowds disrupted the soccer game.	*orderly, quiet, mannerly, lawful*
royal		*adj.*	**regal, grand, superb, august, splendid, magnificent, noble** The opening of Parliament was conducted with royal pomp.	*mean, lowly, base*
rub		*v.*	**scrape, scour, grate, chafe, polish** Rub the tarnished brass with this cloth. *n.* Give it a good rub.	
rubbish		*n.*	**trash, litter, refuse, garbage, waste, debris, junk** Dump the rubbish in these bags.	
rude	**1.**	*adj.*	**discourteous, vulgar, impolite, coarse, boorish, unrefined, insulting** The rude child was told to leave the class. *n.* Rudeness is not necessary.	**1.** *polite, courteous, refined, mannerly, cultured, suave, urbane*
	2.	*adj.*	**harsh, rough, violent** The company's bankruptcy came as a rude shock to the workers.	**2.** *gentle, mild*
	3.	*adj.*	**coarse, crude, rough** The hunter lives in a rude hut in the woods.	**3.** *refined, elegant*
rugged	**1.**	*adj.*	**tough, strong, sturdy, robust, vigorous, hale, healthy, hardy** Rugged pioneers settled in the new world.	**1.** *weak, frail, puny*
	2.	*adj.*	**rough, uneven, harsh, severe, hilly, broken, mountainous** Guerrillas often hide in rugged terrain.	**2.** *even, smooth, flat*

Word			Synonyms	Antonyms
ruin		*v.*	**wreck, raze, demolish, destroy, spoil, damage, injure, harm** A fire ruined the historic building. *n.* The building was a complete ruin after the fire.	*build, erect, save, protect, restore, renew*
rule	1.	*n.*	**law, regulation, edict, code, act, statute, canon** All students have to observe the school's rules.	
	2.	*n.*	**custom, habit, practice, routine** As a rule, we eat out on Sunday.	
	3.	*v.*	**order, decree, command, direct** The government ruled it necessary to wear seat belts in the car.	**3.** *suggest, request*
rumour (also spelled rumor)		*n.*	**talk, hearsay, tale, gossip** She spread false rumours about him cheating on the test.	*fact, truth*
run	1.	*n.*	**sprint, lope, amble** Dogs need a daily run.	
	2.	*v.*	**hurry, speed, race, gallop, sprint, dart, dash, rush, bolt, scamper** We ran all the way to school as we were late.	**2.** *walk, stroll, saunter*
	3.	*v.*	**flow, gush, glide, pass through** The river runs through the town.	**3.** *stagnate, stop, end*
	4.	*v.*	**manage, direct, supervise, operate, control, govern, command** Who runs the local radio station?	
rural		*adj.*	**rustic, countrified, suburban, agricultural, pastoral** Rural areas have a smaller population than urban areas.	*urban, industrial, commercial, metropolitan*
ruse		*n.*	**trick, wile, subterfuge, gimmick, device** Hunters used a ruse to capture the bear.	*truth, honesty, sincerity*
rush		*n.*	**haste, hurry, speed, dash** There was a rush for seats when the theatre doors opened. *v.* The patrons rushed for the seats.	*delay, slowness*
rustic	1.	*adj.*	**countrified, rural, pastoral** The tourists enjoyed the rustic charm of the village.	**1.** *urban, industrial, commercial*
	2.	*adj.*	**simple, plain, unsophisticated, natural** The rustic furniture suited the decor of the chalet.	**2.** *urbane, sophisticated, complex*

ruthless *adj.* **brutal, cruel, harsh, pitiless, merciless, vicious, savage**
The terrorists launched a ruthless asttack on the innocent people.

merciful, kind, forgiving, tender, compassionate, considerate

S, the consonant with a hissing sound, also came to us from ancient Hebrew and Phoenician origins. Until a little more than a hundred years ago, *S*'s and *F*'s were written and printed alike. If you have ever read a very old book or newspaper, you know how puzzling this can be.

Word		Part of speech	Synonyms and example	Antonyms
sad		*adj.*	**unhappy, gloomy, dejected, glum, depressed, melancholic, sorrowful, downcast, sombre, mournful, woebegone** When the dog died, the whole family was sad.	*happy, cheerful, joyous, glad, spirited, jolly, light-hearted*
safe	1.	*adj.*	**secure, guarded, protected** Keep the valuables in a safe place. *adv.* We made sure the door was safely locked before we left.	1. *unsafe, risky, unprotected, dangerous, exposed*
	2.	*adj.*	**careful, reliable, dependable** Her reputation as a safe driver got her the job as the school bus driver.	2. *reckless, dangerous, unreliable*
	3.	*adj.*	**harmless, innocuous** The water from polluted lakes is not safe for drinking.	3. *harmful*
sag		*v.*	**hang down, sink, droop, dip** The old couch sags in the middle.	*rise*
salary		*n.*	**pay, wages, remuneration** This job offers a good salary and other benefits.	
salvage		*v.*	**retrieve, recover, regain, rescue, restore, redeem, get back** Divers salvaged the cargo from the sunken ship. *n.* The salvage of the *Titanic* caused great excitement.	*lose, waste, squander*
same	1.	*adj.*	**identical** This is the same dress I wore yesterday.	1. *different*
	2.	*adj.*	**similar, alike** We have the same likes and dislikes.	2. *different*
sample	1.	*n.*	**specimen, example, model, illustration, prototype** The store was handing out free samples of the new perfume.	
	2.	*v.*	**test, try, taste, examine, inspect** Judges sampled all the cakes in the contest.	
sanction	1.	*n.*	**approval, consent, permission, assent, approbation, ratification** The students were granted sanction to hold a school dance.	1. *disapproval, objection, censure*
	2.	*n.*	**ban, embargo, penalty, fine, injunction, punishment, restraint, restriction, impediment** The United Nations voted to place trade sanctions against that country.	2. *reward, compensation*

Word	No.	Part	Synonyms / Example	Antonyms
	3.	*v.*	**confirm, endorse, authorize, approve** The city council sanctioned the waterfront development.	**3.** *disapprove, censor, object*
sane		*adj.*	**rational, lucid, sound, mentally balanced** The defendant was declared sane and fit to stand trial. *n.* Who will vouch for the person's sanity?	*insane, irrational*
sanitary		*adj.*	**clean, hygienic, purified, sterile, uncontaminated, disinfected, germ-free** Washrooms must be kept in a sanitary condition.	*dirty, contaminated, unsanitary*
sap		*v.*	**undermine, weaken, drain, exhaust** The long illness sapped the patient's strength.	*revive, revitalize, improve, increase*
satellite	1.	*n.*	**secondary planet, asteroid, planetoid** A satellite revolves around a planet that is larger than itself.	**1.** *major planet*
	2.	*n.*	**spacecraft** News is beamed around the world via communications satellites.	
satisfactory		*adj.*	**adequate, acceptable, satisfying, pleasing** Shen cooked the campers a satisfactory meal.	*unsatisfactory, unacceptable*
satisfy		*v.*	**please, gratify** The salesclerks are trained to satisfy all customers.	*dissatisfy, displease, disappoint*
saturate		*v.*	**drench, soak** Heavy rains saturated the fields.	*dry, parch*
saucy		*adj.*	**impudent, rude, flippant, bold, impertinent, brazen, insolent** Sal's saucy remark upset Dad.	*polite, courteous, mannerly, shy, modest*
savage	1.	*adj.*	**wild, untamed, unrestrained** Lions are savage animals.	**1.** *tame, civilized, domesticated*
	2.	*adj.*	**cruel, brutal, ferocious, furious, violent, merciless, ruthless** The huge beast made a savage attack on the hunter.	**2.** *kind, gentle, humane, merciful*

save	1.	*v.*	**rescue, deliver, extricate, free, liberate, release, salvage** Firefighters saved the person trapped in the burning house.	1. *desert, leave, abandon*
	2.	*v.*	**protect, shield, safeguard, preserve** Seatcovers save the upholstery from damage.	2. *destroy, dirty, mar, damage*
	3.	*v.*	**hoard, gather, reserve, lay aside, set aside, collect, store** Joe is saving all his money for a new bicycle.	3. *throw away, give up, waste, spend, squander*
savoury (also spelled savory)		*adj.*	**tasty, appetizing, delectable, palatable, delicious, luscious, pleasing, scrumptious** Our favourite restaurant serves savoury meals.	*tasteless, insipid, unpalatable, unsavoury, unappetizing*
say		*v.*	**utter, speak, tell, express, declare, assert, announce** Can the audience hear what the announcer is saying?	*keep quiet, remain silent*
scale	1.	*n.*	**covering, layer, coating, incrustation** Do all fish and reptiles have scales?	
	2.	*n.*	**balance** Weigh the bananas on the scale.	
	3.	*v.*	**climb, mount, ascend** Who has scaled Mount Everest?	3. *descend*
	4.	*v.*	**scrape, peel, skin, flake, strip off, husk, shell, shuck, pare** The dentist scaled the tartar from the patient's teeth.	4. *cover, wrap, encase, envelop*
scan	1.	*v.*	**analyse, study, examine, investigate** Searchlights scanned the sky for enemy aircraft.	1. *ignore, overlook, neglect*
	2.	*v.*	**glance at, thumb through, browse** Patients scan magazines in the waiting room of the doctor's office.	2. *study, peruse, examine, scrutinize*
scanty		*adj.*	**meagre, sparse, little, skimpy, insufficient, limited** Scanty clothing is dangerous in winter. *adv.* The scantily dressed child was shivering in the cold.	*ample, sufficient, adequate, full, unlimited*

Word			Synonyms / Examples	Antonyms
scarce		*adj.*	**rare, not plentiful, insufficient, uncommon** Some of our natural resources are becoming scarce from overuse.	*plentiful, ample, sufficient, common*
scare		*v.*	**frighten, alarm, terrify** The violent storm scared the children. *n.* The loud knock in the middle of the night gave everyone a scare. *adj.* Tzen wore a scary mask for Halloween.	*soothe, calm, comfort*
scatter	**1.**	*v.*	**sow, strew, spread, sprinkle** The farmer scattered the seeds in the field.	**1.** *reap, collect, gather*
	2.	*v.*	**separate, disperse, disband, diverge** The demonstrators scattered when the police arrived.	**2.** *assemble, collect, congregate, gather, convene*
scene	**1.**	*n.*	**view, vista, panorama, spectacle** The scene from the mountain top is breathtaking. *adj.* The tourist took the scenic route. *n.* The scenery along the route was spectacular.	
	2.	*n.*	**location, site, place** Police rushed to the scene of the crime.	
	3.	*n.*	**act, part, episode** The movie is unsuitable for children because it has violent scenes.	
scent	**1.**	*n.*	**perfume, pleasant smell, fragrance, aroma** Roses have a lovely scent. *v.* Roses scented the air.	**1.** *stench, stink*
	2.	*n.*	**odour, smell** Police dogs were used to follow the scent of the robbers.	
schedule		*n.*	**program, plan, agenda** According to the airline schedule, the first flight is at nine o'clock.	
scheme		*n.*	**plot, plan, design, project** The army's takeover scheme was thwarted by the government. *v.* The army had schemed to take over the government.	

Word			Synonyms	Antonyms
scintillate		*v.*	**sparkle, flash, glitter, gleam, glint, twinkle, shimmer, shine** The singer's costume scintillated under the stage lights.	
scoff		*v.*	**sneer, jeer, mock, taunt, deride, ridicule, be contemptuous of** Ian scoffed at Lee for losing the game.	*admire, respect, sympathize with*
scold		*v.*	**reprimand, rebuke, reprove** Lendo was scolded for being late. *n.* He was upset by the scolding.	*praise, encourage*
scope		*n.*	**extent, amount, size, degree, measure, range, magnitude** Forecasters are unsure of the scope of the storm.	
scorch		*v.*	**char, blacken, burn, parch, wither, shrivel, sear** Flames scorched the wheat fields as the prairie fire raged on. *adj.* The scorched fields were a dreadful sight.	
score	1.	*n.*	**points, marks, tally, rating** Yun got a good score in her science examination.	
	2.	*v.*	**gain a point, win a point** Jan scored the winning goal in the final seconds of the game. *n.* Wayne Gretsky was a leading scorer for his hockey team for years.	**2.** *lose a point*
	3.	*v.*	**scratch, damage, mar, deface, mark, disfigure** The cook accidentally scored the table with a sharp knife.	**3.** *protect, save, shield, guard, preserve*
scorn	1.	*v.*	**despise, disdain, have contempt for, look down upon** The traitors were scorned for betraying their country. *n.* The press heaped scorn on the traitors during their trial. *adj.* People were scornful of the traitors. *adv.* The traitor was treated scornfully.	**1.** *respect, honour, admire, flatter*
	2.	*v.*	**reject, ignore, spurn, shun, renounce, refute** The manufacturing company scorned the inventor's idea.	**2.** *welcome, accept, acknowledge*

scoundrel *n.* **scamp, rogue, imp, rascal, villain**
The scoundrel disappeared with the money raised for charity.

scowl *v.* **glower, frown, glare**
The librarian scowled at the group of noisy students.
n. The students quietened when they saw the librarian's fierce scowl.
smile, grin, beam

scrap 1. *n.* **particle, bit, piece, portion, fragment, crumb, speck, jot**
Police could not find a scrap of evidence at the scene of the crime.
1. *whole*

2. *n.* **junk, garbage, waste, trash, refuse**
The dealer said Sherri's car should be sold for scrap.
v. Sherri scrapped her car at the junkyard.

3. *v.* **discard, abandon, reject**
Plans for the weekend were scrapped because of the rain.
3. *keep, retain, save, maintain*

scrape *v.* **rub, scour, scratch, grate**
Pat scraped the ice off the windshield.
n. She used an ice scraper for the job.

scrawl *n.* **scribble, scratch**
The pharmacist could not read the doctor's illegible scrawl.
v. Vandals scrawled all over the school walls.

scrawny *adj.* **lean, thin, skinny, gaunt, lanky**
Pictures of the scrawny war orphans touched the hearts of everyone.
brawny, muscular, heavy-set

scream *n.* **shriek, cry, screech, squeal, outcry, yell**
The victim's frightened screams could be heard a block away.
v. Victims of the disaster screamed for help.
sob, sigh, whisper

screech *n.* **scream, shriek, cry, squeal, yell**
We were awakened by the screech of tires.
v. The parrot screeched for attention.
sob, sigh, whisper

screen 1. *v.* **hide, veil, conceal, mask, shield**
A high fence screened the movie star's house from curious fans.
1. *expose, uncover*

	2.	*v.*	**choose, select, sift, sort, examine, analyse** All applicants for the job will be screened for security.	
scrimp		*v.*	**save, economize** They scrimped to put their daughter through college.	*spend, waste, splurge*
scrutinize		*v.*	**examine, watch carefully, view, study, inspect** Those jewels were scrutinized to determine their worth. *n.* The suspects were held under close scrutiny.	*glance at*
search		*v.*	**look for, probe, hunt, seek** The children searched for Easter eggs. *n.* They were successful in their search.	*find, discover, uncover*
season	1.	*n.*	**term, period, spell, interval, time** Fall is the most beautiful season of the year.	
	2.	*v.*	**condition, age, cure, dry out** Wood should be seasoned before it is used for furniture or building. *adj.* Seasoned firewood burns well.	
	3.	*v.*	**marinate, spice, make tasty** Season the steaks with salt and pepper. *n.* Soya sauce is a seasoning used in Chinese cooking.	
seasoned		*adj.*	**trained, prepared, experienced** Jacques is a seasoned diver.	*inexperienced novice, untrained*
secret	1.	*n.*	**mystery, confidence** Can you keep a secret? *adv.* They left the country secretly.	**1.** *disclosure, exposure*
	2.	*adj.*	**concealed, hidden, secluded** The money is kept in a secret place.	**2.** *open, revealed, obvious*
secretive		*adj.*	**veiled, concealed, covert, furtive, mysterious** Their secretive behaviour aroused everyone's curiosity.	*open, frank, overt, public, aboveboard*
section	1.	*n.*	**part, share, piece, slice, segment** They divided the cake into sections.	**1.** *whole, entirety*
	2.	*n.*	**region, area, sector, district** Traffic is heavy in this section of the city.	

Word	No.	Part	Synonyms / Example	Antonyms
sector		*n.*	**area, quarter, section, part, portion** We hurried through the rough sector of town.	*whole, entirety*
secure	1.	*v.*	**guard, defend, protect, shield, make safe** The soldiers secured the fort against the enemy.	1. *abandon, forsake*
	2.	*v.*	**obtain, get** The student secured permission to attend the lecture.	2. *be refused*
	3.	*v.*	**fasten, tighten** The skipper secured the boat with ropes. *adv.* The boat was tied securely.	3. *loosen, untie, unfasten*
sediment		*n.*	**residue, dregs, silt, settlings, deposit** A delta is formed from the sediment at the mouth of a river.	
see	1.	*v.*	**watch, perceive, observe, regard, notice, look at, pay attention to** Maria slipped because she did not see the ice on the sidewalk.	1. *disregard, miss, not notice*
	2.	*v.*	**understand, comprehend, discern** I don't see what you mean.	2. *misunderstand*
	3.	*v.*	**ensure, make sure, take care** See that you do your homework before you watch television.	
	4.	*v.*	**visit, meet** I'm going to see my grandparents next week.	
	5.	*v.*	**imagine, consider, envision** I cannot see him as a leader.	
seek	1.	*v.*	**look for, search, hunt, pursue** Police sought the escaped convict.	1. *ignore, neglect, disregard, find*
	2.	*v.*	**try, endeavour, attempt, strive for** Three persons seek the position of mayor.	2. *ignore, abandon, discard*
seize	1.	*v.*	**hang onto, take hold of, grasp, clutch, grip, catch, clench** The bully seized Todd by the arm.	1. *release, let go*
	2.	*v.*	**grab, snatch, take by force, apprehend, capture, impound, expropriate, commandeer** Spanish conquistadors seized the treasures of the Incas.	2. *return, restore, replace*

Word			Synonyms	Antonyms
seldom		*adv.*	**rarely, not often, hardly ever, infrequently** This team seldom loses.	*often, frequently, regularly*
select	1.	*v.*	**choose, pick out, designate, elect, decide on** Have you selected your favourite flavour of ice cream? *adj.* Only a select few will be admitted to the meeting. *n.* This store has a good selection of books.	**1.** *reject, decline, refuse*
	2.	*adj.*	**exclusive, superior, choice** This company manufactures a select line of sportswear.	**2.** *inferior*
self-sufficient		*adj.*	**independent, self-reliant** Everyone should strive to be self-sufficient.	*dependent, reliant*
send	1.	*v.*	**dispatch, forward, transmit, convey** Send the cheque by mail.	**1.** *get, receive, import*
	2.	*v.*	**throw, cast, fling, propel, hurl** The pitcher sent the ball to first base.	**2.** *clutch, grasp, hold, grab, retain*
sensation	1.	*n.*	**feeling, response, sentiment, emotion** Love is a wonderful sensation.	
	2.	*n.*	**sensitiveness, feeling, sensitivity, response** That patient has no sensation in his legs.	**2.** *numbness*
sensational		*adj.*	**spectacular, astonishing, exciting, incredible, marvellous, thrilling** The play was a sensational success.	*dull, uninteresting, boring, tedious, commonplace, humdrum, banal*
sense		*n.*	**understanding, reason, appreciation, judgment, perception** Artists have an excellent sense of colour.	*ignorance, misunderstanding*
senseless	1.	*adj.*	**foolish, absurd, silly, ridiculous, stupid, illogical** Senseless talk is not productive.	**1.** *wise, sensible, intelligent, logical*
	2.	*adj.*	**unconscious** The senseless boxer was rushed to the hospital.	**2.** *conscious*

Word		Part of speech	Synonyms / Example	Antonyms
sensible		*adj.*	**reasonable, discerning, sane, rational, aware, perceptive** Taking an umbrella was a sensible thing to do.	*foolish, stupid, silly, scatterbrained, absurd, thoughtless*
sensitive	1.	*adj.*	**delicate, sore, tender, painful** Sunburned skin is sensitive to the touch.	**1.** *insensitive, comfortable*
	2.	*adj.*	**touchy, high-strung, nervous, irritable** The sensitive actor stormed off the stage when the audience booed.	**2.** *impervious, indifferent, apathetic*
	3.	*adj.*	**alert, aware, perceptive** Police dogs are highly sensitive to smell.	**3.** *unaware, oblivious*
sentiment		*n.*	**feeling, emotion, thought** Romantic sentiments are expressed in Valentine's Day cards.	
sentimental		*adj.*	**emotional, romantic** The family reunion was a sentimental affair for everyone.	*hard, callous, unemotional*
separate	1.	*v.*	**keep apart, part, divide, disconnect, detach, uncouple, undo** The driveway separated the two houses. *n.* The couple's separation did not surprise anyone.	**1.** *join, connect, unite, fasten, link, couple, attach*
	2.	*adj.*	**distinct, individual, unconnected** After years of unhappiness they went their separate ways.	**2.** *connected, attached, joined, mutual*
sequence	1.	*n.*	**order, progression, flow, succession** The names were listed in alphabetical sequence.	
	2.	*n.*	**series, chain, string, set** The actor appeared in a sequence of films.	**2.** *one*
serene		*adj.*	**calm, tranquil, composed, placid, peaceful, unruffled** The tourists admired the serene waters of the lake.	*ruffled, excited, disturbed, tempestuous, confused*
serious	1.	*adj.*	**thoughtful, earnest, sincere** That issue requires serious thought.	**1.** *light-hearted*
	2.	*adj.*	**sober, solemn, thoughtful, grave** The doctor's serious expression told us something was wrong.	**2.** *happy, joyful*
	3.	*adj.*	**important, significant** That's a serious mistake!	**3.** *unimportant, insignificant*

Word	No.	Part	Synonyms / Example	Antonyms
	4.	*adj.*	**grave, critical, dangerous** Cancer is a serious disease. *adv.* Mavis is seriously ill.	**4.** *trivial, minor*
service	1.	*n.*	**aid, help, assistance** She was awarded a medal for services rendered during the war.	**1.** *hindrance, opposition*
	2.	*n.*	**work, duty** The company promises service with a smile.	
settle		*v.*	**determine, decide, confirm, agree** Have the neighbours settled their dispute over the fence?	*argue, debate, discuss, disagree*
settlement	1.	*n.*	**agreement, arrangement, compact, contract** A settlement was reached in the wage dispute.	**1.** *disagreement*
	2.	*n.*	**payment, compensation, reimbursement** The injured worker received a large settlement from the insurance company.	**2.** *non-payment*
	3.	*n.*	**colony, establishment** Quebec City was one of the first settlements in North America.	
severe	1.	*adj.*	**harsh, rigid, strict, stern, exacting, austere, inflexible, grim, forbidding, relentless** Certain crimes deserve severe punishment.	**1.** *lax, lenient, merciful, flexible, yielding, genial*
	2.	*adj.*	**intense, sharp, cutting, extreme, keen** Grandpa suffered severe chest pains.	**2.** *slight, moderate*
shabby	1.	*adj.*	**ragged, worn, threadbare, dilapidated, poor, run-down, seedy** The character wore shabby clothes in the play. *adv.* Why was the person dressed shabbily?	**1.** *new, well-kept*
	2.	*adj.*	**mean, miserable, unkind, low, contemptible, thoughtless** Oliver Twist received shabby treatment in the novel.	**2.** *kind, generous, noble, considerate*
shady		*adj.*	**shaded, dusky, shadowy, dim, sheltered** Some flowering plants grow best in shady places.	*sunny, bright*

Word	No.	Part	Synonyms / Example	Antonyms
shake		*v.*	**tremble, quiver, shiver, quake, shudder, vibrate** Earthquakes cause the ground to shake.	
sham		*n.*	**counterfeit, fake, imitation, pretence, pretext** The thief replaced the famous painting with a sham.	*original, fact, reality*
shame		*n.*	**disgrace, dishonour, discredit, humiliation, disrepute, embarrassment** The traitor brought shame upon his family. *v.* His behaviour shamed the family. *adj.* What a shameful thing to do.	*pride, honour, credit, respect, praise, approval, glory*
shameless		*adj.*	**brazen, bold, rude, forward, vulgar, impudent, immodest** The rowdy guests were told to stop their shameless behaviour. *adv.* They behaved shamelessly at the party.	*polite, cultured, courteous, modest*
shape	1.	*n.*	**form, figure, outline, mold, contour, appearance, frame** Some sails have a triangular shape.	
	2.	*v.*	**form, fashion, mold, make, build, construct, pattern** The sculptor shaped a horse out of the clay.	
share	1.	*n.*	**part, portion, quota, lot, allotment, allowance, division, dose, helping, serving, ration, fraction, fragment, percentage** Divide the money into equal shares.	1. *whole, total, entirety, aggregate*
	2.	*v.*	**divide, allot, distribute, apportion, part** The winners shared the prizes.	2. *unite, combine*
	3.	*v.*	**participate, take part in** The teachers shared in the discussion with their pupils.	3. *take no part in, avoid, shun*
sharp	1.	*adj.*	**keen, acute, razor-edged, honed, sharpened** A sharp knife is needed to cut roast beef.	1. *blunt, dull, unsharpened*
	2.	*adj.*	**severe, harsh, biting, cutting, piercing, intense** Sharp winds made skiing impossible.	2. *mild, gentle*
	3.	*adj.*	**cutting, biting, sarcastic, caustic** Sharp remarks can hurt a person's feelings.	3. *kind, pleasing, complimentary*

4. *adj.* **clever, bright, alert, shrewd, intelligent**
Who is the sharpest student in the class?
4. unintelligent, stupid, dull

5. *adj.* **watchful, alert, vigilant, attentive, close, observant**
Keep a sharp eye on the luggage!
5. inattentive, careless, negligent

6. *adj.* **pointed, spiked, peaked, barbed**
The vet was scratched by the cat's sharp claws.
6. rounded, smooth

7. *adj.* **bitter, pungent, biting, acrid, strong, acidic**
Lemons have a sharp taste.
7. bland, insipid, tasteless

shatter *v.* **burst, break, split, splinter, smash, disintegrate, destroy**
Windows shattered during the earthquake.
remain intact, keep intact

shear 1. *v.* **cut, shave**
Who will shear the lamb's wool in the spring?
adj. Shorn lambs are a sorry sight.
n. Shears are used to trim bushes.
1. let grow

2. *v.* **remove, withdraw, deprive, strip**
The major was sheared of his rank after his improper conduct.

3. *v.* **cleave, sever**
The truck sheared the car into two parts in the accident.

sheer 1. *adj.* **steep, abrupt, precipitous**
There's a sheer drop from the top of the bluff to the water.
1. gradual, slight, gentle

2. *adj.* **thin, flimsy, transparent, delicate, fine, diaphanous**
Nylon stockings are sheer.
2. thick, heavy

3. *adj.* **absolute, utter, complete, total**
Many rescuers were ill from sheer exhaustion.
3. mild, slight, partial

shelter 1. *n.* **refuge, haven, sanctuary, retreat, cover, protection, safety**
Don't take shelter under trees during an electrical storm.
1. peril, hazard, danger

2. *v.* **protect, shield, screen, guard, safeguard**
Children should be sheltered from violence on television and film.
2. expose, endanger

3. *v.* **cover, conceal, secure, preserve, house, hide**
Ambassador Ken Taylor sheltered Americans in the Canadian Embassy in Iran.
3. reveal, evict, turn out

Word			Synonyms	Antonyms
shield		*v.*	**protect, cover, preserve, shelter, guard, defend** The bear shielded its cub from the hunter's bullets. *n.* The warrior's sword struck his enemy's shield.	*expose, uncover, endanger*
shift	1.	*n.*	**turn, spell, working time, working period** Are you working the day or night shift?	
	2.	*n.*	**change, transfer, substitution, alteration, variation** A shift in the winds brought rain.	**2.** *permanence, steadiness*
	3.	*v.*	**change, alter, vary, move, dislocate** We shifted the living room furniture.	**3.** *retain, leave, perpetuate, set, fix, establish*
shiftless		*adj.*	**lazy, indolent, inactive** The shiftless worker was told to pull up his socks.	*industrious, active, hard-working*
shifty		*adj.*	**sly, cunning, tricky, elusive, evasive, deceptive** The stranger's shifty looks aroused our suspicion.	*open, frank, undesigning, straightforward, candid*
shimmer		*v.*	**gleam, glow, scintillate, glisten, shine** Water shimmers in the moonlight. *adj.* The singer was dressed in a shimmery gown.	
shine	1.	*n.*	**lustre, polish, gleam, gloss, brilliance** The table looked beautiful with the shine of polished silver.	**1.** *tarnish, dullness*
	2.	*v.*	**glow, gleam, scintillate, beam, radiate, sparkle** The sun shone on their wedding day.	**2.** *remain dull*
	3.	*v.*	**polish, scour, wax, burnish** The cadets shined their shoes before the parade.	**3.** *tarnish, scuff*
ship		*v.*	**send, dispatch, transport** Tankers ship oil across the oceans, while trucks and trains ship goods across the country. *n.* The shipment of orchids arrived by air.	*receive, import*

Word	No.	Part	Synonyms / Example	Antonyms
shiver		*v.*	**shake, shudder, tremble, quake, quiver** The people at the bus-stop shivered in the cold. *n.* The scary movie sent shivers down my spine. *adj.* Joe was shivery with fear after watching the movie.	
shock	1.	*n.*	**blow, jolt, jar, impact, crash, collision** The buildings tumbled from the shock of the earthquake.	
	2.	*v.*	**startle, agitate, disturb** The burst of gunfire shocked us.	2. *calm, quieten*
	3.	*v.*	**insult, outrage, horrify, revolt, anger, astound, dismay, appall** The vandalism caused by the gangs shocked the community. *adj.* The gang members were punished for their shocking behaviour.	3. *please, delight, comfort, relieve*
shore	1.	*n.*	**coast, bank, beach, coastline** Tides wash seaweed onto the ocean shores.	1. *water, sea, lake, river, pond, ocean*
	2.	*v.*	**support, prop up** Ted shored the sagging roof with a pillar.	2. *let down, collapse*
short	1.	*adj.*	**brief, curtailed, short-lived, fleeting, concise, limited** The whole family spent a short vacation in Bermuda.	1. *long, extended, prolonged, extensive*
	2.	*adj.*	**not tall, little, low, tiny, small** Who is the shortest basketball player?	2. *tall, long, large*
	3.	*adj.*	**inadequate, deficient, lacking, insufficient** The charity will be short of funds this year because of poor contributions. *n.* This year's drought will cause a shortage of fruit.	3. *abundant, adequate, sufficient, ample, copious*
	4.	*adj.*	**curt, sharp, abrupt, terse** His short answer to my question made me wonder what was wrong.	4. *friendly, kind, expansive*
shortcoming		*n.*	**fault, failing, weakness, foible, defect** Kay's biggest shortcoming is her carelessness.	*strength, virtue*

shout		*n.*	**cry, yell, call, bellow, scream, roar** The rescuers heard the shouts of the trapped people. *v.* The victims shouted for help.	*whisper, whimper, moan*
show	1.	*n.*	**exhibition, exhibit, display presentation** Automobile shows are popular. *v.* Manufacturers showed their latest cars.	1. *concealment, suppression, secrecy*
	2.	*n.*	**sham, pretence, affectation, simulation** The child's tears were just a show to win our sympathy.	2. *candour, sincerity, honesty*
	3.	*v.*	**explain, tell, guide, direct** "I'll show you how to use the computer," said the teacher.	3. *confuse, confound*
	4.	*v.*	**register, indicate, reveal, record, point out, designate, disclose** These marks show that you'll have to work harder if you want to graduate.	4. *conceal, hide, deny, contradict, obscure*
showy		*adj.*	**bright, vivid, striking, ornate, gaudy, glaring, flashy, garish, colourful, florid, pretentious, ostentatious** Jim wears showy clothes to attract attention.	*dull, drab, colourless, simple, inconspicuous, unnoticeable, subdued, quiet*
shred	1.	*n.*	**fragment, piece, tatter, strip, scrap, bit, rag** The dog tore the cloth into shreds.	
	2.	*v.*	**tear, rip** The cook shredded the cabbage for the salad.	
shrewd		*adj.*	**keen, sharp, clever, knowing, astute, discerning, observant** Nat is a shrewd businesswoman.	*stupid, silly, foolish, unthinking*
shrill		*adj.*	**piercing, high-pitched, sharp, penetrating, strident** The campers were awakened by the shrill cries of the birds.	*low-pitched, soft, faint, muffled, low*
shrink		*v.*	**compress, diminish, contract, become less, shrivel** My silk blouse shrank in the wash.	*enlarge, stretch, expand, increase*
shrivel		*v.*	**dry up, wither, contract, wrinkle** Plants shrivel without water.	*expand, spread, develop, unfold*

Word			Synonyms	Antonyms
shun		*v.*	**avoid, evade, ignore, neglect, dodge, keep away from, elude** Some famous people shun publicity.	*seek, look for, accept, adopt*
shut	1.	*v.*	**close, fasten, lock, seal** The stores shut their doors at six.	1. *open, unfasten, unlock*
	2.	*v.*	**enclose, confine** We shut the dog in the backyard before we left.	2. *release, liberate*
shuttle		*v.*	**alternate, come and go, go back and forth** The bus shuttles between the hotel and the amusement park. *adj.* The hotel provides the shuttle bus service. *n.* The space shuttle returned safely to Earth after its mission.	
shy	1.	*adj.*	**bashful, timid, reserved, retiring, timorous** The shy author refused to be interviewed by the press. *n.* After some persuasion, he overcame his shyness and met the reporters.	1. *bold, brazen, impudent, confident*
	2.	*adj.*	**cautious, wary, fearful, timid, suspicious, skittish** Deer are shy of humans.	2. *heedless, careless, fearless*
sick		*adj.*	**ill, unwell, unhealthy, ailing, impaired, indisposed, diseased** Doctors tend to sick people. *n.* Meg's sickness is not serious.	*well, healthy, sound, hearty, robust, strong*
sign	1.	*n.*	**indication, clue, trace** There were no signs of life in the deserted town.	
	2.	*n.*	**symbol, mark** The car screeched to a halt at the stop sign.	
	3.	*v.*	**authorize, endorse, approve, confirm, acknowledge** Both parties signed the contract.	3. *unauthorize, condemn, censure, denounce*
signal		*n.*	**sign, indication, cue, beacon, alarm, warning** A flashing red light is a signal of danger. *v.* The driver signalled that he was turning left.	

Word			Synonyms and examples	Antonyms
significant		*adj.*	**important, notable, vital, prominent, meaningful, momentous** July 1, 1867, is a significant date in Canadian history. *n.* Do you know the significance of that date?	*unimportant, trivial, trifling, insignificant*
signify		*v.*	**mean, imply, show, indicate, denote, express, declare** The conductor's arrival on stage signified the start of the concert.	
silent		*adj.*	**noiseless, still, quiet, hushed, soundless, calm** We quietly entered the silent room. *n.* The silence was broken by a cough. *adv.* We left as silently as we had arrived.	*noisy, loud*
silly		*adj.*	**foolish, stupid, ridiculous, inane, absurd, senseless, irrational, witless** The teacher told the students to stop being silly.	*sensible, rational, prudent, wise, sound, clever*
similar		*adj.*	**alike, like, much the same** The twins are very similar in looks. *n.* Their similarity is quite remarkable.	*different, unlike, dissimilar*
simple	1.	*adj.*	**easy, uncomplicated, straightforward** How could you fail such a simple test?	**1.** *difficult, hard, complicated, confusing, complex*
	2.	*adj.*	**plain, unadorned, untrimmed, unaffected, ordinary, unsophisticated** Simple designs are often the most beautiful.	**2.** *adorned, showy, flashy, loud, gaudy, ornate, garish, sophisticated*
simulate	1.	*v.*	**imitate, mimic, duplicate, replicate** Laugh tracks on television shows simulate the laughter of a live audience. *n.* Astronauts train in simulations of conditions in outer space.	**1.** *originate*
	2.	*v.*	**pretend, feign** Wendy simulated illness so she could stay home.	

Word			Synonyms and examples	Antonyms
sincere		*adj.*	**genuine, true, reliable, honest, trustworthy, forthright, candid** Sincere friends should be valued. *n.* Sincerity is an admirable quality.	*unreliable, false, insincere, hypocritical*
site		*n.*	**place, spot, situation, location, position** A hospital is to be built on this site.	
situation	**1.**	*n.*	**place, spot, site, location, position** This cottage is in an ideal situation. *v.* It is situated on a bay.	
	2.	*n.*	**condition, circumstance** Ron was in an awkward situation when he was unable to pay the bill.	
skilful		*adj.*	**skilled, trained, accomplished, efficient, capable** The skilful gymnast amazed everyone at the tournament. *adv.* The gymnast performed skilfully on the bar.	*unskilled, incompetent, clumsy, inept*
skip	**1.**	*v.*	**jump, hop, spring, leap** Skipping rope is good exercise.	
	2.	*v.*	**omit, pass over, overlook, exclude** Bea skipped the difficult question in the test.	**2.** *include, put in*
slack	**1.**	*adj.*	**relaxed, limp, lax, loose** They tightened the slack tennis net before starting the game. *v.* Who slackened the rope?	**1.** *taut, tight*
	2.	*adj.*	**careless, lazy, indifferent, negligent, lax, sluggish, slow** The sales clerks were dismissed for their slack work habits.	**2.** *diligent, careful, industrious*
	3.	*adj.*	**slow, sluggish** Business was slack at the stores after Christmas.	**3.** *brisk, busy, bustling, lively, active*
sleek	**1.**	*adj.*	**glossy, velvety, lustrous, slick, silken, satiny, smooth** Horses are groomed daily to keep their sleek appearance.	**1.** *rough, course, rugged, harsh*
	2.	*adj.*	**streamlined, trim** Peng arrived in his sleek sportscar.	**2.** *bulky*
sleepy	**1.**	*adj.*	**drowsy, dozy, tired** The sleepy child fell asleep in the car.	**1.** *wide-awake, alert, lively*
	2.	*adj.*	**quiet, inactive** Joe couldn't wait to move out of his sleepy hometown.	**2.** *busy, bustling*

Word			Synonyms / Example	Antonyms
slender	1.	*adj.*	**slim, slight, thin, narrow** That slender branch won't hold the boy's weight.	1. *fat, stout, thick, wide, obese, broad*
	2.	*adj.*	**meagre, small, scanty** They have difficulty living on their slender income.	2. *ample, massive, considerable*
slick	1.	*adj.*	**glossy, slippery, oily, sleek, smooth** Roads are slick when wet.	
	2.	*adj.*	**clever, smooth, ingenious, tricky** The company used slick gimmicks to attract customers.	2. *mundane, dull, unimaginative*
slight	1.	*adj.*	**frail, slender, dainty, flimsy, delicate, slim** Although she has a slight build, the ballerina is very strong.	1. *stocky, heavy, stout*
	2.	*adj.*	**small, trivial, insignificant, trifling, meagre** The company made slight profits this year.	2. *significant, large*
	3.	*v.*	**ignore, overlook, neglect, snub, rebuff, disdain, scorn** After his success, he slighted those who had helped him.	3. *favour, include*
slim	1.	*adj.*	**slender, thin, slight** Lu exercises daily to stay slim.	1. *fat, chubby*
	2.	*adj.*	**small, narrow, tight** She won the race by a slim margin.	2. *large, wide*
slip	1.	*n.*	**error, fault, mistake, blunder, indiscretion, faux pas** The cashier was fired for making too many slips in her calculations.	1. *correction*
	2.	*v.*	**bungle, err** Su-Lin slipped when she told Victor about the surprise party.	
	3.	*v.*	**glide, slide** Judy slipped on the ice and broke her elbow.	
	4.	*v.*	**decline, fall** House prices have slipped this year.	4. *rise*
slope		*n.*	**incline, grade, hill** Skiers glided down the steep slopes.	*flat, plain*
slow	1.	*adj.*	**sluggish, gradual, torpid, leisurely** We went for a slow walk after dinner. *adv.* We walked slowly around the neighbourhood.	1. *fast, swift, rapid*

	2.	*adj.*	**delayed, belated, overdue, late** Mail delivery will be slow during the postal strike.	2. *early, prompt*
	3.	*v.*	**slacken, decrease speed** The car slowed as it approached the intersection.	3. *accelerate, quicken, speed up*
	4.	*v.*	**retard, hinder, impede, delay, decrease, reduce** Inefficient machinery slowed production at the plant.	4. *increase, aid, assist*
sluggish		*adj.*	**inactive, slow, torpid, languid, lethargic** His sluggish performance told us he was not feeling well.	*active, lively, fast, swift, rapid*
sly		*adj.*	**crafty, shrewd, cunning, foxy, tricky, wily, subtle** The politician's sly tactics won many votes.	*direct, sincere, straightforward, open, frank*
small	1.	*adj.*	**little, tiny, miniature, minute, petite, wee, diminutive** It's easy to lose a small child in a crowd.	1. *big, large, great, bulky, gigantic*
	2.	*adj.*	**scanty, meagre, inadequate** There were only small quantities of food at the refugee camp.	2. *large, ample, adequate, abundant, extensive*
	3.	*adj.*	**trivial, insignificant, unimportant, unessential** I have a small part in the play.	3. *significant, important, essential*
	4.	*adj.*	**modest, poor, humble, simple, unassuming, unpretentious** Abraham Lincoln was raised in a small cabin.	4. *grand, splendid*
smart	1.	*adj.*	**clever, bright, intelligent, sharp, keen, alert** The smart student won a full scholarship to college.	1. *stupid, dull, unintelligent, slow*
	2.	*adj.*	**stylish, fashionable** Maria wore a smart suit for her interview. *adv.* She dressed smartly for the interview.	2. *unfashionable, out-of-date*
	3.	*adj.*	**sharp, severe, stinging** The fighter took a smart uppercut to the jaw.	3. *mild, gentle, slight, inoffensive, innocuous*
	4.	*adj.*	**active, vigorous, energetic, lively** The soldiers marched at a smart pace.	4. *slow, sluggish, languid*
	5.	*adj.*	**impudent, rude, bold, brazen** Smart remarks are not appreciated.	5. *polite, refined, courteous*

Word			Synonyms	Antonyms
smell	**1.**	*n.*	**aroma, odour, fragrance, scent, perfume** The smell of roast turkey filled the house at Thanksgiving.	**1.** *stench, stink*
	2.	*n.*	**stench, stink** The smell of dead fish spoiled the beach. *v.* Dead fish smell.	**2.** *fragrance, perfume, scent, aroma*
	3.	*v.*	**sniff, scent, detect an odour** Can you smell the cookies baking in the oven?	
smooth		*adj.*	**even, level, flat, plane, flush, sleek, unvarying, glossy, glassy, lustrous, uniform** The smooth surface of the lake resembled a mirror. *v.* Workers smoothed the lawn tennis court with rollers.	*irregular, jagged, rough, uneven, broken, sharp*
smug		*adj.*	**self-satisfied, complacent, egotistical, self-righteous** The team members accepted their award with smug smiles.	*modest, humble, meek*
snatch		*v.*	**seize, grab, take, grasp** Thieves snatched the woman's purse and dashed off.	*return, restore, give back*
sneer		*v.*	**mock, jeer, gibe, taunt, scorn, belittle, scoff, disparage, ridicule** The contestants sneered at each other before the match.	*cheer, applaud, compliment, praise*
snobbish		*adj.*	**snooty, arrogant, ostentatious, pretentious** The snobbish man would only associate with the rich and famous. *n.* He was such a snob he would only wear designer clothes.	*humble, modest, unassuming, gracious*
snub		*v.*	**shun, disdain, disregard, ignore, slight, rebuff** The singer snubbed the audience by refusing a curtain call. *n.* The snub hurt everyone's feelings.	*flatter, fuss over, pay attention to*
snug	**1.**	*adj.*	**cozy, comfortable, sheltered** The children nestled in their snug, warm beds.	**1.** *exposed, uncomfortable*
	2.	*adj.*	**tight, close, trim, compact** Jack complained that the jacket was too snug.	**2.** *loose, lax, incompact*

Word			Synonyms	Antonyms
soak		*v.*	**saturate, wet, drench** May soaked the flower beds after she had planted the bulbs.	*dry*
sober		*adj.*	**serious, solemn, grave, earnest, quiet, staid** We could tell from their sober faces that something was wrong.	*light-hearted, happy, loud, boisterous*
sociable		*adj.*	**affable, genial, friendly, social, hospitable** Sociable people usually enjoy parties.	*unsociable, unfriendly, aloof, distant*
soft	1.	*adj.*	**pliable, flexible, yielding, malleable, pliant** Soft leather is used in making gloves.	1. *rigid, stiff, hard, unyielding*
	2.	*adj.*	**gentle, mild, tender** The nurse's soft manner calmed the child.	2. *stern, severe, harsh, brutal*
	3.	*adj.*	**low, mellow, subdued** The band played soft music while we dined.	3. *loud, harsh, piercing*
	4.	*adj.*	**pale, pastel, delicate, faint** The nursery was decorated in soft colours.	4. *bright, glaring, brilliant, bold*
	5.	*adj.*	**smooth, velvety, satiny, silky, fine, downy** Soft fabrics are pleasant to touch.	5. *rough, harsh*
soggy		*adj.*	**wet, damp, soaked, mushy, saturated** Cedar trees thrive in soggy soil.	*dry, parched, arid*
solemn	1.	*adj.*	**sober, serious, grave** There were many solemn faces at the funeral.	1. *light-hearted, gay, happy, joyful, merry*
	2.	*adj.*	**ceremonial, formal, imposing, ritualistic, ceremonious** Remembrance Day services are solemn occasions.	2. *informal, unceremonial*
solid	1.	*adj.*	**rigid, stable, sound, fixed** All buildings need solid foundations.	1. *unstable, weak, fragile, flimsy*
	2.	*adj.*	**firm, hard, dense** The patient is not allowed solid food.	2. *fluid, liquid, soft*
	3.	*adj.*	**sound, wise, valid, sensible, genuine** The graduates were given solid advice.	3. *invalid, foolish, ridiculous*
solitary	1.	*adj.*	**alone, lonesome, lonely, separate, unsocial** A hermit lives a solitary life.	1. *social, accompanied*
	2.	*adj.*	**sole, only, lone, single, one** There is a solitary passenger on the bus.	2. *several, many, numerous*

Word	No.	Part	Synonyms / Example	Antonyms
	3.	*adj.*	**remote, secluded, desolate, isolated, deserted** That cottage is on a solitary stretch of beach.	**3.** *populated, dense crowded*
soluble		*adj.*	**dissolvable, solvable** Sugar is soluble in water.	*insoluble*
solution	1.	*n.*	**answer, resolution, explanation, key** Do you have the solution to the problem?	**1.** *question, problem*
	2.	*n.*	**fluid, liquid, mixture** Salt and water makes a saline solution.	
solve		*v.*	**figure out, decipher, unravel, resolve, answer** It took us a long time to solve the puzzle.	*leave unanswered, misunderstand*
sombre (also spelled somber)	1.	*adj.*	**dark, gloomy, overcast, cloudy, drab, dull, murky** In winter sombre days are common.	**1.** *bright, sunny, cloudless, sun-filled*
	2.	*adj.*	**sad, depressing, melancholy, dire, funereal** Sombre music is played at funerals.	**2.** *cheerful, gay, merry, happy*
soothe	1.	*v.*	**relieve, help, comfort** She soothed the pain of her twisted ankle with a cold compress.	**1.** *aggravate, irritate, hurt, worsen*
	2.	*v.*	**pacify, console, quieten, calm** Dad soothed the cranky baby by gently rocking him.	**2.** *agitate*
sordid		*adj.*	**dirty, filthy, wretched** The refugees lived in sordid conditions at a camp.	*fresh, clean, uplifting*
sore	1.	*n.*	**wound, infected spot** The mosquito bites turned into itchy sores.	
	2.	*adj.*	**painful, tender, smarting, aching** Lyn couldn't sing because of a sore throat.	**2.** *painless*
sorrow		*n.*	**sadness, grief, woe, suffering, distress, anguish, heartache** War causes great sorrows.	*joy, happiness*
sorry	1.	*adj.*	**sad, grieved, mournful, melancholy** I'm sorry that your pet has died.	**1.** *happy, gleeful, pleased*

Word	No.	Part	Synonyms / Example	Antonyms
	2.	*adj.*	**penitent, apologetic, regretful, remorseful** Sam was sorry for breaking his promise.	2. *unapologetic*
	3.	*adj.*	**poor, dismal, pitiful, pathetic** The house was in a sorry condition when we bought it.	3. *adequate*
sort		*n.*	**kind, class, type, species, variety, group, classification, category** There are many sorts of apples. *v.* Eggs are sorted according to size.	
sound	1.	*n.*	**noise** Don't make a sound!	1. *silence, quiet*
	2.	*adj.*	**healthy, well, hearty, strong, sturdy, robust** Athletes have sound bodies.	2. *weak, diseased, sick*
	3.	*adj.*	**stable, durable, substantial, safe, secure, sturdy, firm, solid** The bridge is supported on sound bases.	3. *unsafe, flimsy, defective, fragile*
	4.	*adj.*	**reliable, wise, sensible, rational, prudent, reasonable** Take the counsellor's sound advice.	4. *foolish, stupid, ridiculous*
	5.	*adj.*	**thorough, deep** Tzen fell into a sound sleep after the examination. *adv.* He slept soundly for a day.	
sour	1.	*adj.*	**pungent, acid, bitter, tart** She winced when she bit into the sour lemon.	1. *sweet, sugary, mild, bland, mellow*
	2.	*adj.*	**grouchy, ill-natured, irritable, grumpy, peevish, disagreeable** Pat was in a sour mood after losing the game.	2. *good-humoured, good-natured, cheerful*
	3.	*v.*	**turn bad, spoil, curdle, ferment** Milk sours if not refrigerated.	3. *stay fresh*
source		*n.*	**origin, rise, beginning** Where is the source of the Nile River?	*end, finish, conclusion*
spacious		*adj.*	**large, roomy, extensive, vast, ample** The rooms are spacious in this apartment.	*cramped, small, tiny, limited, confined*
span	1.	*n.*	**measure, extent, spread** The span of an eagle's wings is impressive.	
	2.	*v.*	**stretch over, extend across** A suspension bridge spanned the river.	2. *tunnel, burrow*

Word	#	Part	Synonyms and example	Antonyms
spare	1.	*v.*	**save, relieve, omit, exempt from** Please give me a ride and spare me from a long walk.	1. *condemn*
	2.	*adj.*	**extra, additional, superfluous, reserve, supplementary** Spare tires are stored in trunks of cars.	2. *less, short*
	3.	*adj.*	**scanty, meagre, lean** The students survived on their spare budgets. *adv.* Apply the ointment sparingly.	3. *abundant*
sparkle		*v.*	**glitter, gleam, twinkle, glisten, shine, flash, scintillate** The children's eyes sparkled when they saw the Christmas tree. *n.* There was a sparkle in their eyes.	
sparse		*adj.*	**scanty, thin, meagre** Vegetation is sparse in the desert. *adv.* Vegetation grows sparsely in deserts.	*ample, adequate, thick, luxurious*
speak		*v.*	**talk, utter, tell, say, express, declare, voice** Laurel spoke about her trip to Asia. *n.* The speaker kept the audience entertained.	*remain silent, be quiet*
special	1.	*adj.*	**particular, specific, definite, distinct, certain** Each instrument has a special purpose in the orchestra.	1. *general, unrestricted, indefinite*
	2.	*adj.*	**unusual, extraordinary, exceptional** A fiftieth wedding anniversary is a special occasion.	2. *ordinary, common, usual, everyday, regular*
species		*n.*	**class, variety, kind, sort, category** Endangered species of birds and animals must be protected.	
specific		*adj.*	**particular, definite, exact, explicit, precise, distinct** We left specific instructions for the babysitter.	*vague, indefinite, general*
specimen		*n.*	**example, sample** The museum has rare specimens of fossils on display.	
speck		*n.*	**spot, fleck, bit, particle, iota, dot** There's not a speck of dust in May's home.	

Entry			Synonyms / Example	Antonyms
spectacle		*n.*	**scene, sight, view, display, exhibition, show** The opening ceremonies of the Olympic Games was a spectacle.	
spectacular		*adj.*	**sensational, striking, impressive, magnificent, thrilling** Under certain atmospheric conditions, the Northern Lights are a spectacular sight.	*dull, boring, uninteresting, dreary*
spectrum		*n.*	**range, variety, array, extent** A wide spectrum of views was offered at the meeting.	
speed	1.	*n.*	**swiftness, quickness, rapidity, velocity, rate, pace** The car reached a speed of eighty kilometres per hour.	**1.** *slowness, tardiness*
	2.	*v.*	**hurry, hasten, move swiftly** Cars sped along the highway.	**2.** *slow down*
speedy		*adj.*	**fast, quick, rapid, swift, prompt** The dry cleaners give speedy service.	*slow, tardy, sluggish*
spellbound		*adj.*	**mesmerized, entranced, amazed, enthralled, fascinated, captivated** The violinist held the audience spellbound with her performance.	*disgusted, offended, bored, disinterested*
sphere	1.	*n.*	**orb, globe** Earth is a sphere. *adj.* Earth is a spherical planet.	
	2.	*n.*	**region, field, range, circle** Sports is not within our sphere of interest.	
spin	1.	*n.*	**ride, short trip** We went for a spin in Jo's new car.	
	2.	*v.*	**gyrate, swirl, twist, rotate, revolve, whirl, turn** Cars spun around on the icy roads. *n.* The skater made some spectacular spins on the ice.	
spite		*n.*	**malice, hatred, contempt, animosity, resentment, ill will** The youth spread vicious rumours out of spite. *adj.* The spiteful gossip caused much harm.	*love, affection, sympathy, good will, benevolence*

Word			Synonyms	Antonyms
splendid		*adj.*	**glorious, grand, magnificent, superb, marvellous, resplendent, sumptuous** The royal family lives in splendid surroundings. *n.* The tourists admired the splendour of the Taj Mahal.	*ordinary, dull, unimposing, inferior, mediocre*
spoil	**1.**	*v.*	**decay, rot, decompose, putrefy, ferment, deteriorate** Fruit spoils when it is kept too long.	**1.** *stay fresh, purif refresh, improve*
	2.	*v.*	**ruin, destroy, damage, harm, injure, impair** Heavy rains spoiled the crops.	**2.** *save, preserve, keep*
spoils		*n.*	**booty, plunder, loot, pillage** Invaders carried off the spoils from the ransacked city.	
spontaneous		*adj.*	**automatic, instinctive, natural, unforced, uninhibited, impulsive** Spontaneous applause greeted the movie star.	*deliberate, intentional, intended, imposed*
sport	**1.**	*n.*	**diversion, game, recreation, entertainment, amusement, play, pastime, pleasure, enjoyment** Skiing is a popular winter sport.	**1.** *work, business, seriousness, toil, labour*
	2.	*n.*	**mockery, joke, ridicule** The rude student made sport of the newcomer's accent.	
spread	**1.**	*v.*	**scatter, disperse, sow, strew, disseminate, distribute, cast, diffuse, circulate** Machinery spreads seeds in the fields.	**1.** *reap, gather, collect*
	2.	*v.*	**unfold, stretch, extend, unroll, expand, open, unfurl** Sir Walter Raleigh spread his cloak for the queen to walk upon.	**2.** *gather up, furl, pick up, roll up*
	3.	*v.*	**proclaim, tell, announce, divulge, circulate, broadcast, publish, declare, advertise** The rumour spread like wild fire.	**3.** *suppress, hide, conceal, hush*
	4.	*v.*	**cover, coat, daub, smear, diffuse** Spread the paint over the entire wall.	**4.** *spot, localize*
spring		*v.*	**leap, bound, vault, jump** The gymnast sprang over the bar. *n.* The cat made a spring for the bird.	*settle, drop, land*
spry		*adj.*	**nimble, active, agile, lively, vigorous** Elderly people can still be spry.	*inactive, infirm*

Word			Synonyms	Antonyms
spunk		*n.*	**courage, pluck, spirit** The runner showed spunk by finishing the race despite an injured leg.	*timidity, fear, cowardice, weakness*
spurn		*v.*	**reject, repudiate, scorn, shun** The wrestler spurned his opponent's demand to surrender.	*accept, welcome*
squabble		*v.*	**bicker, quarrel, fight, argue, disagree, dispute** The twins squabbled over the bicycle. *n.* Those children have squabbles over their toys.	*agree, cooperate*
squalid		*adj.*	**dirty, filthy, unclean, foul, wretched** Some people live in squalid conditions in the cities. *n.* No one should have to live in such squalor.	*clean, spotless, pleasant, welcoming*
squander		*v.*	**waste, throw away, lavish** He squandered away his lottery winnings.	*economize, save*
squirm		*v.*	**wriggle, wiggle, writhe, twist, fidget** Babies are difficult to hold when they are squirming.	*be still*
stable	1.	*n.*	**shelter, barn, pen, corral** Horses are kept in stables. *v.* The groom stabled the colt.	
	2.	*adj.*	**steady, solid, firm, balanced** The barometric pressure is stable.	**2.** *unstable, changeable*
	3.	*adj.*	**permanent, durable, certain, enduring, constant, continuing** A stable government is good for a country.	**3.** *intermittent, spasmodic, irregular, uncertain*
stage	1.	*n.*	**platform, rostrum** The graduates walked up to the stage to receive their diploma.	
	2.	*n.*	**degree, grade, step, period, level** The egg is the first stage in the insect's life cycle.	
	3.	*v.*	**present, show, execute** The people staged a demonstration to protest the new taxes.	
stagnant	1.	*adj.*	**still, inert, inactive** Mosquitoes breed in stagnant waters.	**1.** *active, lively*

	2.	*adj.*	**dormant, lifeless, idle, sluggish** The assembly line is stagnant during the strike.	**2.** *active, busy, productive*
stain	1.	*n.*	**blot, blotch, mark, spot, smear, blemish, splotch, smudge** Dan removed the stains from the tablecloth with bleach.	
	2.	*v.*	**mark, soil, spot, dirty, discolour** Blueberries stain teeth.	**2.** *clean, scour, whiten, bleach*
	3.	*v.*	**colour, dye, tint, varnish, lacquer, paint** We will stain the wooden deck in the spring. *n.* We will use a dark brown stain.	
stall	1.	*n.*	**booth, compartment, cubicle** The horses were kept in stalls in the barn.	
	2.	*v.*	**break down, stop working, malfunction** Cars stalled in the extreme cold.	**2.** *go, function*
stalwart	1.	*adj.*	**strong, sturdy, robust, vigorous** A stalwart crew is needed on an ocean schooner.	**1.** *weak, puny, frail, sickly*
	2.	*adj.*	**brave, bold, valiant, resolute, staunch, reliable** The stalwart soldiers fought to the bitter end.	**2.** *cowardly, fearful, timid*
stamina		*n.*	**endurance, perseverance, strength, vigour** Long distance runners need stamina.	
standard	1.	*n.*	**flag, pennant, colours, banner** The standard waved in the breeze.	
	2.	*n.*	**emblem, insignia, symbol** Each uniform displayed the battalion's standard.	
	3.	*n.*	**measure, criterion, norm** This country has a high standard of living.	
	4.	*n.*	**model, type, pattern, prototype** A Stradivarius is the standard for violin makers.	
	5.	*adj.*	**regular, usual** In this school, the standard class has twenty pupils.	**5.** *irregular, unusual*
staple		*adj.*	**essential, main, principal, chief, standard** Rice is the staple food for millions of people.	*unessential, extra, secondary*

Word	No.	Part	Synonyms / Example	Antonyms
stark	1.	*adj.*	**severe, austere, unyielding, bare, barren, desolate, harsh** Photographs showed the stark landscape of the tundra.	**1.** *soft, gentle, yielding, welcoming*
	2.	*adj.*	**complete, absolute, utter, sharp** There is a stark contrast between the lives of the rich and the poor.	
start	1.	*n.*	**beginning, opening, commencement** The start of the summer is most exciting.	**1.** *end, ending, conclusion, finish, finale*
	2.	*v.*	**begin, commence, set out** When will the band start to play?	**2.** *end, finish, stop*
startle		*v.*	**alarm, frighten, surprise, shock** The loud noise startled the baby. *adj.* The startling news left everyone in shock.	*soothe, comfort*
state	1.	*n.*	**condition, situation, status** This old house is in a ramshackle state.	
	2.	*v.*	**tell, say, inform, express, declare, announce, pronounce, assert, affirm** The witness was asked to state the facts only.	**2.** *remain silent, suppress, repress*
stately		*adj.*	**dignified, majestic, grand, imposing, magnificent** Many stately old homes have been converted into hotels.	*modest, unpretentious*
static		*adj.*	**immobile, inactive, dormant, inoperative, sedentary** Stock markets remained static during the holidays.	*active, operative, mobile*
status		*n.*	**rank, station, standing, position** The singer achieved celebrity status with her first album. *adj.* She bought a sleek car as a status symbol.	
staunch		*adj.*	**loyal, faithful, trustworthy, true, steadfast, firm, strong, stalwart** The mayor's staunch supporters turned out for the rally.	*undependable, unreliable*
stay	1.	*v.*	**remain, wait, linger** We were asked to stay for supper.	**1.** *leave, go*
	2.	*v.*	**visit, dwell, live, reside, lodge, sojourn** We will be staying with friends during our trip.	**2.** *depart, leave, go*

	3.	*v.*	**delay, postpone, defer, suspend** The show's opening was stayed because the star fell ill.	3. *advance, bring forward, hasten*
steady	1.	*adj.*	**unvarying, uniform, regular, constant, continuous** Most people have a steady heartbeat.	1. *irregular, variable, inconstant, changeable*
	2.	*adj.*	**sure, firm, dependable, secure, stable** Pouring coffee requires a steady hand.	2. *unsure, unsteady wobbly, wavering*
stealthy		*adj.*	**furtive, sly, evasive, shrewd, cunning, wily** Cats are stealthy creatures when they stalk their prey. *adv.* The cat crept stealthily toward the bird.	*straightforward, obvious, direct, undesigning*
steep		*adj.*	**sheer, abrupt, precipitous, sharp** Steep cliffs rose from the sea.	*gradual*
step	1.	*n.*	**pace, stride** Take one step forward. *v.* Please step forward.	
	2.	*n.*	**rung, level** How many steps are on the ladder?	
	3.	*n.*	**stage** I was involved with every step of the production process.	
stereotyped		*adj.*	**conventional, typical, customary, indistinctive, routine** Television shows tend to be filled with stereotyped characters.	*atypical, original*
stern		*adj.*	**severe, rigid, strict, austere, harsh, forbidding, unyielding** The security guard's stern expression frightened the students.	*genial, lenient, easy flexible*
stiff	1.	*adj.*	**rigid, inflexible, unbending, firm, unyielding, hardened** The stiff collar made me most uncomfortable all day. *v.* I stiffened the collar with starch.	1. *limp, flexible, pliant, soft, yielding*
	2.	*adj.*	**hard, severe, exact, strict, difficult** Only a few students passed the stiff examination.	2. *easy, lax, simple*
	3.	*adj.*	**formal, stilted, constrained, unnatural** The speaker's stiff speech showed he was nervous.	3. *relaxed, unceremonious*

Word	No.	Part	Synonyms / Example	Antonyms
	4.	*adj.*	**obstinate, stubborn, headstrong** The government's proposal received stiff opposition from the people.	4. *weak, yielding*
	5.	*adj.*	**potent, strong, powerful, hard** Stiff winds caused high waves on the lake.	5. *gentle, soft*
still	1.	*adj.*	**hushed, quiet, silent, calm, tranquil, peaceful, serene** An owl's hoot broke the still night.	1. *noisy, turbulent*
	2.	*adj.*	**motionless** The boat couldn't sail in the still waters of the lake. *adv.* The child was told to stand still.	2. *moving*
stimulate		*v.*	**stir, rouse, excite, kindle, foster, spur, invigorate, exhilarate** That movie stimulated my curiosity about the Orient.	*curb, restrict, hinder, impede*
stimulus		*n.*	**incentive, motive, inducement** Winning the first game of the season was a stimulus to the team.	*preventive, obstruction*
stingy		*adj.*	**miserly, closefisted, tightfisted, grasping, penny-pinching** At the outset of the famous novel, Scrooge is a stingy person.	*liberal, generous, lavish, unsparing, bountiful*
stop	1.	*v.*	**cease, quit, terminate, halt, discontinue** Please stop complaining. *n.* Police are trying to put a stop to drunk driving.	1. *begin, start, commence, continue*
	2.	*v.*	**stay, pause, rest, remain** Let's stop at this restaurant.	2. *continue, proceed, advance*
	3.	*v.*	**halt, arrest, block, check, suspend, detain** Will the police stop the fugitive?	3. *expedite, assist, release*
	4.	*v.*	**prevent, obstruct, hinder** A severe storm stopped all incoming flights from landing.	4. *promote, advance, assist*
stormy	1.	*adj.*	**blustery, inclement, turbulent, rough** The canoe capsized in the stormy weather.	1. *clement, mild*
	2.	*adj.*	**wild, fierce, violent, raging, turbulent** There was a stormy meeting about the proposal to close down the school.	2. *gentle, composed, serene, peaceful*

Word	No.	Part	Synonyms / Example	Antonyms
story		*n.*	**tale, narrative, article, account, report, anecdote** Have you read the story of the space launch?	
stout	1.	*adj.*	**fat, plump, corpulent, portly, heavy, thickset** Shakespeare's famous character Falstaff was stout.	**1.** *slender, thin, lean, slight, frail, puny*
	2.	*adj.*	**sturdy, strong, well-built, firm, durable, tough, solid** Stout beams support the weight of the building.	**2.** *fragile, weak*
	3.	*adj.*	**brave, bold, courageous, valiant, dauntless, resolute** The soldier praised those of stout heart who died in battle.	**3.** *timid, fearful, cowardly*
straight	1.	*adj.*	**unbent, plumb, even, level, unswerving** Draw a straight line.	**1.** *bent, curved, crooked*
	2.	*adj.*	**clear, direct, frank, honest, reliable, correct** Give me a straight answer to the question.	**2.** *indirect, evasive*
	3.	*adj.*	**undiluted, unmixed, pure** That glass contains straight orange juice.	**3.** *diluted, mixed*
	4.	*adj.*	**directly, without interruption** Steffanie went straight home after school.	
strange	1.	*adj.*	**odd, peculiar, unusual, queer, exceptional, uncommon, unfamiliar, irregular** People report seeing strange flying objects in the night.	**1.** *usual, common, commonplace, customary, familiar*
	2.	*adj.*	**foreign, alien, unaccustomed, unknown, unfamiliar** Marco Polo travelled to strange lands. *n.* He was a stranger in Cathay.	**2.** *familiar*
strategy		*n.*	**tactics, plan, procedure** Napoleon was brilliant with regard to military strategies.	
strength		*n.*	**vigour, vitality, robustness, sturdiness, power, force** Much strength is required to swim across the English Channel.	*weakness, frailty, feebleness*

Entry	No.	Part	Synonyms / Example	Antonyms
strenuous		*adj.*	**vigorous, arduous, demanding, exhausting, laborious** Strenuous exercises were part of the daily routine.	*easy, relaxing, undemanding*
stress	1.	*n.*	**importance, significance, weight, emphasis** How much stress is put on academic achievement? *v.* The school program stressed the arts.	1. *insignificance, irrelevance*
	2.	*n.*	**pressure, strain, tension, anxiety** He quit the job because he couldn't cope with the stress. *adj.* The job was too stressful.	2. *peace, quiet, tranquility, ease*
	3.	*n.*	**tension, strain, pressure, tautness, pull, force** Constant stress on the cable caused it to snap.	3. *release, relaxation*
stretch	1.	*n.*	**expanse, tract, extent, length** The travellers drove across a vast stretch of desert.	
	2.	*v.*	**expand, extend, increase** Nylon stockings can stretch to fit any size.	2. *contract, shrink*
	3.	*v.*	**occupy, spread over, extend** The prairies stretched as far as the mountains.	
strict		*adj.*	**severe, stern, rigid, stringent, austere, exact** Schools must have strict safety rules.	*easy, lax, loose, inexact, lenient*
strife	1.	*n.*	**quarrel, discord, disagreement, dispute, altercation, dissension** The building of a fence caused much strife between the neighbours.	1. *agreement, concurrence, harmony*
	2.	*n.*	**war, battle, fight, struggle** Many lives were lost in the strife between the nations.	
strike	1.	*n.*	**walkout, boycott, work stoppage** Will there be a strike by the employees? *v.* The employees struck for better working conditions.	
	2.	*n.*	**blow, hit, slap, punch, stroke, thump** The boxer landed many strikes to his opponent's body. *v.* The fighter struck her opponent.	2. *caress*
	3.	*v.*	**find, discover, uncover, expose** The prospectors finally struck gold. *n.* What a lucky strike!	3. *miss, overlook, lose*

Word	No.	Part	Synonyms / Example	Antonyms
	4.	*v.*	**begin, start, establish** They struck up a firm friendship after one meeting.	4. *end, terminate*
	5.	*v.*	**impress** That strikes me as a bad plan.	
	6.	*v.*	**light, kindle, ignite, scratch** Strike a match and light the candles.	6. *extinguish, douse, put out, squelch*
strive		*v.*	**try, endeavour, attempt, aim, venture, compete for, aspire** Su strove to be an honour student.	*give up, quit*
strong	1.	*adj.*	**robust, sturdy, powerful, vigorous, hardy, forceful, mighty, brawny** Three strong horses hauled the load.	1. *feeble, weak, powerless, delicate*
	2.	*adj.*	**solid, firm, durable, stable, tough, steady, well-made, substantial** Space vehicles are made of strong materials.	2. *flimsy, insubstantial*
	3.	*adj.*	**powerful, potent, acute, intense** This cheese has a strong smell.	3. *mild, bland, delicate*
stubborn		*adj.*	**obstinate, unyielding, pigheaded, determined, headstrong** The stubborn child would not budge when told to go to bed.	*pliant, flexible, agreeable*
student		*n.*	**pupil, trainee, learner** The college students are preparing for their final examinations.	*teacher, instructor*
stumble		*v.*	**trip, fall, falter, lurch, flounder, topple, slip** The skater stumbled and fell. *n.* The stumble cost him some marks.	*be steady*
stun	1.	*v.*	**knock out, daze** The boxer stunned his opponent with a blow.	1. *stimulate, revive*
	2.	*v.*	**surprise, astonish, amaze** Paul was stunned when he won the lottery. *adj.* It was a stunning win.	
stupendous	1.	*adj.*	**breathtaking, marvellous, amazing, overwhelming** The Egyptian pyramids are a stupendous sight.	1. *unimpressive, ordinary, mediocre*
	2.	*adj.*	**enormous, immense, colossal** We hope to be able to pay off our stupendous debt.	2. *minute, tiny, small*
stupid	1.	*adj.*	**dull, dense, unintelligent** Is any one animal more stupid than another?	1. *bright, quick, sharp, clever, intelligent*

	2.	*adj.*	**foolish, silly, senseless, absurd, ridiculous, daft, ill-advised, inane, unwise, nonsensical** It is stupid to cross a street without looking in both directions. *adv.* The child stupidly dashed across the street without checking for traffic. *n.* He was punished for his stupidity.	**2.** *wise, sensible, judicious, sane*
sturdy	1.	*adj.*	**hardy, husky, robust, strong, powerful, firm** Athletes have sturdy bodies.	**1.** *weak, frail, fragile, delicate*
	2.	*adj.*	**durable, tough, long-wearing** Hotels need sturdy furniture.	**2.** *fragile, delicate, unsubstantial*
	3.	*adj.*	**firm, stubborn, unyielding, resolute, determined, steadfast, steady, definite, unchanging** The witness's sturdy denial impressed the jury.	**3.** *inconstant, fickle, vacillating, shifting, changeable, capricious, uncertain*
style	1.	*n.*	**way, form, manner, method, technique** The Beatles had a distinctive style of singing.	
	2.	*n.*	**fashion, vogue, mode, habit, custom** Some people always dress in the latest styles. *adj.* These people are stylish.	
subdue	1.	*v.*	**tame, master, overcome, quell, conquer, suppress, vanquish** Alexander the Great subdued many enemies.	**1.** *yield, succumb, surrender, give up*
	2.	*v.*	**hold in check, handle, repress, restrain, contain, control, curb** He subdued his temper and spoke calmly.	**2.** *release, liberate, free, be overcome by*
subject	1.	*n.*	**topic, theme, matter, substance** Decide on the subject of your essay.	
	2.	*v.*	**control, tame, subordinate, subjugate, dominate, suppress** The dictator subjected the people into subservience.	**2.** *liberate, free, release, rescue*
submerge	1.	*v.*	**engulf, swamp, inundate, flood, immerse, submerse** The tidal wave submerged the village.	
	2.	*v.*	**sink, descend into water** Scuba divers submerged to investigate the coral reef.	**2.** *rise, emerge, surface*

Word			Synonyms	Antonyms
submit	**1.**	*v.*	**offer, tender, present, send in** Applications must be submitted promptly.	**1.** *withdraw, take back*
	2.	*v.*	**surrender, yield, cede, obey** The company submitted to the workers' demand for a pay raise. *n.* The submission by the company prevented a strike.	**2.** *hold fast, oppose, disobey, retaliate*
subsequent		*adj.*	**following, succeeding, later, ensuing** A new cast will perform at subsequent shows.	*previous, prior, former, earlier*
subside		*v.*	**dwindle, ebb, recede, sink, fall, abate, wane** The seas became calmer as the winds subsided.	*increase, rise, swell*
substance	**1.**	*n.*	**material, matter** The new sink is made of a strong substance that will not scratch.	
	2.	*n.*	**essence, main point** The substance of the president's speech was that peace is vital.	
	3.	*n.*	**wealth, property, affluence** He comes from a family of substance.	
substantial	**1.**	*adj.*	**strong, solid, firm** Tall buildings require substantial foundations.	**1.** *insubstantial, weak*
	2.	*adj.*	**considerable, ample, large, abundant, plentiful** Substantial donations were given to the charity.	**2.** *small, meagre, insignificant*
	3.	*adj.*	**important, valuable, principal** The mayor plays a substantial role in the community.	**3.** *unimportant, secondary, trivial*
	4.	*adj.*	**wealthy, rich, well-to-do, affluent** A millionaire is a person of substantial means.	**4.** *poor, humble, ordinary*
substitute		*v.*	**replace, represent, stand for, take the place of** The designated hitter substituted for the weak batter. *n.* Margarine is a substitute for butter.	
subtle	**1.**	*adj.*	**inferred, indirect, implied, insinuated** Her subtle frown told us she was displeased with the situation.	**1.** *open, frank, blunt, obvious*

	2.	*adj.*	**faint, light, delicate, fine, slight** There is a subtle difference between the styles of these two writers.	2. *heavy, strong*
	3.	*adj.*	**discerning, acute, keen** His subtle observations made him a well-respected journalist.	3. *rough, simple*
	4.	*adj.*	**sly, cunning, crafty** He has a subtle way of getting what he wants.	
succeed	1.	*v.*	**prosper, thrive, flourish, achieve, score, gain, triumph, accomplish** I intend to make this business succeed. *n.* The reason for her success is hard work. *adj.* Running a successful business takes a lot of time.	1. *fail, deteriorate, decline, diminish, lessen*
	2.	*v.*	**follow, come after, supplant, replace, displace, become heir to** Queen Elizabeth II succeeded her father as sovereign. *n.* She was the successor to the throne.	2. *precede, come before*
sudden		*adj.*	**hasty, quick, abrupt, swift, impromptu, fast, rapid, unexpected, unpremeditated, instantaneous** Our car came to a sudden stop when the light turned amber.	*slow, sluggish, premeditated*
suffer	1.	*v.*	**endure, bear, sustain, put up with, undergo, experience** Many people suffered hardships during the war.	1. *be relieved, be restored, recover*
	2.	*v.*	**allow, permit, authorize** "I will not suffer any laziness from my students," said the teacher.	2. *forbid, reject, exclude, expel, disallow*
sufficient		*adj.*	**enough, adequate, satisfactory amount** There's sufficient food for all the guests.	*inadequate, insufficient, deficient*
suggestion	1.	*n.*	**proposal, plan, proposition, recommendation** The teacher listened to the students' suggestions. *v.* They suggested ways to raise funds to help the poor.	
	2.	*n.*	**hint, trace, insinuation, tinge** Everyone was shocked when the company collapsed because there had been no suggestion of trouble.	

Word			Synonyms	Antonyms
suitable		*adj.*	**becoming, proper, fitting, appropriate** Suitable attire is required at the dance. *adv.* Guests must be suitably dressed.	*inappropriate, improper, unbecoming*
sullen		*adj.*	**glum, morose, grouchy, grumpy, sour, surly, unsociable** Everyone left Sheen alone when they saw her sullen face.	*friendly, happy, sociable, pleasant*
summit		*n.*	**top, zenith, apex, crown, peak, pinnacle, culmination, climax** Winning an Oscar is the summit of an actor's career.	*low point, starting point, bottom, start, beginning*
sunny	1.	*adj.*	**bright** Plants grow best in sunny areas.	**1.** *dark, dull, shady, overcast, gloomy*
	2.	*adj.*	**cheerful, cheery, happy, gay** Jen is well-liked because of her sunny disposition.	**2.** *miserable, sullen, morose, grouchy, grumpy, glum*
superb		*adj.*	**magnificent, splendid, elegant, grand, exquisite** The band put on a superb performance.	*plain, ordinary, common, unimposing*
superficial	1.	*adj.*	**exterior, shallow, surface, skin-deep** The cat's claw made a superficial scratch.	**1.** *deep, deep-seated, serious*
	2.	*adj.*	**shallow, cursory** Superficial friends disappear in times of trouble.	**2.** *profound, deep*
superfluous		*adj.*	**excessive, redundant, surplus, unnecessary** He was told to edit the superfluous words in his essay.	*essential, necessary*
supple		*adj.*	**flexible, pliable, pliant, yielding, elastic, limber** The gymnast has a supple body.	*firm, inflexible, unyielding, stiff, rigid*
supplement		*v.*	**augment, add to, fortify, enrich, increase, strengthen** Dot supplemented her income with a second job. *adj.* She needed the supplementary income to put herself through school. *n.* Some breakfast cereals contain vitamin supplements.	*lessen, deplete*

Word			Synonyms	Antonyms
supply		*v.*	**provide, give, furnish, outfit, contribute, fulfil, satisfy** The people supplied the victims of the tornado with food and clothes. *n.* Supplies poured in from all parts of the country.	*withhold, retain, withdraw, demand*
support	1.	*n*	**aid, assistance, help, comfort, cooperation** Give the committee your support. *v.* Many people support charities.	**1.** *opposition, hindrance, discouragement*
	2.	*v.*	**hold up, prop, sustain, bear, shoulder, shore up, uphold, brace** The legs of a table support its weight. *n.* Legs are supports for tabletops.	**2.** *drop, let go, release*
	3.	*v.*	**nourish, maintain, provide for, take care of, sponsor, pay for, subsidize, finance, nurture** Ellie makes enough money to support herself and her child.	**3.** *abandon, neglect, hinder, fail, ignore, thwart*
	4.	*v.*	**defend, stand by, promote** How many voters will support this candidate? *n.* Her supporters cheered when she won the election.	**4.** *oppose, disfavour, discourage, subvert*
suppose		*v.*	**assume, conjecture, surmise, theorize, presume, believe, deem, think** Do you suppose that our team will win tomorrow?	*be certain, know, prove, substantiate*
suppress	1.	*v.*	**crush, defeat, overpower, put down, subdue, quell** Troops were sent to suppress the revolt.	**1.** *surrender, submit, join, support*
	2.	*v.*	**ban, withhold, conceal, hide** The government suppressed the news about the uprising.	**2.** *disclose, release, publish*
	3.	*v.*	**check, hold back, restrain** Nan suppressed a yawn during the boring speech.	**3.** *release, let out*
supreme		*adj.*	**highest, chief, paramount, top, principal, prime, utmost** Final judgments are made by the supreme court of the land.	*lowest*
sure	1.	*adj.*	**certain, assured, confident, convinced, positive** I'm sure that she will do well in her new job. *adv.* She will surely do well.	**1.** *doubtful, dubious, unsure, uncertain*

	2.	*adj.*	**inevitable, unavoidable, certain, indisputable, infallible, unmistakable** Coastal areas are sure to be hit by the hurricane.	2. *avoidable, uncertain, dubious, disputable, doubtful*
surface		*n.*	**outside, exterior** Aluminum siding covered the surface of the house.	*inside, interior*
surly		*adj.*	**sullen, morose, irritable, uncivil, testy, discourteous, irascible** We did not leave a tip for the surly waiter.	*affable, sociable, civil, courteous, pleasant*
surplus		*n.*	**excess, extra, glut, oversupply** There was a surplus of corn in this year's harvest. *adj.* The surplus corn was donated to the poor nations.	*insufficiency, dearth, scarcity, deficiency*
surprise		*n.*	**astonishment, amazement, wonder, shock** That news came as a surprise. *adj.* It is surprising news! *v.* The news surprised us. *adv.* The news came surprisingly fast.	*expectation, anticipation*
surrender		*v.*	**give in, give up, submit, yield, capitulate, cede, relinquish** The escaped convict surrendered to the police.	*fight, conquer, subdue, win, suppress*
surround		*v.*	**enclose, encircle, circle, girdle, shut in, envelop, hem in, wall in** Bodyguards surrounded the President.	*free, open, liberate*
surroundings		*n.*	**area, neighbourhood, vicinity, environment** We were enchanted by the beautiful surroundings of the Lake District.	
survey		*n.*	**review, study, examination, critique, investigation** A survey will be made to determine the needs of the elderly. *v.* A committee will survey their needs.	
suspicious	1.	*adj.*	**questionable, doubtful, suspect, open to question** There's something suspicious about that person!	1. *dependable, reliable, trustworthy*

Word	No.	Part	Synonyms / Example	Antonyms
	2.	*adj.*	**distrustful, suspecting, doubting, doubtful, dubious** Are you suspicious of that person's intentions?	**2.** *trusting, trustful, undoubting*
sustain	1.	*v.*	**bear, support, hold up** Bridges sustain the weight of heavy traffic.	**1.** *drop, abandon, collapse*
	2.	*v.*	**nourish, provide food for, maintain, prolong** Soil, water, and sunlight sustain plant life.	**2.** *starve, neglect*
	3.	*v.*	**suffer, experience, undergo, endure** The company sustained major losses in the recession.	
sweet	1.	*adj.*	**pleasant, agreeable, pleasing, winning, engaging, considerate** What a sweet disposition that child has!	**1.** *disagreeable, repulsive, inconsiderate*
	2.	*adj.*	**unsalted, uncured, unseasoned, fresh** "Isn't that sweet butter?"	**2.** *cured, salted, seasoned, pickled, briny*
	3.	*adj.*	**sugary, candied, rich** Sweet foods are not good for the teeth.	**3.** *sour, bitter, sharp*
swell		*v.*	**inflate, rise, expand, bloat, dilate, distend, increase, enlarge, grow, inflate, amplify, extend, distend, augment** Heavy rains swelled the rivers. *adj.* The swollen rivers overflowed their banks.	*shrink, dwindle, deflate, contract, recede, decrease, shrivel, diminish, lessen, reduce*
swift		*adj.*	**quick, fast, rapid, fleet, speedy** Sam could not keep up with Tim's swift pace. *adv.* Who runs most swiftly?	*slow, tardy, sluggish*
sympathy		*n.*	**compassion, understanding, condolence, pity, empathy, commiseration** People often express their sympathy by sending flowers. *v.* Everyone sympathized with Tzen when he broke his collar bone.	*antipathy, antagonism, harshness, unkindness, coldness*
synthetic	1.	*adj.*	**artificial, false, phony, counterfeit** Synthetic jewels can look realistic.	**1.** *real, actual, genuine*

	2.	*adj.*	**chemically made, unnatural, manufactured** Many modern materials are made from synthetic fibres.	2. *natural*
system	1.	*n.*	**method, mode, way, scheme, policy, usage, custom, practice, procedure** The coach has a unique system for training our swim team.	1. *confusion, muddle, tangle*
	2.	*n.*	**organization, order, sequence, orderliness, regularity, rule, conformity, definite plan, arrangement** Earth is one planet in the solar system. *adj.* Are the planets arranged in a systematic way?	2. *disorder, confusion, derangement, unconformity*
systematize		*v.*	**plan, arrange, order, organize, design, arrange, put in order** The computer systematized the data.	*confuse, jumble, disorder, disorganize*

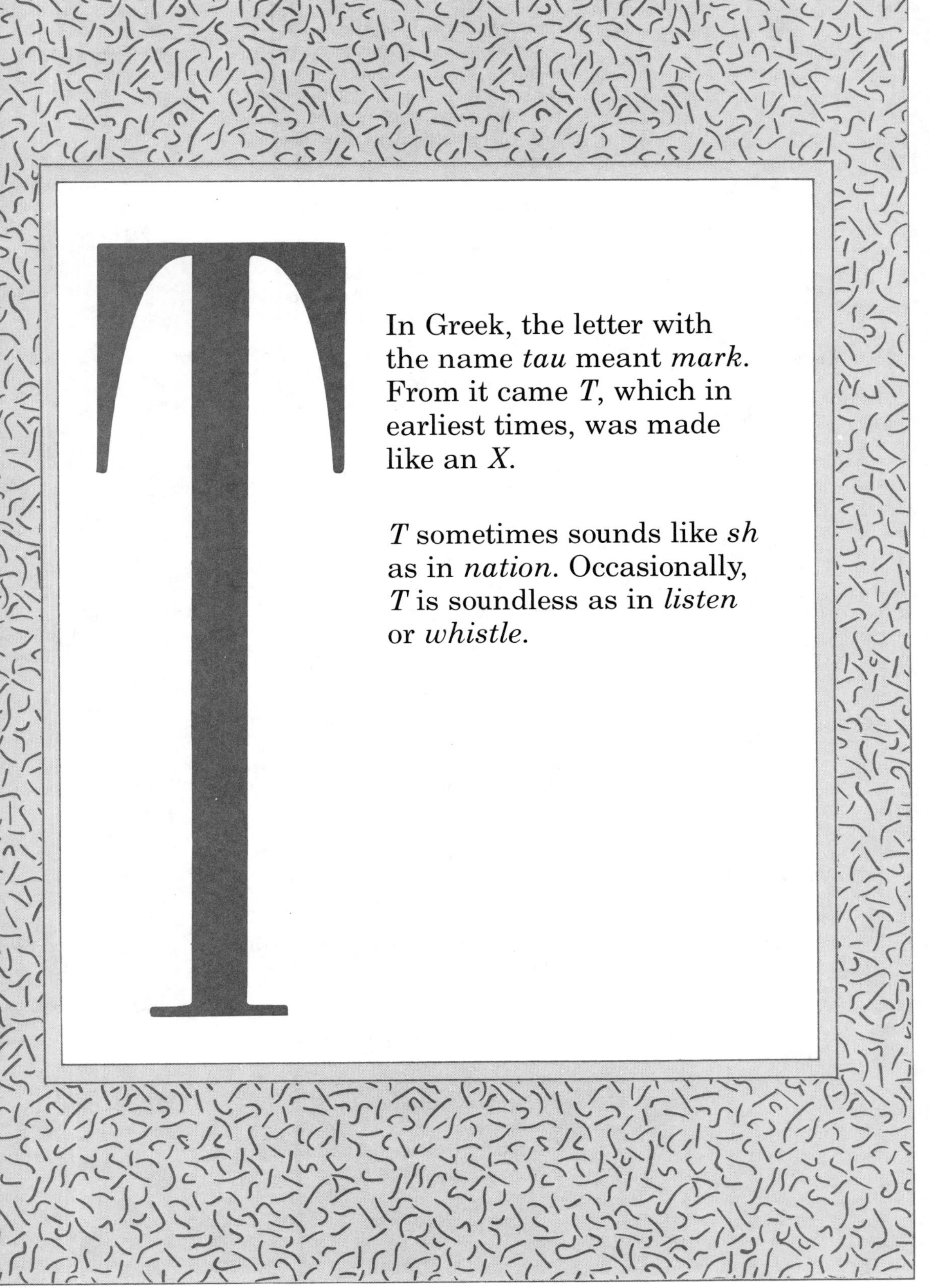

In Greek, the letter with the name *tau* meant *mark*. From it came *T*, which in earliest times, was made like an *X*.

T sometimes sounds like *sh* as in *nation*. Occasionally, *T* is soundless as in *listen* or *whistle*.

Word			Synonyms	Antonyms
taboo		*v.*	**prohibit, forbid, disallow, ban** Some religious laws taboo the eating of meat. *n.* The eating of meat is a taboo for the followers of some religions. *adj.* Going out undressed is taboo in our society.	*allow, permit, sanction, legalize*
tact		*n.*	**discretion, delicacy, feeling, finesse, diplomacy** Some situations must be handled with a great deal of tact. *adj.* Sara is such a tactful person. *adv.* She handles people tactfully.	*crudeness, indiscretion*
tactics		*n.*	**way, method, policy, scheme, approach, manoeuvres** He used delaying tactics to avoid paying his bills.	
talent		*n.*	**skill, gift, ability, capability, aptitude, flair** Huei-Tjin has a talent for drawing. *adj.* She is a talented artist.	*inability, incapability*
talk	1.	*n.*	**conversation, chat, discussion** They had a long talk about their future plans.	
	2.	*n.*	**gossip, chatter, hearsay, rumour** There has been a lot of talk about building a new school.	
	3.	*n.*	**speech, address, oration, lecture** The science talk was about amphibians.	
	4.	*v.*	**lecture, deliver a speech** The missionary talked about his work in Africa.	**4.** *listen*
	5.	*v.*	**discuss, chat, speak, converse** The former classmates talked about old times at the school reunion.	
talkative		*adj.*	**chatty, gabby, wordy, loquacious** The talkative child was told to keep quiet in the library.	*quiet, silent, taciturn, mute*
tall	1.	*adj.*	**high, lofty, elevated, towering** The city is crowded with tall buildings.	**1.** *low, short, squat*
	2.	*adj.*	**farfetched, outlandish, exaggerated** His claim that he had found a pot of gold was dismissed as a tall tale.	**2.** *realistic, believable*

Word		Part	Synonyms and Example	Antonyms
tame		*adj.*	**domesticated, docile, obedient** Dogs and cats are tame animals. *v.* The trainer tamed the wild tiger. *n.* The lion tamer cracked his whip.	*wild, fierce, uncontrollable*
tangible	1.	*adj.*	**material, solid, physical, concrete** Houses and cars are tangible assets.	**1.** *intangible, spiritual, ethereal*
	2.	*adj.*	**actual, definite, real, positive** He had no tangible proof that the suspect had robbed him.	**2.** *imaginary*
tantalize		*v.*	**tease, torment, plague, taunt** Never tantalize caged animals.	*calm, soothe, comfort*
tardy		*adj.*	**late, slow, sluggish** The tardy sales clerk annoyed the customers. *n.* Many customers left because of the sales clerk's tardiness.	*prompt, punctual, quick, early*
tasteful		*adj.*	**exquisite, beautiful, pleasing, elegant, well-chosen** The designer's tasteful clothes are always popular. *adv.* Their home is tastefully decorated.	*displeasing, inappropriate, unbecoming, tasteless*
tasty		*adj.*	**palatable, savoury, delicious, delectable, appetizing** Dad baked a tasty pie for dessert.	*tasteless, insipid, unappetizing*
taunt		*v.*	**insult, tease, mock, jeer, scoff, ridicule** The children taunted Terry because he couldn't swim.	*applaud, praise, encourage, humour*
tear	1.	*n.*	**rip, split, slit, rent, hole** There is a tear in your green shirt.	**1.** *patch*
	2.	*v.*	**rip, split, slit, shred, lacerate** She angrily tore up the letter.	**2.** *patch, sew, mend*
	3.	*v.*	**snatch, grab, pull, yank, seize** The purse was torn from her hand by the thief.	
	4.	*v.*	**race, run, rush, dash, hustle, speed, fly, scramble** The boys tore down the street to catch the bus.	**4.** *stroll, saunter, walk*
tease		*v.*	**taunt, tantalize, annoy, irritate, badger, irk, aggravate, disturb, torment, goad, bother** The bully teased the children and made them cry.	*comfort, please, calm, soothe, encourage, console*

Word		Part of speech	Synonyms	Antonyms
tedious		*adj.*	**tiresome, wearisome, dull, boring, slow, monotonous, humdrum** He quit his tedious job on the assembly line.	*entertaining, amusing, interesting, fascinating, exciting*
teenager		*n.*	**adolescent, teen, youth** Teenagers are people between the ages of thirteen and nineteen.	
tell	**1.**	*v.*	**distinguish, identify** Can you tell the twins apart?	**1.** *confuse, mix up*
	2.	*v.*	**reveal, relate, inform, narrate, disclose, say, mention, impart** Mom told us that she was expecting a baby.	**2.** *keep secret, be silent*
temper	**1.**	*n.*	**calm, composure, balance** Rita lost her temper when she saw the child hurt the puppy.	
	2.	*n.*	**anger, bad humour, rage, fury, irritation, wrath, annoyance** He needs help to control his frequent bursts of temper.	**2.** *composure, good humour, patience*
	3.	*v.*	**moderate, soften** The judge tempered justice with mercy in passing sentence on the thief.	**3.** *violate, injure, attack*
	4.	*v.*	**harden, strengthen, toughen** Intense heat and sudden cooling is required to temper steel.	**4.** *weaken, soften*
temperamental		*adj.*	**excitable, headstrong, emotional, high-strung, sensitive, erratic, moody, impulsive, unpredictable** The temperamental movie star stormed off the set in a huff.	*easygoing, calm, cool, even-tempered*
temperate		*adj.*	**moderate, gentle, mild, clement, pleasant, balmy** Florida is famous for its temperate climate.	*severe, harsh*
temporary		*adj.*	**brief, transient, short-lived** The power cut-off is only temporary.	*permanent, lasting*
tempt		*v.*	**entice, lure, attract, captivate** The witch tempted Snow White with a red apple. *n.* Snow White could not resist the temptation.	*repulse*

Word			Synonyms / Example	Antonyms
tenacious		*adj.*	**firm, persistent, determined, stubborn, obstinate, steadfast, resolute** Matt clings to the tenacious belief that he will recover soon.	*irresolute, wavering, flexible*
tendency		*n.*	**inclination, habit, disposition, leaning** Ray has a tendency to act rashly.	*reluctance*
tender	1.	*adj.*	**gentle, kind, loving, sympathetic, solicitous, compassionate** The nurse treats the patients with tender care.	1. *harsh, severe, unkind, cruel*
	2.	*adj.*	**delicate, fragile, frail, weak, soft** Young plants have tender stems.	2. *strong, sturdy, tough*
	3.	*adj.*	**painful, sore, sensitive** The pitcher's arm is tender after the long game.	3. *painless*
tense	1.	*adj.*	**anxious, nervous, strained, on edge, jittery, excited** Everyone was tense as we waited for the election results to be announced.	1. *relaxed, calm*
	2.	*adj.*	**tight, taut, stiff** The athlete did exercises to relax his tense muscles.	2. *relaxed, flaccid*
tension	1.	*n.*	**stretch, stress, pressure, tautness** The sewing machine has a device for adjusting the tension of the thread.	1. *slack, looseness*
	2.	*n.*	**strain, anxiety, apprehension, stress, pressure, nervousness** The class was under much tension on the day of the examination.	2. *relief, ease, calm, relaxation*
terminate	1.	*v.*	**end, conclude, finish, close, stop** Our apartment lease terminates in September.	1. *open, begin, start, commence*
	2.	*v.*	**cancel, abolish, annul, revoke, invalidate** We terminated our contract with the company because of poor service. *n.* The company sued us for the termination of the contract.	2. *validate, sanction, permit*
terrible		*adj.*	**horrible, frightful, dreadful, awful, shocking, terrifying** Terrible typhoons occur in the South China Sea.	*pleasing, appealing, pleasant, welcome*
terrific		*adj.*	**terrible, frightening, terrifying** Terrific waves pounded the shore during the storm.	*mild, insignificant, conventional, ordinary*

Word			Synonyms	Antonyms
terrify		*v.*	**upset, frighten, scare, alarm, shock, horrify** The huge dog terrified the little boy.	*reassure, encourage, comfort, calm*
terror		*n.*	**panic, anxiety, dread, fear, fright, alarm, horror** The eruption of the volcano filled the villagers with terror.	*courage, unconcern, security, comfort, calm*
test	1.	*n.*	**examination, trial, quiz** Vera passed the driver's test and got a licence to drive.	
	2.	*v.*	**try, examine, inspect, analyse** Dad tested the well water before the family drank it.	
thankful		*adj.*	**grateful, obliged, appreciative** We are so thankful for your help.	*ungrateful, unappreciative*
thaw	1.	*v.*	**melt, liquefy, dissolve, soften** The warm temperatures thawed the ice and snow. *n.* The thaw caused flooding.	**1.** *freeze, harden, solidify, congeal*
	2.	*v.*	**open up, relent, grow genial** Relations between the two countries thawed after the leaders met.	**2.** *harden, grow cool*
theft		*n.*	**robbery, burglary, piracy, stealing, thievery, pilfering** The man will be charged with the theft of the jewels.	
theory		*n.*	**concept, idea, plan, scheme, hypothesis, principle** Darwin's theory of evolution is still debated today.	*application, proof*
thick	1.	*adj.*	**heavy, dense, close, profuse, packed** Thick forest once covered many areas of Canada.	**1.** *thin, sparse, scanty*
	2.	*adj.*	**broad, wide, deep** It will take me many days to read this thick book.	**2.** *narrow, thin*
thin	1.	*v.*	**dilute, water down** The painter thinned the paint with turpentine.	**1.** *thicken*
	2.	*adj.*	**slim, slender, slight, lean, lank, gaunt, skinny** Jan is quite thin since her illness.	**2.** *fat, bulky, obese, pudgy, plump*
	3.	*adj.*	**skimpy, light, flimsy** Biz shivered under her thin dress.	**3.** *thick, ample*

Entry	No.	Part of speech	Synonyms and example	Antonyms
	4.	*adj.*	**weak, flimsy** We did not believe his thin excuse for missing school. *adv.* He showed his arrogance through his thinly-veiled sneer.	**4.** *solid, substantial, valid*
	5.	*adj.*	**sparse, meagre, scanty** How can I fluff up my thin hair?	**5.** *thick, dense, packed*
think	1.	*v.*	**ponder, meditate, reflect, consider, reason** Ken thought carefully about his choice of a university.	
	2.	*v.*	**believe, feel, judge, deem** We think that you should tell her the truth.	
thorough	1.	*adj.*	**complete, full, perfect** Do you have a thorough understanding of this play? *adv.* The students were thoroughly drilled in safety procedures.	**1.** *incomplete, imperfect, partial*
	2.	*adj.*	**careful, meticulous, detailed** Pat did a thorough research on the subject before writing her paper.	**2.** *careless*
thought	1.	*n.*	**idea, view, notion, opinion, conclusion** Do you have any thoughts about your future?	
	2.	*n.*	**concern, caring, kindness, regard, consideration** It's the thought, not the gift, that's important.	**2.** *unconcern, disregard*
thoughtful		*adj.*	**considerate, kind, caring** My thoughtful neighbour brought me some soup when I was ill.	*thoughtless, inconsiderate*
thrifty		*adj.*	**frugal, economical, sparing, penny-wise** It is wise to be thrifty when buying food and other necessities.	*wasteful, extravagant, spendthrift*
thrill	1.	*n.*	**glow, tingle, rush, quiver, tremor** We felt a thrill of excitement when the space shuttle took off.	
	2.	*v.*	**excite, arouse, stir, delight** The whole family was thrilled when the new baby arrived.	**2.** *calm, soothe, bore*
thrive	1.	*v.*	**flourish, bloom, grow well** Most plants thrive in sunny areas.	**1.** *die, fade, wither*

Word			Synonyms	Antonyms
	2.	*v.*	**succeed, prosper, flourish, boom** I hope the store will thrive in the new location. *adj.* It should be a thriving business.	2. *fail*
throw		*v.*	**hurl, fling, thrust, pitch, toss, sling, cast, heave** The pitcher threw the ball wildly to second base. *n.* It was a wild throw.	*catch, receive, grab, trap*
thwart		*v.*	**stop, hinder, check, obstruct, prevent, foil** The club members thwarted Rick's plans to become president.	*help, aid, support, encourage*
tidy	1.	*v.*	**clean up, arrange, put in order, straighten** Did you tidy your room this morning?	1. *mess up, disarrange*
	2.	*adj.*	**neat, orderly, trim, well-kept** Ali has a tidy desk.	2. *sloppy, messy, unkempt, untidy*
tight	1.	*adj.*	**firm, taut, secure, fast** The police held onto the robber with a tight grip. *v.* He tightened his grip when the robber struggled. *adv.* He clutched the robber tightly.	1. *slack, loose, shaky*
	2.	*adj.*	**snug, close, narrow, too small** Jim's new shoes are too tight.	2. *loose, large, oversized, wide*
	3.	*adj.*	**scarce, scant, deficient** We had to cancel the trip as money was tight.	3. *ample, plentiful, abundant*
timely		*adj.*	**well-timed, suitable, appropriate, opportune** The timely arrival of the police prevented a riot.	*inopportune, untimely, unsuitable inconvenient*
timid		*adj.*	**shy, afraid, fearful, cowardly** The timid child would not play with the other children. *n.* He must overcome his timidity. *adv.* He hid timidly behind his parents.	*brave, daring, confident, outgoing*
tiny		*adj.*	**small, little, wee, minute** Just look at the baby's tiny toes!	*immense, large, enormous, huge, big*
tire	1.	*v.*	**weary, exhaust, fatigue, wear out** The long flight from Hong Kong to Vancouver tired the travellers. *adj.* The tired travellers went to bed.	1. *refresh, invigorate, stimulate*

Word	No.	Part	Synonyms / Example	Antonyms
	2.	*v.*	**bore, irritate, annoy, disgust** They tired us with their constant complaining.	2. *excite, inspire, interest, please*
tiresome		*adj.*	**irksome, boring, wearisome, tedious, exhausting** It was tiresome to listen to such a long speech.	*inspiring, interesting, invigorating, stimulating*
toil	1.	*n.*	**work, labour, task, effort, drudgery, hardship** The workers received very little pay for their toil.	1. *idleness, leisure, rest, play*
	2.	*v.*	**work, labour, slave** The farmers toiled in the fields for long hours.	2. *rest, idle, relax*
tolerate		*v.*	**permit, allow, bear, endure** Our teacher does not tolerate any nonsense.	*disallow, prohibit, prevent, oppose*
top	1.	*n.*	**summit, head, crown, zenith, apex, crest, tip, peak** They climbed to the top of the tower.	1. *base, bottom, foundation*
	2.	*n.*	**lid, cap, cover** Did you tear off the box top?	2. *bottom*
	3.	*v.*	**surpass, exceed, better, outdo** To date, no one has topped Tzen's backstroke record.	
	4.	*adj.*	**highest, uppermost** Put the books on the top shelf.	4. *lowest*
	5.	*adj.*	**best, foremost, leading** Abe is the top student in the class.	5. *worst*
topic		*n.*	**subject, theme, text** The topic of my project is: "Ways to preserve the environment."	
torment		*v.*	**badger, annoy, provoke, plague, torture, distress, pester, irritate** The bully tormented the children in the playground.	*comfort, ease, aid, assist*
torrid		*adj.*	**sultry, tropical, scorching, sweltering** The Sahara is a torrid desert region.	*frigid, freezing*
tough	1.	*adj.*	**obstinate, stubborn, inflexible** Jose is a tough person to convince.	1. *easy, easygoing, mild, gentle*
	2.	*adj.*	**durable, strong, firm, sturdy** The tough cord held the parcel securely.	2. *brittle, fragile, weak*
	3.	*adj.*	**difficult, hard, strenuous, exhausting** Digging that flower bed was a tough job.	3. *easy, simple*

	4.	*adj.*	**hard, sinewy** The steak is too tough to chew.	**4.** *tender, soft*
tour		*n.*	**trip, excursion, journey, visit** They had a tour of Europe last summer. *v.* They toured Europe by car.	
tournament		*n.*	**contest, competition, pageant, match, meet** The tennis tournament is being held in June.	
trace	1.	*n.*	**sign, mark, impression, trail, indication** There was not a trace of the burglars to be found.	
	2.	*v.*	**discover, trail, hunt, track down, seek, look for** The company promised to trace the lost parcel.	
trade	1.	*n.*	**commerce, busines** The fur trade has declined in recent years.	
	2.	*n.*	**occupation, calling, profession, employment, business** Mr. Reed's trade is plumbing.	
	3.	*v.*	**exchange, deal, swap** Ross wants to trade his car for a station wagon. *n.* Will he get a good trade?	
	4.	*v.*	**do business, deal, buy and sell, barter** Canada trades with many nations.	
tradition	1.	*n.*	**practice, habit, custom** It is a tradition in our family to have an annual picnic. *adv.* Traditionally, we hold the picnic on a Sunday.	**1.** *novelty, new ide*
	2.	*n.*	**legend, myth, folklore, fable, superstition** According to Greek tradition, gods and goddesses lived on Mt. Olympus.	**2.** *fact, true story*
tragic		*adj.*	**sad, dreadful, sorrowful, ill-fated** President Kennedy and his brother Robert died tragic deaths. *n.* Their deaths were tragedies. *adv.* They were tragically assassinated.	*happy, joyous, comic, cheerful, pleasant*

Word	No.	Part	Synonyms and example	Antonyms
train	1.	*n.*	**series, string, chain, sequence, succession** The family has been dogged by a train of misfortunes.	
	2.	*v.*	**prepare, practise, drill** She trained for years to be a champion skater.	
trait		*n.*	**quality, feature, characteristic, mark, attribute** Two good traits to have are kindness and dependability.	
traitor		*n.*	**deceiver, renegade, betrayer, hypocrite, false friend** A traitor is one who betrays country or friend.	*patriot, supporter, defender, true friend*
tranquil		*adj.*	**calm, peaceful, quiet, still, placid, restful, undisturbed, serene** They lead a tranquil life in the country. *n.* They lead a life of tranquillity.	*rough, violent, tempestuous, disturbed, agitated*
transform		*v.*	**change, convert, turn, alter** The fairy transformed Cinderella's pumpkin into a carriage. *n.* What a transformation that was!	*maintain, keep, preserve*
transient	1.	*n.*	**traveller, migrant, drifter, visitor** Many farms hire transients at harvest time. *adj.* Transient workers move around the country looking for jobs.	1. *resident*
	2.	*adj.*	**transitory, brief, short-lived, passing, fleeting** Youth and beauty are transient.	2. *permanent, lasting, abiding*
transitory		*adj.*	**temporary, brief, passing, fleeting, short-lived, transient** She had a transitory loss of memory after the accident.	*long, long-lived, lasting, durable, permanent, eternal*
transparent	1.	*adj.*	**clear, lucid, see-through** Glass is transparent.	1. *opaque, muddy*
	2.	*adj.*	**sheer, translucent, gauzy, diaphanous** The living room had soft, transparent curtains.	2. *opaque*
	3.	*adj.*	**plain, apparent, obvious, evident** No one was taken in by their transparent lie.	3. *vague, hidden, obscure, mysterious*

trap	1.	*n.*	**snare, ambush** The farmer set a trap for the fox. *v.* The mice were trapped in a mousetrap.	
	2.	*n.*	**plot, intrigue, ruse, device** The detective's trap fooled the drug dealer.	
trash		*n.*	**garbage, waste, rubbish, refuse, litter, debris** Put that trash in the wastebasket.	*valuables, treasure*
travel	1.	*n.*	**journey, trip, voyage, tour, expedition** Marco Polo wrote fascinating stories about his travels to China. *n.* He was a great traveller.	
	2.	*v.*	**journey, move, proceed, go, progress, rove, tour** We will travel by sea on this trip.	
treacherous	1.	*adj.*	**deceitful, unreliable, disloyal, undependable, unfaithful, false** A traitor is a treacherous person. *n.* Julius Caesar died because of the treachery of Brutus.	**1.** *dependable, loyal, true, reliable, trustworthy*
	2.	*adj.*	**unsafe, risky, hazardous, dangerous** Many accidents occur on this treacherous stretch of road.	**2.** *safe, reliable, secure*
treasure	1.	*n.*	**riches, wealth, loot** Great treasure was found in the sunken Spanish galleon.	**1.** *trash, garbage, junk*
	2.	*v.*	**value, esteem, cherish, prize, regard, care for, love** Di treasures her stamp collection.	**2.** *scorn, disregard*
treat	1.	*n.*	**pleasure, delight** The performance was a real treat for the audience.	
	2.	*v.*	**handle, act toward, manage** This company treats its employees very well. *n.* The employees are satisfied with their treatment.	
treaty		*n.*	**contract, agreement, bargain, promise, pact** The two nations signed a treaty to end the war.	

tremble		*v.*	**shake, quiver, shiver, quake, wobble, shudder** Oliver Twist trembled with fear as he stood before his master.	
tremendous		*adj.*	**huge, enormous, vast, immense, gigantic, colossal, stupendous** We were awed by the tremendous size of the new stadium.	*tiny, minute, small, wee, miniature*
trend	1.	*n.*	**leaning, drift, inclination, tendency** The trend today is toward healthy living.	
	2.	*n.*	**style, fashion, mode, vogue** Movie and rock stars often set the trend for teenage fashion.	
tribute	1.	*n.*	**honour, respect, praise, esteem, gratitude, recognition** The famous violinist paid tribute to her teacher.	**1.** *dishonour, scorn, blame*
	2.	*n.*	**ransom, bribe, payment, toll, settlement, levy** The conquerers demanded tribute from the captured people.	
trick	1.	*n.*	**ruse, device, deception, hoax, ploy, stratagem, wile, gimmick** They played a trick on Fran on April Fool's day.	
	2.	*n.*	**feat, stunt, act, number** The magician performed several new tricks.	
	3.	*n.*	**knack, art, technique, gift, skill** There is a definite trick to making good pastry.	
	4.	*v.*	**deceive, hoax, cheat, swindle, dupe, trap, bluff, fool, defraud** The salesperson tricked the teenager into buying the faulty car.	
tricky	1.	*adj.*	**crafty, wily, deceitful, deceptive** The tricky politician won votes through false promises.	**1.** *straightforward, open, aboveboard*
	2.	*adj.*	**intricate, difficult, complicated** There are many tricky turns in the race track.	**2.** *easy, safe*
trim	1.	*n.*	**order, good condition, shape** The crew made certain the sailboat was in trim for the regatta.	**1.** *disorder, mess*
	2.	*v.*	**clip, cut, prune, shear, crop, lop** The gardener trimmed the hedge.	**2.** *lengthen, extend*

Word	No.	Part	Synonyms / Example	Antonyms
	3.	*v.*	**decorate, adorn, ornament** The children enjoy trimming the Christmas tree.	
	4.	*adj.*	**neat, orderly, tidy, spruce** The house was in trim condition.	**4.** *untidy, unkempt*
	5.	*adj.*	**slim, shapely, fit** Erin keeps trim through regular exercise.	**5.** *shapeless, overweight, obese*
trimming	1.	*n.*	**decoration, ornament** They hung trimmings on the huge Christmas tree.	
	2.	*n.*	**beating, defeat** He took quite a trimming in the fight.	**2.** *success, victory, triumph*
trip	1.	*n.*	**journey, voyage, tour, excursion** Lim makes many business trips.	
	2.	*v.*	**stumble, slip, fall, tumble** Cathy tripped over the rock and fell.	
triumph	1.	*n.*	**victory, conquest, success** The landing on the moon was one of the triumphs of modern science.	**1.** *loss, defeat, failure, setback*
	2.	*v.*	**conquer, win** Chris triumphed over Hana to win the tennis championship.	**2.** *lose*
triumphant		*adj.*	**victorious, successful, winning** The triumphant team celebrated all night long.	*unsuccessful, beaten, defeated*
trivial		*adj.*	**small, petty, unimportant, slight, insignificant, trifling, minor** He lost marks for trivial mistakes.	*important, serious, significant, major, exceptional*
trouble	1.	*n.*	**hardship, pain, suffering, misfortune, worry, distress, difficulty, misery** Most people have troubles of some kind.	**1.** *pleasure, delight, happiness, ease, joy, comfort*
	2.	*n.*	**sickness, ailment, disease** John's uncle has heart trouble.	**2.** *health*
	3.	*v.*	**worry, upset, perturb, concern, distress** The news of the accident troubled Sally's parents. *adj.* Their troubled looks told us something was wrong.	**3.** *console, calm, relieve*
	4.	*v.*	**vex, bother, annoy, pester, disturb, irritate** Don't trouble Mom when she's reading.	**4.** *leave alone*

Word			Synonyms	Antonyms
true	1.	*adj.*	**actual, genuine, real, accurate, authentic, right, correct** The true story of the accident was finally revealed.	**1.** *untrue, false, incorrect, fake*
	2.	*adj.*	**reliable, sincere, dependable, faithful, loyal** She has always been a true friend.	**2.** *unreliable, insincere, unfaithful, disloyal*
truly	1.	*adv.*	**sincerely, genuinely, really** I'm truly grateful for your help.	
	2.	*adv.*	**certainly, indeed, absolutely, surely, positively, definitely** Rubens was truly a great artist.	
trust	1.	*n.*	**faith, hope, confidence, belief** Pinocchio put his trust in bad companions.	**1.** *doubt, distrust*
	2.	*v.*	**believe in, confide in, rely on, depend on, put hope in** Pinocchio trusted the wrong people.	**2.** *mistrust, doubt, disbelieve, distrust, suspect*
trustworthy		*adj.*	**reliable, dependable, faithful, sincere, honest, truthful, conscientious, responsible** Parents should insist on trustworthy babysitters.	*undependable, unreliable, insincere, dishonest, irresponsible*
truthful		*adj.*	**reliable, exact, honest, candid, correct, accurate, sincere** Reporters should write truthful accounts of events.	*dishonest, false, inaccurate, untruthful*
try	1.	*n.*	**attempt, trial, effort, endeavour** Take another try at the high jump.	
	2.	*v.*	**attempt, tackle, undertake** Patsy tried skiing last winter.	**2.** *avoid, evade*
turbulent	1.	*adj.*	**violent, stormy, wild, fierce** Turbulent waves lashed the coast.	**1.** *calm, gentle, pacific, smooth*
	2.	*adj.*	**noisy, restless, agitated, rowdy, boisterous, riotous** The turbulent mob was scattered by the police.	**2.** *quiet, orderly, peaceful*
turmoil		*n.*	**confusion, chaos, disorder, uproar, commotion** The town was in a turmoil after the earthquake.	*order, peace, calm*
twirl	1.	*n.*	**spin, whirl, turn, twist, revolution** The dancer made many rapid twirls. *v.* Heavenly bodies twirl through space.	

	2.	*v.*	**coil, twist, wind, wrap, curl** Jane twirled the string around her finger.	**2.** *untie, unwind, remove*
twist	1.	*n.*	**twirl, whirl, turn, spin** Give the top a twist.	
	2.	*v.*	**turn, wind, coil, spin, twirl** The spider twisted the web around the helpless fly.	
	3.	*v.*	**distort, contort** The victim's face twisted in pain.	
	4.	*v.*	**curve, crook, bend, swerve, veer** The road twists to the right at the top of the hill.	
typical	1.	*adj.*	**normal, regular, usual, ordinary, standard, conventional** A typical school day begins at nine o'clock. *adv.* The school day typically starts at nine o'clock.	**1.** *uncommon, unusual, strange, exceptional, extraordinary*
	2.	*adj.*	**characteristic, like, to be expected** It is typical of Mike to be late.	**2.** *unexpected, unlike*
tyrant		*n.*	**dictator, despot, oppressor** The country was ruled by a tyrant. *n.* The people suffered under his tyranny.	

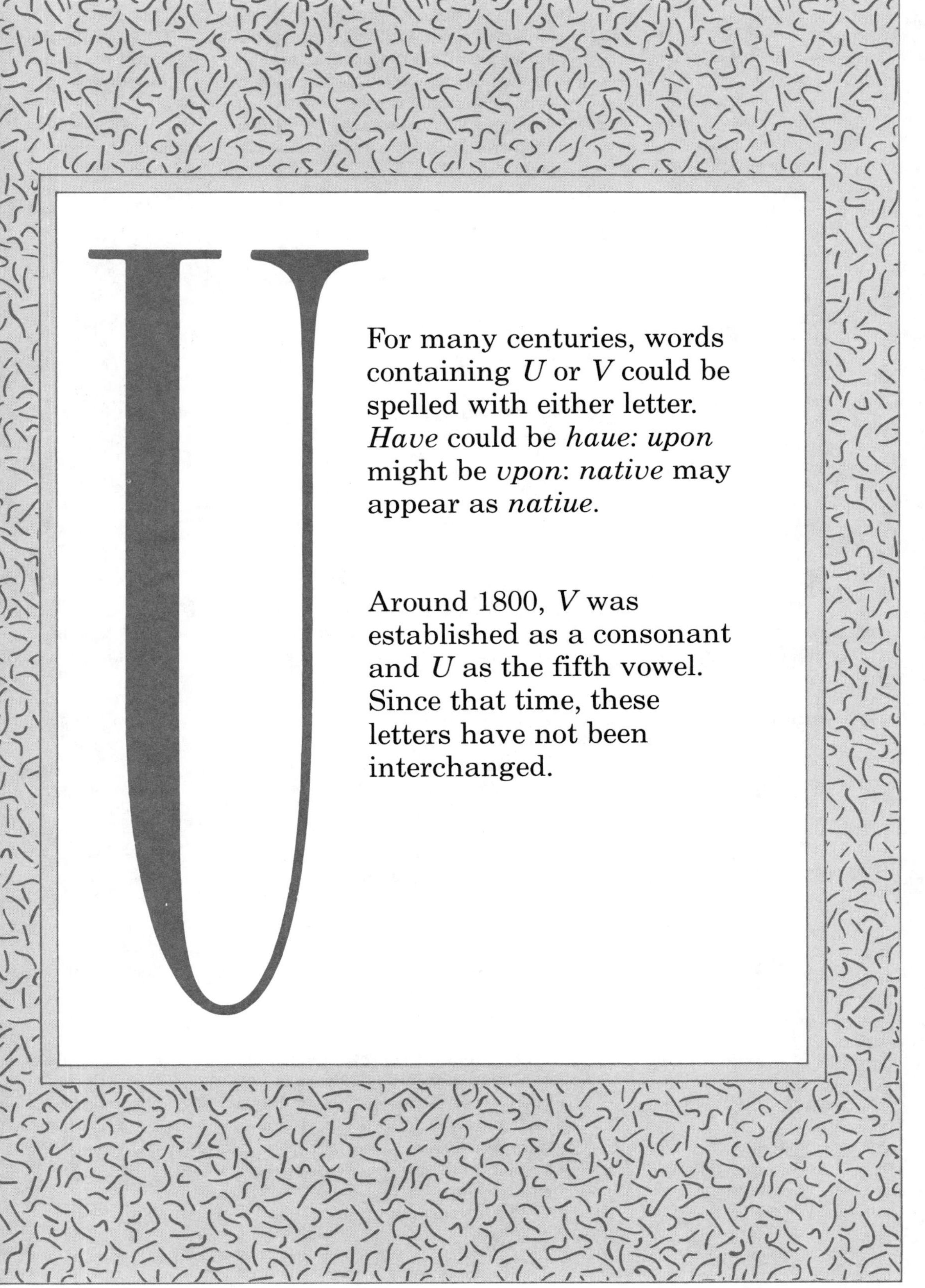

For many centuries, words containing *U* or *V* could be spelled with either letter. *Have* could be *haue: upon* might be *vpon*: *native* may appear as *natiue*.

Around 1800, *V* was established as a consonant and *U* as the fifth vowel. Since that time, these letters have not been interchanged.

Word			Synonyms	Antonyms
ugly	1.	*adj.*	**unsightly, unpleasant, repulsive, hideous, offensive, loathsome** In the fairy tale, the ugly frog turned into a handsome prince.	**1.** *beautiful, lovely, gorgeous, attractive, handsome*
	2.	*adj.*	**dangerous, threatening** The wrestler gave his opponent an ugly glare.	**2.** *mild, reasonable, complaisant*
ultimate		*adj.*	**final, last, extreme, farthest, terminal** An Olympic gold medal is the ultimate achievement for an athlete.	*beginning, start, first, prior, preliminary*
unable		*adj.*	**incapable, not able, unfit** The injured athlete was unable to complete the race.	*able, capable*
unanimous		*adj.*	**united, unified, collective, homogeneous, undivided** The jury came to a unanimous decision of "not guilty."	*divided, opposing, divergent, dissenting, discordant*
uncertain	1.	*adj.*	**doubtful, unsure, undecided, indefinite, dubious, unresolved** Yen is uncertain about which university to attend.	**1.** *definite, secure, sure, certain, resolved*
	2.	*adj.*	**unsettled, changeable, unreliable, unpredictable** We cancelled the trip because of Kit's uncertain health.	**2.** *settled, unchangeable, reliable, predictable*
uncommon		*adj.*	**rare, unusual, extraordinary, unique, exceptional** In an uncommon act of charity, the miser donated money to the poor.	*common, usual, familiar, regular, normal, customary, characteristic*
unconcerned		*adj.*	**disinterested, nonchalant, careless, heedless, insouciant, indifferent, apathetic** We can no longer be unconcerned about preserving our environment.	*interested, keen, eager, zealous, concerned*
uncover		*v.*	**reveal, disclose, expose** Police uncovered a plot to assassinate the president.	*conceal, hide*
understand	1.	*v.*	**comprehend, catch, know, grasp, construe, perceive, fathom** I don't understand what the author is saying.	**1.** *misunderstand, mistake, misconstrue*
	2.	*v.*	**infer, gather, assume** I understand you've won a scholarship.	

Word			Synonyms	Antonyms
understanding	1.	*n.*	**knowledge, perception, comprehension** This book is beyond my understanding.	
	2.	*n.*	**agreement, common view** After months of negotiation, the companies reached an understanding.	
undertaking		*n.*	**venture, project, enterprise, task, endeavour** Space exploration is a costly undertaking.	
uneasy		*adj.*	**anxious, troubled, perturbed, upset, worried, nervous, agitated, unsettled** Dad is uneasy about the business deal he just acquired. *n.* His uneasiness was evident in his inability to eat and sleep.	*composed, calm, collected*
unemployed		*adj.*	**jobless, out of work, inactive** When the plant shut down, many people became unemployed.	*employed, at work, busy*
unequal		*adj.*	**uneven, irregular, unbalanced** Weigh scales must not be unequal.	*regular, balanced, even, equitable*
unequalled		*adj.*	**unmatched, matchless, supreme, unrivalled, unique, unparalleled** His home run record remains unequalled.	*common, usual, frequent, many*
unexpected		*adj.*	**unforeseen, surprising, startling, unpredicted** Unexpected illness caused the singer to cancel the performance.	*predicted, foreseen, expected, anticipated*
unfasten		*v.*	**release, untie, undo, loose, disconnect** The crew unfastened the ship's ropes.	*tie, fasten*
unfit	1.	*adj.*	**incompetent, inept, unable** Why is that dancer unfit to perform?	**1.** *competent, able*
	2.	*adj.*	**unsuitable, improper, inappropriate** The water is unfit for human consumption.	**2.** *correct, apt, suitable, proper*
unforeseen		*adj.*	**surprising, unexpected, startling, unpredicted** The defeat of the champion was unforeseen.	*predicted, foreseen, expected, anticipated*

Word			Synonyms	Antonyms
unforgettable		*adj.*	**notable, impressive, exceptional** The moon landing was an unforgettable event.	*forgettable, unimpressive*
unfortunate		*adj.*	**unlucky, ill-fated, hapless** The acrobat had an unfortunate accident.	*fortunate, lucky*
unhappy		*adj.*	**sad, miserable, gloomy, dismal, dejected, distressed, sorrowful, melancholy, downhearted** The children are unhappy about the loss of their pet.	*cheerful, happy, joyful, merry, glad, jolly, ecstatic, light hearted*
uniform	1.	*n.*	**costume, garb, attire** The band's uniform is colourful.	
	2.	*adj.*	**even, steady, regular, stable, constant, consistent** There is a uniform temperature throughout the building.	**2.** *uneven, irregul varying, erratic, variable, inconsistent*
	3.	*adj.*	**equal, identical, alike, similar, correspondent** Those two packages are of uniform size.	**3.** *different, unlike varied, varying*
unique	1.	*adj.*	**distinctive, unmatched, single, novel** Every single human being is unique.	**1.** *common, usua*
	2.	*adj.*	**rare, uncommon, unusual** Michelangelo had a unique talent.	**2.** *ordinary, everyday, commo*
unite		*v.*	**join, combine, merge, associate, consolidate, amalgamate** The two companies united against their competitors.	*divide, separate, part*
unity		*n.*	**harmony, concord, agreement, accord** The new leader restored unity to the country.	*discord, dissension conflict, contentio*
universal	1.	*adj.*	**worldwide, global, catholic** Universal concern for the environment now exists.	**1.** *local, district, regional*
	2.	*adj.*	**general, widespread, entire, extensive, comprehensive** The government's proposal met with universal approval.	**2.** *partial, limited, incomplete*
unkempt		*adj.*	**untidy, disorderly, tousled, careless, dishevelled, slovenly, rumpled, ill-kept, bedraggled** The tramp's unkempt appearance frightened the children.	*tidy, neat, orderly*

Word			Synonyms	Antonyms
unruly		*adj.*	**disobedient, unmanageable, rowdy, uncontrollable** Police were called in to control the unruly mob at the rock concert.	*docile, orderly, obedient, well-behaved*
untidy		*adj.*	**messy, slovenly** Steve was told to clean up his untidy room.	*tidy, neat*
uphold		*v.*	**maintain, support, back up, confirm, sustain, champion** Citizens are expected to uphold the law.	*confront, oppose, counter, resist, obstruct, contradict*
upright	1.	*adj.*	**vertical, erect, perpendicular** Upright beams held the scaffolding in place.	**1.** *horizontal, flat*
	2.	*adj.*	**honest, true, trustworthy, fair, honourable, principled, virtuous** The company is upright in its business dealings.	**2.** *dishonest, corrupt, dishonourable*
uprising		*n.*	**revolt, rebellion, riot, upheaval, revolution, insurrection** The army was sent to quell the uprising.	*order, peace*
uproar		*n.*	**commotion, confusion, hubbub, clamour, disturbance** The spectators were in an uproar over the umpire's unfair call.	*quiet, calm, order*
uproot		*v.*	**pull up, remove, extract, rip up, eradicate** The tornado uprooted many trees.	*maintain, preserve, take root*
upset	1.	*v.*	**overturn, tilt, topple, tip over, knock over, capsize** Rough water upset the canoe.	**1.** *right*
	2.	*v.*	**disturb, bother, fluster, perturb, agitate** News of the tragedy upset everyone.	**2.** *please, calm, soothe, ease*
	3.	*v.*	**defeat, beat, overthrow, topple, win, conquer** The newcomer upset the favourite in the match.	**3.** *lose, be defeated*
up-to-date		*adj.*	**fashionable, modern, stylish, in vogue, new, current** Which car has the most up-to-date engineering?	*out-of-date, old-fashioned*
urge	1.	*n.*	**need, desire, impulse** She stifled an urge to yawn.	

	2.	*v.*	**implore, beg, plead, entreat, coax** I urge you to continue your education.	**2.** *deter, discourage*
	3.	*v.*	**drive, compel, press, push, force** The general urged the troops into battle.	**3.** *deny, withhold, block, inhibit*
urgent		*adj.*	**pressing, serious, important, critical** The doctor received an urgent call for help.	*trivial, insignificant, unimportant*
use	1.	*n.*	**utility, value, applicability, practicability** The salesperson claimed the appliance could be put to many uses.	**1.** *misuse, abuse, misapplication*
	2.	*v.*	**employ, utilize, apply, expend, consume** We used all our resources to build the tower.	**2.** *discard, reject, refuse, neglect, waste*
useful		*adj.*	**helpful, valuable, advantageous, beneficial, serviceable** It is useful to know some first aid.	*useless, valueless, worthless, unbeneficial*
useless	1.	*adj.*	**worthless** We found a lot of useless junk in the attic.	**1.** *usable, useful*
	2.	*adj.*	**futile, fruitless, hopeless, in vain, pointless** All rescue attempts were useless.	**2.** *productive, useful*
usual	1.	*adj.*	**ordinary, normal, common, everyday** Insects are the usual carriers of pollen.	**1.** *uncommon, unusual, odd, abnormal, irregular*
	2.	*adj.*	**habitual, customary, traditional, conventional** It is usual to bow as a greeting in Japan. *adv.* North Americans usually shake hands when they meet.	**2.** *unconventional, uncustomary, extraordinary*
utmost	1.	*adj.*	**greatest, ultimate, most, maximum** This news bulletin is of the utmost importance!	**1.** *least, minimum*
	2.	*adj.*	**farthest, furthest, remotest, extreme** Explorers probe the utmost regions of the world.	**2.** *nearest, closest*

utter

1. *adj.* **complete, total, thorough, absolute, sheer, unqualified**
Utter joy was felt when the rescue team arrived.
adv. The survivors were utterly exhausted.

1. imperfect, incomplete, partial

2. *v.* **speak, say, voice, tell, articulate, declare, announce, express, state**
The bully was heard to utter an apology.

2. remain silent

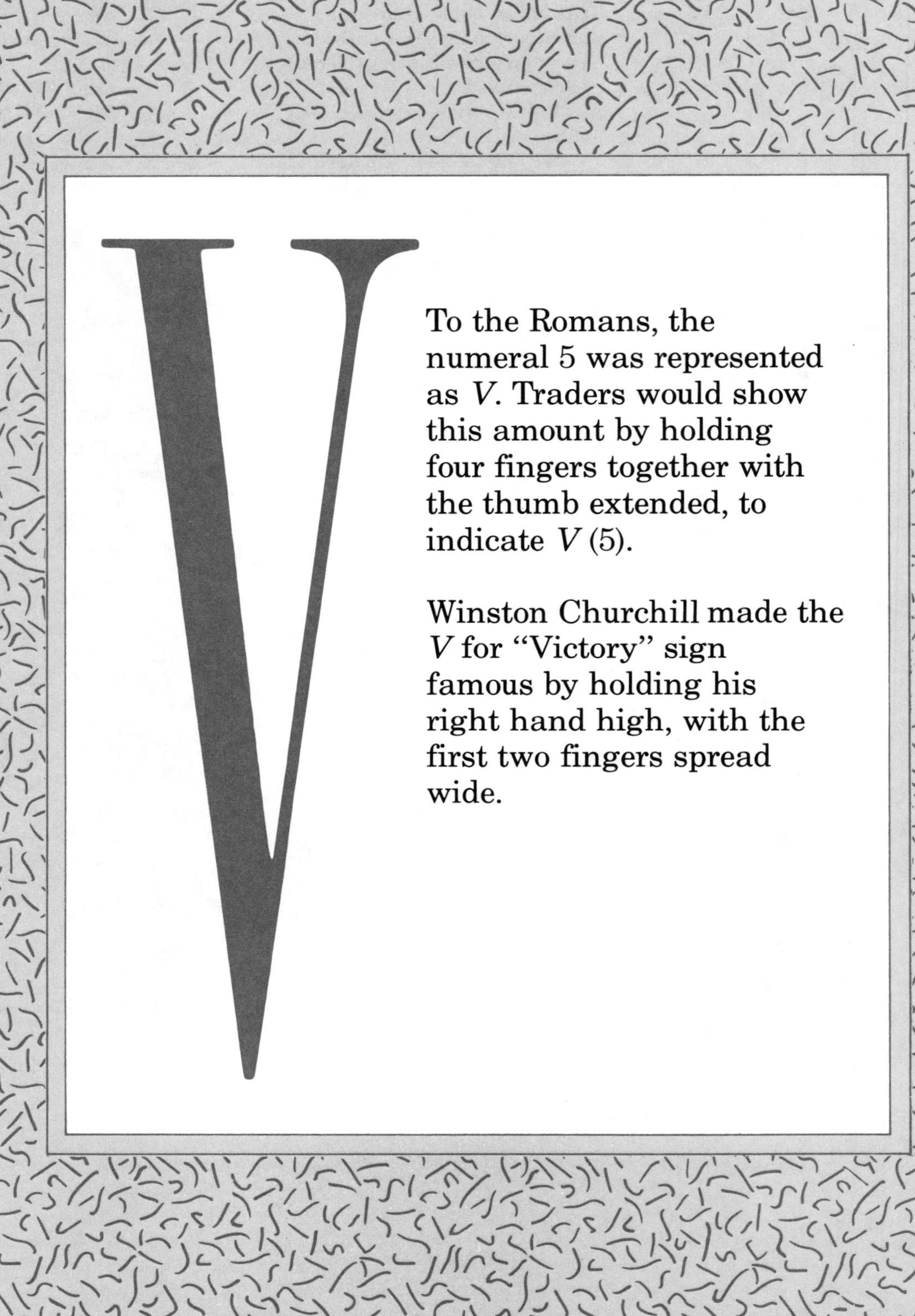

To the Romans, the numeral 5 was represented as *V*. Traders would show this amount by holding four fingers together with the thumb extended, to indicate *V* (5).

Winston Churchill made the *V* for "Victory" sign famous by holding his right hand high, with the first two fingers spread wide.

Word			Synonyms	Antonyms
vacant		*adj.*	**empty, unoccupied, free** There is a vacant house next to ours.	*inhabited, filled, occupied, full, taken*
vague	1.	*adj.*	**uncertain, undetermined, unsure, unsettled, indefinite, obscure** John's vague answer left everyone wondering.	**1.** *definite, certain, sure, clear*
	2.	*adj.*	**dim, indistinct, hazy, faint** The vague outline of a ship could be seen in the fog.	**2.** *clear, distinct*
vain	1.	*adj.*	**conceited, egotistical, proud, arrogant** The vain actor spent hours getting ready for the party.	**1.** *humble, modest, meek*
	2.	*adj.*	**futile, useless, unsuccessful** The lifeguard made a vain attempt to save the boy.	**2.** *effective, successful*
valiant		*adj.*	**brave, bold, daring, courageous, heroic, gallant, fearless, dauntless** The soldier received a medal for his valiant deed. *adv.* The troops fought valiantly.	*cowardly, fearful*
valid	1.	*adj.*	**proper, suitable, sound, genuine** Do you have a valid excuse for being late?	**1.** *improper, false, fictitious*
	2.	*adj.*	**legal, binding, lawful, legitimate, official** That contract is not valid without both signatures.	**2.** *illegal, unlawful, invalid*
valour		*n.*	**courage, bravery, gallantry, heroism** The Victoria Cross is given for great valour.	*cowardice, timidity, fear*
value	1.	*n.*	**worth, importance** What value do you put on your life?	
	2.	*n.*	**price, cost, charge** What is the value of this gold pen? *adj.* It is a valuable pen.	
	3.	*n.*	**ideals, norms, standards, mores** Children learn traditional values from their parents.	
	4.	*v.*	**price, assess, appraise, estimate, compute, evaluate** The owner valued his car at $20 000.	
	5.	*v.*	**prize, respect, treasure, cherish** I value her friendship.	**5.** *disregard, scorn*

Word			Synonyms	Antonyms
vandal		*n.*	**looter, raider, destroyer** Vandals broke the windows. *v.* They vandalized the building. *n.* Vandalism is a continuing problem everywhere.	
vanish		*v.*	**disappear, evaporate, dissolve** The magician waved his wand and the rabbit vanished!	*appear, materialize*
vanquish		*v.*	**defeat, conquer, overpower, overcome, beat, master, crush, subdue** The army vanquished its enemies.	*surrender, yield, give in*
vapour		*n.*	**moisture, fog, mist, steam, condensation** The vapour from the shower clouded the bathroom mirror.	
variety	1.	*n.*	**assortment, variation, diversity, mixture** This store has a great variety of candies from which to choose.	**1.** *sameness*
	2.	*n.*	**kind, sort, type, brand, category** Red Delicious is my favourite variety of apples.	
various		*adj.*	**many, several, numerous, diverse, differing** There are various ways to solve the problem.	*few*
vary		*v.*	**change, differ, alter, modify, fluctuate** The price of most things varies according to supply and demand.	*be steady, hold*
vast	1.	*adj.*	**huge, great, tremendous, mighty, immense, colossal, enormous** A vast crowd assembled in St. Peter's Square on Easter Sunday.	**1.** *small, little, sligh tiny*
	2.	*adj.*	**boundless, unlimited, immeasurable** The universe is vast.	**2.** *limited, confined, restricted*
vehement		*adj.*	**intense, fierce, fiery, eager, earnest, fervent, enthusiastic** There are many vehement opponents of the seal hunt. *adv.* They protest vehemently against the hunting of seals.	*indifferent, unconcerned*
veil	1.	*n.*	**cover, cloud, screen, blanket** Veils of white mist hung over the valley.	

Word	No.	Part	Synonyms and example	Antonyms
	2.	*n.*	**face covering, head covering** The bride wore a veil of antique lace.	
	3.	*v.*	**cover, hide, conceal, obscure, screen, dim** Heavy smog often veils Los Angeles.	**3.** *expose, reveal, show, disclose*
velocity		*n.*	**speed** Light travels at a velocity of 299 792 kilometres per second.	
vengeance		*n.*	**revenge, retribution, reprisal, retaliation** The tribe swore vengeance on the invaders.	
venture		*n.*	**endeavour, risk, undertaking, chance, project, enterprise, speculation, gamble** His venture in real estate proved successful. *v.* He ventured a large sum of money on the building.	*certainty*
verbal		*adj.*	**oral, spoken, vocal, unwritten** The two groups arrived at a verbal agreement. *adv.* They agreed verbally.	*written*
verdict		*n.*	**decision, judgment, finding, conclusion, result** The accused person waited anxiously for the jury's verdict.	
verify		*v.*	**confirm, support, guarantee, prove, vouch for, establish** Two witnesses verified the suspect's alibi.	*deny, contradict, dispute*
versatile		*adj.*	**resourceful, adaptable, able, expert, clever, accomplished** The versatile performer can sing, dance, and act.	*limited*
vertical		*adj.*	**erect, perpendicular, upright** The wallpaper has vertical stripes.	*horizontal*
veto	1.	*n.*	**refusal, prohibition, rejection, denial, prevention** The president's veto of the club's proposal angered the members.	**1.** *approval, sanction, endorsement*
	2.	*v.*	**reject, deny, prevent, turn down, forbid, disallow, prohibit** The council vetoed our proposal for raising funds.	**2.** *approve, endorse, allow, sanction*

Word			Synonyms	Antonyms
vex		*v.*	**displease, annoy, anger, provoke, trouble, irritate, disturb** The students were vexed when the trip was cancelled.	*please, delight, satisfy*
vibrant	1.	*adj.*	**vivid, lively, bright, brilliant, strong, intense, striking, glowing** The vibrant colours of the autumn leaves delighted the visitors.	**1.** *dull, flat, colourless, lifeless*
	2.	*adj.*	**active, energetic, lively, vigorous** She inspires her students with her vibrant personality.	**2.** *insipid, lifeless, inactive, dull, slow, lethargic*
vibrate		*v.*	**quake, tremble, throb, quiver, sway** The buildings vibrated when the earthquake struck. *n.* The vibrations terrified the occupants.	
vice	1.	*n.*	**flaw, shortcoming, fault, failing, defect, weakness** Dad's only vice is smoking.	**1.** *strong point, talent, gift*
	2.	*n.*	**corruption, immorality, iniquity** The police try to keep our cities free of vice.	**2.** *virtue, morality*
vicious		*adj.*	**spiteful, bad, vile, wicked, destructive, unruly, savage** Their vicious lies about the new neighbours caused a lot of grief.	*gentle, harmless, noble, virtuous*
victor		*n.*	**winner, champion, conqueror** The victor acknowledged the crowd's cheers with a wave. *adj.* He was victorious in three matches.	*loser*
victory		*n.*	**conquest, triumph, success, win** Congratulate the team for its victory in the debate.	*defeat, failure, loss*
vie		*v.*	**contend, compete, fight, struggle, challenge, contest** Two strong teams are vying for the Stanley Cup.	*share, cooperate*
view	1.	*n.*	**sight, scene, outlook, vista, panorama** The view from the mountaintop is spectacular.	
	2.	*n.*	**opinion, feeling, belief, judgment** It is my view that the country needs a new leader.	

	3.	*v.*	**see, look at, look on, survey, scan, examine, watch** The press was invited to view the designer's new collection.	
vigilant		*adj.*	**watchful, alert, wary, observant** The store needs a vigilant guard. *n.* Vigilance is necessary in order to do the job.	*careless, negligent, inattentive*
vigorous		*adj.*	**energetic, lively, robust, healthy, active, spirited, strong, forceful** Grandfather is still vigorous although he is 85 years old. *adv.* The workers vigorously protested against the new rules.	*weak, lifeless, inactive, feeble*
vile	1.	*adj.*	**nasty, odious, disgusting, bad, offensive, unpleasant, repulsive** Vile odours came from the chemical plant.	**1.** *pleasant, good, agreeable*
	2.	*adj.*	**filthy, obscene, gross, vulgar, coarse, despicable, sordid** Vile language is not necessary or appreciated.	**2.** *polite, cultured, acceptable, refined*
violence	1.	*n.*	**brutality, outrage, savagery** There have been outbreaks of violence in some parts of the country.	
	2.	*n.*	**force, might, fury, intensity, impact** The violence of the tornado hit almost without warning.	**2.** *weakness, calm*
violent	1.	*adj.*	**strong, forceful, raging, furious, rough, turbulent, severe** Violent thunderstorms lashed the coast.	**1.** *weak, tranquil, calm*
	2.	*adj.*	**fierce, savage, brutal** Dave was told to control his violent temper.	**2.** *gentle*
visible	1.	*adj.*	**distinct, in view, clear, in sight** The enemy's camp was visible through the telescope.	**1.** *invisible*
	2.	*adj.*	**evident, apparent, plain, obvious, noticeable** After a day's treatment there was a visible improvement in the patient. *adv.* The crowd was visibly shaken by the bad news.	**2.** *concealed, buried, hidden*
vision	1.	*n.*	**sight, eyesight** Yun has excellent vision.	**1.** *blindness*

	2.	*n.*	**foresight, insight** The founder of our school was a person with vision.	
	3.	*n.*	**ghost, spirit, phantom, fantasy, apparition, image, illusion** Many prophets claim to have seen visions.	
vista		*n.*	**outlook, view, perspective** College opens up new vistas of knowledge for many students.	
visual		*adj.*	**optical, visible, perceptible** Many visual learning aids are used in our school.	
visualize		*v.*	**picture, imagine, fancy, envision** We visualized her Italian village as Rosa described it.	
vital	1.	*adj.*	**important, urgent, critical, basic, pressing, serious, essential, chief** Preserving the environment is a vital issue today.	**1.** *trivial, unnecessary, unimportant*
	2.	*adj.*	**forceful, lively, strong, energetic, dynamic, vibrant** She is one of the most vital leaders we have had in years. *n.* Her vitality inspires everyone.	**2.** *listless, weak, dull*
vivacious		*adj.*	**animated, active, lively, gay, spirited** We always enjoy her parties because she is such a vivacious host.	*dull, uninteresting, lifeless, listless*
vivid	1.	*adj.*	**bright, brilliant, strong, intense, striking** The vivid colours of the autumn foliage covered the hills.	**1.** *dull, flat, colourless, lifeless*
	2.	*adj.*	**lively, vibrant, active** The author has a vivid imagination.	**2.** *dull, boring*
	3.	*adj.*	**distinct, clear, lifelike, realistic** Parkash has vivid memories of his home in India.	**3.** *dull, vague*
void	1.	*n.*	**blank, vacuum, emptiness, empty space** The death of her husband left a void in her life.	
	2.	*v.*	**cancel, annul, reverse, rescind, break, repeal** Breaking the lease voided their rental agreement.	**2.** *validate, effect, bind, enforce*

volunteer

1. *n.* **unpaid worker, helper, free assistant**
Many volunteers help out at the hospital.
adj. The volunteer staff works in every department.
Antonyms: 1. *paid help*

2. *v.* **offer, step forward, enlist, promise to help**
During the war, many young people volunteered to serve in the army.
adj. Their voluntary efforts were greatly appreciated.
Antonyms: 2. *force, compel, recruit*

voyage

1. *n.* **journey, cruise, trip, excursion, tour**
After their retirement, they went on a voyage around the world.

2. *v.* **travel, journey, cruise, visit**
They voyaged to many lands.

vulgar

1. *adj.* **rude, uncouth, ignorant, coarse, rough, impolite, crude**
That's a very vulgar remark!
n. Such vulgarity is not appreciated.
Antonyms: 1. *polite, cultured, refined, tasteful*

2. *adj.* **common, ordinary**
The vulgar masses rioted against the king.

vulnerable

adj. **exposed, susceptible, defenceless, unprotected, unguarded**
Without vaccination, we are vulnerable to measles.
Antonyms: *protected, guarded, immune*

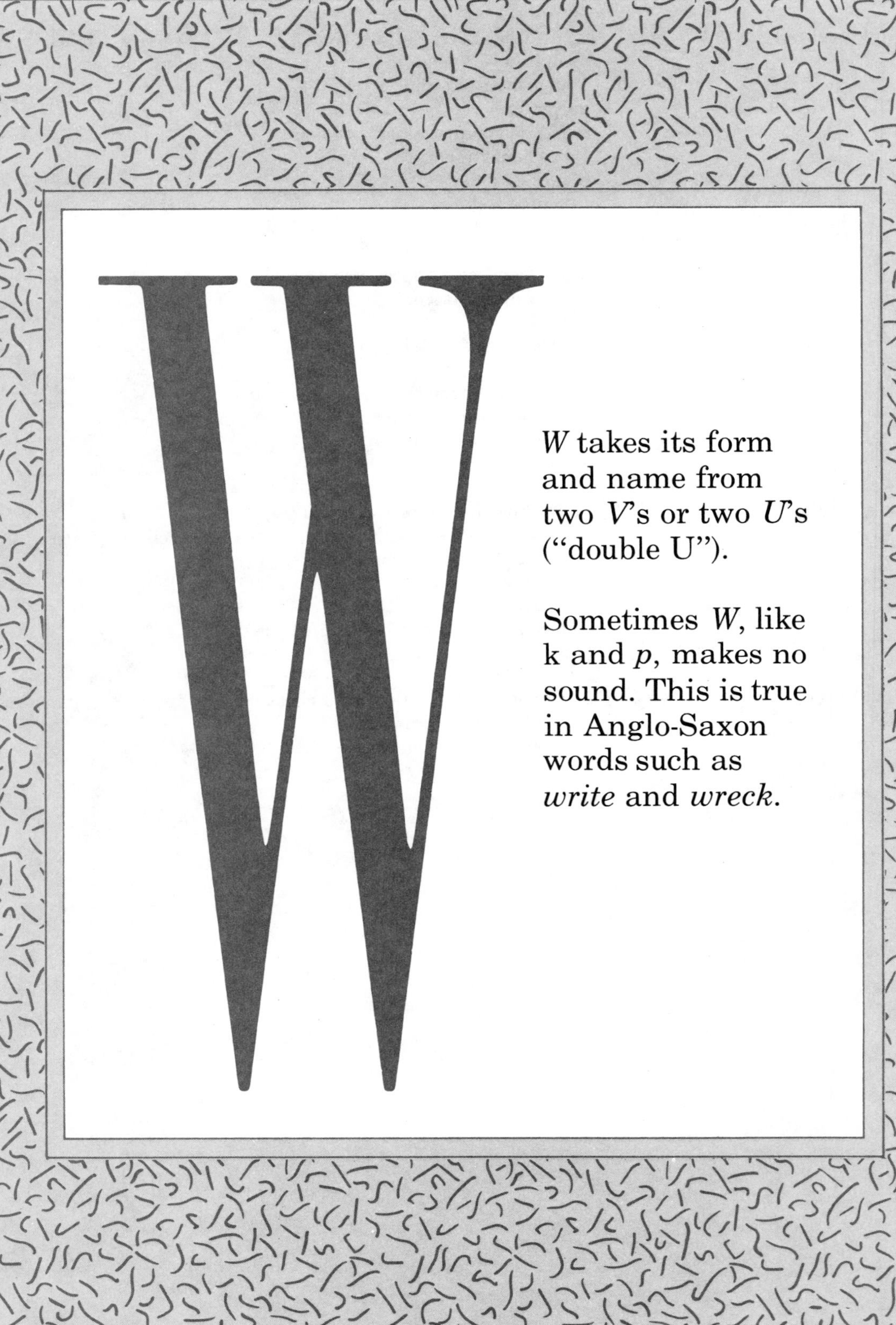

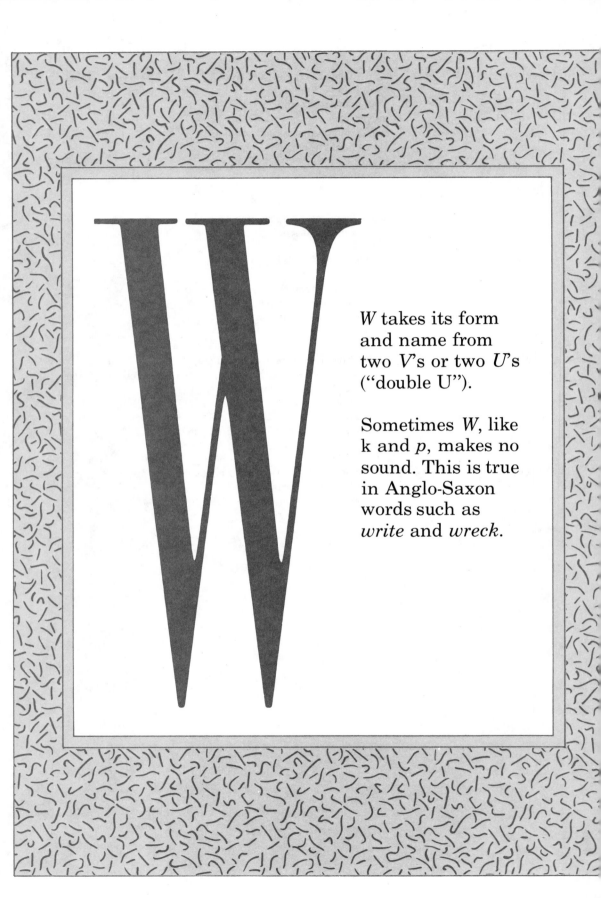

W takes its form and name from two *V*'s or two *U*'s ("double U").

Sometimes *W*, like k and *p*, makes no sound. This is true in Anglo-Saxon words such as *write* and *wreck*.

Word	#	Part	Synonyms / Example	Antonyms
wages		*n.*	**pay, salary, earnings, income, payment, remuneration** Andrew makes good wages delivering pizza.	
wail	1.	*n.*	**howl, whine, cry, moan** The wail of the air raid sirens wakened the villagers.	**1.** *whisper, murmur*
	2.	*v.*	**cry, weep, moan, howl, lament, sob, bawl** The earthquake victims wailed as they searched for their loved ones.	**2.** *laugh, smile*
wait	1.	*n.*	**stay, pause, delay, stop** Sue had a long wait in the lineup for tickets.	
	2.	*v.*	**linger, remain, stay, tarry** I'll wait for five minutes.	**2.** *leave, go*
	3.	*v.*	**look for, expect, watch for** Jim is waiting for the test results.	
	4.	*v.*	**serve, attend to** Kay waits on tables after school.	
wake		*v.*	**arouse, awake, rouse, stir** Please wake me at six.	
wander	1.	*v.*	**roam, ramble, saunter, meander** Joan and I wandered slowly through the park.	
	2.	*v.*	**stray, drift** My mind wandered off during the long, dull speech.	
wane		*v.*	**fade, weaken, decline, lessen, decrease, sink, subside** Her health waned after the operation. *adj.* We had to stop our gardening as we couldn't see in the waning light.	*increase, strengthen, wax, brighten*
want	1.	*n.*	**need, poverty, destitution** The class raised money for the people in want.	**1.** *abundance, wealth, plenty, affluence*
	2.	*v.*	**wish for, desire, crave, yearn for** My brother wants a ten-speed bicycle.	
	3.	*v.*	**need, require** The man wants some water.	
warm	1.	*v.*	**heat, make hot** Let's warm the casserole for lunch.	**1.** *cool, chill*
	2.	*adj.*	**not cold, not chilled, somewhat hot** Are you warm in that coat?	**2.** *cold, chilly*

	3.	*adj.*	**kind, tender, loving, friendly, pleasant, gracious, cheerful** What a warm person your friend is!	**3.** *unfriendly, unkind, aloof*
warn		*v.*	**caution, advise, notify, inform, alert** The announcer warned us of the coming storm. *n.* We cancelled our fishing trip because of the storm warning. *adj.* We slowed the car when we saw a warning light flashing ahead.	
wary		*adj.*	**cautious, alert, careful, prudent** It is wise to be wary with strangers.	*unwary, rash, careless, reckless*
waste	1.	*n.*	**garbage, refuse, rubbish, trash, junk, debris** Industrial waste has polluted our lakes and rivers.	**1.** *valuables*
	2.	*v.*	**squander, misuse, throw away** Don't waste your money on comics. *n.* Comics are a waste of money.	**2.** *save, preserve, hoard*
	3.	*v.*	**fade, weaken** He is wasting away from cancer.	**3.** *strengthen*
	4.	*adj.*	**useless, unused, worthless** Deserts are waste lands.	**4.** *useful, purposeful*
wasteful		*adj.*	**extravagant, lavish, reckless** The foolish man is wasteful with his money.	*miserly, stingy, thrifty*
watch	1.	*n.*	**heed, attention, notice, guard, supervision** Please keep a close watch on the children.	**1.** *inattention, neglect*
	2.	*n.*	**timepiece, wristwatch, pocket watch** Does your watch keep good time?	
	3.	*v.*	**observe, see, look at, notice, survey, regard, gaze at, view** Did you watch the news on TV?	**3.** *overlook, disregard, ignore*
	4.	*v.*	**be careful, take heed, be cautious, be on guard** Do watch where you're going!	**4.** *be rash, be reckless, be careless*
watchful		*adj.*	**vigilant, alert, wary, careful, attentive, cautious, heedful** He has been keeping a watchful eye on his diet.	*careless, negligent, heedless*
waver	1.	*v.*	**vacillate, hesitate** She wavered over which university to attend.	**1.** *be decisive, be certain*

	2. *v.*	**flutter, flicker, falter, totter** The suspect's voice wavered when he was questioned by the police. *adj.* The candle's wavering flame threw eerie shadows on the wall.	**2.** *steady*
way	1. *n.*	**path, track, route, road, direction, course** Show me the way to the campsite.	
	2. *n.*	**custom, manner, habit, style, fashion, practice** Ramon has adapted to our way of life.	
	3. *n.*	**method, means, procedure, measure** We have to find a way to raise funds for the trip.	
wayward	*adj.*	**difficult, troublesome, unruly, wilful, disobedient, rebellious** Many wayward youths have been helped by wise counselling.	*obedient, steady*
weak	*adj.*	**feeble, fragile, shaky** The sick child is too weak to stand.	*strong, vigorous, sturdy*
wealth	1. *n.*	**money, riches, fortune, assets** They made their wealth from oil. *adj.* The wealthy family donated money for a new hospital.	**1.** *poverty, want, need*
	2. *n.*	**abundance, large quantity** There is a wealth of talent in our school.	**2.** *scarcity, shortage, dearth*
weary	*adj.*	**tired, fatigued, exhausted** The weary runner collapsed in a faint. *n.* He was overcome by weariness.	*fresh, lively, rested*
weep	*v.*	**sob, cry, shed tears** Annette wept for joy at her wedding.	*laugh, chuckle, giggle, smile*
weird	*adj.*	**strange, peculiar, eerie, odd, mysterious, unearthly, uncanny** People reported seeing weird flying objects in the dark.	*normal, usual, common, natural*
well	1. *n.*	**water hole, spring, pool** How deep is this well?	
	2. *v.*	**gush, flow, stream, spurt, pour, spout, ooze** After much drilling, oil welled from the ground.	
	3. *adj.*	**healthy, strong, sound, vigorous** Ben is well again after his operation.	**3.** *ill, sick, ailing, weak, unwell*

Word	No.	Part	Synonyms / Example	Antonyms
	4.	*adj.*	**favourable, good, satisfactory, happy, right** I hope all's well with your family.	**4.** *unfavourable, unhappy, bad, unsatisfactory*
	5.	*adv.*	**intimately, personally** Do you know Montreal well?	
	6.	*adv.*	**thoroughly, completely, fully** The recipe said to mix the batter well.	**6.** *poorly*
	7.	*adv.*	**nicely, favourably, adequately, successfully** David is doing well in school.	**7.** *poorly, badly, inadequately*
whim		*n.*	**notion, fancy, urge, impulse, quirk, caprice, inclination** On a sudden whim, we decided to go swimming.	
whole		*adj.*	**entire, complete, total, undivided** The greedy girl ate the whole box of chocolates.	*partial, incomplete*
whole-hearted		*adj.*	**sincere, true, complete, earnest, enthusiastic, unreserved** The teacher gave his whole-hearted support to our project.	*indifferent, lukewarm, half-hearted*
wholesome	1.	*adj.*	**nutritious, healthy, nourishing, healthful, sound** A wholesome diet includes grains, vegetables, fruits, and milk.	**1.** *unwholesome, unhealthy, harmful*
	2.	*adj.*	**decent, moral, clean, responsible, honest, worthy** The children were raised in a wholesome atmosphere.	**2.** *immoral, wicked, bad, degrading*
wicked		*adj.*	**sinful, evil, immoral, bad, corrupt, vile** The wicked witch was killed.	*good, loving, kind*
wild	1.	*n.*	**bush, wilderness, wasteland, barren area** Lions, tigers, and zebra roamed the wilds in Africa.	
	2.	*adj.*	**untamed, savage, unbroken** The cowboy tamed the wild horse.	**2.** *tame, broken, civilized*
	3.	*adj.*	**natural, desolate, rugged, bleak, wooded, forested, uncultivated** There are many wild areas in Canada's North.	**3.** *populated, inhabited, cultivated*
	4.	*adj.*	**unruly, violent, disorderly, lawless, reckless, fanatical** A group of wild fans started a riot at the soccer game.	**4.** *orderly, law-abiding, well-behaved*

wily		*adj.*	**cunning, sly, crafty, scheming, tricky, shifty, crooked, shrewd** They were hoodwinked by a wily car dealer.	*open, sincere, honest, straightforward*
win	**1.**	*n.*	**conquest, victory, triumph** One more win and the cup is ours!	**1.** *defeat, loss*
	2.	*v.*	**get, gain, achieve, capture, earn, secure, receive** Mario's kindness won our sincere admiration.	**2.** *lose*
wind	**1.**	*v.*	**twist, turn, curve, bend, weave, meander, ramble, zig-zag** The Mackenzie River winds northward to the Arctic Ocean. *adj.* The winding road is dangerous at night.	
	2.	*v.*	**coil, twist, twine, roll, loop** She wound the yarn into a ball.	**2.** *unwind, unroll*
winner		*n.*	**champion, conqueror, victor** Rae was the winner in four of the sports events.	*loser*
winning		*adj.*	**attractive, charming, appealing, enchanting, pleasing, delightful, fascinating, captivating** Some people have winning personalities.	*repulsive, irritating, sickening, disgusting*
wisdom		*n.*	**judgment, sense, reason, comprehension** Solomon is famous for his wisdom.	*foolishness, stupidity, folly*
wise		*adj.*	**intelligent, astute, profound, clever** The leader of the country is a wise person.	*foolish, stupid, silly*
wish		*v.*	**desire, crave, long, hope, hanker, yearn, want** Tom wished for a puppy. *n.* He got his wish for his birthday.	
wistful		*adj.*	**pensive, sad, forlorn, sorrowful, melancholy, thoughtful, doleful** Jan had a wistful look as she left for camp. *adv.* She looked back wistfully at her folks.	
wit	**1.**	*n.*	**humour, fun** The comedian's wit amused the audience.	

Word	No.	Part	Synonyms / Example	Antonyms
	2.	*n.*	**intellect, brains, mind, sense** Cliff used his wits to earn some money.	**2.** *stupidity*
withdraw		*v.*	**recall, leave, draw back, retreat, remove, pull back, take out** The general withdrew his troops from battle. *n.* She made a withdrawal from her bank account to buy the car.	*advance, proceed*
withdrawn		*adj.*	**shy, quiet, reserved, unfriendly, unsociable, uncommunicative** The child has been withdrawn since she lost her dog.	*friendly, open, sociable*
withhold		*v.*	**keep, retain, hold back** The witness withheld information from the police.	*give, provide*
without	1.	*prep.*	**lacking, not having** The survivors went without food until they were rescued.	**1.** *with*
	2.	*adv.*	**outside, outer part** This house has been painted within and without.	**2.** *inside*
withstand		*v.*	**resist, tolerate, bear, endure, suffer, cope with** It is difficult to withstand long, cold winters.	
witness	1.	*n.*	**onlooker, observer, spectator, eyewitness** Were you a witness to the attack?	
	2.	*v.*	**see, notice, observe, view, note** Mark witnessed the accident.	
witty		*adj.*	**clever, humorous, funny, droll, bright, amusing** Bert entertained us all night with his witty remarks.	*dull, serious, solemn*
wonder	1.	*n.*	**amazement, astonishment, awe, surprise, fascination** When she saw the pictures of Mars, she was filled with wonder.	
	2.	*n.*	**marvel, miracle, sight, spectacle** Niagara Falls is a famous natural wonder.	
	3.	*v.*	**doubt, marvel, speculate** I wonder when we shall travel by space shuttle.	

Word	No.	Part	Synonyms / Example	Antonyms
wonderful	1.	*adj.*	**incredible, marvellous, splendid, superb, striking, spectacular, amazing, remarkable** Modern science can do wonderful things.	1. *unimportant, ordinary, simple*
	2.	*adj.*	**good, fine, great, terrific, superb, super, fabulous** We had a wonderful time at the party!	2. *bad, dreadful, horrid*
work	1.	*n.*	**job, labour, task, toil, effort** The work of building the Great Wall of China took many lives.	1. *leisure, relaxation, ease*
	2.	*n.*	**employment, job, trade, occupation, profession** Many people are looking for work nowadays.	2. *vacation, unemployment*
	3.	*n.*	**product, creation** The sculptor's works sell for a great deal of money.	
	4.	*v.*	**toil, labour** The employees worked for eight hours each day.	4. *rest, relax*
	5.	*v.*	**operate, perform, run, go, function** How does this machine work?	
worn		*adj.*	**shabby, threadbare, used** The worn clothes were discarded.	*new, fresh*
worry	1.	*n.*	**trouble, care, anxiety, concern, problem, misery, despair** Recession and inflation cause many worries.	1. *assurance, calm, comfort, security*
	2.	*v.*	**torment, disturb, upset, trouble, vex, bother** Ed's poor health worries everyone.	2. *leave alone, please*
worth	1.	*n.*	**value, price** A person's worth is not measured in dollars and cents.	
	2.	*n.*	**good, use, importance, benefit, value, merit** Is there any worth in reading fairy tales?	
worthless		*adj.*	**valueless, useless, good-for-nothing** Counterfeit money is worthless.	*valuable, worthwhile, serviceable, useful*
worthwhile		*adj.*	**valuable, useful, profitable, good, beneficial, worth the effort** The project to help the retired people proved worthwhile.	*worthless, useless, bad, trivial, pointless*

worthy		*adj.*	**deserving, valuable** Helping to save the environment is a worthy cause.	*worthless*
wrap	1.	*v.*	**cover, parcel, bundle** The butcher wrapped the steak in waxed paper.	1. *uncover, unwrap, open*
	2.	*v.*	**clothe, cover, swathe, shroud, cloak, envelop, enfold** The baby was wrapped in a shawl.	2. *uncover*
wrath		*n.*	**anger, rage, ire, fury** The government incurred the wrath of the people with the new taxes.	*gentleness, kindness, mildness*
wreck	1.	*n.*	**ruin, derelict, mess, dilapidated structure** That vacant house is now a complete wreck.	
	2.	*v.*	**ruin, destroy, demolish, raze, level, spoil** The old school building will be wrecked during the summer vacation.	2. *build, construct, preserve, restore, repair*
wretched	1.	*adj.*	**pitiful, gloomy, shabby, miserable, forlorn** The slums of the city are wretched places.	1. *cheerful*
	2.	*adj.*	**poor, pitiful, unfortunate** The wretched people were forced from their homes.	2. *fortunate, lucky*
wrong	1.	*n.*	**crime, sin, wickedness, vice, transgression, misdeed, error** There are many wrongs in this world.	1. *justice, goodness, right, honesty, virtue*
	2.	*v.*	**hurt, harm, abuse, ill-treat** The criminal claimed that he was wronged at the trial.	2. *aid, assist, help*
	3.	*adj.*	**evil, wicked, unjust, unlawful, bad, immoral, sinful** It is wrong to steal.	3. *right, proper, suitable, fair, moral*
	4.	*adj.*	**incorrect, erroneous, false, mistaken** That's the wrong answer.	4. *right, proper, suitable, correct, accurate, exact*

X came to us from the ancient Egyptian hieroglyphics via the ancient Greeks and Romans. Not many English words begin with *X*, but it is a versatile letter which always has intrigued us.

It can be used by itself to represent an unknown quantity. We solve equations to find "*X*" in algebra. *X* marks the spot on maps and diagrams. *X* names geometric angles and lines. It can be used as a personal signature by someone who cannot write. But best of all, it sends our kisses in cards and letters to loved ones.

x	*n.*	**unknown quantity, unknown** Solve the equation to determine the value of x.	*known quantity, known, given*
xerox	*v.*	**photocopy, reproduce, copy, photostat, duplicate** It is illegal to xerox copyrighted material. *n.* I made a xerox of my notes for Belinda.	*originate, print, invent*
Xmas	*n.*	**Christmas, yule, yuletide, the Nativity** Xmas is the abbreviation for Christmas.	

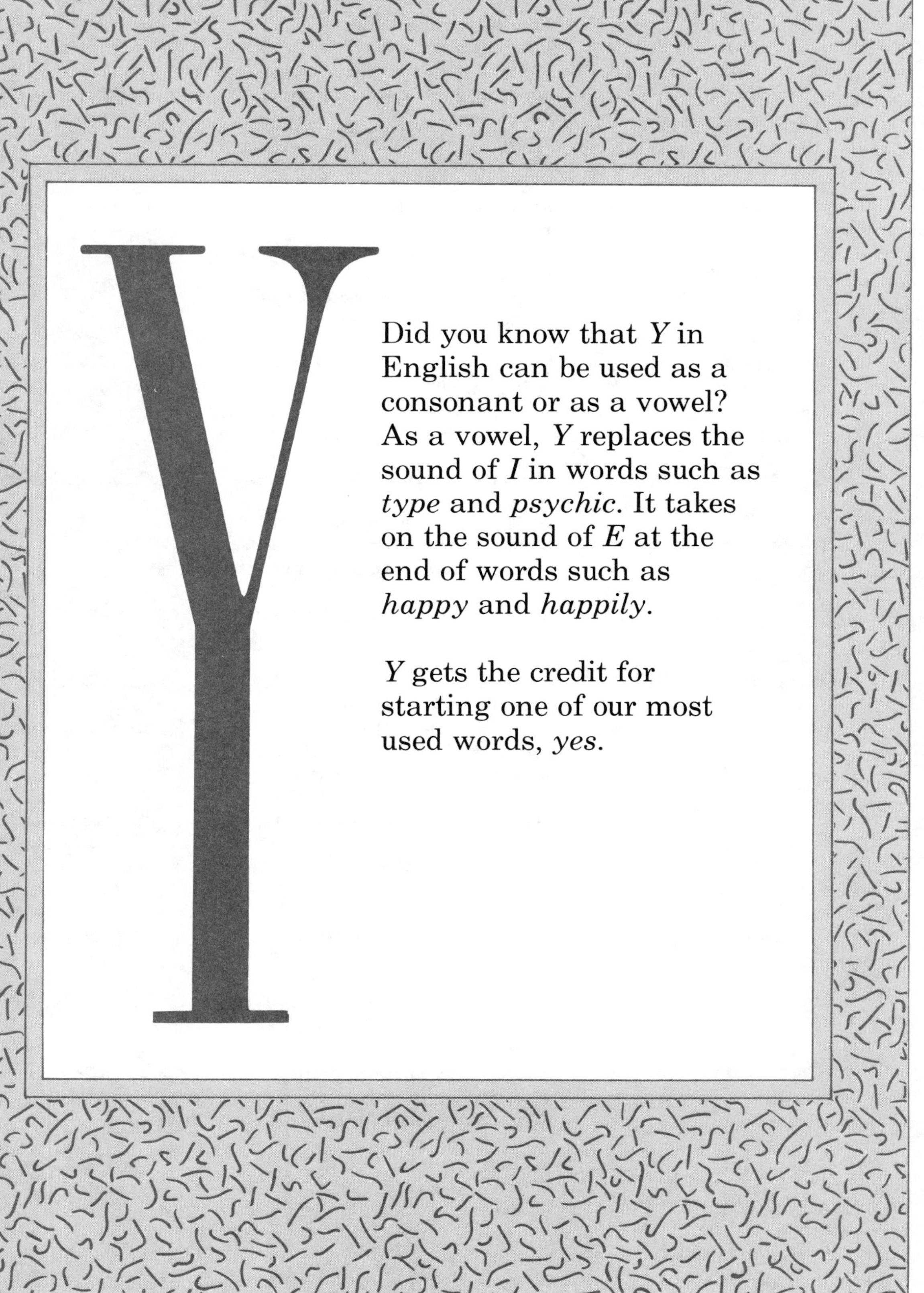

Did you know that *Y* in English can be used as a consonant or as a vowel? As a vowel, *Y* replaces the sound of *I* in words such as *type* and *psychic*. It takes on the sound of *E* at the end of words such as *happy* and *happily*.

Y gets the credit for starting one of our most used words, *yes*.

Word	No.	Part of speech	Synonyms / Example	Antonyms
yearly		*adv.*	**annually, once a year** Petunias bloom yearly.	
yearn		*v.*	**pine, long for, hanker, desire, crave, want** I yearn for the peace of the countryside.	*be indifferent, avoid, be repulsed*
yell		*n.*	**shout, scream, bellow, holler, roar, cry** James gave a yell when he tripped over the stone. *v.* People on the roller-coaster yelled in excitement.	*whisper, murmur*
yield	1.	*v.*	**produce, supply, furnish, bear, bring in, afford** Orchards yield fruit. *n.* This orchard gives an excellent yield.	1. *deny, take away, refuse*
	2.	*v.*	**surrender, cede, give up, submit, give in, succumb** After a long struggle, the people yielded to the demands of the leader.	2. *oppose, resist, fight*
	3.	*v.*	**give way, come apart, bend, cave in** The shelf yielded under the weight of the books.	
young	1.	*n.*	**offspring** Animals protect their young.	1. *parents*
	2.	*adj.*	**juvenile, youthful, childish** Young people flocked to the pool. *n.* This movie is suitable for the young.	2. *old, aged, elderly*
	3.	*adj.*	**inexperienced, callow, green, immature** Young football players are coached by the veterans.	3. *experienced, veteran, expert, mature*
youth	1.	*n.*	**child, youngster, teenager** The youths were commended for their bravery during the fire.	1. *adult, elderly person*
	2.	*n.*	**childhood, adolescence, puberty** The old friends shared memories of their youth.	2. *old age*
	3.	*n.*	**younger generation, young, children** A country's youth is its future.	3. *older generation*
youthful		*adj.*	**young, juvenile** This movie is not for youthful audiences.	*aged, old, mature, venerable, antiquated*

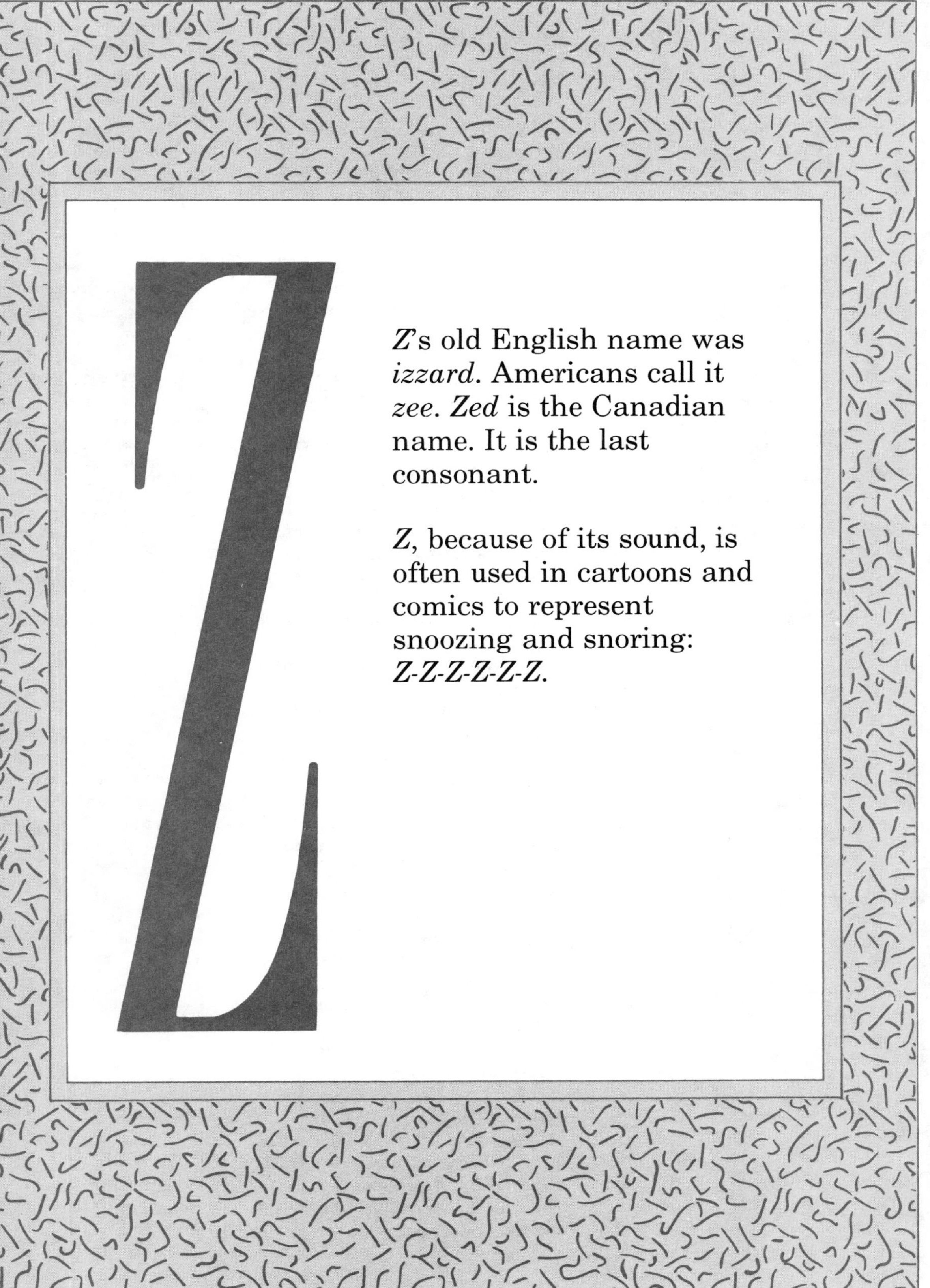

Z's old English name was *izzard*. Americans call it *zee*. *Zed* is the Canadian name. It is the last consonant.

Z, because of its sound, is often used in cartoons and comics to represent snoozing and snoring: *Z-Z-Z-Z-Z-Z*.

zany		*adj.*	**wacky, funny, humorous, silly, madcap** The Marx Brothers were zany actors.	*serious, sombre*
zeal		*n.*	**ardour, fervour, eagerness, enthusiasm** Astronauts train with zeal. *adj.* Her zealous efforts paid off with a scholarship.	*indifference, apathy, unconcern, reluctance*
zenith		*n.*	**top, pinnacle, summit, apex, height, climax, crest, crown** Elvis Presley reached the zenith of the recording industry.	*bottom, base, foundation, depth*
zero		*n.*	**nil, nothing, naught, none** The score is two to zero.	*something, anything*
zest	1.	*n.*	**flavour, tang, bite, nip, spice, pungency, piquancy** Spices add zest to food. *adj.* This curry has a zestful taste.	**1.** *blandness, mildness*
	2.	*n.*	**relish, gusto, zeal, enjoyment, ardour, enthusiasm, fervour** Grandpa has such a zest for life.	**2.** *disgust, distaste, dissatisfaction, apathy, indifference*
zigzag		*adj.*	**crooked, askew, jagged, winding, rambling, meandering, indirect** We followed a zigzag course up the hill. *v.* Paths zigzagged through the woods.	*straight, direct, unswerving*
zip		*v.*	**fasten, close, do up** Zip up your coat in this cold weather!	*unfasten, unzip, open, undo*
zone	1.	*n.*	**territory, district, location, area, region** The reporter was sent to the war zone.	
	2.	*n.*	**area, region, belt, band, latitude** Canada is in the north temperate zone.	
	3.	*v.*	**plan, restrict to, apportion, set apart** This section of the town is zoned for industrial expansion.	**3.** *leave unrestricted, leave open*
zoom	1.	*v.*	**speed, rush, hurry, hasten, bustle, race, fly, dash off, hustle** Race cars zoomed around the track.	**1.** *saunter*
	2.	*v.*	**climb, soar, rise, ascend** The new show's ratings have zoomed this season.	**2.** *crash, sink, fall, descend*